PS: It's Still Poetry
Volume II

An Anthology of Eclectic Contemporary Poems
Written by Poets from Around the Globe

D1218273

For information contact:
https://www.poetrysoup.com/

ISBN: 9798793344418

Preface

(The **table of contents** by **title** and **author** are at the end of this publication. Let's get to the poetry.)

This is PoetrySoup's second anthology. Like the first, **PS: It's Poetry**, this anthology is a collection of the work of various poets from all over the world. By reading these diverse works, we hope that people will become more understanding, compassionate, and empathetic towards all people. Additionally, we hope that this poetry makes the deepest kind of personal impression upon its readers.

Those whose works appear in this anthology have decided to publish their poetic works under a title published by PoetrySoup and Arczis Web Technologies, Incorporated. Special permission has been obtained for each copyrighted poem in this volume. The right to publish has been explicitly given to the publisher of this anthology by the respective poets. While most of the poems were submitted by the poet, the editors have chosen which poems to include.

In this anthology, we have followed an arrangement representing some of the more popular poems on the PoetrySoup.com website. Instead of an arbitrary selection by PoetrySoup's editors, each poet member has been permitted to express themselves by the work they consider their best, with few stipulations. PoetrySoup editors then decided what should be printed and what was omitted, but, as a general rule, the poets have been allowed absolute freedom in their choice of inclusion.

As mentioned, the contemporary poets in this anthology are members of the PoetrySoup.com website. PoetrySoup is a vast international community of about 42,000+ poets. It is known for its loyal, robust, welcoming, and growing community of poets (called Soupers). However, none of the poets in this anthology are personally known to the editors and selection committee. They are united by the fact that they are "Soupers" or members of the PoetrySoup community.

All Poems submitted are published as the poet's original work and under the poet's copyright. We wish to extend our thanks and acknowledgments to the poets (Soupers) who kindly allowed us to use their poetry in this anthology.

Like Ice --- The Waltz

by Irma L Hole

"Black Ice"

Sorrow flows from the first sunrise
Eyes deeper than winter and rainfall
A painful combination never felt before
At core death awaits
  - laughing while she begs for clemency!
In her eyes, fault is found in every sunset
  - after coming down from cloud nine.
Impossible to move --- her body stiffen
That very moment, a precious Waltz - Expires!
Coldplay and winter mist set in
Ruins of love clinch an endless echo
  - taunting the very merry memory.
The auditory sensation of broken trust
  - stride across the way.
Icing every thought in a sullen, cold rink.
She fell - She crumbled
  - In a world where hope once existed

Today, she will sway alone without a lullaby
In a room with no warmth
One time a sweet symphony, now a sour moon
  At last, a different tune begins to fiddle
As she grooms the icicles in her room.
On every mid-moon, she stares and stares
  towards the old shriveled lipstick on his pillow
Unseen coldness, unsatisfied, incomplete tears
She can feel the complete braille of hate
--- cascade around the emptiness

Throughout her poise frostbite travels in
Midnight Summer dreams are near an end
Autumn bones covered by winter sleet
A deadly force condemns all because of one

Lost years crumbled like an avalanche
Way deep down inside.......
She paints the rain like no other heartache
Leaving winter residue behind every step
"Black Ice" sits close to the cold canvas on her pale

If you seek closely, she is there
Immobilized in a waltz, in a waltz, in a waltz

Never to linger or trust
The "HE" that spoke of love, then melted away

The Rose Bowl

by Andrea Dietrich

The sky is a gigantic bowl of pink turned upside down,
spilling soft rose petals that peeked out
from beneath snow white billowed clouds
till - fully blossomed - they burst forth.

Growing radiant at the edge of twilight,
they've scattered as rubescent streaks falling,
lush and luminescent, as we watch in solitude.
No parade this evening - just you and I aglow,
wishing for an eternity to be like this:
so splendidly in love. . .
in the pink.

Unspoken Words

by Paul Callus

I often scribble in the sand
The words I find so hard to say
And hope the wind will come along
And blow them all your way.

A Smile Appeared

by Rick Keeble

Silently, I sat by,
To listen to the sounds of the world,
Of all the voices that touched me most,
Were those caught in the angelic wind?
For all things have a voice,
And the voice for all things speaks through the wind,
So, silently I sat and listened.
With the salty taste of a tear
As it touched my upper lip,
A smile appeared.
All the while the wind kept blowing,
Secret after secret, revealing to me,
If only I could comprehend its wisdom.
But that is half the allure,
Happy I am just to hear it blow,
And acknowledge its influence over my spirit.
The wind has taught me many things,
Though, I cannot speak for the wind,
Instead, let it speak for me.

Tranquility

by Constance K. Wong

Oh little one, how soon you'll be
In turbulence of puberty.
I will hold tight your days of youth
And share with you my honest truth

That innocence ingrained at birth,
Precious childhood days filled with mirth,
Will be so fleeting... you will see
The need for God's tranquility.

How grandma's age is redefined
When your teen years become aligned
With thoughts of struggles, I go through,
The many shades in every hue,

That colors life for me today.
In these sweet days, I watch you play
As I instill the grains of hope,
An inner strength to help you cope

With all the changes life will bring.
The ups and downs from early spring
Throughout your life in winter years
When you, like me, through joys and tears

Have lived a life you feel has worth;
Have given back to better earth.
When you have children of your own
And you too, see how they have grown,

My hope is that you let them know
That through their life where e'er they go
They carry with them bits of me,
Please share with them, tranquility.

The teenage years and the golden years are
the most difficult to endure. Both are fraught
with emotions...of facing life...of facing death.

Conversation With My Soul

by John Watt

Dwell not, O soul, on yesterday,
  on sorrows past and gone -
the sketch you drew so long ago,
  today may be redrawn.
Dwell not upon tomorrow's wars,
  nor borrow from their pain -
that energy you need today
  let not your worries drain.

Dwell not, O heart, on failures past
   though each one left its scar -
rich lessons you have learned have forged
   the person you now are.
Dwell not upon your victories,
   for those shall also pass -
let not your pride construct a shrine
   to trophies made of glass.

Dwell not, O soul, on others' gain
   nor envy those with much -
contentment, paired with gratitude,
   brings peace no wealth can touch.
Dwell not on anyone's downfall
   as though it lifted up
your own estate; we're siblings all
   and drink from the same cup.

So what is left, O soul - where does
   the prudent soul pay heed?
Become less of a taker,
   always give to those in need.
Where is the plot of ground to plant
   your seed - which soil to plow?
Sow seeds of love, be brave, and dwell
   in the eternal now.

Where The White Rose Blooms

by Kelly Deschler

The single white rose captured the old gardener's attention,
He lovingly cared for it, like it was his own grand-daughter,
The roses were just like family and friends in his eyes,
He gave them bright sunshine, and plenty of fresh water.

He had always planted roses in reds, yellows, and pinks,
Yet, it was the one white rose that he favored most,
The old gardener admired it's innocence and elegance,

A quality that the other roses just could not boast.

This precious rose was pure white, like new fallen snow,
Which only a cold, late November day could bring,
It's delicate petals were soft to the finger's touch,
Similar to that of a feather, in an angel's wing.

The old gardener was perplexed and astonished,
Only this rose bloomed through spring, summer, and fall,
Each of the other roses had withered months ago,
The frost and cold weather did not affect it at all.

With a smile, the old gardener took one last look,
Unknowingly, death would soon come without warning,
After he had settled down for a nap in his chair,
He drew his last breath, later on that morning.

His funeral was held on the very next day,
Loving words were spoken, as he was laid to rest,
His grand-daughter approached, with tears in her eyes,
As she placed the single white rose upon his chest.

The cemetery was a quiet and peaceful place,
Where family and friends gathered to remember,
A gentle snow began to fall upon the casket lid,
Brightening the gloom on this final day of November.

The old gardener's soul departed from this earth,
Lead away by a choir of angels, on delicate wings,
Then on through the pearly gates of heaven's garden,
Where the white rose still blooms, in eternal springs.

Snow -A Sleep
by Andrea Dietrich

Snow -
a sleep
descending on the twilight streets;
Snow, in silent fields you lie pristine
beneath moon's glow, a blanket shimmering.

Oblivion serene!
Tranquilly envelop me in
Sleep -
a snow;
the more you fall, the deeper that I go
under.
Oh, sweet Slumber,
suffocate with pearly flakes
those of us the weary that repose,
long time having waited like the windrows.
As Boreas does blow,
lull and bury all in drifting, dreamy
snow.

Island Spirit

by Constance Kay Wong

Palm trees are swaying island style
Within the gentle trade wind's flow,
As Egrets glide on salty air—
Then land where verdant grasses grow.
Breathe in sweet scents of tuberose
And let fine mist caress your face,
Dive deep into aqua waters—
Become enchanted with this place.

Let your eyes consume the beauty,
Let rhythmic music soothe your mind.
You'll feel the aloha spirit—
A kinder people you won't find.
Go hiking in hillside forests,
There are no bears or snakes that hide,
Just waterfalls you'll find waiting,
That flow toward the ocean side.

In the distance whales are breaching,
Humpbacks with little calves in tow.
They share waters with the dolphins,
And green sea turtles down below.

Can you hear paradise calling?
Whispering your name at sunrise,
To later bask on pearly sands.
Swaying hula hips at moonrise,

Coaxing you to join in the dance.
Exotic Mai Tai in your hands,
Sweet flower leis caress your neck,
Come investigate our islands,
And board on wild waves at surfside,
Cast your cold and cares to the breeze.
Sailing out on sunset cruises—
Take homeward bound warm memories.

Someone Who Used To Be You

by Vijay Pandit

When splendor of love spun dreams ecstatic
Musings of fantasy waltzed joyous themes
On blossoms of meadows in prime of spring
And giggles of streams donning green prairies

I felt your presence my eager beats crooned
When halo of the moon ravished our mood
As melodic rhythms inflamed doting hearts
And voice of hot passion blazed our romance

You were sweet life that I cheerfully claimed
And I was to you what your triumph meant
But feelings euphoric soon lost their edge
When in winds of change vows of youth drifted

I saw you go there where lonesome souls cry
Where emotions despised strife of pale sighs
When day's silence often filled awkward void
And haze of nights we spent gazing gray skies

When dawns soon arose enveloped in shroud
Love too got masked, cloaked in stygian clouds

And allure, once acclaimed, began to fade
As contempt of sameness dwindled our flames

As you leave this dream, dear, you know it too
No longer the birds choose to croon your tune
They are searching someone they loved and knew
The one they once wooed, who used to be you

Unsure The Shore

by Susan M. Ashley

Grim fog, I praise the shelter of your drear,
the sundown ghost morose not grandiose,
I walk alone - but, no -- with my despair;
a bittern bids a bitter adiós.

The breakers so in agony they gnash
and gnaw the strand with thrash of foamy green,
the tempest witch brings ironfisted lash
alas, the eye-of-storm epiphany unseen.

Free, free! The tern who flies in Gemini
above beloved peak and shore and wave,
sun-painted wings, away you went -- so spry,
so fierce! Bluebird pierced and buried in your grave,

..and the stars understand; a fateful fall into the sea --
Damn the deep! It's jostle docile...my scream to meet the scree!

*bittern: any of several tawny brown herons
*scree: an accumulation of weathered rock fragments at the foot of a cliff

Oceana

by Annette P. Kauffman - Sam Kauffman

Oceana flings her sequined petticoats
Upon the sands
As if to toss the seaweed
From the
Swirling edges
While she dances with the wind
With each turn she swings her skirts
In thunder
As she passes – faster, faster -
Until her laughter
Foams upon the waves
And in the early midnight dawns
She turns to cover up
Her turquoise evening gown
With capes of fog so thick
The soaring gulls
Seem to carry
This her summer train
To quickly change into a dress
Of silver satin,
Bound with trims of frothy sprays,
Rising and swelling,
When morning reaches for windy afternoons,
She teases sudden lightning outbursts
Leaving behind,
Upon the outstretched strands,
A foaming lace of pearls
That decorate her new
Rippling dress
Of brilliant sapphire blue
Drawing it around the world
In flowing currents
To follow, forever follow, the lilting music
Of her lover moon,
Softly singing enchanted melodies,
Ever beckoning his earthbound bride

Unto himself
To watch her gaily waltz upon the rolling seas
Circling to his rune.

Miss Amelia Havisham's Garden Shed

by Gary Radice

between the plant pots and the trays
the cobwebs had seen better days
and for all the wood and damp and soil
the smell was one of paint and oil
as flies and wasps lying in state
were curled up past their fly-by-date
and nails and screws and metal hooks
shared space on shelves with brewery books
beneath a clock with broken hands
where time stood still amongst the cans
and jam jars full of pip-like seeds
stood next to things that no one needs
and while her tears had stained the glass
that looked out on the unkempt grass
upon the floor amid the mess
..a letter
and her wedding dress.

The Enchanted Forest

by Constance K. Wong

The woods were silent except for the shifting
soft sounds of his hooves as they fell upon
the forest floor. There he stood amid the mist in
his white majestic coat calling to me to come
to him and ride upon his back, vanish with him,
(as the sun lay dying into quiet shades of twilight)
into an unknown sacred secret realm where no
one's footsteps could follow.

I stroked his soft warm velvet nose and felt the
subtle flair of his nostrils breath on my hand.
When I climbed upon his back we rode
as one as our love and trust in each other
had slowly grown into a synergy unsurpassed.
Moonlight filtered through the verdant trees
as darkness enveloped the starry sky.
Suddenly we found ourselves in a glade
where we were surrounded by the soft glow
of tiny faeries as numerous as fireflies.

We were warmly welcomed into their sacred
sanctuary and I felt enchanted by their sylvan
beauty as two tiny faeries braided long strands
of my golden hair, intertwining fragrant flowers.
I was asked if I would help to keep the forest
safe from clear cutting, and I promised I would.
I awoke to the faint sound of hoofbeats as dawn
was rising and there were pretty flowers in my hair.

Crepe-Myrtle Flowers

by Vijay Pandit

Eventide's misty winds gently oscillate
Colorful clusters of crepe-myrtle flowers
Crowning atop rows of elegant tree-trunks
Blooms lavender, pink, red, and purple
Hanging in air from tips of twigs slender
Bowing to earth, donning green foliage
Arrayed in symmetrical flower-bouquets.

On a summer stroll, my hand you hold,
Gazing rhythms tilting back and forth
Swaying gracefully symphony of colors
As synchronized whispers merrily rustle
Echoing intentions of doting twilight sun
Beholden to season's gift of blossoms.

Gales now swirl, petite petals disperse,
Whirling confetti, drifting dances aerial,

Sprinkling fine motifs of tinted splendor
Twisting, turning, in eve's amber passion
Flying all over, as we gaze, wooing love,

Where violet-sky above artfully evokes
Opaline glimpses of dreams ephemeral
Inscribed in spectrum on crimson horizon.

If I Were A Flower

by Vijay Pandit

A blossom I'll be on the wreaths for peace
An offering to deity to feed world's hungry
I'll be the garden on every troubled street
Preening as gleefully as exuberant tulips
Swaying with spring in rhythms of daffodils

I'll be the laudable bouquet of friendship
An emissary of cupid when love is elusive
A gift I'll be, from souls of dreams romantic
I'll be the cure when dear-heart is aching
A sensuous rose I'll be, alluring bride to be

I'll be sweet smile of expressions in violet
Pleasing smitten hearts on lilac landscapes
Presenting bell-shaped English bluebells
Tenderly in aura of angel's blessed grace
I'll be the enlightenment in lotus of solace

Lovingly I'll answer every call of your will
In colors of hyacinth upon your window sills
And fragrance of white Lily evoking revelry
Composing gaily dulcet themed melodies
Strumming floral kisses on your sateen lips

The Angel Inside

by Roy B Jerden

Coral life forms in copious swarms
feast in the Cambrian chyme,
dividing their cells and forming their shells
to end on the seafloor as lime.
Tectonic churning and magma upturning
renders marble whiter than bone.
The marble is mined, but the cutters are blind
to the angel confined in the stone.

A young sculptor arose, with a bend in his nose
and a transcendent creative spark,
charged with ambition to fulfill a commission,
an angel for St. Dominic's Ark.
An artist sublime who will live for all time,
his genius is to see things not shown.
For an angel to achieve he first has to perceive
its splendor enclosed in the stone.

At dawning's first glow he surveys the tableau
of the blocks the stone cutters supplied.
In some he sees dreams of potential themes,
but only one holds an angel inside.
"A beautiful thing never gives so much pain
as does failing to hear it and see it."
The block that he chose was rejected by those
who then lied and claimed to foresee it.

With talent and skill he falls to with a will,
surrounded by rubble and relic.
His method you see, for the angel to free
is to remove all the bits not angelic.
Michelangelo's art for all time stands apart
but there's something further to heed.
For there's a bit more to the fine metaphor
in the tale of the angel he freed.

"A beautiful thing never gives so much pain
as does failing to hear it and see it."
For in all our insides a bright angel abides
and is just waiting for something to free it:
to remove all the parts which harden our hearts,
to chip out the darkness and pride,
to smooth the rough patches, to polish the scratches
and unshackle the angel inside.

When I Dream Deep

by Charles Messina

As the mornings sun - begins to shine
And memories of yesterday - I leave behind
I get to see - another rising sun
And store more memories - when the day is done

Thoughts in my mind- Which I hold true
My life - what I've been through
All those nights - when I dreamed deep
My all-nighter's - I couldn't sleep

Remembering thoughts - from new, from old
Good times, bad times - I still hold
But tomorrow's sun - again will rise
I may not see it - with my own eyes

For if I don't - and I... not awake
I hope the sun - is yours to take
To let you dream - into the night
Savour memories - see the light

That will rise again - with tomorrow's sun
And leave you memories - when the day is done
Your thoughts in mind - that you hold true
Your life - what you've been through

But if you don't - your eyes...not awake
I hope the sun - is mine to take

So that I can remember you - memories I'll keep
All those nights - when I dream deep

Starry, Starry Night

by Jennifer Proxenos

I often look up towards the sky at night,
And wonder who or what is there,
I shout out loud, if you see or hear me, I love you,
I do this every night, the starry sky, an absolute delight!
I drive out of the city to the Kruger Park,
There, not only am I close to nature and serenity,
But to the universe, I look up, no pollution,
I stretch my arms up high, excited, it is very dark!
No street lights, or cars headlights, or any noise,
The moon is so bright and full, it smiles at me,
Quite rare, for normally the moon looks a little sullen,
The stars, I've lost count, as they twinkle with such poise!
The Milky Way so clear, I feel I want to reach up high,
As it allures me, and weaves across the sky,
Milky, so graceful and silent, as it, and I watch
Sparkling stars, and planets rotating, unknown
To mankind, yet to be discovered in our eternal
Galaxy to which I want to fly!
Our universe has constellations of stars, named mostly
After mythology's gods, who beckon, tempt and wink
And entice me, but I am on planet earth, how near
Could I reach this flamboyant display, body, soul
And mind, holistically!
So maybe if I look up into our never ending
Sky at night,
And wish upon one star, with imagination
That runs rampant,
I will see above and far beyond with breathless anticipation,
What I could never imagine, an explosion that blinds me,
An aura, translucently bright!

All Too Soon

by Elaine Cecelia George

One windy night upon my breast
I felt the kiss of winter's breath
A breath that blew me into flight
Upon my breast one windy night

A leaf once green now bathed in red
With coat of spring and summer shed
True color bursting at the seams
Now bathed in red a leaf once green

Upon your breath I learned to fly
A flame of glory in the sky
Not knowing that the price was death
I learned to fly upon your breath

But all too soon I came and went
The seasons of my life were spent
A bud in spring that came to bloom
I came and went - but all too soon

Always

by Richard Robinson

I'll always be here for you,
where else would I go.

But for you, my heart is lost,
in dream..
to counting sheep,
and always will be so.

I don't need a better picture of you..
than the one that plays in my mind.

Two hands held so close to my heart,
and you always were so kind.

Keep me near like a smile..
one you used to hide.
A whisper of your beautiful name
to my faithful heart.

It's never too far..
           after all,
my hands hold back approaching tide..
to catch you when you fall.

I'll always be here for you,
where else would I go.

And Sweet Is Her Demise

by Andrea Dietrich

In primrose twilight, summer is still near.
She whispers in my ear; I hear her in
the one lone owl that hoots to only me.
I wake to find her shining through the clouds -
though breathing not so warmly on my cheek.
I glimpse her waning smile as in a field
I dance to soundless music in her sun.
My mind goes wandering, and in the breeze
I hear her sigh, for she is lingering
within the scent of asters that I pluck.
I'm hanging on to that one glint I see
of her before me in gold glitter dusk.
But in the cries of geese across the sky,
she calls goodbye, and sweet is her demise.

A Wordless Sky

by Eileen Manassian Ghali

If I don't write, I'm doomed to die
and lie beneath a wordless sky
A silent corpse, unseen, unheard
alive yet dead- is that absurd?

If rhymes don't paint a rainbow hue
and lines don't tempt with taste of dew
If words can't clothe just what I feel
this thing called life must not be real

Without a dose of poetry
what will become of you and me?
Just members of the walking dead,
we march each one with empty head

A lifeless, joyless, hopeless mass
who try to make the hours pass
Without the ecstasy of rhyme
to be alive is just a crime

For life without the words I write
is dull and drear, like starless night
Like endless, tortured misery
is life without my poetry

A Beautiful Mirror

by Irma L Hole

-Escape of the mountain-

Do you care about my breast?
The new curve - countryside corset
The beauty of every summer dress

Laying down, wearing out gravity
Embracing the same feeling;
Your hands indulged in
Passion and devotion
around perfumed scenery
    The perfect pair

Today we will pray,
Counting every second on the clock
No longer the womanly figure before'
I will possess a new battle,
around the virtues of my palace.

Will you still be there,
  when the hump and lump are gone?
Will I still be the queen of your heart?
Patiently I shall wait and see
 in hopes to gain the time breast cancer stole
Leaving behind torn tissue, with a daily reminder of;
The one that got away.

A Flower Blooms

by John Gondolf

While traveling 'cross such harsh terrain
    left parched and barren from the sun
  and weeks without a cooling rain,
    I saw a sight that left a stun
    beside the road on this long run.

I stopped to have a closer look;
    perhaps my vision had deceived
  with image that my mind mistook
    and merely something I perceived,
    but I would never have believed.

Yet there a single flower bloomed
    upon the dry and sun parched soil.
  Impossible I had assumed
    with harsh conditions to embroil;

to stay alive, how she must toil.

Her face shown fair in sun's dry heat
    magenta petals shining bright
appearing happy and upbeat
    without a worry to incite,
    and unaware of her dire plight.

I ponder how one could exist
    in harsh conditions such that be
and thrive with little to assist,
    yet ne'er for help to send a plea;
    she seems to live her life carefree.

Perhaps we all should take a clue
    from gentle flower's look on life
ignoring hell we're going through
    with all its worry and its strife,
    and all the bad with which it's rife,

    and focus on our gifts in life.

Still I Run

by Dale Gregory Cozart

I race for summer's setting sun
as crimson bleed the alder leaves
and still I run. And still I run.

My rival, time, is yet undone.
Past pyramids of flaxen sheaves
I race for summer's setting sun

across the low unbroken run.
Each cow out in the pasture grieves
and still I run. And still I run.

In late September's crisp blazon
my heart to fragile hope now cleaves.

I race for summer's setting sun.

With slaughter of the calves begun
I fled from 'neath the killing eaves
and still I run. And still I run.

Our time on earth is under gun.
My burning chest now breathless heaves.
I race for summer's setting sun
and still I run. And still I run.

To Be Loved

by Edward Ibeh

To be loved
is to be a wildflower
blooming in springtime.
How wondrous to be much desired
by all the honeybees in the meadow.
There's no greater wealth on all of earth.
That feeling,
that inexplicable feeling
is like being all wrapped up
in warm satin sheets.
Oh, what a thrill it is
to be loved, unconditionally.
It's like being sung to all at once
by the robins of the universe;
words can't possibly describe it.
Is it crazy to imagine
it feels like a walk across
heaven's pearly gates?
Is it but the loveliest of dreams
one would rather die
than awake from?
Oh, I bet it is.
I know this much is true,
it's heavenly to be loved
by you.

The Whip Of Your Selfish Whims

by Susan M. Ashley

O
the bane
of being so slavishly in love
and facing another bloodless sunrise alone
myself I'm spun in silken strands enthralled
yet still stung by the whip of your selfish whims
your fleeting presence flashes like iridescence in the light
elusive fire and passion whose colors escape my grasp

I pine for possession of one I cannot possess
though my burning being's bewitched
by a yearning that pliantly possesses me
ensnaring me in the exquisite twist
of fervent temptations you weave
as your amorous play strums the lusty lure
of a gossamer thread I wish to follow to your soul
whilst my purring thirst is captured   then ignored

O
the woe
of being caught
in the frill of desire's web
aching for the thrill of arching pleasures
craving to be melted by our molten fusion
longing forever wanting and waiting breathlessly
for your wanton appetite to ravish me
always and again.

Inside My Head

by Vivian Wigley

Hello there, do please come inside- no need to wipe your feet
excuse the mess, I fear you'll find it isn't very neat.
This place is always untidy, victim of my disorder
from old hang-ups to memories, I'll admit I am a hoarder.
In here hanging like mobiles, noisy, at odds with my feelings
are life's little distractions, niggling, swinging from the ceiling.
Careful with your torch, don't shine it underneath the bed
beneath it there is lurking a dark sprouting creeping dread.
Most people couldn't live with it, a disturbing thing to some,
as it cowers in the corner from the things still yet to come.
Tread lightly in the corridor, just mind out where you walk
you'll trip on my anxiety that bobs up like a cork.
The fire is stoked, the hearth is swept and logs stacked in a heap
my warmth to all well-tended (well, except when I'm asleep).
Cardboard tubes in disarray, and more you cannot see-
plans I drew up in the past, none ever meant to be.
Mannequin in veil of black, arms raised as if to dance
with all my past relationships that never stood a chance.
This rocking chair, my temper, that sometimes I must sit in
and you'll notice that the varnish of my patience has worn thin.
My sense of humour's in the loft, protected by my hats
seemed like the right place for it, since my friends all think I'm bats.
That one small window by the beam lets my faith's light shine in
I'm sorry it's not brighter, window dirty from past sin.
Still, I can climb and open it to aim my telescope
for somewhere in the darkness lies the faintest glimpse of hope
that keeps me living here in peace and shelters me from sad;
you wonder why I live in here? Well, out there-
it's just mad!

Gentle Harbinger

by Delice Arleen Skelly

Musing on this life of mine
Alone I wonder if it's time?
Robin sings in my heart
Fluttering wings like cupid's dart.

Have been hurt, no doubt caused pain
Hearing robin's song again
Before I journey who knows where?
Know angelic wings will take me there.

The time has come and gone again
I'm stoic now what's left to gain
The universe will keep me here
Perhaps a day, perhaps a year.

A harbinger called to seal my fate
My gentle songbird set no date
Listen carefully you might hear
Angelic music have no fear.

There Was Silence

by Malabika Ray

among green foliage and slender twigs, perched a graceful mellifluous
Nightingale.
Chickadees, Robins, Orioles stopped their synchronised cadence of rhythmic
tweets, in anticipation..
a tranquil silence fell in the forest, a quiet trance around...

tall majestic trees stopped swaying their aspiring branches,
plants and shrubs and bushes softly emanated saffron scent,
rustling fragrant breeze whispered lilac mystery,

chartreuse clouds stooped and gently touched the treetops,
tangerine twilight moon flickered ribbons of love,
ravishing flowers opened their petite petals blazing red blush in awe!

Nightingale sang the most melodious song, sprinkling amber passion,
It sang a symphony pouring its heart, weaving
the story of eternal love and loss,
mesmerizing the audience with lavender dreams and hopes
a dazed forest stood still ...

All hushed!

Rainbow Promise

by Joanna Daniel

He has announced his arrival. She waits,
Listening to the thunder cracking through
the layers of air. Looking at the lightning,
brightening and frightening the darkness away,
Lapping up the sweet petrichor that comes her way.
He gushes and rushes down to meet her.
In warm welcome, she opens up
to quench her unsatisfied thirst.
The twain meet and a silence follows,
As thick as the mist that envelops this inexplicable gloom.
Emotions flood the watery lane...
His constant showers drench her very soul...
New life awakens as old lives are cleansed, refreshed.
The earth has had her fill...
For now...
Drip...
        drip...
                drip...
Slowly the gentleman rain recedes...
He will come...
                yet again...
                        to meet her...
With this rainbow promise, they part...

On Poetry Soup

by *Wilfred Aniagyei*

A first day on Soup is filled with much awe
The wonderful poems will make you smile
Easy is it to fall for all
Some enabled my mind, lingering a while
Just the few Soupers I mention here
Will blow you away with works of this year!

Janet Cervenka almost made us lust
When she penned a piece on Heavenly's bust

Marvelous is the diversity of Jan Allison
Such a dressed gem, and she's only blooming

Nandita then tells us that she's no Jan
Indeed her craft is paralleled by none

Man! the lyrics never cease to flow for Dave
So highly endowed with a skill many crave

You see, my first day on Soup I was greeted by SKAT
Who so humbly laid down the welcome mat

And if there exist a bond no man can put asunder
I have to say it's between SKAT and Linda

O! How can I forget 'Half of A Heart'
A Sara Kendrick special, such design and art!

Who better to mend our Broken Wings
Than the namesake with a quill in full swing

Yes Soupers always brighten my days
Place me in velds full of beautiful haze
And there I spot a Mystic Rose
Defined so uniquely like a Kim Nunez prose

From a consummation a lover was denied
To the hautiness of a lonely man's pride
Whatever we plan to glimpse or scoop
We tend to leave with more from Soup

Where My True Love Lives - A Ballade

by Elaine Cecelia George

Seared upon my soul for ever more
That break of dawn upon a summer morn
As I made my way along that rocky shore
Strewn with remnants from a raging storm
When through a rising mist of gray - so forlorn
I saw a badly broken sinking ship
With canvas wings of white so sadly torn
There beneath those majestic purple cliffs

And as that mighty fearless ocean roared
With salty breezy breath so filled with scorn
I saw it rise up from the ocean floor
Wrapped in a velvet coat so frayed and worn
A red, red, rose impaled upon a thorn
Where passion bled like rain from ruby lips
Upon a vivid memory reborn
There beneath those majestic purple cliffs

The wind - it whispered - in my ear - Lenore
As black clouds in the sky began to form
Into a face I'd never seen before
With hollow cheeks that endless tears adorned
That fell in frozen crystal drops so foreign.....
Then from those clouds his face began to slip
And I cried the tears of a woman scorned
There beneath those majestic purple cliffs

Lenore, the love he would forever mourn
That from his pen on page in words did drip
As I read his poetry and love was born
There beneath those majestic purple cliffs.

~ ~ ~ ~

A tribute to: Edger Allen Poe and his Lenore

Within Her Heart
by Daniel F Turner

Within her heart is where I wish to be
To dwell inside the garden of her soul
Where each soft heartbeat plays a symphony
And all around is beauty to behold

The sunshine of her love would keep me warm
My one desire, to take life's pain away
Consoling her when clouds of sadness form
Removing troubles of each stressful day

Should something cause her fragile heart to break
I'd gather up the pieces tenderly
With love I'd smooth the sharpness of heartache
Then put them back together lovingly

Within her heart is where her beauty lies
Her love, the light that shines within her eyes

Mindful
by Annette P. Kauffman - Sam Kauffman

Mindful

Startled out of nonchalant light,
Wakefulness stands at attention
Ignited flame from the eternal candle,
Energized vigil of the watchman
At the soul's dawning daybreak
Tingling in the presence

Of every dappled infinite breath.

Rotating eye of illumination
Watchful, like a lighthouse beacon hovering,
Charts rocks and shoals through clear oceans insight,
Every nerve exposed in circumspection
Sometimes cringing in wary expose
Often basking in the light touch of satisfaction
As niggling prophecy finds confirmation in revelation

Throwing off the blinded penury of antonyms,
Embracing flashing synonyms of wisdom,
Tears of the heedful heart touch drab puzzles poverty
To polish with refinement's shine burnished enthusiasm
For the incandescent dancing mindful
Then banish chary strobes of destitute indifference
Reaching beyond self-centered parentheses.

A lantern of thoughtfulness in floodlights
Of full harvest shared – no scattered crumbs of bread
Baked to stone in scathing flashes of the false
Eloquent vigilant splendor - never morning extinguished –
Torch to awaken lambent radiance of clarity's joy,
Identity of the pilgrim heart, ejects sightless shades

Mindfulness blends the conscious scattered fragments
For Mosaics in clear lit portraits of charity's open hands
Throwing off the numb stalker branded carelessness
Born of intentional ignorance
Seeker's actuated incentive to the attentive –
To hear! To see! To feel! To move in birth!
Action invigorated by accentuated humility of grace.

Not Enough Time

by Daniel Turner

Last January, winter lost its chill
By May the summer's sun had turned me brown
I watch the leaves late August, change at will
Time's speeding up or am I slowing down?

It brings to mind, a boy, who I once knew
While young, he put a dream up on a shelf
It sat there many years. Oh, how time flew.
While he got sidetracked searching for himself

And then one day while sitting in a swing
His body tired, each passing year a mile
With autumn closing in, he thought of spring
And how time turned his dream into a smile

How quickly through the glass our trickling sand
One day a boy, the next, a tired old man.

Part Time Poet

by Michelle Lynn Faulkner

She calls on me, intermittently
In fickle favor, in spotty dictionaries
My demure, distracted destiny

She is the unrequited lover, the absent mother
She is Santa, granting wishes
Upon orphan dinner dishes
Then, flitting through my mind's back door
Leaving me her messy, unfinished chores

She is sly mischief's mocking whim
She is moonlight's pull, waxing and dim
She arrives on trumpet's fanfare glory
To bestow in my beggar's palms, a story

I am too poor to pass her by
Too thirsty, her nectar to deny
I am the third string, the second select
Her stepchild of benign neglect

She is my bitter pleasure, my inconvenient pride
My every frustration, my only tribe

I am a poet on part time pay
As full time runs a five second delay.

All Of Life Is A Poem

by John Watt

all of life is a poem
sometimes the inkwell is empty
the quill rests
the deer pants for a stream
but finds only hardscrabble land

all of life is a poem
as we rearrange its lines
to find rhyme in mayhem
     beauty in chaos
     reason in ambiguity
     hope in a dungeon

all of life is a poem
sometimes
sometimes it gets put into
          words

Love Melts The Thorns Of A Rose

by Evelia Roper "Eve"

Another night to drown in your mystic splendor
  Could not calm a pounding heart swoon, neath a blush moon.
   Poise in untold colour, true beauty you surrender
    Suspended, soon bedding, good-night veils of clouds cocoon.

Thirst of the soul melts the thorns of
      A rose, transcends beyond a never-ending fountain of Love.

Endless blue mosaic slumber awaking in cool caress.
  Burst of radiant hope release in fluttering flight,
   Caught across in the current ripples; whose touch may press

Deeply, brushing against nature's doorstep light.

Thirst of the soul melts the thorns of
    A rose, transcends beyond a never-ending fountain of Love.

Thy presence summons by my yearning love,
  Peacefulness invited in, welcoming salvation,
    Enlightenment of the presence of the Lord above.
    Enrapture faint breath and sigh deep emotion.

Thirst of the soul melts the thorns of
    Arose, transcends beyond a never-ending fountain of Love.

Spring Sunrise

by Tania Kitchin

magenta pink sky
songbirds singing melodies -
peony opens

A Blessing If You Would Learn

by Besma Riabi Dziri

The heart when young, so blissful and knows no sin
the mind's ego knows no bounds, its strength within

The earth, sound and steep, its fruits the soul entice
the taste of spice great! to every slice a price

The eyes rain and the mouth would savour its pain
when dry is your land, sow no seed, reap no grain

Valiant steps fear no edge nor the burn of sands
wish die for the glory of walking God's Lands

Specks of dust make souls blind can turn lives to dust
just a spark of deep Faith heralds paths to trust

Ascend and observe, gems in you aim to earn
What seems as harm, a blessing if you would learn

God for you paves paths and lends many a hand
a deep well of Love granted to flood your land

Those warm drops of Love and Life, in time of birth
brought heaven under your feet, mothers of earth

Peace and joy in voice of heart to God raise praise
light in soul, a power with beauty would blaze

Brushes and pens paint and a language translate
the soul ebb and flow beyond language and state.

Play On Words

by John Watt

Write here, right now. Write now, right here!
Capture the moment while it's near
and seize the day. You now know how:
write now, right here; write here, right now.

The rhyme is tight. The time is right
to write some rhyme this time of night –
a rite of writing, lacking light.
The time is right, the rhyme is tight.

Another draft you craft in ink.
No lucre comes from thoughts you think;
though relatives may think you daft,
you craft in ink another draft.

What you can see, you then can say.
At dawn, as dark dissolves today,
with light, you write. In poetry,
you then can say all you can see.

The play's the thing, you need to play

with words. Then, playfully they say
what makes the heart smile, cry, or sing;
you need to play, the play's the thing.

Now play on words and let them dance
in rhymes and rhythms of romance;
teach them to sing like carefree birds
and let them dance. Now play on, words!

It's Only Time

by Nicholas Windle

For the lark she sings in her morning song,
That brightens up my day.
The pitter patter of tiny drops,
Clouds fill the sky with grey.

The dampened ground, that familiar smell,
Now quenched refreshed anew.
Brings forth forgotten memories,
Of a time that I once new.

Like grains of sand they ebb and flow,
Those minutes of the day.
In lines of endless moments,
That brought forth that child at play.

For is this just like déjà vu
For some time I've been alone.
Now standing here now humble,
To all these things I've known.

With gentle face a youthful pose,
As we danced the night away,
A tender touch a knowing gaze,
No need for words to say.

For what is love but a feeling?
As hearts melt into one.

With the blessings of good fortune,
  Now Care free and full of fun.

For they say that hopes eternal,
And all things come to he who waits.
Or is that for other people,
For nothing seems that straight.

Given in reflected thought,
To those oh so special years.
Brought back in just a heart beat,
I wipe away the tears.

The Glory Days Of Now

by Michael J. Gentile

I'm grateful for the sun
        which shone on younger days
The days of scurried heartbeats
            and butterflies of love

And for the carefree hearts
            on beaches of my youth
The nights of clothes and cars
            and bars of clubbing beats

I'm grateful for the sun
        which lights the memories
of newlyweds with king sized beds
and never-ending dreams

And for all the glory days
        I've lived and loved, gone by
Yet, as I know sun still
I'm grateful for the glory days of now

Watercolours In The Rain

by James Fraser

~*~ Summer to Autumn ~*~
Expresses blooms of beauty,
~ primary pastels ~
whilst impending changes loom
~*~ Water colours in the rain ~*~

The Digger's Children

by Craig Cornish

I paced between the old and new
along the rows where gray stones grow,
so careful not to tread upon
the freshly filled and seeded few.
Soft shadows slid across the lawn
where long ago a scythe would mow;
its ringing echoed down the row
like angels voices singing now,
a prayer of faith, a sacred vow.
While young men die in foreign fields,
when once they played with cardboard shields -
now dig, like I, an endless trench,
a hole where mud and blood would drench;
the devil's own unholy stench.
Today my labors dig like they,
yet here, a grave where mourners pray
as chapel bells ring hymns of peace;
a futile wish for hate to cease.
The soil is scarred across the world,
with trench and grave, more holes to fill,
while there, on high, a tempest swirled.
It all will heal...it is his will.

One Tear

by Michelle Lynn Faulkner

One tear slides down a slanted cheek
A silver line, the only sign

Of anguish which she does not speak
Insistent smiles, bright by design

Thin fortitude, her whitewashed shrine
Gilded answers rain, lily meek

She lies and says that she is fine
When truth is too fearsome to seek

Whispers Of Nature

by Rama Balasubramanian

Winds whisper be active throughout the day
Flowers whisper enjoy every moment of stay
Mountains whisper be silent, calm, stand tall
Rains whisper go up pure every time you fall

Moon whispers in dark be the light
Sun says don't be egoistic of your might
Multifarious things can block me
Be realistic, your limitations always see

Earth whispers endure all pain
Be silent, in crying there's no gain
Forests whisper don't worry at all
Benevolent God provides for all

Waves whisper work without rest
Till you are alive don't lose your zest
Rivers whisper don't stop till your goal you reach
Many things profound, elements of nature teach

Harmony

by Anitha Jayasankar

Her sounds are peaceful
symphonic and soothing

The chirping of the birds
at the crack of dawn,
the plopping of rain
pouring heavily at roof tops,
the humming of bees
as they move swiftly
flower to flower,
the rustling of the leaves
in a cool breezy evening,
the splashing of the stream
as it swerves through forest,
the burbling of the river
as it trickles through valleys,
the crackling of dead leaves
as you walk through it in fall,
the whistling of the wind
through the coconut tree tops,
the crashing of waves
against the rocks in the sea,
the croaking of distant frogs
in the stillness of night

As She sings in harmony
to the tunes composed by God

Perception

by Heidi Sands

I thought I heard you calling in the rain from afar
What do you need on this gray day without a star?
The fog is lifting, revealing a crystal light
If you look in the sky, you may also see the sight
Perception can change, quick as lightening to ground
Blink your eyes, look again, to see what you have found
I thought I heard you calling, beyond the pounding rain
Let it be a washout for that lingering pain
Perception can change just about anything
Without losing the moment to things that sting
    And this my friend, allows us to sing!

All Too Wonderful

by Gordon S. Wolf

The trees are given
  to you, to me
The clouds are given
  to us, for free

The grass turns green
  overnight, prithee
The birds sing sweet
  as the honeybee

And if all this seems
  too wonderful to be
The whole Earth belongs
  to the Lord, you see

Legion Of Doom

by Subrahmanyan Radhakrishna

howling black wolves complain to new moon,
of devastation wrought by creatures!
different from rest in size and shape,
walk on two legs, strange hairless features!

in packs behind rigid barriers,
cunning to modulate world to needs,
the rivers run dark under their feet,
trees have perished to nourish their seeds!

clouds now migrate away to the south,
it thunders and rains where once desert,
vast oceans expand as glaciers melt,
cold death now haunts where once birds would nest.

hunt us down, say are born of devil,
spare not a thought for nature's reasons,
we hunt when hungry, the weak and lame,
but they kill for game in all seasons!

fire horrors ravage homely woods,
cuckoo laments morning with its lore,
big herds that walked now dress their rooms,
world is wounded, earth is bleeding sore!

Horror! Horror! we cry to the moon,
our laments tear down the dark silence,
ruled by these creatures with hearts of stone,
they are destructive sans repentance!

we fear not ghosts that lurk in the dark,
nor dripping blood from a sharpened steel,
greater horror lurks where these things haunt,
a pestilence that rocks nature's keel!

If Hearts Could See

by John Gondolf

If hearts had eyes perhaps then yours might see
the person standing right in front of you
with open arms and love, that longs to be
the one with whom a lifetime to pursue.

if hearts had ears perhaps then yours might hear
the tender whispers drifting through the air
amongst the trees, that softly call you near
and wrap around your soul with loving care.

if hearts had hands perhaps then yours might feel
emotions ever longing to caress
your tender feelings with a love so real
that only loving hearts can e'er express.

And still I hold great hope that there's a way
your heart will someday see love's sweet display.

Worry

by Anne E Sangster-Keeley

Worry eats your energy and robs your peace of mind
It brings about anxiety so you cannot unwind
It takes away your happiness, it steals away your joy
And left unchecked eventually your health it will destroy
So learn to stop the worry as it only serves you harm
And make the time to meditate to find your inner calm
For your mind is the driving force in how you will progress
And so that inner chatter is the thing you must address
Your thoughts can either set you free or keep you chained in fear
So take back all your power and make worry disappear

Cherry Beach House

by Evelyn Judy Buehler

Out where the blooming path comes to an end,
Along with wildflowers and Queen Anne's Lace,
A white sandy beach is waiting in the sunshine,
With a house so inviting at the day's primetime.
Seagulls are swooping and diving so endlessly,
Like the turquoise waves that come crashing in,
Before rushing back out to wild fathomless sea!
At the end of the beginning of gold midmorning,
It is noontime in the silent house of the sun.
Red butterflies are flittering on a soft breeze,
And the bees have begun their quest for honey.
Blooms yellow orange and red sit upon the porch,
As if somehow lit up, by the sun's flaming torch!

Breathe

by Susan Lawrence Piatt

I call to you my beloved
Your unleashed whispers arrive
Riding the tendrils of an approaching fog
A dance of mist unfurling its fingertips of desire
Coming ever closer to my pulsating heart
I long for you, for all you have ever been
To taste your breath, your desire, your heartache and your sorrow
Would be my everlasting gift
You come to me in many forms... hovering close by
Beckoning me upward to that place between Heaven and Earth
White hawk.....Your feathered wings outstretched
I lay upon your back merging with you
Entering your being
Becoming you
I feel our wings beating as we enter the sky together
Gliding across powdery clouds

A stillness... the air brushing our cheeks
Our bodies rising and falling
Dipping, curving, and diving
Before climbing again
Joy
A quiet ascendance soaring into the realm
Of Spirit and Soul
Entering magical moments cloaked in ancient memories
Our guardians are hummingbirds and owls
Adorned in snowy white guiding us towards the velvet envelope
Between space and time
Undying light reaching out to the end of the horizon
A merging of ALL..... Promise and Desire
An everlasting illumination of hope
Swimming in the naked air
Being kissed by bursts of sunlight
Peering through the gauzy sky
My body basking in radiant warmth
A quiet solitude
A tapestry of pale rose, magenta, and mauve
Reflecting my inner soul
A call to BREATHE....Deeply...Fully
Feeling the eternal connection
Becoming one with the pulse of life
Surrounding us all
A deep reverence towards all that is
Pink pearled strands of rain pierce the sea of mist and clouds
A kaleidoscope.... columns of light and shadow
Swimming through glorious turquoise universes
I close my eyes and feel your embrace
As we become one

Grief Of Losing A Life Partner

by Subrahmanyan Radhakrishna

It is important we know this eternal truth,
that our earthly lives may be linked but not our deaths!
you may have special memories from early youth,
but one has to watch the other take the last breath!

you will for sure shed tears of separation, grief,
fear future prospect of life without the other,
but thank God for the lovely life however brief!
pray after life you still wish to be together!

we do not choose to be born nor do we choose death,
in the garden of creation we bloom and rest,
relish every moment of fortune and good health,
but when the end comes, please trust him for He knows best!!

let not this despondency rob your faith in Him,
as you are precious to others as was to you,
life must still be lived and cherished however grim,
destiny has plans for you till you bid adieu!

Flying Over Vietnam, 1974

by LEN J. CARBER

I flew,
a modern man in a steel bird,
with all the arrogance of
ancient Icarus, but my wings
did not melt nor I swoon.

I flew high, very, very high
over Asian lands and homes,
and below me, very, very far
down where the bombs fell
like the rains of hell...
I saw the face of the moon.

Cloak Of The Oak

by Chantelle Anne Cooke

sunset souls seep sighs
our eyes as blue butterflies
leaves...God's love letters

This Beautiful Brown Eyed Boy

by Betty Robinson

He was skipping along, swinging his arms and laughing
At what I don't know.
His grandmother, lagging a few steps behind, was laughing at him I
suppose.
And I thought to myself, she loves him, she does,
This Beautiful Brown Eyed Boy.
He stopped when he got to the corner and waited for me to turn right.
A smile crossed his lips,
As he waved at me - at me and my shabby old car.
And when I had passed him, he started to prance quite merrily on his way.
This Beautiful Brown Eyed Boy.
The confidence of youth flowed joyfully through him,
Just looking at him made me smile.
And you know what I did? I pulled to the curb and parked my silly old car.
I watched for a while as he started to run and then charge on out of sight.
This Beautiful Brown Eyed Boy.
How old he was then, I'm really not sure, Maybe five, maybe six,
Not yet Seven.
But ageless his quest to embrace this life whatever might come his way.
A sadness crept into my heart just then for I knew life would never be fair to
This Beautiful Brown Eyed Boy.
It will be harder for him to be special. The color of his skin will not help.
I wish I could be there
To tell him be careful, stay safe in this white man's domain.
But maybe the people he'll meet in his life will let him be just who he is
This Beautiful Brown Eyed Boy.

Pale Shelter

by Paul Callus

Dangling from fragile threads
soaked in suppressed emotions
I weigh my limited options
as flashes from the past flicker
behind a barrier of uncertainty.
In swirling mist, I see your hazy
expressionless face. I call out,
my voice cracking under the
strain of persistent instability.
Scornfully stonewalling me
you turn and walk away, while
suspended in the throes of time,
I hesitate, then stop in my tracks
dejected...rejected...hurting...

How Long Is Forever

by Laura Leiser

The vision calls me once again against this restless night
in brilliant strata gems, in timeless dreams of light.
I close my ancient eyes, and there, so long ago
I see the walls that rose above the eventide.

For it was there where we scaled the lofty cliffs
and breached the gates of a grand estate
with rows of high arched windows, fine
and endless rooms of decadence in decline.

His youth, his hair, flowed e'er alive, my heart revived
I followed in his footsteps as we ran among the heights.
Hidden memories we explored, abandoned dusty rooms
we fell into each other's arms, dancing to a distant tune.

Under the vast eternal sun, my heart was knit
in rapt kinship, time melted in his presence
our days divine, indelible design
were carved for us and us alone.

In random room we laid upon a dingy floor
his strong limbs, my budding breasts
together we explored youth's sparks
as thick as honey, blossoming to a fragrance.

No other bliss could be like this, I now know
with mirrors in my mind of sunsets' glow
undimmed by time, I'll ne'er forget...
...I open ancient eyes with honey on my lips.

All In A Day

by Michelle Lynn Faulkner

Dawn's soft silence kept under gauzy veil
Lifted by harmony of harp and flute
Colors dance along roses, bright and pale
Rainbows springing where fertile sky takes root
Elfin robins follow the fitful wind
Across freckled grass, where new faith consumes
Mossy velvet bark, and sunny bees send
Assured calendars of glory bound blooms
Coy autumn flirts with stately august shade
In kisses of crimson impertinence
Where barefoot rivers rush in eager aid
Hope overflows the banks of reticence
This sunrise drips with beauty's sweet syndrome
For it brings me the day you're coming home.

Sweet Breeze

by Mike Bayles

The sweet breeze through the window
asks nothing as unseen birds call.
It asks nothing of the sun
as it sweeps across yards,
yet it whispers to waking dreams.
My dreams ask,
Did I love too much?
behind my mind's eye,
visions
and what do they mean
when we give of ourselves
so fully we are spent.
Now I'm alone.
Canadian geese gather
crowding a path along the river
as the day passes,
so consumed with each other
they ignore the mothers
and children who pass.
A ski jet slaps waves,
and the river breathes.
The gaggle whispers among itself,
and nature speaks a language of her own.

Supernova Bossa Nova

by Eric Cohen

Now I'm ninety solar masses and I grow as I accrete
all the inter-stellar gasses near my neighbors when we meet.
My doctor says I've grown too fat too fast, "... it's unsustainable!"
But I've big plans for a big blast that I know is attainable:

I'll do the Supernova Bossa Nova, watch me when I blow.

Let's do the Supernova Bossa Nova and host a cosmic show
for galaxies both near and far, a dazzling dance display,
and I'll blow a smoke ring where we are here in the Milky Way.

My hydrogen will all convert and soon I will implode
inward, I'm an introvert, but watch my shell explode.
My core will keep on shrinking 'til a blackhole is created,
a wormhole linking to a world where dance is venerated.

We'll do the Supernova Bossa Nova, watch me when I blow.
You can blame the Bossa Nova but let's get on with the show!

I Think I Know

by Charles Messina

I think I know why the ocean flows
Why the sun shines...why the moon glows

I think I know why leaves fill trees
Why flowers grow...why winds breeze

I think I know why angel's- wing
Why hearts beat...why birds sing

I think I know why the deserts- sand
Why mountains peak...why snowflakes land

I think I know why friends are fun
Why elders walk...why children run

I think I know why skies are blue
Why grass is green...why two is two

I think I know why the ocean's flow
why love is love...I think I know

Soliloquy Of Abandoned Lighthouse

by Aditi Mishra

O hear I chant clinging to a sullen northern shore,
tempestuous serene rocky beach that you so adore,
sultry soliloquy sturdy stifled structure sings,
a witness of forgotten sailors and majestic kings.

Them, I blessed with gracious shelter in storms,
for I unmanned, rejoiced in accompanying norms
dreaming of worlds afar with anchored symphony,
of parting tears that await a returning euphony.

O watch my ancient red-bricked watchtower in sky
where the cherry-eyed albatross prepares to fly,
whispering of solitary voyages on vessels adrift,
guiding them through entailing waters, cold and swift.

Them, I engulf in mystic hues of radiant green light,
their shivering agony embraced by divine joy so bright,
dancing to tunes of prodigious waves as they kissed,
my feet reuniting with the ocean bed of forlorn mist.

O taste the pungent waves that carry eternal seasons,
timeless frequencies sprinkled on heavenly reasons,
essence of leaves rolled in snow and streams they fuse,
beads reborn of universe in a cradled hammock cruise.

Them, I absorb with their enchanting viscous tides,
they melt with innocent bliss my truculent slides
that flourishes my solitary light to let me sense
melodies of blushing mornings with visitors hence.

O touch my abandoned walls, barren yet strong,
bereft of warm embrace in a lifetime so long;
them I nurture with tears of melancholic grief,
to be held by tender nights of melodious relief.

I await the echoing hums of a delicate little girl,
her fingers orchestrated the howling wind with a twirl,
I became the serene light that guides despondent ships,
a proud beacon of benign hope dissolving dark eclipse.

Candle Light

by Robertina Basilico

The sun sets..
Darkness surrounds..
There is a candle burning..
Candle light ..
A flickering flame..
A tender flame that glows so lovely..

Peace and quiet..
Silent and still
Only the sound of a slight crackle..
By a warm glowing candle..

In my moment of silence..
In my moment of serenity
I softly whisper a prayer of gratitude..
A heartfelt prayer of pure Love..

My entire being had been lifted by divine love..
The flame of the candle had died..
For I am now the flame of the candle..

Glowing with divine love and light..

Psalm To The Artist

by Laura Leiser

The Lord weaves His grand tapestry across the skies
He outlines charcoal-colored clouds with silver threads
sews the sunlight of dawn into rays that caress the sea
and folds ocean ripples into fans of intricate patterns.

Each morning God's canvas awaits His ready hand
a master Artist, His creativity knows no bounds
He dips His brush into the spectrum of rainbows
like a whirlwind, He mixes and paints dazzling designs.

God deftly blends pastel shades to greet the rising sun
He sweeps white, cotton clouds that hover over land and sea
He paints the morning light to touch lush liquid waves
and adds violet-colored shadows that fade into the horizon.

His living canvas continually changes its hues and tones
each moment rearranged by heat, wind, or sudden storms
a cornucopia of shapes sweeps across the heavens
like rapid time frames that move within an eternal film.

Will not many among the nations fail to see His mighty wonders?
Will not many among us look up to relish in His majestic sky?
God's handiwork daily displays His infinite creation
may we lift up our eyes to behold His unending glory.

Beautiful Flowers

by Paula Goldsmith

I love pink rose flowers
Kept safe by thorns on the flowers
Big smiling sunflowers
Wide face opening up to the red sun, flowers
Ruffled white carnation flowers

petticoats worn beneath the flowers
Many colors of lily flowers
Their cups make the perfect rain catching flowers
Beautiful purple lilac flowers
Each bud comes to make its own flowers
Daffodils known as buttercup flowers
Beautiful little yellow spring flowers
Big or small orchid flowers
The smell from one fills the room like a bouquet of flowers
The yard is filled with dandelion flowers
Make a tea-make a salad flowers
Yellow or white petals from daisy flowers
He loves me-he loves me not flowers

Last Love Letter

by John Gondolf

Adrift upon a sea of dreams
like paper boats on downhill streams;
my swirling heart is like debris
forever drifting endlessly
while weathered by your wily schemes.

And so I write as my soul screams
this last love letter so it seems
as hearts approaching apogee
  adrift upon a sea.

I'm hiding from the moon's soft beams;
a pool of sorrow sadly steams
with fantasies you stole from me
when you walked out and set me free
and left my heart in dire extremes
  adrift upon a sea.

End Of Age

by Thomas Cunningham

At the edge of town stood, a government research centre
It was heavily guarded, no unauthorised persons could enter
The authorities put down rumours, saying it's just a research station
But word got out they were trying, to open an other dimension.

One night a massive blast took off the research station roof
If anyone doubted the rumours, here now was the proof
The gates of hell opened, with the sound of blood curdling screams
And out poured tall green creatures, only found in hellish dreams.

They were humanoid winged reptilians with eyes a blood red
The townspeople heard the blast, many of them were in bed
All the streetlights went out and the sky turned pitch black
Under the cover of darkness the creatures launched an attack.

They entered every house and mutilated everyone inside
There was pools of blood everywhere; hundreds had died
The police and army arrived and fired shell after shell
But they too were slaughtered by these demons from hell.

They kept coming out of the portal and went from town to town
They were annihilating mankind and they weren't slowing down
By the next day they'd invaded, across the world every land
No weapons could stop them, they had the upper hand

World leaders held an urgent meeting and agreed a strategy
But that strategy would mean, the end of humanity
The plan was to launch nuclear missiles, it was the only way
If mankind couldn't rule the earth then neither would they.

The countdown time was agreed, and it was announced worldwide
Everyone told to stay at home, with your loved ones by your side
People were crying, religious leaders urged people to pray
Ten minutes later earth was vaporised on mankind's darkest day.

I Reminisce, I Miss

by Paula Goldsmith

I reminisce, I miss....
The smell of fresh home baked cookies,
today they come from a box of stale goodies.
Please and thank you,
now very seldom heard.
When kids were kids just having fun,
not tied to a computer so they cannot run.
Life was work hard with simple things,
like flowers you would bring.
The days of old are long gone,
never to return.
The ones I loved,
the ones that loved me are all gone.
I reminisce, I miss....

Like A Hundred Violins

by Constance La France

it is cold and the flowers are dying
becoming withered memories
leaves are drifting and rain is falling
and the river flows like a stream of glass
the grass is fading
and birds are flying away
and the forest is taking on a sombre hue
and storms shake the ocean of my sleep
where my hair is soft as a spider web
and my filmy dress a paling green
and I stand still in this decay as a tree
with my arms outstretched to the sky
oh, the fine thread of summer is a fading thought
yet, there is a hazy beauty all around me
and within the crumbling fragile leaves that soar
oh, the splendor of the whirling burnt orange

and red leaves spinning
like weeping blood red raindrops
oh, listen to the sweet chiming
of falling leaves
that I will hold like a blanket of memory
while the wind utters low wails like a hundred violins
and hidden birds sing
a beautiful symphony just for me

Morning Whispers

by Paulette Calasibetta

Undulating veils, gray and gauzy
Seducing hills and valleys,
Whispering secrets in the morning mist.

Writing On Snow

by Carol Mitra

The sun on snow looks like glossy paper
Rolled out in endless sheets
With my skis I sketch and write in zigzag letters
Long and flowing are my verses
The wind in hot pursuit, forging my lines
Intricate patterns I draw on snow
I discern a hidden meaning in all of my musings
The cold burning my words into flowing sheets
Holding a promise for the future that seems
like a tiny tip writing effortlessly with swaying motion
In the distant horizon I see two fellow skiers
Writing stories in different languages
Drawing parallels in shades of constant flow
I follow the light shining deep in my core.

Of Sorrow

by Susan M. Ashley

Sorrow is
the night's rainstorm
lashing an impoverished psyche
wandering lost with loss
'neath weeping eaves in murky-minded alleyways
without an umbrella.

The Beautiful Sea

by Sandra Weiss

I lost my heart to the ocean.
The first time we met, I knew.
I was drawn by its endless motion.
In awe of its magnificent view.

I watched as waves rolled onto the sand.
I felt the cold sea spray on my face.
I had never been where ocean met land.
A vision that nothing could ever erase.

The waves with their rhythm of ebb and flow
What they brought in, they then carried away.
Their tales from the beginning of time we don't know.
Their underwater secrets, not ever on display.

The vastness and power of this great sea.
Rendered me speechless, and feeling small.
I could feel the spell that it cast over me.
I knew that I would always answer its call.

The ocean sings a song, for all to hear.
It's music finds that empty place inside
It's age old melody draws you near.
As the water dances along with the tide.

On this island my dream became real.
Peace and contentment have found me.
Life's many wounds will finally heal.
Forever surrounded by the beautiful sea.

I Wonder

by BRYAN PAUL NORTON

I wonder as I wander
From head to heart to soul
If life is like an empty game
Or more, an empty goal

If passion is the price we pay
For pure and perfect peace
If people are the problem
Or the path to our release

For who I am and what I know
Is not what others see
When life is like a rocket ship
And no one cares but me

The path to my salvation
Is a long and winding road
But I am glad to make it
With an extra heavy load

The promise of a better life
Is part of who I am
The lesser peace of harmony
Is worthy of a clam

The urgency of living
Is a worthy fact to face
The silence of a shooting star
Is harder still to trace

The universe is full of those
Who buried on the shore
Gave deference to those who died
By living so much more

The story of eternity
Is written in your heart
The actor that you suffer long
Is waiting for a part

The soul that you should conquer
Is the hardest one to win
The restless dream within you
Is the place you should begin

But when you do remember
That discretion is your fame
The wiser part of virtue
Is the value in your name.

Once Willows Wept Not

by Paula Ann Swanson

'Tis now known why the Willow weeps,
a tragedy of love, its memory keeps.
For once a young man and young maid,
on tender grass, beneath branches lay.
Though pledged by birth to another,
from clans they hid, to be together.
Thus, the gentle Willow was their choice,
meeting beneath, till love they could voice.
The Willow held these secret lovers dear,
so would lower its boughs, when they drew near.
Thus tucked away in the Willow's womb,
could lay as one, yet this love was doomed.
For jealousy lurked within the pines,
spying young lovers thus entwined,
behind Willow's curtain of slender limbs,
He swore the maiden, would yet be his.
Thus, it came to pass one day,

as young maid softly made her way,
to their Willow, deep within the glen,
espied the branches did already bend.
Timidly, as she did draw near,
soft sound of sorrow fell upon her ears.
Parting Willow's branches to look within,
a dampness did touch upon her skin.
The Willow was shedding sap laden tears,
for the young man, in death, was near.
'Twas an arrow that had been used,
a potent poison, the tip infused.
The maiden, now blind with grieving mist,
pulled out the arrow, held it, in clenched fist.
Whilst cradled in love's arms, did he draw last breath.
Then, young maid, plunged the arrow, into her breast.
And so it is, that this story is told,
as the Willow's grief would not be consoled.
For unable to stop what had befell,
the young lovers, it had hid so well.
With will broken, as lovers lay dead,
the Willow, its branches, never again spread.
And because it is the memory it keeps,
it is to this day, that the Willow weeps.

Passing Trains In Winter Rain

by Terence O'Leary

Distrait within the dismal night
while drifting down deserted track...
Beyond the bend, a lantern light
illumed alone the vacant black.
Such are the tricks that fate will feign
with passing trains in winter rain.

The darkling sky sighed, dripping dew,
beguiling to the trek anew.
Through diamond dusk old demons came -
There was no dread, there was no claim,
for distant thoughts will entertain

on passing trains in winter rain.

Through shadow's fog a form appeared
(which slowed its pace as morning neared),
a lonesome, meek and wistful thing,
like fallen bird with broken wing.
Such are the shapes and weary strain
of passing trains in winter rain.

We paused a moment, side by side
confronting Fate in eventide.
But Passion's Pains of yesteryear
left youthful Ardor draped in fear -
We had our courses to maintain
like passing trains in winter rain.

I often harken, flashing back,
to sense the formless twisted track
muse "Few have loved though all have toyed
inside this vast and vacant void -
The reason why? At heart, mundane
as passing trains in winter rain" ...

Sometimes

by Phil Capitano

Sometimes, when I look in the mirror
I see my brother's face,
I quiver with recognition.
As time takes me,
so it takes my eyes, I reason,
a trick of the mind.
Just sometimes.

Sometimes, when I'm working with my hands
I see the hardened hands of my sister
who slaved to keep her family together.
Only sometimes,
then I give my head a shake.
Not real, I defend.

Sometimes, when I look at my feet
I see the worn shoes of the homeless,
the refugees in search of a place.
I remember the long, hard road
and compassion forms in my throat.
Just sometimes.
I wish I could see that way more often.

Divine Wine

by Pashang Salehi

Pleasantness is within me, I need more of that wine.
  What a night I hope it be, I need more of that wine.
You are me and I'm you, till my last day loving you.
  I am us and you are we, I need more of that wine.
Like a candle in my night, break the darkness from my sight,
  Shine at me until I see, I need more of that wine.
I'll rub my lips to your lips; my pain will be all gone,
  Let's break our cage, and go free; I need more of that wine.
Blissfulness is around us; seek it from within you,
  Come and find the hidden key, I need more of that wine.
Wingless flying is unwise, sit down, watch the sunrise.
  Laughing crying grief and glee, I need more of that wine.
You left a trail for "Haloo", he found you with no clue.
  He knows the way and told me, I need more of that wine.

A Damsel Enchants Felicity

by Olive Eloisa Guillermo-Fraser

Aurora breaks,
Cinderella damsel enchants felicity,
gliding halcyon--
implanting jazzy kisses,
languorous murmurs. . .
Nectared opulent press

quakes reactions.
Succulent tissues urge
virginal wanting: xerothermic,
yearning zenith!

Believe In Yourself

by Christopher Goss

If only for today...
Would you believe?
Not in a deity
Not in someone else
Not in some grand idea
But in yourself
We put faith in what is around us
But little of it finds a home
Within the depths of our soul
But there is one reality
Nothing is realer than you
Nobody ever knows you like you
Your deepest thoughts
Your greatest fears
What you see in the mirror
All uniquely personal
Language is imperfect
And something is lost when spoken
Be good to yourself
Be honest with yourself
Be the one you see in the mirror
Painted beautifully
With all your hopes and dreams
And no
You won't be some grand idea
You won't be someone else
You won't be some deity
For one day...
Would you believe...
In yourself?

The Whistling Hamlet
by SILPIKA KALITA

A whistling wheezing hamlet, whispering and emanating, tunes euphonic,
In a remote isolated valley, far-flung from the abode of the temporal,
Warbling quietly to whistle scads of tranquil cryptic songs;
Lying spasmodic, a sparsely inhabited mellifluous hamlet, Kongthong!

Not to hyperbole, a singing utopia, uncustomary to the core!
Where innate and mellow are the naive dwellers' rustic tinkling timbres!
A rover's riddle, the natives' pride, a unique heritage, their blissful strains!

Ringing with an ancient tradition of tune-giving in honour of the root
ancestress,
 Customary to the matrilineal surviving unknown folk of the thorp!

The chirping region's dispositions and practices outlandish, vague, and
obscure,
Primitive and bizarre, mere to merge with nature's absolute accord!

Voices buzzing in whistles, murmuring, and chattering, lilting,
 Arcane, pervading the virgin thicket of the sacred thorpe!
To entangle, passerby and wanderers in dream like metaphors!
Those magical murmurs in quirky tunes, mingling the breeze of the
secluded hamlet, intoning own tinkles!

Blessed are the tuning terrain's offsprings, nameless!
Rared by ditties, hailed sacred by the clan's conviction!

Outlying, by the uninhabited enchanting wilderness of East Khasi Hills,
 Sleeping quietly the untrodden, nature's lulling lullaby, the whistling
Kongthong!
Yell! Immaculate and serene, the saga of their undeciphered airs, mumbling
in exquisite ethos!

Inimitable and gripping to eye, how the denizens of the tribe,
Are crooning to dub and call each other by indigenous intonations!
Pitching and whooshing, to tune their melodic identities unique!

Whew! The picturesque terrain is tweeting, whooping, and whizzing!
Heaven! Bless anomalous nature's absolute pamphlet,
The ringing Kongthong, God's own whistling hamlet!

Zephyr's Silky Tendrils

by Joanna Daniel

Curling
around the house,
the breeze was unfurling,
moving dead leaves in its twirling
fingers, apparently
satisfied with
whirling

The dance
lured the lovers
to come out and romance
under the willow's shadowed trance,
soft whispers of the breeze
inspired their love's
warm glance

Showers
gently fall on
them, even as flowers
bloom open with piquant powers,
they laugh and enjoy love's
passionate few
sweet hours

The soft
zephyr played with
trees in the woods and croft,
with laughter ringing, it does waft
mingling with mild murmurs
of love in skies
aloft

The breeze
lingers to look
at the lovebirds and tease
them with silky tendrils that squeeze,
meandering with ease,
watching o'er them
'mid trees.

Exposing The Soul

by Robert L Carmack

The fallen sons slipped off Creation's lens.
To taste the sting from our own tree and fruit.
Their giants quarried till no place to stand.
Before these day's deceiving shades of gray,
The prophet's shutters opened wide to write.
Foretold of hate in focus driving nails.
Our Pilate's wash in Silver Halide's bowl.
For only one Son's blood can fill the baths,
His saving grace developing the soul.
And now reflecting every color's hue,
Presented flawless under Father's sight.
This world to turn and from you it will take.
Endure this to the end and ride the light.

No Gold Nor Silver

by Daniel F Turner

No gold nor silver, weights my needy purse
Spun silk and finery I have no need
Such poverty of wealth be not God's curse
For bless'd the man who covets not for greed

My wealth is in the lilies of the field
The colors of the sunsets thrill my soul
Fruit trees and animals provide their yield
And stewardship to nature is my toll

But verdant forests do not warm a bed
The moon and stars, though friends, are silent stones
And lonely is the footpath which I tread
For one true heart, I'd share my pauper's throne

A golden heart and pauper's paradise
For love and happiness, a humble price

Please Love Me Like I Love You

by Bobby J. May Sr.

Your lips I wonder and ponder
Wishing to place them upon mine
As I conjure your taste in wander
Intoxicating as if a fine wine
Your eyes so intriguing as jewels
Bright diamonds sparkling into mine
Your scent of perfume I cannot refuse
Please love me like I love you
Take this heart and hold it as if it were yours
Let our dreams come true
Never let me go and I will hold you
Please love me like I love you
Take this hand and walk with it
Hold it as if it were yours
With two becoming one
You will always be mine let me hold you

Will You be my Valentine

Sandia

by Susan Lawrence Piatt

Sandia ...Sandia I love you. Sandia...Sandia your beautiful deep shadows and
illuminated peaks stir within me wonder and desire. To be part of your
world, your story, your history would be my gift.

Whisper to me ...

Sweet watermelon hills. I long to be closer to you, to touch you,
to smell the air on your highest peak,
to lay my tired body in your lush green valleys.
I know you speak to me and whisper in my ears.
I know you call to me, and I hear your words...

"Come to me. Let me embrace you. You will become me
and travel through my past, my present and on into my future.
Let me stroke your forehead and gently touch your tired eyelids
closing them so you may rest if even for a few moments."

"Rest in my hills, in my shelter of smooth warm stones.
Surround yourself. Rest on me. Breathe in my air.
Look upward and gaze upon the lovely pink and gray
clouds that hover around me.
Let me kiss you with my breeze...the call of the air...
and the promise of dreams to come."

The Lovers

by Francis J Grasso

How gently darkness lays itself upon the restless sea
While breezes scented cool and clean, are blowing wild and free
When moonlight's blush fades gradually and hides its ash white face
A thousand candles dimly lit, now frame the soft embrace

All through the night, with spirits bright as shameless dreams unfold
'till sunlight makes the darkness break to show the story told
Tempest waters calm and smooth, stillness now the sea
Sky and water, bound in love... as lovers, you and me

Starry Night

by Maria Amelia Corado

his gaze -
starry night sky's
soft rays.

her face
caught the night light,
such grace!

hearts tossed,
perched on the stars -
words lost ....

hija de la luna

The Bookshop Upstairs

by Gary Radice

Try leave behind "Book Of The Week"
And head upstairs where floorboards creak.

Where people tilt their heads to look
At every spine on every book.

Where murderers and secret lovers
Plot and scheme between the covers.

Where transport from another age
Transports you to another page.

Where old detective books reside
Each with their price pencilled inside.

Where books based on geometry
Share space with trigonometry.

Where childhood annuals stand in line
With memories of a simpler time.

Where silent thoughts pervade the air
And words speak volumes everywhere.

The Reclusive Verses

by David Kavanagh

Wanting to shrug off this shell, break loose from me
Silence that damn hermit, hiccuping under his tree
Trapped inside too long, dormancy dreams to wake
Disgorging bubbly lava, filling in soporific landscapes

Longing to escape soft tissue, cast off mortal bones
Break shackles of mundanity, rid life's infernal drone
Out there lies all answers, beyond the hermits void
His space mostly perfect, til our Big Bang destroyed

Go forth and multiply, primal stars hypernova like hell
Filling a cosmos with elements, configuring him as well
Hold your tongue hermit, stop humming about in bliss
Stay quiet down that hole, cease fumbling at the abyss

Deeper and deeper, below where basements depress
Sits an altar of incremental tables, poets go to confess
Forget truths algorithm, they'll fool any polygraph test
And the hermit lies all day long, he meditates for a rest

Breathe in, breathe out, forget about terminal breaths
Don't underestimate the ether, chants a monk in Tibet
Fill your mind with mindfulness, peace will set you free
Watch them hiccups abate now, our hermit's all at sea

On The Waves Of Lost Memories

by Millard Lowe

These salted memories tell stories
The oceans and seas gave birth to.

Over the tempestuous waters
Echoes from the bellies of slave ships
Ride the tides of history

Spreading ripples over the shores
Of time proclaiming forgiveness
For lost souls.

We sashay along bleached beaches
Where white sands mask the shed blood;
And splashing waves drown out
The ghost echoes of rattling chains:

We no longer remember
Our beginnings here.

Shades Of Marmalade

by Joseph May

Evening drifting in on twilight's shade
  As sunset glimmers softly on the sea
Shimmering in colors of marmalade
  And fading deep into its mystery

Dusk enchants with spells of its sweet allure
  As restless waves await the mystic night
Flowing relentlessly on a rocky shore
  As seagulls dot the sky in twilight's flight

And in the darkness of the cryptic deep
  The ocean churns with raging sounds sublime

And soon, it lulls the midnight moon to sleep
As starlight twinkles a silvery chime

When the moon awakens from its sweet dream
The sea in morning light will surely gleam!

To A Divorce Woman

by Mark Frank

Death appeared in your marriage
Ugly Words were spoken creating a cause to leave
For some there was an applause for your breakup
Because some spoke behind your back!
You are now a woman in solitude
Understanding the value of moving away from the multitude
At times, you saw the danger in your marriage
But you still believed it could be fixed until
You realize that ugly words compounded more ugly words
Now you know that nothing is opened by mistake more than the mouth!
Both of you said things you should have never said
Ultimately, you started to realize the bed meant nothing anymore!
Before you knew it, it was too late!
Too often one in the relationship will try to be the dictator
Soon after that, the other one will be a spectator
But despite the calamity of divorce
You will stand strong and
Know that your next relationship will be without force!
You are now a woman in solitude
Understanding the value of moving away from the multitude
Remain strong; your heart belongs to the man
That understands that nothing is opened by mistake more than the mouth!

The Relativity Of Beyond

by Sandra M. Haight

Bacteria, too small for human eyes
engage their fight for life within our midst,
so unaware of Earth's gigantic spies
with microscopes and slides, who co-exist.

And tiny fish, contained by walls of glass,
oblivious to all that thrives outside,
in worlds of colored sand and plastic grass
know not the ocean's roar or rhythmic tide.

Too, we the wisest creatures of life's sea,
who travel well the wonders of our home,
are blinded by the endless mystery
of space and time- horizons we can't roam.

What great dimension of the vast beyond
makes Earth a microscopic vagabond?

Trees

by Joseph May

The tree that held the forbidden fruit
   Held our destiny within its root
The ancient secrets that it kept
   May hold the tears that the willow wept

The tree that holds the robin's nest
   Holds life most precious, it is blessed
The tree from which nightingales sing
   Holds the melody until spring

But the tree that I will forever miss
 Is the tree under which we kissed
So long ago our hearts did leap

With sweet caress and passions deep
The tree where hearts will meet in bliss
Is the tree that holds tomorrow's kiss

Apogee Of Grief

by Edward Ibeh

hibernating pain

awakes from slumber

a long rusty nail

plunging deeper and deeper,

piercing

into the heart's chamber,

driven by resounding blows

from Thor's hammer;

apogee

of her grief.

The Universe Of Creativity, The Poet, And The Poem

by George Stathakis

Poetic lines
plucked out of the universe of creativity
a structure perhaps in place.

The poet's mind
a receptor
like a television receiving radio waves.

A message and a form emerges and a pattern appears
then to be arranged and carefully designed
like a quilter creating a quilt.

Further guided to play with words and structure
so as to fine tune
like a musician fine tuning a musical instrument.

The poet beckoned
by the universe of creativity
summoned to create the poem.

The My Way Highway

by Howard Robert Manser

blind minions do not hear
deaf disciples cannot see
callous subzero frozen feelings
breed gibberish jarring jubilee

this bloody blind-eyed messiah
rode to town astride an ass
belching barking oratory
for an aimless lower class

a starry-eyed astrologer
alchemist extraordinaire
summoned shrouded quatrains
revealing he baffles with a flare

loitering lotus-eater
puppeteer par excellence
self-indulgent Machiavellian
pitched fabricated arrogance

adroit and ambidextrous
he summons the mercurial mass
conjuring decrees and fairytales
dictating his rules pass

lose not a bloodied hammered head
resign yourself to a running retreat
le guillotine administers
swift sweet and replete

no man speaks of that not heard
or sees that left not read
bony fingers point with indigestion
reflecting in fractured mirrors

An Autumn Path

by Angel L Villanueva

The path he takes this early day
Is dressed in dew and straws of hay.
The morning mist obscures his view;
The barn, though near, seems far away.

The sleepy sun begins to rise,
And light prepares to climb the skies.
He sees the path much clearer now,
As life awakened fills his eyes.

He senses changes autumn brings,

A mix of scents from lovely things.
The air, perfumed by turning leaves,
Is fragrance loved by serfs and kings.

Above he hears migrating birds,
Their calls of joy, like soothing words.
They tell of lands where warmth awaits;
A transient home for flocks and herds.

The cows have stirred and move about,
And roosters crow as piglets rout.
A dog begins to run to him,
His faithful friend and eager scout.

So much to do while autumn stays,
Before the freeze of winter's gaze.
And yet, for now, he walks the path,
And sings a psalm of morning praise.

Mist By The Sea

by James Marshall Goff

In
Stillness
I dream of
Your last salt tears
kiss

Nocturnal Contagion

by David Mohn

While it feels in the noontide, just steps through the trees,
As the sky bleeds to twilight – the sweetest disease.
On a walk through the maples, an itch of romance,
As a warm breeze courts Eros at gloaming's advance.

Just a glance woos the shivers, through come hither eyes,
Nervous hands - now perspiring, by moonlight's devise.

Down a path softly swaying, then slowly a waltz,
Till a feverish tango as all reason halts.

Soon the knees start to wobble and vision subsides,
As the world falls from focus in dizzying strides.
There's no end to the sickness on warm summer strolls,
Should the moon cast its toxin on amorous souls.

Watering The Garden Of Dreams

by Lonna Lewis-Blodgett

taciturn springs rising
from within the quarry
of deep earth's wisdom
urging lyrical waters to transpose
while held like singing seas of living reveries
of history and infinity
misting to meld with rainfall dreams
Falling like ancient messages
into the orchard of molecular landscapes
drawn to penetrate its legacy
embedded in the rockeries and rills
blanketing the groves of dirt and ferns
teeming in the arcadian oasis
feeding feast or famine
flourishing the solicitude of springtime
in spider spun dreams
of longings in ancient oaks
merging with the ebb of shedding sycamores
in salted seas teeming and exalting
the rhetoric of existence
in musing opaque vapors
mingling into pervasive clouds
bleeding life
cached in the creche
of pastoral beginnings
of everlasting eddies
watering the garden of dreams

Mother And Dementia

by Beryl Edmonds

When dementia creeps in, through the back door
Loving is needed, like never before...

An expressionless face, an empty heart
A once dazzling life that had lost its spark
I saw your sad tears and felt every fear
Of foggy days that for you never cleared.

All disappeared, those happy golden years
Memories you held, so precious, so dear
The loveliest of smiles, gone without trace
Who was that stranger who dwelt in your place.

Tenderness was missing, none existing
Care and affection you were resisting
It sure broke my heart, to see you like that
When we'd shared love and friendship in the past.

My one and only forever mother
There couldn't have been a better another
I still pray in hope, again and again
You didn't suffer any physical pain.

As you loved and cared, like a mother should
I cared for you, as I promised I would
I hope that these words to heaven get through
"Dearest Mother, I will always love you.

Anthropomorphic

by Margarita Lillico

If food for finer thoughts we did not crave,
If sense of purpose we did not apply,
If we did not critique how we behave,
If dormant laid Alert Judgmental Eye...

If float and breed were our exclusive wish,
If instincts solely spurred us to survive,
We might as well be just a school of fish -
Not learning about deep currents of Life.

If we ran loose, not playing by the rules,
If years weren't measured by the days we seize,
We might as well be just a pack of wolves -
With hungry jaws and reflex to appease.

If loyalty and trust weren't our guide,
If fam'ly failed to withstand the Time,
We might as well be lions, without pride -
Where govern male rivalry and crime.

If we ignored the term - Personal Growth,
Meandering complacently in awe,
We might as well be just a slack of sloth -
With sluggish status quo, seeking no more.

If benefits of thought we didn't reap,
If mindful property we didn't hold dear,
We might as well be just a herd of sheep -
That sacrificed their free will out of fear.

Brushing aside the Kingdom of the Wild,
Place on a pedestal a Human Mind.
With love and progress equally aligned
Let's be the best we can, one of a Kind.

As to Judgmental Eye, its primal goal -
To keep our planet safe and civil,
By virtue of Grey Matter, above all -
To distinguish between good and evil.

Dolly

by Paul Gaffney

Death surrounded her
Bombs falling captured the stories inside her head
Real life tears fell over blood-soaked mornings
Screams pierced right into the reality she called life
Friends, limbs missing made her look abnormal
Laughter left the country vowing never to return
She watched the burning figure running towards her
Collapsing before her, pleading for death
But death didn't want him that day
He wasn't one of the fortunate ones
She climbed into the basement seeking solace
Clutching the doll who like herself seemed to have survived in one piece
But something wasn't right
Dolly was living a lie
She pulled one arm and one leg off
Dolly smiled
And the world became normal again.

Martians Calling Earth Nursery Rhyme

by Jennifer Proxenos

Mummy, Mummy come quickly and see,
A pretty picture for Blib and me,
Blog was jumping up and down
Her helmet bobbing on her curved crown.

Look at this picture in the sand,
We saw them, they were not from our land.
They flew up into the sky in a rocket ship

Honestly mummy, mum looked at Blog and Blib.

What dream did they have last night,
Their TV aerial was certainly a mite,
Strange and the Moon and Mars picked up sounds,
Which seemed weird, and out of bounds.

Something unusual, her twins Blib and Blog,
Had noticed, that they were so excited about,
Absolutely no doubt!
Can Daddy please beam us to this land,
So we can offer them a moonlit Mars hand?

We'll have fun and tell them to come and play
Any Moon or Mars day!
But Dad chose to use his rocket ship
On this trip!

So four Martians, Blip, Blog Mum and Dad,
Began a Mars, to Earth fad,
They took off to find this land, and Sam and Sue!
Poor Blib, with a slight dose of the flu.

They hurtled at thousands of miles an hour!
Their GPS directed to Earth, on four
We land, said Dad, don't bump your head.
Blib stay still, you should be in bed.

The pups had seen a foreign approaching object,
Martians and curious pups about to connect,
The Martians were speaking gobbly goo,
And the pups excitement grew and grew.

They hugged and played and ran,
Becoming the first universal connection,
In our galaxy and under our sun,
What a delightful galactic affection.

Soothing Star

by Sneha RV

My legs give out
    and I sink
        onto the grassy blanket,
whose thorns   feel like velvet
  against parched skin.

I close my eyes and
  d
    r
      i
        f
         t
      away.
    from this cruel confinement
where fleeting time   waits   for none.

I am drawn awake.
  It's that feeling all over again.
  It allays my ears,
       casting away the shrieks and screams
that haunt them.

This is the muse the world needs.
  Melodies and lyrics are stars
     to its a
       b
       y
       s
       s.

The music bewitches,
  I tiptoe on notes
    dancing in octaves.

I call the tune ~ I shall stay here
until the music dies.

For in the mansion beside my run-down hut,
they begin

to blow the trumpet.

Eye Spy

by Jennifer Proxenos

There was once an old woman,
Who lived in a small village,
Her name was Matilda Schoeman
Like Popeye, she only ate spinach!
One day she went to her Pastor,
To confess that her neighbor was
Always nude,
This is a chapter
Of my life I don't want to end
Father, am I being rude?
The Pastor came to her house to see,
Saw nothing, oh yes, said she, but if you
Stand On my toilet seat
And put a milk crate on top, and kneel
On one knee,
I can see his weenie, now am I a cheat,
For I feel it's a treat!
My eyesight is not so good, can not
Always see,
And do not recognize who he may be,
The Pastor looked up to heaven with glee,
So you don't know said the Pastor,
And put down his half-finished
Cup of tea
Just continue to knit said he,
And under his breath said, thank you God

She does not know that the
Nude man is me!

Precious Black Night
by Evelyn Judy Buehler

Black onyx night, of the pearlescent moon,
A velvety backdrop for rare diamond stars,
And nocturnal tunes all the nights of June,
Black opal night, converging on ruby Mars!

Black pearl night, flowering peace's dream,
Black diamond luster, far away from the day,
Obsidian night, with bold touches of cream,
Smooth and luxurious, and beauty's hideaway!

Love Is Blind
by Sandra M. Haight

They say that love is blind; that's nature's way
    to leave uncluttered pathways to our hearts,
so cupid's arrows see their targets lay
    with no distractions when love-struck with darts.

The eyes of love see beauty sweet and pure;
    their vision filled with roses and blue skies.
Without life's rain and clouds they can assure
    a state of mind and heart with no goodbyes.

If love were not so blind it would not last,
    for open eyes would see past cupid's goals.
But hearts once pierced with blinded love amass
    the strength to later see uncovered souls.

Love firmly planted builds a broader view;
    rose-tinted glasses traded for the clear,
to open up the narrow paths, breakthrough

to fuller scenes that blinded love might fear.

Yes, love is blind; a gift to draw us in-
the bait is sweet, we hunger for the taste.
Yet this love grows to fuller depths within
when planted, in deep soil, and firmly braced.

Above The Ocean Path

by Francine Roberts

" .... can you hear the bells? ... "
~~ ~~~

I trudge along the ocean path
up the hill to the promenade.
Above the crashing waves I stand,
then memories, my thoughts, invade.

Behind me, white and old, as I,
the abandoned church beckons me.
It says " do you remember when?"
"Think back ... what do you see?"

I remember lilacs blooming
and music from inside,
when this was a church full of life,
when I became a bride.

But now the lilacs fade from sight,
a deserted shell is all I see.
There is no music playing.
Sadness settles over me.

The curtains blow through broken panes.
They billow in the breeze
as if they're trying to escape
out to the beckoning seas.

Once upon a time we were
Alive ! , this church and I.
But we are old and empty now
and ready now to die.

~~~   ~~~

"behind the church is a promenade
   they call the Widows Walk"

Sandalwood

by Carol Ann Richardson

They are playing that song again
The one that reminds me of you
It began to rewind as I turned up the dial
from a place long ago that's been bleached for awhile

"California Dreamin" sifts through the air
like the sandalwood incense, that used to be there.

   "All the leaves are brown, and the sky is grey
      I've been for a walk ....On a winter's day"

There's an image I've kept, still tucked within my mind
It used to fill me with envy, until it reckoned with time
You at twenty-one, wild and beautiful in a way that I could never be
Perched upon your back-porch steps, beneath the russet trees
Soaking up the morning sun, stroking your guitar

I only knew you then, as that 'hippie" type of girl
The one who lived next-door that year
Your candles shimmering, bangles glimmering
A tangle of strawberry hair, that flirted with the wind
Childlike and fair, devil-may-care, long gypsy skirts,
and a peasant look that took one's breath

The faint scent of sandalwood, swept into my yard
from your wide-opened windows, wide-opened doors,
while I was wrangling a baby on my hip

or hanging bleached-white sheets onto a clothesline

I had often wished I were you, ... flitting about, barefoot in the morning air
But, I was teaching my toddler to tie his shoes
Both of us twenty-one, ... on two sides of a cedar fence, ...
a thousand light years apart

"All the leaves are brown, and the sky is grey
I've been for a walk,...on this winter's day
All the leaves are brown. Songs have come and gone
Seasons had their songs, but what became of you?"

So You Want To Know Me?

by Joseph S. Spence Sr

So sensationally super; Sagittarius son of John Spence
Pleasantly personable, and matriarch Maud Spence's son
Enabling, exquisite, eloquent, evolving and enterprising
Naturally nice, no nonsense, and a nutritionist nobleman
Carrot consumer, constant comrade and cold-war veteran
Equitably enlightened, and just an elegant eggnog taster

Jumping Jupiter, a jubilant sundae lover, and just a jewel
Oppresso de liber, optimistically captivating; oratorical
Saintly passionate, succulent salmon sampler; sweetheart!
Exquisitely enchanting, enchantingly amatorious; éclat!
Playful, painstakingly passionate, pajama wearer, patient
Handsomely helpful handyman, harmonizer of happiness

Sweet as syrup, shining armor off the shelf; savoir-faire!
Red-blooded poetry connoisseur and radioactively lovable!

Peace And Brightness

by Heidi Sands

I send you these calm, baby blue skies in these words I write
The clouds light up near the horizon, approaching this coming night
It's peaceful here on a special hill, where I see so many things
And there will be more color soon, with what autumn brings
After leaves fall, the views open up, to each distant mountain scene
I wish I could send them all, so you could see exactly what I mean
So here is my pen sending sights and words, I hope will describe to you,
Beauty that you can see that will bring you peace and brightness too

The Missing Me

by Shiraz Iqbal

With shadows in the dark,
Facing atrocities of the cold,
Yet drenched in the sweat,
I walk down the street

Am bound to follow what others passed by,
Crime it is as if else I try,
Tears follow the path of my cheek,
And it's the only way my eyes speak,
Lips of mine when turn dry.

I smile I really try to,
To be happy as if I was made to,
I speak of something I don't know
But there's what my heart knows,
That's what my eyes ponder,
And that's what untold but true,
Yes I know,
Yes I do,
I am missing me in me,
Yes I know,

Yes I do,
I am missing being me..........

In The Garden

by Ann Foster

In the Garden...

Sometimes
in the garden,
if you are quiet,
and watch carefully;
there are birds.
They come to visit,
and listen to the trees.
They sing in unison
to the leaves,
and the movement
of the grass.

The song is not easy to hear,
but if you let,
your heart...
it will match the beat,
and you will feel the miracle.

They...
all of them...
Come to visit the flowers,
and be part of the picture,
that makes everything perfect.

There are bees,
that kiss the blossoms,
and tell stories to the gnomes.
Ladybugs that dance among the roses,
and eat the aphids.
They laugh in celebration,
of the most beautiful buds,

ever allowed to open,
and smile at the sun.

The court of the big tree,
the land of the green,
the lake brought by irrigation,
a reality of everything,
truly...
lovely.

Like A Peacock

by Malabika Ray

My heart dances like a Peacock,

When I hear your voice!
It emerges from far,
Brings the tempestuous ocean to me,
Brings the soaring mountains to me,
Reminding me of the long arduous path
I have to walk,
To reach you!

Still it dances like a Peacock!

My heart starts waltzing
The moment I hear your voice!
My heart starts trembling with a mysterious exhilaration,
Quivering with an unfathomable elation,
And a peacock within me starts dancing

In the rain!

The rain shivers me, shudders me,
Almost whirls me away,
To a land,
Where I will walk on a path
strewn with golden and tangerine fall leaves,
admire a koel and sing her
mellifluous rhapsody with my voice uninhibited,

gambol and frolic to the sonata,
dream endless dreams with the cadence
of a humming stream, with uneven pebbles

but not quaver for a moment!

Where dreams are not splintered into fragments!

Butterscotch Moon

by James Marshall Goff

For Carolyn

By Carolyn Devonshire & James Marshall Goff

My hand
Wet with tears pouring down my face
Reaches out and finds nothing
Empty spaces where familiar voices
Once comforted me
My only hope
Is sleep, where dreams, in sketchy
Re-wind, promise a glimpse of lost
Loved ones, maybe a voice, if fleeting
Even, to soothe me
Those still with me
Look to me for strength, my motor
Memory urging me on, focusing
On the well, deep in my heart,
Cycle renews
Another beloved soul passes
Light they find
But darkness they leave behind
Grief
Hungry monster

Selfishly consumes my life
Devours all glimmers of hope
Leaving me
Destitute on a perilous plane
Mere existence
Not life as it once was
Sanity
Confronting memories, loneliness
Trek on an unbalanced bridge
Connecting life and death
Emotions purged
Shadows of yesterday surround me
Wisdom of loved ones
Permeate my thoughts
Filled
With clear vision, handed down to me
From my ancestors

Speak In Silence

by Gary Radice

what happens to those words we say
that speak in silence when we pray?

do they remain inside our head
to die with us when we are dead?

or do they echo off the walls
of bedrooms, churches, schools and halls

to fall upon the silent ground
and lie unheard and lost 'til found?

or do they find those cracks of light
that shine despite the darkest night

and reach out to that world above
to talk to those we miss and love?

Morning Sky

by Paris-Maree Boreham

The dazzling exquisite sunrise had captured me to stare
pumpkin, orange, tangerine, and amber of bright glare
I recall the tiger sprawl that burned the skyline vast
How the break of day lit up to reminisce the past
Now sky is dark and with no spark though memory of morn
Magnificently glorious today it was at dawn.

A Memory

by Frederic M Parker

When stars are hidden from view
And hazy clouds hang in the night
I remember a lover I knew
An ethereal beauty of sunlight

Days were pure with laughter's guise
With imaginary dreams, we'd mine
Surreal the moment, we dropped our disguise
To share a trancelike fervor so divine

Our flowering hearts we'd claim
From the shadowy garden, we desired
This dreamlike world turned to molten flame
An unreal realm, where our souls conspired

Monochrome

by Paul Callus

From the allure of coloured art
We step aside and then depart
In search of ways by which to sate
The urge to please, communicate;

Monochromatic visual fare
Sharpness defined, intent to share
With composition in full view
Amid the shadows that imbue
Ideal traits of dark and light
Contrasting shades of black and white.

Half A Heart

by Chantelle Anne Cooke

my heart speaks right beats
is my left side the shadow
only one spot light

my ruby wing sings
blood petals push through my pulse
sustaining solo

butterfly rainbows
reach royal blessings of life
my heart heaven harp

notes of normalcy
swirl in my saucy soul
my heart the crescent blood moon

I'm My Daddy Made Over

by Sabrina Niday Hansel

Dedicated to my Dad Jerry W. Niday 3/20/1952 - 6/18/2013

I am who I am because of him
He's the reason for my son's name
He gave me my courage & my strength
To stand tall even when standing wasn't easy
Stand for the ones who can't

To think and fend for myself
I'm my Daddy made over

Taught me to fight back
To never back down
How to pick myself back up
When I've been knocked down
Fight for what I believe
I'm my Daddy made over

He gave me my stubbornness
Gave me my pride
Gave me my temper
Taught me not to take crap
To speak my mind to no matter who
Work for what I want
I'm my Daddy made over

How to keep my emotions in check
How to handle large amounts of pain
When in trouble he always had my back
He knew how my mind worked better than anyone
I got it from him
I'm my Daddy made over

Even though he's gone
I'll stand and continue on
I may stumble I may fall
May even get hurt along the way
But I'll pick myself back up
I'll dust myself off and stand tall
I'm honored and proud to say
I'm my Daddy made over

The Going Green

by Kelly Deschler

Sooner now does daylight fade
and with it a summer die,
as green becomes a brighter shade
and for a short time says goodbye.

A welcomed change of pace
to what these eyes have seen,
blazing red and orange replace
the swiftly going green.

Like fire dancing on the limbs
a new breath with each new breeze,
flickering in brights and dims
alighting amongst the trees.

Rekindled life flows in their veins
as another season takes it's rest,
and shaken off the summer rains
prepares for fall, a temporary guest.

Waving leaves do remember when
knowing this farewell is not forever,
the going green comes back again
after the most beautiful autumn ever.

God Saw A Prize

by Valerie D Staton

My world a chasm of utter darkness
Dreariness enveloped me like a cloud
Bound by chains in an abandoned fortress
Tormented body - a field freshly plowed
Accomplishments ignored; voice never heard
Wondered why on earth was I even born

Treated like clipped wings of a fallen bird
Ripped to shreds, I could no longer be torn
Unsettling to be taunted by others
When all you do is exemplify love
Why is it so hard to love one another
As commanded by the Savior above
I tried so hard to find favor in their sight
All efforts were unfavorably received
I began to pray and was bathed in light
Chains started falling, my sentence reprieved
God looks at me and sees a worthy prize
The Lord loves all of his children the same
I'm no longer concerned about man's eyes
Ill-conceived judgments nor secular names
The name of the Lord is a strong tower
His mighty name is worthy to be praised
I thank him for his redemptive power
For being my light on the darkest of days
In times of despair God spoke from above
Through His Word, He counseled and He advised
Keep His commandments - Keep walking in love
I am His, I am loved, and I am a prize!

Grandpa

by Irma L Hole

GRANDMA WAITS IN THE GARDEN

Hi grandpa, it's me again!
Your dentures sit in an open glass above the nightstand
Remember the tears grandma sang before she pass?
The way she looked into your eyes,
Moments before she said goodbye
Grandpa, I found a note from grandma,
She will always wait for you.

Hi grandpa, it's me again!
The rocking chair is old and dusty
Remember the way grandma sat me on her lap?

Read many stories before I took a nap
How she enjoyed stroking my hair with her hands
I miss the way she rocked me to sleep every night

Hello, grandpa!
I stored your hearing aid away
Remember that special musical box in grandma's drawer?
I opened it last night, to watch the ballerina soar
I wish you could hear the tiny chimes grandma loved
I hope you don't mind, I'm keeping grandma's favorite scarf

Hello, Grandpa!
I'm caressing grandma's picture frame
Remember the way she looked in the yellow pretty sundress?
Grandpa, I miss the things grandmother did for you
Like the walking cane she handcrafted before she left

Hello, grandpa, it's me again!
My tears have softened now,
knowing you will soon see her again
Take your place with her in the sky
Please, say hi and give her a kiss
Tell her I miss her so much
I love you grandpa

Monadnock

by Kenneth Wayne Cheney

More than merely a mound of rock;
More timeless than a broken clock;
Standing alone to define a place;
A stone edifice of granite grace;

I have traversed to the top;
Led by white crosses and white dots;
There I have sat and been renewed;
By views imbued with a purple hue;

Pictured and painted from many towns;
Majestic scenery doth abound;

Blazing reds, the finest of Fall;
Brilliant white dome, when Winter calls;

I've traveled widely in the world;
Natural wonders I've seen unfurl;
But I love the best a granite ball;
No grander vision my mind recalls.

The Hounds Are Barking Still

by David Andrew McHattie

My slumber knows no measure
With no sleep that I can see.
The hounds are barking through the night
For immortality.

I toss out a leg of mutton
And a banal cliche for slight effect.
But their hunger goes unsated...
I lay waste my self-respect.

A few platitudes and twaddle
Are quickly gobbled by the beasts.
I make an honest effort at contrition
To give aid to my relief.

But my words of self-castration
Seem to energize the hounds.
I further try to appease and quantify...
But I'm losing precious ground.

I prostrate a harried confession.
My delusive sins are now a flood.
The wolf stands menacingly astride my door...
The beast has tasted blood.

Again... I apologize now threefold times
Using paper, pad and quill.
But it matters not to feed the beasts...

The hounds are barking still.

The End

Blame It On The Moon
by Ray Dillard

I dare you to say,
"It's because of the full moon."
My heart is not made of iron.
No magnetism
Pulls me like the ocean's tide,
Holding me here by your side.

Instead, please tell me
That our hearts will beat as one
Regardless of the moon or sun.
Say that you'll be here
When we become old and gray...
Then, say the moon made us that way.

Persistent Memories
by Paula Ann Swanson

In shadow, shade, and angled light,
memories echo, when given time.
They persist, though out of sight,
when even bells will lose their chime.

To torture, teach or reprimand?
Why then comes, the weathered old?
The heart and soul hold scars and brands,
when even stars burn out, turn cold.

On Wings Of Song

by Evelyn Pearl Anderson

I fly on wing of song.
Twenty-three miles out of Atlanta
soaring like an eagle traveling from DC
thirty-six thousand miles high
Fly, fly away
Through the blue hues of morning
white fluffiness lie below towards earth
puffy white and gray cotton-like softness
gently moving on windsong
feeling like a Welsh princess
watching o'er her universe.
I see the world through a rectangle
looking out over the airplane's wing
reaching outward and upward.
Soaring like hope
Moving like faith
Solid span of charity
Humming motor onward bound joyful sound
A higher plane than I have found;
Lord, plant my feet on higher ground
wind under my winged sails
I'm pressing on the upward way.
Arrows painted on wingspan
pointing left as we travel right
viewing "safety line attach point"
feeling secure way up here
three flapjacks adjusting the wind flow
reminding of Father, Son and Holy Spirit
pouring through keeping my soul.
Upward outward incline
continuous motion held by metal strength
while thin white clouds pass by.
Heaven's sky still far far away
no matter how far up one gets God is farther still
beyond the blue somewhere higher.

Sitting assured as my mind presses on—
landing soon will come
back to earth world
where I belong.

The Goat That Lives Next Door

by Neva E. Romaine

Hello my friend, good day to you; I see you got my note
It's time we had a face to face about that crazy goat!

He made a mess, broke in my barn; ate up my buds and cans
And when I tried to chase him out, he kicked my bloomin' fan

Now see here Mr. Farmin' Man, I know you from way back
But if you don't restrain that goat - I'll stretch his scrawny neck!

Me and that goat been fightin' long; he thinks he won this time
So I'll show him today for sure that I'm still in my prime

That goat won't get the better of me; I'll trap him with some hay
I'll lay a path straight to the barn and lead him in that way

Oh darn! He's smarter than I thought, he ate up to the door
He stopped and turned then shook his tail like he don't want no more

Aww shucks - there's got to be a way to trap that crazy goat
He's found new ways into my barn - I'll send another note

This time though Mr. Farmin' Man, I will not shout and wail
I'm goin to git the Sheriff now and throw that goat in jail!

Clair De Lune

by Carol Ann Richardson

I would practice each day without satisfaction,
longing to capture the moon's oratory.
DeBussy, God, help me, I should say that I'm sorry!

Though my fingers were nimble, I'd lose concentration,
and fumble along with a grumble and sigh.

Provoking the chords, that should tumble and rise
into a glorious, exquisite river of mist.
But, when thumbs went adrift, beyond the abyss,
　　I'd return to the first bar, and start once again.
-

I'd retrace every note of the measure and time. And time after time,
I'd assault a B-flat, where a C-sharp should chime.
All my hopes and my schemes came from this longing to please.
My dreams to succeed, and to offer this gift.
To grant her the wish.
The rapture, to swoon, as I played 'Clair de Lune'.

　　My mother's favorite. -- And I aimed for the moon

—
I remember my mother with dishes piled high,
soap on her nose,
calling out from the kitchen.
"That time, much better!"

Or my dad, in the dark room, Walter Cronkite, his companion,
calling out from the shadows,
"I think now, you've got it!"

Tonight in the dim light,
I'll watch how the moonlight,
slides over the piano, sliding over the keys.

It seems that the moon knows,
that time cannot stand still.
That years come and the years go.
But the tune, is the same tune, and the moon is the same moon.
　　And DeBussy still winces in the place I called home.

Wayward On Golden Sands A Dedicated Verse To Heidi Sands

by James Edward Lee Sr.

Wayward strolling travel sorts;
I am homeward bound;
Roaming twix these golden fields;
Walking these tinted bronze grounds;
Hoping at least best;
I find my rest;

Dormant stop by I;
This my traveling's I now grasp my chest as;
I lay down my life;
Onto the ground;
I passed my last breath;
For this you see I'm falling asleep;
On these the golden fields;

Springtime

by Eve Roper

Springtime touch unfolds veracious winsome,
colorful rainbow blossom to come.
Tranquil redolence fragrance,
a ballad narrated on carpet grass pleasance.

Crisp dawn enlightens fanciful golden
colors, of purples, pinks, greens, quaint and olden.
Blends float and dance amongst the valley
outstretch, toward enraptured abbey.

Glorious hanging ivy, juniper, kiss
me not plants, all in a garden's vast bliss.
As the fields blossoms quince to thirst
sweet and tender jewels among all to burst.

Worthlessness Without The Saviour

by Beata B. Agustin

My life's worthless without You, my Saviour*
my soul's great fortress
from sin-woes' distress...
You made a grand change in my behaviour
with Your divine might
showing me Your light.
Yes, You left Your glory just to seek me out
Leading me toward heaven without doubt...
You're my being's essence.

Pride prevails over me without Your grace
thus, I trust Your heart
midst unbelief's dart...
I constantly need Your goodness' embrace
warming me with joy
against guilt's ploy...
You deserve my praises with full earnestness
To You I submit, trusting Your faithfulness...
You're my being's essence.

My world revolves around You – forever...
You hold my future
Of faith's adventure...
Even final death can never sever
our relationship
of sweet fellowship.
May You find me pleasing You with my utmost
While serving You thru others at any cost.
You're my being's essence.

*Luke 1:47 And my spirit hath rejoiced in God my Saviour.

The Gilded Leaves Of Autumn Sigh

by Pandita Sanchez

The Gilded Leaves of Autumn Sigh

As the gilded leaves of Autumn sigh,
I'm haunted by the shadow of a long-lost love.
I'll always remember the soft song of a summer breeze...
from golden days when we were carefree butterflies.

I'm haunted by the shadow of a long-lost love...
memories of our first kiss still leave me breathless,
from golden days when we were carefree butterflies;
when our silhouettes tangoed in moonlight's silvery embrace.

Memories of our first kiss still leave me breathless!
I was enchanted by soft caresses and sparkling red wine.
When our silhouettes tangoed in moonlight's silvery embrace,
I believed stars would shine until the end of time.

I was enchanted by soft caresses and sparkling red wine...
enthralled as you held me tenderly in your arms.
I believed stars would shine until the end of time;
when I thought you would be forever mine.

Enthralled as you held me tenderly in your arms,
I'll always remember the soft song of a summer breeze,
when I thought you would be forever mine...
as the gilded leaves of Autumn sigh.

My Small Bit Of Forest

by Kim Rodrigues

The colorant of dawn, the cardinal sees,
intoning its hues with, "pretty...pretty...pretty."

As I covet red feathers, in the teaberry tree,
the sunlit chickadee harmonizes, "hey sweetie."

The woodpecker like a heckler is pining for laughs -
pounding, drumming the marionette for gaffs.

A tufted titmouse tweets, "peter...peter...peter."
The goldfinch dines on dandelion seeds, lilting sweeter.

Outfitted with winsome wildlife, comfortable and commodious,
my small bit of forest resonates with songbirds, melodious.

Embers Of A Memory--Dad's Song

by Carol Ann Richardson

Our hands and our feet were warmed from the cold,
while the campfire burned into embers and coal
The song that he whispered combined with the sparks,
and drifted away, to be lost in the dark

Splinters of light outlined his shape,
and hollowed the lines in his face.
With fingertips calloused, he strummed his guitar
into the solace of night.
We gathered to listen, and gathered our tears,
with smoke in our eyes and our hearts compromised.

    The song told the fable of babes lost in the woods
    who had wandered away on a bright amber day.
    Where the robins of red, so gingerly spread
    green strawberry leaves to cradle their graves

Crickets, like orphans awakened from rest,
lamented with sorrow from pine-needle nests
This legend was saved, but others were lost,
tossed to the wind, like ghost-feathers of ash.
My father is gone, but the song lingers on
remembered tonight, from a night in the past

The wind still unfolds the song to the night
whispering words that make robins cry
Drifting through the trees and taking me home
Still stoking the embers of a mid-summer's moon

A Soldier's Last Hurrah

by Robert E. Welch, Sr.

He was sitting at the table,
His coffee in his hand.
Not caring where he was,
This sad and lonely man.

The years that he had lived
Totaled ninety-nine and one
His memory was going
Of days when he begun.

He fought the war in Germany
With medals on his chest.
Then came home to family
Who said he was the best.

Now he sits alone at home
With none to share his fame.
Often asking for his friends
Though none had ever came.

Then a young boy came along
To hear the tales of glory.
The old man closed his teary eyes
And began to tell his story.

He passed away that very day
To walk the streets of gold.
Saying "Thank you, Lord, this last hurrah,
My one last story told."

Evermore

by Paula Ann Swanson

I shall love thee evermore,
beyond this life, I do vow.
Mortality, I can't ignore,
with Autumn's years, set 'pon my brow.

Beyond this life, I do vow,
our souls entwined, shall endure.
With Autumn's years set upon my brow,
of this bond, I can ensure.

Our souls entwined, shall endure,
life, fleeting, as a matchstick flame.
Of this bond, I can ensure,
my lips shall whisper thy sweet name.

Life, fleeting, as a matchstick flame,
as my grains of time, slip through the glass.
My lips shall whisper thy sweet name,
when comes the last beat of my heart, at last.

As my grains of time, slip through the glass,
mortality, I can't ignore.
When comes the last beat of my heart at last,
I shall love thee evermore.

In An Old Cathedral

by Terence O'Leary

She knelt upon a plank, plain oaken
(sable cloak, her mourning guise),
and sensed the breath of distant sighs,
pale shades of pain behind blue eyes...

While clasping close a cross-like token
(holding hope for those in need)
she prayed her Lord "please intercede,
my woes be washed, my soul be freed"...

Archangels, in the skies evoken
(candles flickered, shadows shivered),
through the panes, the moonlight quivered,
summoned forth, the wish delivered...

Forgotten words he once had spoken
(dimly echoed 'neath the dome)
swept sweetness of the honeycomb
o'er distant realms they used to roam...

At midnight's knell, in dreams awoken,
memories of love unfeigned...
Though loneliness of grief remained,
she still held hope... hope hadn't waned...

And when the dawn had early broken,
by the font, in peace, she lay...
As sudden as a sunset ray,
the light of life had slipped away...

Winter Horses

by Paulette Calasibetta

Horses wearing woolen coats
of red, green, and grey,
Gather round their daily bale of early morning hay.

Nodding, blissful heads, musing as they munch;
The earth beneath their steady hooves feel the snowy crunch.

Corralled behind sprawling, mended, wooden fences,
Curious they gaze with acute and focused senses.

Nostrils wide, clouds of breath, circling in rings,
Listen closely, hear them softly neigh and sing.

I See Love

by Marilene L. Evans

I see God's love to
mankind with His majestic,
innate creations

moon
m a g n i f i e s
mystique

stars
s p a r k l e
sky

sun
s h i m m e r s
sea

sea
s c a t t e r s
seashells

sanderlings
s c a n
seashore

wind
w h i r l s
weeds

breeze
b l o w s
bush

butterflies
b o a s t
beauty

I see love around
in people admiring and
praising God's wonders.

I Am An Old Man

by Richard Colbert

i am an old man
when i look in the mirror
i don't see me
a resemblance of my past
but know things aren't
always what they seem
  my skin is wrinkled and thin
  i bruise easily
  though not emotionally
  my arms have spots not freckles
  my sight and views are
  becoming blurred and vague
choices made in my younger daze
left gaps between
my teeth and memory
i'm guarded about
revealing either one
  the soles of my shoes flare
  making it easier
  to take things in stride
  i have arch supports
  so as not to be caught flat footed
the Cloud has
nothing to do with
information storage
but more the cause of
hide and seek with the
the sun and the past
  i talk to myself
  trying to get a consensus
  to show i'm not crazy
  the conversation

usually ends in a stalemate
and nobody wins
when i retired
everyday became Saturday
i start and finish
everything and nothing today
yesterday is gone
and tomorrow comes to quickly
when i look in the mirror
i see the lines i drew
in the sand and in my life
a resemblance of a past
maybe things are
what they appear to be

after all, i am an old man

The Fight For Equality

by Melissa Cornatzer

We can be equal without being the same.
Let's say it out loud, we shall be heard:
Look past my gender and know my name.

This is not about gaining wealth or fame
Together let's stand, let's spread the word:
We can be equal without being the same.

No more fighting about who is to blame
What matters most, is the pain inferred
Look past my gender, and know my name.

Do not forget how far we came
Forward we march, for the pot has been stirred
We can be equal without being the same.

Who we are is no reason for shame
The lines between male and female are blurred
Look past my gender, and know my name.

We don't need a label; this isn't a game
Inequality still existing is completely absurd
We can be equal without being the same.
Look past my gender and know my name.

It Came And Passed

by Ralph James Inman

It came and passed, and not a word was spoken
   as trills sang sweet from the tongue of the sparrow.
      Indifference now, our love was but a token,
         my heart's pierced through with Cupid's broken arrow.

With morning break I felt the deepest sorrow
   and setting sun heard silence, yet unbroken,
      then tolling bells left no time more to borrow.
         It came and passed, and not a word was spoken.

The cool breeze blew, no cloud in azure heaven,
   no voice raised loud atop the rolling barrow,
      like yeastless bread our words could never leaven,
         as trills sang sweet from the tongue of the sparrow.

So deep our passion grew in early sun rise,
   till lost in evening sleep and never woken.
      Like snowflakes that melt upon our hands are lies,
         indifference now, our love was but a token.

Forever has now come with painful remorse
   With night our light is dim, and vision narrow,
      as in the dark we fumble to change our course,
         my heart's pierced through with Cupid's broken arrow.

Long each minute passed in sorrowed memory,
   no tears to shed for moments lost forever.
      Flamed to ash in naught but burnt black cindery
         as, like the day, we're but a lost endeavor,
               ...it came and passed.

The Empty Quarter

by Roy B Jerden

Desirous dust devils dance for a glowing gold god,
withering winds wandering whither they wish.

Silenced as shadows stretch, silhouetting strange shapes,
elongated ellipses etching the expansive emptiness.

Quickly cooling, the sunset slathers the sky in carnelian colors.

Deep desert darkness descends, a moonless diaphanous dome.
Looming above us, the luminous universe lifts our eyes aloft.

A celestial shining so supreme it spawns starry shadows,
succoring our unsatisfied souls in its empyrean embrace...

The watcher waits...

Exotic Glacier Bay - The Glaciers Speak

by Sandra M. Haight

Here they are before me,
    surreal in the dazzling morning sun.
        Against clear skies of blue, and
peaked snow-capped mountains-
    these tall glaciers of Alaskan ice,
        stand heavenly before my eyes.

Their marbled, glistening whites,
    with multi shades of blue,
        arcane crevices and jagged peaks-
stir visions of cold, ghost-like forms
    that glare at me in this mysterious Bay
        of murmurous creaks and moans.

More than the eye can see,
  these lustrous glaciers speak,
    like eerie, moving forms,
in corridors that shift and moan-
  and with their loud sonorous wails,
    give birth- calving chunks that fall.

With an abrupt, roaring explosion,
  all at once, it starts- the large,
    calved segment plummets to the sea.
Waves and splashes follow every birth.
  These exotic glaciers live and speak-
    more than the eye can see.

Another Dawn, Another Day

by Ade Robert Amure

(Out of Eden: Act V)

Have you heard the sound of hooves go..... 'clippety clippety, clop'?
That is the sound that the Pale Horse makes, when down on Earth to shop.
That Reaper mean, the one called 'Grim',
Takes tortured souls with wanton whim.
That rider of the Pale Horse smirks - goes ...clippety, clippety, clop.
...clippety, clippety, clop.

Have you heard the sound of chests go...... 'boom-a de boom-a de boom'?
That is the sound that the poor heart makes in throes of gloom and doom.
Horrors unleashed you freeze with fright,
Hormone screaming 'flee or fight!!!'
The stricken heart pounds deathly beats - goes '...boom-a de boom-a de
boom'....boom-a de boom-a de boom'!

Have you heard the sound of guns go ....rat-a-tat, rat-a-tat, tat?
That is the sound that the nozzle made when out, it's bullets, spat.
To claim a life and rip apart
The victim ...and a loved one's heart.

That nozzle spits out rhythmic hate - goes...rat-a-tat, rat-a-tat, tat! ...rat-a-tat, rat-a-tat, tat!

Have you heard the sound of bells go ..ring-a-ling, ding-a-ling, dong?
That is the sound that the Church bells make to mark a victory song.
Men may die, and many shall mourn
But Life itself is not forlorn.
Be brave, take heart...the Church bell peals, ..goes: ring-a-ling, ding-a-ling, dong ...ring-a-ling, ding-a-ling, dong!

Have you heard the sound of the Cock; go ...kook-a-doodle, kook-a-doodle, doo?
That is the sound that the rooster makes when light, the days, renew.
Days will come, and days will go
And Life goes on the way we know.
So listen, hark! The cockerel crows - ....it goes: ...kook-a-doodle, kook-a-doodle, doo ...Kook-a-doodle, kook-a-doodle, doo............Kook-a-doodle, kook-a-doodle, doo - Another Dawn ...another Day ....kook-a-doodle, kook-a-doodle, doo!

Fantasy

by Alcibiades Castelo Branco

Fantasy,
is the garment we wear
day by day...
dreams feed
the reality and we
free from common, strengthen
our reality...
the hallucination of
being clay hallucinates us,
but the reality of being
  soul...
magnifies us, cheers us up...!

Her Renunciation

by JCB Brul

She walks barefooted in spiny shore
as dusk descends to snatch her heart;
Bloody feet turn curling foams
into hot crimson red~
melting her footprints
and her wild dreams
into smoke
that kills
her.
She
dances
with the moon
as the tide dries;
Her dolesome heart hails
on nocturnal murmurs
echoing from northern lights
as seabirds return to their nests;
She jumps in and succumbs to the sea.

Baseball

by Neva E. Romaine

To see the game, you have to plan
It takes some time you see
This is for all the die-hard fans
You'll need a strategy

To stand in line for baseball
Can be a timely task
You first must get the tickets
To clear your way to pass

Excitement now before the game
Which section are you in?

The dugout group or foul ball side
Row 5, seats 9 and 10

Concession stands are all around
Decide which should be first
Tee shirts and hats or hot dogs
You'll have to quench your thirst

Now don't forget the plans you made
Cause folks are filled with glee
You'll drink your beer, your coke and sprite
But then you'll have to pee

Another line to wait in
The porta potties blue
Don't get distracted from your plan
They'll jump in front of you

Oh Wow! Another "homer"
My team is going to win
Can't wait for seventh inning stretch
I have to pee again

Great game it was they played today
Our team is now the star
We're tired but we have to go
It's time to find the car

Life's Love Story

by Jerry T Curtis

Written for the contest
MORE SONG LYRICS

Have you ever seen, the sun setting down
Upon this red roofed town
And hear the sound of love begin
I have never found a more perfect place
Than, when I see your face

I simply fall in love again

Don't ask me which way the wind will blow
Or the tide will flow
Or even where, our love will go
I just know there could never be a place
Where I can't feel your warm embrace
With those lips I love to taste

Have you seen the mountains rising from the sea
That's where I want to be
With you eternally, in grace
We hear our tune, carried along the wind
Strummed on life's violin
As a tear rolls down your face

Don't ask me why the good times seem to fly
Or why some passion dies,
Or how lovers, can say Goodbye
All I know is when I leave this tropic heat
I am filled with the Latin beat
Until the next time on this street, we meet

Not So Long Ago

by Jonathan Michael Bellmann

Not so long ago beneath a bright blue summer's sky
There your eyes met mine how wondrous was the sight;
We walked together hand-in-hand long into the night.

Not so long ago I held you firmly in my arms
That we should never part or you wander from my side;
We promised then our love to share never more to hide.

Not so long ago in a hostile foreign land
I held your picture tight, and kissed your lovely face;
I wondered how you spent your day, longing for your embrace.

Not so long ago I heard your familiar, lovely voice
Though we couldn't touch I wiped away your tears;

I'll be home before you'll know it to quiet all your fears.

Not so long ago you found me standing in a crowd
There our love embraced and never to let go;
I cherished every single moment more than you should know.

Not so long ago I watched the autumn's setting sun
With shadows growing long and hours passing by
We tasted love's sweetest nectar, and sorrow's bitter cry.

Not so long ago beneath a bright blue summer's sky
There your eyes met mine how wondrous was the sight;
We walked together hand-in-hand long into the night.

A Fond Remembrance

by Frederic M Parker

We became lovers in a youthful world
Where love's elation flowed forever free
And allowed untamed fervor to unfurl
In a sphere of change too young to see
Could all our shades and shadows have been known
When we held tight in our love's embrace
To know we could only reap what was sown
From windswept furrows, we could not replace
Now in these years of twilight thoughts are pure
I welcome the world we both looked upon
When we touched the face of love so unsure
Until the moment came when it was gone
You are a memory a lasting gift
A fond remembrance, that I will die with

Fragments Of Fractals

by Eric Cohen

Fractals.

Spawn of iterating quadratic functions.
Choreographers of cosmic conjunctions.
Impervious to human dysfunctions.

Makers of multiverses. Encoders of creations.
Limited only by imaginations.

Recursive. Coercive. Immensely immersive.
Purveyors of poetic creative cursive.

With formative fractals you'll melt your mind's shackles
and be anywhere that you may want to be.
You can form fractals to your own reality,
and make anything in the sky or the sea.
You can even repurpose them to poetry ...

Yes, if
fractals were dactyls they'd flow off the page,
whirling and twirling, sublime.
Freeing us, being us, thoughts disengage,
teasing and pleasing with rhyme,
reaping the rhythms of time.

From mundane equations that yet yield complex
repetitive patterns that please and perplex,
come fractals so beautiful in all respects.

Constructors of coastlines and snowflake concerns,
foundries for forests, and feathers, and ferns,
the deeper you dive they have more twists and turns.

Generators of patterns, like veins in a leaf,
and the branches of trees, shapes of every motif.
Look around, everywhere, there are fractals, good grief!

From the large to the small and still smaller they flow,
simple patterns repeating, yet different, you'll know
that there's just no escaping the great fractal show.

So, let's face them, embrace them, we'll host history.
Let us master them, plaster them, I guarantee:
merge your mind into fractals, you'll set your soul free.

Ars Poetica

by Gary Bateman

Ars Poetica

Horace circa 19 BC gave some sound advice to
poets on the art of writing poetry and drama.

The following thoughts may echo in our minds,
most likely, the intent of what he may have meant . . .

A poem may excite and delight readers with its
imagery, meaning, metaphors, and so much more

A poem may speak of "home" and what it means
to each of us as we grow up and reach adulthood

A poem may excite one's imagination to learn
of people, places, events, and things in our world

A poem may speak to one's emotions—
love, lust, hate, happiness, sadness, and more

A poem may speak to palpability—
touching, feeling, embracing, kissing, and more

A poem may address courage—
to stand for something meaningful against all odds

A poem may address a weakness—

cowardice, avarice, and even a temptation

A poem may address humility—
in realizing that being humble can be strength too

A poem may address faith—
believing in yourself and others, and a cosmic destiny

A poem may address morality—
as good and evil, right and wrong are with us always

A poem may address objects and images—
that tickle one's poetic imagination and certitude)

Billy's Revenge

by Thomas Cunningham

Billy Smith was poor and it did show
His rich relatives didn't want to know
They had their cars and barbecues
And howled at Billy's worn out shoes.

Billy went for a walk and on the ground
Saw a shiny thing, a brand new pound
Bought a lotto ticket he had nothing to lose
But should have bought glue to fix them shoes.

That night he was sitting, watching T.V.
And up came the results for the lottery
He looked at his ticket, in total surprise
He had six numbers; couldn't believe his eyes.

Some twenty years later Billy passed away
His relatives had looked forward to this day
For the funeral some had travelled miles
Wearing Sunday best and big false smiles.

He was a lovely man they'd all say
But a big surprise was coming their way
They couldn't care less about poor Bill

Only interested in what was in his will.

Three weeks later Billy's will was read
And in it this is what the statement said
There is not one relative here today
That is going to gain in any way.

I was down on my luck you shut your door
You didn't want to know me anymore
You heard of my win, you circled around
My money I've given to the dog pound.

And here is something else that is in hand
By your houses I've purchased all the land
A sewage farm will be built that you'll see
When you open your windows, remember me.

Ode To Jakk

by Chantelle Anne Cooke

bold gold eyes glimmer
sleek sweet soul softly simmers
flame of love flickers

feline fur fashion
personality passion
always attraction

paws of pearl parchment
pranced and danced with enchantment
regal and romantic

loving lick kisses
his bold colors autumn bliss
we now reminisce

his heart cared and shared
like summer steam rain that paired
with us all...we faired

purring music floats
within our wishing soul boats
we catch his cat notes

She Likes To Knit Her Noodles

by Natasha L Scragg

Her chopsticks are at the ready.
Her hands are good and steady.
She likes to knit her noodles!
The task has just begun...

She starts off with a mango Welt
With pride, with zest, with tang.
It's a mesmerising watch
While the wiggling noodles hang.

Next. She's on to saucy Stocking Stitch.
Her garment sure does grow!
Knit one - Purl one - Knit two together
On each tasty row.

And this main course is called
" Knit Purl Chopstick Cha "
With a curry Cabled centre,
With sides of paprika Purl and Knit korma.

And as an extra taste-bud treat
BBQ Rib Raglan is on the menu.
Trust me! This kind of cuisine
Can't be found in any old venue!

From there on, the sleeves do drop
Like the soy sauce shaken a top.
Neatly Knitted are the Ribs.
Who voted for fish and chips?

To finish this fine course...
Knit - Slip - Knit - Pass Slip Stitch over.

This will make the button holes
For the Cadbury chocolate to melt all over.

And on completion, these knitted noodles
Slide straight on down her throat...
Before we've had a chance to prove her skill
This talent to others gloat!

A Tiny Messenger

by Debra L Brown

I saw a little Cardinal
setting in a tree.
I said to that little red bird
"Why have you come to me?"
He flew a little closer
and let out a great big "chirp"!
I'm a messenger sent from heaven
and from those who have passed on.
I hope this brings you blessings
and great peace in your heart
because, God heard your grieving prayer
and your loved one is at rest.
At that very moment
my heart was at peace.
Because, God sent this little bird
in my time of need.
Now if you see a Cardinal
listen closely to his song.
It might be the answer to your prayer
sent by the Lord above.

The Power Of A Dream

by Vera Judy Ball

It's easy for the things we want to just be put aside.
The things we've always dreamed of put on hold and left to ride,
Until some time, some future date we hope will come to pass,
And the dream becomes reality not just a dream at last;

But time slips by and other things can over cloud our dreams,
And slowly they just slip away, become forgotten schemes.
But dreams can give us purpose, the power to start improving.
A dream can give us energy, the will to get things moving.

Don't lose the power of the dream.
It helps you to accrue,
The things to make things happen,
And it's custom made for you.

Swans

by Dale Gregory Cozart

A pond quivers in demure gusts,
cygnets of morning light undulate
with lithe ripples. Winter thaws,
the sun arcs over feathered rainbows
as ice sculptures bevy like water lilies
on April's frigid cobalt.

In abrupt squall webbed feet prance
on a mirror, capturing saffron exhalations
of rapt poppies, a wild umbrella splayed
like tumultuous cumulus, ending a reflection
of snow angels promenading
in boundless cerulean.

Everlasting Love For Me

by Beata B. Agustin

"I have loved thee with an everlasting love." *
Precious assurance from the Father above
Expressed by Jeremiah 31:3
Wondrous God's compassion, bountifully free.

Drawing me near Him with His loving kindness
Portrays His goodness despite my sinfulness
Reaching-out to me, leaving throne of glory
To rescue me from hell's condemning fury.
"I have loved thee with an everlasting love." *
Precious assurance from the Father above
Expressed by Jeremiah 31:3
Wondrous God's compassion, bountifully free.

Midst God's love reigns bliss of sweet serenity
Vanquishing turmoil with great peace certainty
His grace protects my soul from guilt-causing pain
Offering comfort with whole forgiveness gain.
"I have loved thee with an everlasting love." *
Precious assurance from the Father above
Expressed by Jeremiah 31:3
Wondrous God's compassion, bountifully free.

Such inspirational verse from the Scriptures
Divinely sublime, propelling faith ventures
Securing me with the Lord's relationship
Sealing redemption for eternal worship.
"I have loved thee with an everlasting love." *
Precious assurance from the Father above
Expressed by Jeremiah 31:3
Wondrous God's compassion, bountifully free.

*Jeremiah 31:3 The LORD hath appeared of old unto me, saying, Yea, I have

loved thee with an everlasting love: therefore, with lovingkindness have I
drawn thee.

We Raise Them Up

by Ann Gilmour

Today we sing
great joy we bring
To those sweet souls
words long forgotten

For just a while we take them
to a peaceful magical place
      a place they knew
         a place they loved
           a place to put smiles on their face

Even those who do not speak whose memories faded long ago
They'll sing along inside their heads the words they used to know
And as the music starts to play deep inside a memory stirs
As slowly they will rock and hum before the words begin to come
And by the time we reach page two they sing along with me and you

  'Blue Moon' ~ we sing ~ oh how they swoon
  'Delilah' ~ 'Lean on Me'
  'Sweet Caroline' ~ they start to move it really gets them in the groove

We sing with gusto they smile with joy
As memories return when girl meets boy
Our last rendition our final song
Full of joie de vivre the choir and me

We start to sing 'You Raise Me Up'
I start to cry ~ I don't know why it always makes me cry...
We raise the roof our souls entwine they almost touch the sky
Our spirits smile with exultation to cheers ~ applause ~ a celebration

For today we really made their day and they have made ours too
Monies sent to Parkinson's UK we pray a cure is found one day

We bid them farewell ~ We wave them goodbye
I'm so blessed to be part of this choir
It is food for my heart each time I take part
With lovely friends who like me have "P"

Singing together in our Parkinson's choir
I feel truly alive ~ I feel almost on fire...

Like The Lotus

by Subrahmanyan Radhakrishna

God does not blink in his eternal watch,
because time does not come in to it at all!
pure stillness reigns where he is awake,
no breath, no whisper there is nothing at all!
in a turbulent pond- like a lotus calm!

slaves we mortals are to the whip of time,
we measure it all day, measure it all night
by the beat of the heart, rhythm of the breath,
at the birth of a child, to the end of our lives,
by the revolutions of earth, Sunset, Sunrise!

look deep within the calmness of your Soul,
there is a glow of divinity that is real you,
there is stillness within that is stillness of God,
the absolute truth that doesn't change at all,
in a turbulent pond - like a lotus calm!

the absolute truth is not the slave of time,
because it is so still time does not exist at all,
life's many gains and losses, defeats and pain,
have no longer any meaning in this domain,
in a turbulent pond- like a lotus calm!

align your mind with that divine stillness,
perceive the glowing unending brightness,
cast away the body, surrender your soul,

nothing exists! you are part of absolute truth,
the lotus glows - the pond was a mirage!

Greater Art Thou!

by Joseph S. Spence Sr

Heart broken torn apart like scrambl'd eggs;
As the weak link snapp'd momentum slow'd—stopp'd
Love wherest art thou? Torment'd now begs,
This cup of scourge, drink or not—spill'd—now mopp'd.

Et tu Brute? Whisper'd from Caesar's lips;
Yet Romeo and Juliet once lov'd,
Like Macbeth's witches brew—don't drink nor sip:
Fate or faith shatter'd, vulture pick'd bones—cross'd.

Heart pleadeth upward—greater is thy love,
Open Heaven's gate with thy purest light;
Hearest thou not the meek? Awaiting thy dove!
Remove these shadows of darkness and strife:

Greater art thou in Heaven than on Earth,
Creator of creation giveth now birth!

The End Of The Trail

by Thomas Cunningham

Two weeks we'd been droving; and the end was now in sight
In the distance was Dodge City, we'd be there before night
I was on the trail with other cowboys from the Double Circle Ranch
And we were looking forward to the saloon, the notorious Long Branch.

We reached the railhead with the longhorns , just before sundown
Me and the other cowboys were itching, ready to hit town
The buyers were there waiting, hands were shook the deal done.
We were aware there would be lowlifes, so we all packed a gun.

First a shave then a hot bath to wash off the layers of dust

Then buy some new clothes and long johns, the latter a must
We then headed for the saloon and were ready for some rye
After two weeks on the trail our throats were kinda dry.

We walked through the bat wing doors, there were the usual stares
The good time girls were beckoning us, to follow them upstairs
We all asked for some whisky and some ordered hot foods
Then the young bucks went upstairs; to satisfy their *lustful moods*.

Old Jethro our foreman, the next day rode into town
And spent the best part of two hours tracking us all down
Bleary eyed and throbbing heads, no spoken words were said
And thoughts of that long ride home filled us with dread.

At the stables in a side street our horses were stood ready
We paid the stable boy and mounted, we all felt quite unsteady
We'd ride for nigh on two weeks crossing the great Texas plain
Get home round up more Longhorns and do it all again.

I Simply Refused To Ride With Death

by Janice Canerdy

When I refused to ride with Death
He tied my hands and feet,
Then tossed me in with some poor guy
He'd grabbed up off the street.

Oh, what a hurry he was in!
He slammed it to the floor.
We sat in wide-eyed, abject fear,
Each clinging to a door.

While whizzing past the school, we saw
The children run and play.
We passed the fields where tractors hummed
On this, our judgment day.

We captives introduced ourselves,
Shook hands, and sadly talked.

When Death heard unfamiliar names,
He gasped, slowed down, and balked.

He made a sudden stop beside
A swelling of the ground.
He scratched his head, he murmured low,
And then he turned around.

" 'Tis centuries until your time!
I've made a grave mistake.
Seems I misread the pick-up sheet.
You're free, for goodness sake!"

Between Midnight And Dawn

by Carol Sunshinze Brown

Overcome by the peace in the midnight hour
Moonlight fills the otherwise velvet black sky
Twinkles of newness invade our senses from afar
The night so beautiful it causes us both to sigh

On our tropical island watching the trees sway
Love was captured between midnight and dawn
Bodies entwined the feeling took our breath away
Forever our nights under the moonlight will live on

Do Not Delay

by Eileen Manassian Ghali

I wait for you to come with open arms,
for pain that flays and sears me will not cease
though once I feared you, now I see your charms
I long to enter rest and sleep in peace

For you are nothing but a placid state
devoid of feelings and of lucid thought
where pain and heartache do not carry weight
and cravings and ambitions tarry not

You promise me a tranquil, fond embrace
I will not pull away from proffered kiss,
for tears have never ceased to bathe my face
to be relieved of anguish equals bliss

I wait with baited breath; do not delay
Oh, Death, it is for you I kneel to pray

Whispers From Beyond

by Scott Williams

Listening for whispers from beyond the grave.
So hard to hear for the mortality slave.
Wind blows a chill thru the winter's trees.
Hands clasped in prayer I'm on my knees.
Denial on my lips, disbelief in my heart.
Scared and alone my world torn apart.
A pastor speaks standing beside you.
I know you're gone but don't want it to be true.
Who are these strangers standing around?
Inch by inch you're lowered into the ground.
Everyone says, " I'm so sorry for your loss. "
Can't they see I'm on an ocean that I can't cross.
If I close my eyes and listen really hard.
I can hear you say, " go play but stay in the yard."
Memories hurt Mom and I don't want to cry.
Please don't go I don't want you to die.
I know I can't stop it there's nothing I can do.
You'll just have to live on in my memories of you.
Now I have to find a way to be strong and brave.
Keep listening for whispers from beyond the grave.

Mona Lisa's Paramour

by Suzette Richards

A period of youthful vim ferments
as coruscating golden flecks in eyes
that mesmerise and tantalise, give rise
to secrets in my breast to stir, foment.
The xanthous tresses that cascade torment.
My eager and impressionable sighs
that echo every pirouette and pliés,
a fleeting intercession of lament.
A maverick when it comes to amour
and quintessentially a rakish cad.
Unrequited love longstanding rancour,
but finally become your paramour.
An enigmatic smile ever so sad;
your broken heart I gladly give succour.

L U S T

by Olive Eloisa Guillermo - Fraser

L U S T
helter-skelter heat
it boils emotions to peak
carnal rots the flesh

New York Street Horse

by Suzanne Delaney

Plunked down in chaos
from a gentler time,
blinkered from the traffic
he pulls the coach along.
Patient, in his harness bond
he tugs at hearts, with pathos-
as to his love of duty we respond.

Amidst the screech of sirens
and the blasting horns,
he stands and dreams
of meadows in a nosebag.

Such rhythmic clicking of
 metal shoes on concrete,
full rolling of the carriage
wheels and he, confined,
down through the centuries
he thought he'd left behind.

Reflections Of God

by Beryl Edmonds

I feel God's presence when walking o'er hills
In nodding heads of golden daffodils
In fields of green and crystal waterfalls
In trees standing proud, statuesque and tall.

I hear God in vibrant sounds of the woods
In murmurs of the breeze and babbling brooks
I find Him in the glow of risen sun
Fresh days and fresh pages to write upon.

I sense God's love flow through charmed symphonies
In enchantment of choral melodies
I seek Him in the dewy morning mist
In the sky when it has been rainbow kissed.

God's revealed in roosters crowing refrain
In rain dancing upon the window pane
I rejoice in nightfalls scenic display
Stunning sunsets taking one's breathe away.

There's not a fragrant rose in June that blooms
Nor stars twinkling brightly around the moon
No clouds adorning the canvas of sky
That doesn't send reflections of God on high.

In the morning I will sing of your love...

Yet Pushed, Ever Onward, I Dare Tread

by Robert J. Lindley

Yet Pushed, Ever Onward, I Dare Tread

BEHOLD, I wade into darkening mists,
My journey, clarification of Fate
When I balked, black ghost said, I insist
Hurry destiny cries it is too late,
Strolling deep within, horrific the sounds
So strangely pungent the circling winds
In distant valleys, baying of the hounds-
I fear what that hideous sign portends.

Now so afraid, through weeping years I trod
Searching, ever onward, I did thus tread.
My shield, simply faith in Light and my God
And bushels of truth, to me, life has fed.

I pray for salvation of divine light.
Blessed ending of this courageous flight.

Would I Be A Flower

by David Andrew McHattie

Would I be a desert flower
    To beguile your wandering eye
Where you hesitate a moment
    To peruse a flower such as I.
As you so lovingly marvel
    At the fragrance of my bloom
And your gentle touch lays a shiver
    To put a blush upon my plume.

Would I be a mighty oak tree

Stretching tall towards the sky
To fill your heart with wonder
   As you're slowly passing by
And sit with me this summer day
   to pass away the hours
While you slyly press against me so
   To avoid a mid-day shower.

Would I be a double rainbow
   To slake and take your breath away
With my colors drab and muted
   Compared to the beauty you display.
But you see in me some worthiness
   Causing your heart to skip a beat
As you leap and laugh through dappled grass
   With a bounteous world beneath your feet.

Would I be the sun from high above
   To warm you in your stead.
But I could never bear to leave you so
   When twilight sends me to my bed.
I would then take hold of life's celestial keys
   And send a baffled Nature to her room
So I could be the sun in the light of day
   And at night I'd be the moon.

Could I be a rainbow, sun, tree or flower?
   I will now answer brash and true.
I would be all these things and many more...
   Just to love and honor you.

   The End

Autumn Royal

by Frances Schiavina

Come my love past the beauty of the hill
Ablaze with ginger sunset and fall fire
On a fast downhill wagon hayride thrill
In festive saffron and amber attire
Celebrating with tambourine and lyre
Autumn's gift of new harvest abundance
With an improvised Abu Barn floor dance
Circling around a ginger umber mound
Pumpkin carving for the Jack-O- lantern
Eating chestnuts fresh gathered from the ground
Racing rolling barrels to the caverns
To ferment before hitting the taverns
Cinnamon flavored pies and crimson wine
Ginger spiced to flavor the night is fine

I Lifted Up

by Gabrielle Jordan

from suffering and pain
that is piped into veins
by the organ-less master
who relentlessly plays

from a congested gutter
of fake themes
hiding in deception
and callous clutter

from distaste of the old
the sick the poor and uninvited

from the self-imposed
silent deaf and short-sighted

I rise
as a bed of plume feathers
carry me gently towards
an untainted treasure

klimt gold ash pours over my body
soothing the distress I allowed to infest

I stroll along the mountains aurora
feet sinking into a bed of stardust flora
gazing out at mankind

a dull drum beat of the blinding matrix
trudging in sync to a contrived greatness

oblivious to the thundering roar
of perishing seas

animals lie floating
in warm global soaking

smoldering sun with rusted rays
shivers in the sky
with disheartened malaise

the illusion is breaking
a decision is undertaking

a red beaked sparrow beckons me
to look off into the darkening blue

a great tempest is coming
and long overdue

Reflections On My Seventieth Birthday

by Thomas Wells

Marked by seven decades on land and sea,
my asymmetrical soul always out of place.
Trying on attire like subtextual pedigree,
My fake jewels mimic a state of grace.

Ignore the Homeric, Shakespearian legacy.
Forget the poet as prophet.
Now, most poets are stupid beasts jotting every lunacy.
Now I know my haven. For this, I am another misfit.

Lopsided is my consciousness, deformed is my thought.
Seven decades of faltering certitude, years of faltering competence.
I am forgiven to write poetry, excused for being overwrought.
These are my coarse unauthorized edges in coexistence.

Always in motion, animation distracts broken reflection.
So many blunders and ill-conceived opinions.
My metamorphosis into Aidos, sick with shame and dejection.
No, I never belonged, just a squatter in all dominions.

There were meager victories even in the freezing midnight rain,
more like random good luck, I had no faith in them.
Poetry grants license to accept what I can't explain.
Seven decades casting about the rubble ad hominem.

II

I am stable now. These back-brain wounds play only for me
as unavoidable torment probing my limits.
It isn't exactly old I feel. It's more like experience ladling fresh ways to see.
The best lives are extended childhoods confident in attaining new summits.

Any universal architect surely granted us supple wonder to adapt.
Our galaxy alone presents at least 480 billion alternatives.
But from other monkeys, we branched, with imaginations we tapped.
As our cortex grew, our pictographs became the language of narratives.

I am lucky to be among the privileged wondering.
Seven decades have nearly reduced most of my conceit.
My wisest word to travelers is to ask questions and start wandering.
Above all, believe your purpose in the journey and roam without deceit.

It

by David Mohn

It dances deep in tranquil eyes
from velvet plumes of ether's calm
as soft as alabaster skies

It softly sings an ancient psalm
rewritten when the moon invites
in lavender of evening balm

It gently blooms with conscious slight
in zephyred streams of fragrant dreams
as lilacs waft the night towards light

Upon the page, untraced it streams
It dwells between the words – it seems

Vigilant

by Mark Pringle

We must be vigilant to
the shards of radiance and splendor
that flash
before our squinting cynic eyes.

Choice Words

by Christopher Lane

Write words
that will be scraped
into a stone
by a rebellious kid
who refused
to be owned
Write words
that will make
a hopeless sinner
never feel alone
Write words
that will move
a homeless man
from a shelter seat
to a throne
Write words
that will tattoo
the answers
to your soul
about the questions
of the future
that is unknown

The Meatball

by Robert James Liguori

I'm a meatball in a sub,
With three others just like me,
We are warmed by tomato sauce,
And a blanket made of cheese.

The roll is our surrounding house,
Handled by a man,
Shivering at a football stadium,

While sitting in the stands.

My best friends will soon leave me,
One by one as I watch the teeth,
Overreach each sphere of nutrients,
Devouring what's beneath.

This is what I was born to do, so I will not be afraid,
Munch, munch, munch. Oh, what a glorious day!

I'll Cry No More For You

by Neva E. Romaine

Seems long ago - a distant time, at first when I saw you
My heart did leap within my chest; was love to spring anew?

I should have known, I couldn't see, enthralled I was with you
The guard that was upon my heart had lifted and withdrew

When from the start our passion flowed - so intimate were we
We'll stand a test of time and stay as close as two can be

Long walks beneath the twilight skies and joyous times we shared
We spoke of secrets buried deep and still our passion flared

Betrayal! sudden and complete - a knife has pierced my heart!
Your other "lover" on the phone?!? You Cheater!! It's time to part!!

Oh ache, oh heartache go away; sweet sleep, please come to me
These tears, these rolling tears must stop - I need to be set free!

How sad it is when love runs cold; Loves' flames die down and wane
The mind is filled with memories; the heart is wracked with pain

Too long I've felt this emptiness in finding you untrue
And though I'm filled with sadness now - I'll cry no more for you

Alibi

by Bernard Chan

In the end, we were there-not there,
two present absentees
sharing an apartment vacated by a relationship
and the worst kind of loneliness -- feeling solitary next to someone --
partners in the crime of abetting mutual misery,
though neither of us can really be linked
to the crime scene, can we?

We've got each other's alibi.

Harris Tweed

by Peter Rees

Look deep within these loosely-woven layers to find
primeval land with ocean, sky and wind entwined,
skilled hands and eyes of generations gone before
and peat smoke mingling with a sea mist on the shore.

In old and intricate design you may well sense
a solitary piper skirling a lament,
or view the purple heather blowing on the hill,
or hear soft-spoken memories echoing still.

Some bold and joyful as a vibrant summer's day,
and others tinted as an autumn bride's bouquet,
some speak of wilderness and yet untrodden ways,
some melancholic strangers to the sun's sweet rays.

With insight woven and a clarity of mind,
the rhythmic textures of the land we see defined.
With colours of the seasons, each piece of cloth unique,
of planet Earth and nature's harmony does speak.

Revered now far beyond its island home,

a homespun cloth of gold it has become.
Ambassadors for Scotland, yes indeed,
that's whisky, Robert Burns and Harris Tweed.

Opaque People

by Subimal Sinha-Roy

I've never been where they've been,
chasing the mirage in the desert storm.
I look into their tranced eyes,
see their vision transfixed on illusion,
the shroud of ruse spreads on sneaky people.

The gleam of oasis out of their sight,
they lie on wasteland like dry shadow of trees
that have forgotten they were once green,
but I know they've lost their roots,
desiccated they've turned into wooden people.

Layer on layer of designed deception
morphs into misleading molds of crafted mask,
changing into chameleon skin on their faces.
Behind the smoke-screen I can't see through
the veil created by the insecure people,

The light of reality doesn't penetrate,
so they make their own darkened world,
don't perceive when they turn into antiques,
but I know because for a long time now
I've walked in the museum of masked people.

They build castles in the air within deep valleys,
no window of their mind opens on sparkling sky.
The sun rays don't light up their bleak isolation,
their desolate souls remain obscure in the dark,
for the spent sun starts to set for dismal people.

For them the harvest moon doesn't ever rise,
they become gloomy splinters of the starless night,

not knowing why their dreams break in dark abyss,
but I know why no rainbow enters their heart,
for they've turned into opaque people.

Mindfully Enjoying The Moment

by Rama Balasubramanian

When mind is in the moment, thoughtlessness prevails"
~
Keep your mind away from thoughts that rebound
Hear the mesmerizing melodic music of surround
Bask in the bewitching beauteous objects that astound
Sense all the sensations you skin has sensed around
Inhale the myriad magnetic fragrances floating around
Experience boundless bounteous bliss of God abound

Mindfulness leads to cessation
Of thoughts, the causation
Of our miseries, our vexation

Mindfulness makes us aware of creation
Leading to captivation
Then to our admiration
And acclamation
Of love of God flowing without cessation

When thoughts end
Vibrations ascend
We transcend

The body
Situated in Samadhi
experiences bliss eternal
Sees soul internal

Attains salvation
Instant elation
To final destination

Names

by Robert L Carmack

Every past that perfectly colors letters,
haunting losses beckon the predecessors,
utter names in passion or greeting, makes a
furious girlfriend.

The Mirror Of The Lake

by Dale Gregory Cozart

Shy autumn first appeared in scarlet blush
to kiss the silent mirror of the lake
as umber shadows gathered in the hush
of amber afternoon and rose to take

the waning glow of summer into night.
The ginger leaves of maples echo still
a decoupage of August's blazing light
that spread like flames upon the cresting hill

then downward to the water's gleaming run.
They spill upon the glass like lava sear
amidst a mist of steaming cinnamon,
the saffron embers whispers in the ear

of pilgrim day to one last journey make
to view its image mirrored in the lake.

Sitting Still In The Dark

by Brandee Augustus

Sitting still in the dark
can sometimes make the light feel distant,
like you can't even reach it
and your pain has left a mark.

It makes you feel like nothing can change
and everything seems impossible -
crippling you to the point of doing nothing.
But let the Light in - those thoughts will rearrange.

You'll remember that you're not helpless
and you have an inner strength that can't be denied.
With the true Spirit of Light you can do anything.
The darkness will scatter and you won't feel hopeless.

Now you can move on to make your mark-
one that can't ever be erased.
You'll realize that the Light was always there
and you'll never be afraid to sit still in the dark.

Once A Goddess Of Evening

by Suzanne Delaney

I miss the placid lavender dusks
tinged with cerulean mist
and watching spiders
weaving gossamer into faint
whispers of evening

How I would dally,
dressed in velvet and pearls
dangling emeralds on
golden swirls to
entice new tomorrows

into this sultry,
waiting world

Photograph Of A Redwood Stump In Sepia
by Suzanne Delaney

The human spirit needs places where
nature has not been rearranged
by the hand of man
Author Unknown

A metal rail now mocks the space

where a massive trunk once rose two hundred feet,
and a long stairway, and a sign, and a doorway
 make up 'The Stump Hotel.'

As a roadside attraction this once magnificent tree
is more suggestive of an amputee
whose prosthesis
could never recapture the living limb or,
a whisper of the spark within.

Think -
of the many who came and stood,
here on this altered stump.

Did anyone look up to see its phantom trunk
rising to the moon?

Where Will He Sleep Tonight

by Eileen Manassian Ghali

She's tucked in bed of floral white
To mommy's hand, she holds on tight
No hunger pangs disrupt her night
In dreams she sees candied delight

He finds a place out on the street
He's scared of strangers that he'll meet
A piece of bread has been his treat
In dreams he sees his mother sweet

The morning comes, a brand new day
She hurries, for she can't delay
There's time at school for work and play
Her mom escorts her on the way

He hears a noise which makes him wake
It's cold; his body starts to shake
How many coins will begging make?
"Please help me, sir, for heaven's sake!"

Why should she have more toys to keep?
Why should he live in pain so deep?
When day is done, each child will sleep
In dreams she'll smile, while he will weep

And as you read this little rhyme
explain to me, what is the crime
of that young boy who's doing time
with heart of gold beneath the grime

Is there no way to right this wrong?
Will he get lost among the throng
in quest for love, a smile, a song
some food to make his body strong?

If circumstance would turn around

to make you sleep there on the ground
your crying drowned by city sound
would you not dream of being found?

So while you're kneeling by her bed
to plant your kisses on her head,
Think of that boy who lives in dread
and share your wealth, your home, your bread

A child should live a life carefree
and sleep in warm security
So hear my plea, and let this be
the day you change his destiny

How She Weaves

by Martha L. Kiser

In hues of sepia she maintains
her web of life, Mother Nature;
from smallest seed to greatest
creature her umbilical sustains.

The fate of all life resides
in her consciousness and flow;
like a machine each part depends
on the other parts smooth glide.

Pollinators nurture flora,
food is recycled and regenerates;
feeding others of her children,
from trees to abundant Passiflora.

Through our big blue marbled macrocosm
she weaves her web of life;
from Terra-firma are many birthed
abundant arising microcosms.

With light and pigmentation's work
amazing color floods her realm;

from greens, golds, reds and browns
she paints such serene patchwork.

Wondrous miracles she has birthed
within her spirits sylvan seas;
a universal soul, our Mother,
captured by the poets in verse.

The finest artist of her kind,
with unlimited imagination;
her womb is quite a fertile one,
life's threads are fragilely intertwined.

God's Voice Whispers

by Kimberly J Merryman

God's voice comes in gentle whispers:
soft and soothing
never harsh.
He whispers words of love and grace,
then wraps you in a warm embrace.
You must be quiet,
you must be still,
to hear God's whisper to your soul.
He'll whisper "peace",
when you are troubled.
He'll whisper "faith",
in times of doubt.
And when you're wracked
with guilt from sin,
if you'll be still,
and let Him in,
you'll hear Him whisper:
"I forgive."

One In Nature

by Carol Sunshinze Brown

Human life as a perennial plant goes dormant,
yet we will renew in magnificent splendor.

My Final Curtain

by Terry Flood

No encore demanded, I stand alone
No applause as I hang up my 'microphone'
But what do they care, for no empty chair
Has ever acknowledged good tone

I took to this stage in a different age
I think then, the Stones were the rage
Yet, I've appeared here, daily for years
And sung like a songbird uncaged

But this, my last bow, arthritic now
Elicits no 'Bravo' or 'Wow'
I gave it my best, my stage put to rest
A field I can no longer plough

For fifty years hired, tomorrow retired
This caretaker? No longer required
So thanks for the chance, to sing and to dance
Enacting the dreams I desired

My time to go, my time to rest
The silence now, inside my chest
Applause resounds, my lights go down
I take my leave, where I lived best

Night Shoes--

by James Edward Lee Sr

Mama and them, took us aside
When we cried
She wiped our eyes

She grandma and Auntie
Bathed and feed us
Took us to church learnt us bout' JESUS

And when it was time for bed
We kids would put on pyjamas and them **night shoes**
~
NIGHT SHOES
We won't need in glory
On them heavenly golden grounds
NIGHT SHOES
Worn in the daylight
Shines in steps of grace
When grandpa died grandma said he paid his dues
Ole granny told the mortician, sir, please dress him in them old
Night Shoes

Somethingsaurus

by Robert L Carmack

Fossilized pieces past discovery's brink
made some people
think, think, think,

of giant plant eaters in an artist's sketch,
how their necks would
stretch, stretch, stretch.

Meat eaters hungry and looking for a fight,
ambush or chase,

bite, bite, bite.

But it took just one space rock pulled by the sun,
and their time was
done, done, done.

They may have to stay in studios and screens
if we can't find
genes, genes, genes.

Dino from Bedrock, Godzilla from Japan,
imagine it
can, can, can.

What a purple T-Rex from Texas would bring,
and how he could
sing, sing, sing.

From a land before time filled with Ducky's pep,
good to the last
yep, yep, yep.

Flow

by Gabrielle Jordan

I watched a glass goblet clean itself in patience of beauty
The tingling ring in sparkle water
was the evidence
of the slow unfurl of a flower
I imagined a symphony of open palms
swaying
spreading winged tips
flowing blankets of kindness
caressing
golden light that never flames
but shines
The measure of humanity
clearly defined

Passion Dance

by Joanna Chamberlain

Captivated, he embraced his dainty partner in crime
Dramatic bold pauses, leading posture, keeping her time

Unique sultry fiery ruffles, frame her sleek scarlet gown
Golden sun caressed curls, eyes intense mahogany brown

His stance dominating, he guides her through the auburn air
Spontaneous their rhythm, passionate tempos flair

Intense synchronised mirrors, reflecting interaction
Energetic Man, mysterious, luscious attraction

Pulsating hearts, romantic half-moon rotations in flight
Vibrant, rustic, festivals of multicolour unite

Music commences, dazzling lights, gathered crowds start to roar
Appointing their collaborator, taking the dance floor

Haiku

by Warren Doll

falling rock cut tree
thick resin flow insect trap
amber time capsule

Sonnet 21, Old Hiking Shoes

by Ken Allan Dronsfield

(Spenserian Format)

Don't grieve for me here on the attic shelf;
we're joined infinitely as one, you said.
In an old moldy box now, by myself;

my place was there tucked well under your bed.

Don't grieve for me here within the dark dread;
the days and nights meld together as one.
Reflect on happy times, with stronger tread;
sweet dreams now reign as dead leaves in the sun.

Memories fade away after you're done;
the old just crumble away into dust.
Remember all the mountain trails we'd run?
Fear, you showed none, only honor and trust.

Don't grieve I'm here above your clarinet;
on the top shelf, right beside your train set.

Summer's Curtain

by Heidi Sands

The curtain of summer approaches now
It is knitted in the green of the trees
Flowers are saying goodbye with a wow!

Petals will fall and fly afar with breeze
Vibrant color will decorate the land
It is knitted in the green of the trees

Sea will bring coolness to the beach's sand
Wildlife will gather food, they are smart
Vibrant color will decorate the land

Strawberries now gone, for an apple tart
Nourishing food comforts us, as we know
Wildlife will gather food, they are smart

The curtain can come down for the new show
We're grateful and ready to watch it all
Nourishing food comforts us, as we know

We leave humidity to wear our shawl

The curtain of summer approaches now
We're grateful and ready to watch it all
Flowers are saying goodbye with a wow!

A Summer's Day

by Janis Medders Thompson

Can I compare colors to a summer's day?
So many different hues at play.
Summer is *saffron* like an orange balloon,
hot and fiery by the first week of June.

Noon is yellow, a *lemon* so bright
until the creeping sunset casts it *crimson* light.
Tangerine shadows upon *chartreuse* grass
means another summer day has passed.

A *lavender* dusk brings cool to the day
with scent of *lilac* around the way.
Watermelon tastings flavor July,
as fireworks light up an *aquamarine* sky.

The world rests beneath a white *coral* moon.
Gently dreaming in a soft summer swoon.

Enlightenment

by Pashang Salehi

What is this consciousness that feels so sublime?
They told me that I am conscious of my time.
It is all gloomy and dark with lots of pain.
If I'm conscious is it a virtue or its crime?

Do I see you or are you there in my mind?
I do wonder what if this life makes us blind.
Maybe it's all a game we're just here to play,
The things that you have lost you will never find.

There is something within us that never dies.
Never get old within you and never cries.
He is just there and lives like a little child.
When you are old enough, he leaves and then flies.

I am so wondering where my today went?
Yesterday I was young, I was so content.
Was I conscious then or conscious I am now?
They gave me consciousness, without my consent.

Haloo

Words

by Richard D Seal

Words, this life, knows no stronger force
These fragments with such ease we wield
Even love, they will steer off its course
And fell the high and mighty in the field

Unthinking we may use one by mistake
Throw out the smallest humble negative
Not realising how that one may grate
And find a heart unwilling to forgive

At times we twist them to our greatest gain
How simple is the art; Manipulate
With disregard for whom they may cause pain
With no concern for chaos they create

A means that has no other parallel
To take us to the plain of joy
Or plunge us into blackest hell
Unequalled is their power to destroy

We use them each, to communicate
To both confound and un-confuse
On their answers, we must ever wait

Whilst in reply, decide, which ones to choose

And on that throw of dice, win or lose

Flash Memory Therapy

by Line Monique Gauthier

Grab a blank sketch book and call it your own
Create your personal memory album
It's fun, creative, therapeutic, and shareable

Your eyes will light up each time you share memories
Your heart will tingle as you turn the pages
You'll laugh, you'll cry, you'll travel back in time
'Cause memories are meant to be remembered

Take your book and sketch your favourite memories
The object is not to produce works of art but
To evoke the feelings related to each moment in time
Draw stickmen and cartoons but mostly
Exaggerate details to get each feeling across

Even with unpleasant memories
The ones that haunt you because
You still see them through a child's eye
I found the adult in me wanting to step in
And protect my inner child
There was a soothing healing happening
And I felt much lighter about it all

Better than a camera, you hold the pencil
Drop irrelevant details, expand on the relevant ones
Tweak the images in your mind and put them on paper
Feel free to add key words of course
Re-spin the storyline and rewrite your history

Create your own precious memory album
Start now, pick up a pencil
Draw the memories you hope to never forget
Sketch the elements of your magical moments...

Clair De Lune Pensif

by Lycia Harding

A pensive moon lets fall the rain
that calls you to a darkened sill,
where, apprehensive, you remain,
held captive in her thrall

until she waxes at the windowpane
to ask intently if you'll still be back
when she's gone past her wane

Beyond the glass,
you swear you will...

Cross Road

by Virginia Darline Gelok

As he shuffled toward me, I cringed.
Ripped clothes and shoes with flapping soles had alerted me.
I could actually see his sunken cheeks and lips clamped tight.
What was he thinking?

Me, dressed just so. Fancy hair, eyes aglow.
What was he thinking?

My purse clenched tightly.
Do I cross to the other side?
What was he thinking?

Suddenly it came to me,
flooding both my mind and my heart.
I am so very sorry.

I almost forgot that you are as human as I.
I am so sorry.

One thing for sure, apparently you are the stronger one.
I am sure I could not live the life you must.

What was I thinking?

Rain

by Ann Oglesby Peck

Many years skies were generous with rain.
Cactus perfume infused with rain's soft scent.
Grey skies threatening, gleams in misty veins,
becoming lightning to prove their intent.

Streaks of fire racing across summer skies,
more magical than ever dreamed by man.
Music of dancing raindrops soon belie
storm's frenzied anger, its thunderous hand.

We evince rain as a gentle creature,
gracing rooftops, trees, dry wildflower beds.
Lulled to sleep, we forget its main feature:
without it all suffer, life becomes dead.

We thirst for rain in our over-parched lust,
lest greens turn to brown and living to dust.

Rain

by Francis J Grasso

Hear the music from a gentle rain
As it taps upon the windowpane
Listen to the soothing beat
That gives recourse to days defeat

The bird that whispers just to you
While it sings the world a sweet adieu
Telling of a secret place

Where birds can die without a trace

The darkness at the edge of light
Terror in a moonless night
Buried deep within the days
The ashes left from life's cliches

Tales of romance, risk, and wonder
Memories made from chance and blunder
Living through life's raucous raves
While dead dreams lie in open graves

The Mistletoe

by Bobby J. May Sr.

This story is from long ago,
It's about two people under the mistletoe
It was a cold winter night with snow on the ground
The lights from the Christmas tree were draped all around
With popcorn and berries dressing the tree,
with toy's all around a beautiful Christmas tree
The Children in their beds happy with glee
Snug under their blankets watching TV
When all of a sudden we heard a great sound
And as we ran all around only to see
It was Mickey the Mouse, on the children's colored TV
As we walked out the door we looked above
And there we saw a mistletoe
With a note placed upon, that read,
We did this for you, this present we give to you
We heard a small voice whispering so low
I wonder if they will kiss,

Under The Mistletoe.

Neanderthal

by Terry Flood

He stands there, stripped bare, shameless, nameless, voiceless
Standing there, choice-less

No dignity, no vanity, no pity
No integrity

No eyeballs so no stare, no flesh and no hair
And no underwear

No contract, no guarantee, no warranty
No appearance fee

He stands there, stripped bare, shameless, nameless, voiceless
Sudden schoolboys-less
Museum... noiseless

Forget-Me-Nots

by David Drowley

Leave me now love, if you not would grow old.
Memory will keep your beauty on hold
For autumn afternoons when leaves turn gold
And on wintry eves when the days are cold.

Years will drift by like clouds upon the wind,
Painting the dappled landscape of my mind
With visions of impressionistic hue
Of love I left behind when I was new.

A view from afar is never so dear
As the heartfelt warmth of one who is near.
I'd rather share the seasons as they pass
Then scan them through memory's looking glass.

Sofia's Dream

by Gayle Rodd

For Sofia Coppola

The epitome of serenity
lies just beneath the foot of me
sashaying through the sweet, clean grass
White linen bathes my skin
my loose hair dancing in the wind
billowy clouds, how silently they pass

Oh Mozart!
take my heart
dance playfully and light about my mind
Mandolin disrupts the wind
glint of sunshine blinds my eye
fat, sumptuous grapes exploding on the vine

Brie, Bordeaux, wild strawberries
fill the bounty set in front of me
my avid hunger puts me to the test
To my woolly lamb, how safe I am
amongst the wheat so tall and tan
as I hold him firm and snug against my breast

Take me home
thatched roof and stone
the proud gazebo stands beyond the stream
My duvet of straw and hay
my eyes they close, my body lay
to lose myself inside Sofia's dream.

My impression after viewing Sofia Coppola's Marie Antoinette.

The Most Fragrant Rose

by Thomas Koron

I.

In youth, she was a gift from the divine,
Bringing happiness to those she would meet.
Her complexion would radiantly shine
To compliment her soft brown eyes so sweet.
Her shining dark hair was always kept neat
Whenever she went outside to have fun—
The most fragrant rose grew beneath her feet.
Quickly around the playground she would run,
Then her young smile faded into the summer sun.

II.

In adolescence, she had grown defined,
Who she was becoming began to show.
Her youthful features became more refined,
Walking gracefully through the leaves and snow.
Over the months, the years would come and go—
Mother Nature followed her to ensure
The most fragrant rose continued to grow.
Her beauty became increasingly pure,
As her childhood face had proceeded to mature.

III.

In adulthood, a queen she is now crowned,
As her elegance still lights up the room.
A dearer woman can never be found,
Search far and wide, it is safe to presume.
These lines recall a hint of her perfume,
And her beauty still shines bright throughout time—
The most fragrant rose is now in full bloom.
Here, she shall always remain in her prime,
With her image forever captured in this rhyme.

Bold

by Brian Sambourne

Little boy scales the snowbank
    in Spider-Man boots
    stomping snow,
    relentlessly
    a focused performance
    superboy tantrum, gushing discontent
    flattening worlds imagined
    crushing lands gripped by villains

His mother, nearby, gleams
    like heat under a stove pot
    a wary gatekeeper,
    extending love unmatched
    to watch the giddy rush of boy
    to dream a soulful future
    to wonder on the needs of self
    to view a son's awakening
        in the freedom of spaces

Little boy
    unfinished work
    putting his stamp on joy
    as bits of snow fly like a tale unfolding
As a mother watches the elastic bounce of youth,

    till the real world runs away with him.

Dangerous Mind

by Gregory C Masciana

Dangerous Mind

The mind is a most dangerous thing,
Forcing memories into replay,
Endless relived moments drowning bring
Snippets in time more real than today.
Paralyzing sadness is trouble
Which the mind needs to be addressing.

Before I died inside, I really tried.

The sleepless mind toys with our heartstrings,
Always knowing our loved one can't come back.
'Sorry for your loss' causes cringing,
Tearful anger and urge to attack.
Remembering makes sadness double,
Sharp edged memories, full of longings.

Why drive to survive, living isn't alive.

The mind is also a tricky thing,
Lulling into complacency when
Life together starts out with a ring.
Daily work and play begin to blend
Into a wonderful, safe bubble
That protects against everything.

Love is giving a life worth living.

The unhappy mind prevents planning
For a future without one to love,
Alone, unsafe, fruitlessly scanning
Every crowd for my dearest dove.
Real life bursts that beautiful bubble,
And now frightened by everything.

Looked everywhere on Earth for her.

The mind needs a sense of belonging,   Minds
Not at all happy being alone.
together sing dreams that take wing,
Unsatisfied by just talk on phone.
The mind stings by the urge to cuddle
That knick-knacks and holidays still bring.

Be kind to the mind by living to love.

Seagull Semantics

by Gregory F. Hladky

Fair wind floating above a sparkly sea
as the pounding surf grinds sand over there,
I then feel hunger to a large degree,
sense some morsels near, beat my wings on air.

As the pounding surf grinds sand over there,
I fly, knowing fellow hunters will feast,
sense some morsels near, beat my wings on air,
then hover, tuck, and dive in from the east.

I fly, knowing fellow hunters will feast,
will swoop and swoon for every scrap of food,
then hover, tuck, and dive in from the east,
attacking dinner with some attitude,

will swoop and swoon for every scrap of food,
and leave naught behind but sand, sky and brine.
Attacking dinner with some attitude,
squalling seagulls sip the morning sunshine

and leave naught behind but sand, sky and brine;
I then feel hunger to a large degree.
Squalling seagulls sip the morning sunshine,
fair wind floating above a sparkly sea.

Sunday Evening Stretches

by Gordon S. Wolf

Sunday evening stretches and yawns
  drowsy as a tender fawn
Who frolics and plays throughout the day
  then curls up midst leaves to lay

While sleep overspreads her dewy head
  constellations crisscross above her head
How sweetly angels sing in her soft ears
  a moonstruck smile o'er her lips appears

  ~ Sweet dreams, everyone! ~

Defiance, The Old Gods Fall, And Dark Mortal Reign Begins

by Robert J. Lindley

(My Tribute poem, honoring Alfred Noyes....)

Defiance, The Old Gods Fall, And Dark Mortal Reign Begins

Fiery earth, multitude of chasms deep
The gods rose from their long and restless sleep,
Of those few again stirring brave and wise,
Night's last breath then magnificent sunrise
Invincible new Gods as yet unborn
Quaked the earth, as high heavens are torn.

Again the gods woke from their restless sleep
Pale the colors as Gods learned to weep
Mortal defiance, as it swiftly grows,
O' Seer, virgin flesh, in time arose
Dying Gods their powers had failed to keep
Earth's realm free, as mankind's destiny seeps.

Solitude, neglect had laid heavy blows
Universe its powers, had set new shows
As retiring Gods fled the future's flight,
Man's spirit therein, sought the blessed light
Yet in that vein, darkness again held sway
From fleeing Gods heard, "Mortals too shall pay".

Hello, My Name Is

by Richard Robinson

Three day's journey from Coachella to Paradise,
felt like adding beauty to my day, and you did.
Pretty painted toes peek from muslin wool socks,
all your nametag revealed: Hello, my name is...

Once looked at me wondering am I the one.
Let me spare you some disappointment, I'm a coward.
Hey, not squeamish at the sight of a little blood,
tho' scared I'll be unable to save you again cactus flower.

Sense a phantom pain from a missing limb,
still afraid I'm borin' you to death.
Laptop key tied to you in gentle refrain,
just another heart left out
by an absent-minded tin smith.

Your illusions wistfully missed my cactus flower...
without true love, what a waste our finest hour.
'Til then let nametag be proof that we exist,
a paper illusion called 'Hello, my name is....'

The Harvest Dance

by Debra L Brown

The hills have come alive today,
with the dancing of the leaves.
The wind was playing songs of love,
it really was unique!

To see them waltz across the sky,
then stop, and off they'd fly.
They'd do a dip and take a bow,
as the next pair flutters by.

The birds were perched up in the trees,
to see this autumn show.
They'd cheer and sing their melodies
with the wind as it would blow.

The oaks and elms and maple trees,
have all joined in the show.
They'd dressed their leaves so festively,
they drop them and they'd blow.

This is a magical season in time,
the Harvest dance comes but once a year.
Once the trees lose their leaves,
 then winter will soon appear.

Thunderheads

by Tommy Leon Wright

O, boisterous clouds,
Why do you pout on high?
With friction so among you,
Will lightening too,
Not soon cross the sky?

In bumping heads,
You cause the thunders burst
Then in your sorrow weep
And once again your tears,
Quench earth's thirst.

I stand alone surveying aloft,
Your strength and might.
But then like curtains,
You're parting once again,
For God's sunlight.

Seeing a rainbow hanging,
In a distant portion of your sky.
I need not ask the question,
Where do you go
When not in sight,. or why?

What Am I

by Ray Dillard

I pause and listen
To your distant lonely call.
Long and low it pushes
Through the stillness of
The early morning air
To trumpet your arrival.
A disturbance to the sunrise
That is waking here.
It whispers to the ear
That knows your song.

An announcement, an invitation
To meet you at the crossing
Where flashing lights, like soldiers
Make us bow.
And colored arms, like sabers
Fall from attention
To protect your call.

Twelve –hundred horses' nostrils flare,
Huff and puff their acrid air.
Steel shoes clatter as they rumble
Along your private path.
Your wealth follows on carts
That rattle as they roll.
A strand of pearls
That speaks a message
From a place I'll never know.
Cyrillic and artistic,
Sung as love notes from a lark.
A serenade to caress you as you slept.
Sung by men who joined the caravan
And later disembarked.
I feel compelled to count them
Then their romance sings
A rainbow to my heart.
Each message is a picture
Drawn by men that love you
As a colored canvas
Waving with the wind.
And when you pass,
My world is still again.

Betty's Swing

by Valerie D Staton

Down a long winding road there lived Old Betty Ann
In an old wooden house, the color of sand

Her home was surrounded by gardens and trees
And wind chimes that sung with the stir of a breeze

Most days Betty Ann could be found on her swing
It was above her porch and asparagus green

She'd kick off with a foot and then she would soar
Each vacillation higher than the one before

Betty Ann loved her metal swing so much
Only by permission could it be touched

Every year its color would be renewed
In either white, green or cobalt blue

She often sat on the old swing to knit
When in a good mood she'd allow others to sit

There was not much Betty Ann could not do
In the cast iron swing that was built for two

When Betty became ill and the end was near
She gathered together all those she held dear

"Before I go family, I ask one thing...
For one last ride inside my swing."

On the final day before Betty Ann died
She was placed in the swing for her final ride

And thus she transitioned doing what she loved most
She took one last swing then gave up the ghost

Sting Bee

by Richard Breese

I once knew a bee that could sing
It worked for a queen and a king.
But they preferred honey
And paid it no money,
So now it sings backup for Sting.

A Black Oak Tree

by Smita Kulkarni

A noble Black Oak tree stands tall and tranquil
Wearing brown, old and dried crumpled leaves
Withstanding all autumn and winter storms
Without any distress or any grief
Golden fall is long gone, cold, wet season is also concluding
Spring is poking its head up with colorful bulbs blooming
Some of her allies have Cherry blossoms in flourish
Some show progression of luscious new emerald leaves
Mother earth knows unique behavior of her child
With assurance, she lets her be herself while watching over with smile
Tree wants to hold on to longstanding and withered for a while long
Not ready yet to let go of dear presence of that warmth
April comes along to cheer her up
Tree beams, perks up
Ridding her old dry appearance, starts dressing up
Growing yellowish handsome clusters of dangling male catkins,
Gorgeous reddish female flowers in short striking javelins,
Velvety foliage of sharp zigzag tips in red tinge,
With pointed seven to nine lobes with bristles exquisitely unique
Summer grows them into profound shade of shiny green
Rust colored acorns with top halves enclosed in caps start appearing
Showing her wisdom in her towering strength and stability,
With canopy of branches widespread and mighty,
Tree gets ready once more for visitors of ecosystem to offer plenty...

To Her Ardent Mister

by Margarita Lillico

Had we but World enough and Time
Your mating call, sir, were no crime.
If lifetimes were more than a few
I'd spend an Age for each of you.
First with a Parisian lover

For a century I'd hover.
Then hot Latino macho boy
Will fill a few decades with joy.
Then I meander solo East
On diverse cultures I would feast.
When great adventures I'm done with
I'd meditate on what Life is.
For Lady I deserve such state
Not would I love at lower rate.
Then comes the quest for the best part -
To whom I shall invest my heart.
But, sir, you're right, there is no time
To waste on matters less sublime.
I'd rather spend all years I have
On vast eternity of Love.
Your mortal fears I'd gladly spurn,
The grave would be my last concern.
About my pores with instant Fires?!
They'll last a lifetime to transpire.
Into my coyness do not delve
Handle your ardor, sir, yourself!

Covid 2

by Richard Colbert

it's odd to be held hostage
by the same thing
at the same time
as the entire world
it's put everyone
into darkness
the unknown
the unseen
one of the perils
of being a senior
is isolation
it's ironic that
i've been asked to do

just that; isolate
shelter in place at home
go out only when necessary
avoid contact with others,
even family
unfortunately for a great many
that means little has changed

Today, What Music Brought

by Sally Young Eslinger

Today, What Music Brought

  I caught them,
Outside their invisibility,
Dancing
As they sang
Outside their more formal
Chanting of prayers. They chorused
In a reveling in God to the glory
Of His crown, of heaven,
 Of all the cosmos,
For the pure expressed joy
Of all life in and through God —
For the all that was, is and will be...

There! I saw
Some angels dancing
Beneath an overhanging
Of fresh, white, springtime
Dogwood trees abloom. Then,
With their arched and pointed feet,
They coursed their light steps
Circling over the tips of soft moss,
As I, just glancing out my window
Chanced
  (Or was it by fate?)
Upon the seeing of
The motions of their Alleluia!

Dear angels!
My heart rose. My soul floated.
My thoughts began to swirl...
And as time goes forward,
I refuse to forget, and will
Not agree to
Ever saying it was a dream.

Let The Bullets Drop As Flowers

by Subimal Sinha-Roy

Lifeless bullets asleep as captive
In the restive barrels of the cold guns
Cold as the shadow of death
Waiting camouflaged in the dark
Wake up at the strike of the trigger
Pulled by crooked fingers of insane men.

The bullets to accomplish the mission
Whiz on fire to their feral freedom
Carrying the slices of mad men's spite
On their zooming shoulders
Shoot off toward the fated targets
To deliver the message of murder.

Would the bullets stop midair
Abandon the fatal flight
Refuse to become cold blooded killers
Stop and shed the flakes of fury
Fling the lethal intent in the thin air
And disappear forever.

Would the life they get from fire
In the stillness of the deadly barrel
Blossom into flowers of the verdant vale
Would they let the living
Breathe free the fragrant air
In this beautiful world.

Won't we listen the mute voice of fallen lives
Imploring our humane sensibility:
Let the bullets sleep forever unfired
In the rusted barrels of the discarded guns
Let the shooting ones stop midair
Drop as flowers on graveyards.

I Lassoed Some Stars

by Nancy Lee Kaufman

I lassoed some stars from near and far
and kept the dark at bay.
I hugged the moon and danced a tune
until the break of day.
The covers I flung as I kissed the sun
and asked it please to stay.
I sung a verse to the universe
and then I knelt to pray.

I Failed To Write You A Love Poem

by John Terence Miller

I stared at this blank page for days on end
In futile scrabble to discover words
That would transform this cold, white emptiness
Into something filled with love and meaning.
But pen, hand, and lexicon in my head
Could not provide the message from my heart.

I Thought It Was You

by Richard Robinson

I saw you in the street again.
That's when...
like a shadow that turned,
and disappeared in the light.
I knew it was you.

They're coming back you know,
the memories I sold.

Have you been following me?
I wanted it to be, I wanted you.

Those days told in a truth...,
of youth, and glad heart's touch,
they thought we two,
were us.

When I awoke from a long sleep,
I thought it was you, I swear.

The love shared seemed so real,
taught me how to feel.

Now I know it was false,
just a hoax,
of what was supposed to be,
you and me...

I thought it was you.
I guess I forgot our sleepy dreams.
But how could I?
Lost in the past,
now I want them back.

I can tell now, see it in those eyes...
I had to look away, damn it,
had to.

I loved another because..., I thought it was you.
But it wasn't, I'm so sorry...
it wasn't you.

Stoic Silence Serves

by John G. Lawless

The silent stoic stands
mumbling ice crusted mantra
"my light must never fail".

Riddled by the sting of stony hail
blanched white by salty spray
peering into the maelstrom's eye

un-blinking in the excoriating gale
knowing its duty is to serve
those in need – at their worst.

A silent storm's "eye" mocks
the stoics steadfast stance
unable to comprehend such light

retreats again to fleeting fury
howls at the penetrating beam
exposing the peace within its core.

Pine Blossom Pavement

by James Marshall Goff

I never left the soft sunshine,

reflected across the satin smooth pond, deep in the forest,
with flowered edges of pink ladyslippers, wild roses and daisies,

to slope old deer trails...... foraging mushrooms, wild garlic, and sage,

I'm still in awe as I pass by city trees, reminded of old growth
    red and white pine, towering over my humble path,
whispering wisdom.... as their crowns gently sway in the wind.

I pour myself a glass of tap water.... but am refreshed again,
    as I drink from the secret spring, I discovered
bursting forth, the true 'Source of the Mississippi' a stone's
    throw from Lake Itasca.... on Elk Lake

sirens wail but sleep still comforts me.... with haunted loon lullabies,
    and melancholy frog symphonies,

I still eat fast food, but am nourished by line-caught fish
    rising to my bait... as fog lifts with the sunrise,

I barrel down the freeway.... while still paddling silently
    into sunsets filled with looming shadows of the voyageurs,

all around the city sounds.... yet I hear cheerful warblers and
    the midnight bark of the doe, calling her fawns,

gasses from sewer vents confront me.... but I smile!

    as the skunk marks his range,

I'm back in the city,
.... but think in the forest

    back in the city....

        but think in the forest

Her Eyes Are Carried On A Light Wind

by Mark Pringle

My attention span is short. Yet, my pen's is still shorter
It looks absent only after a few words... a few lines
Though ink in its intestines and subject to furnishing hands
It never finishes what it begins. At least, what I want it to finish
So, I hold its face with both hands, as we share eyes
"Write, will you. Do not stop until I give consent."
"Ok" she says, "I will focus" ...as her eyes are carried on a light wind

I presume that's why my poetry is never more than a few lines... a few expressions.

Ode To The Seafarer's Wife

by Jan Camille Tongco

My heart shall travel far
End to end where rainbows meet
Skywards the North Star
Beckoning the waves to glide
Quickly to come home
To thy warm, sweet embrace
And your bright summer kisses

Nephthys

by Michael Whatley

Ashen black bricks,
all surround.
Nestled in the darkness,
Night's silent blackened crown.

She owes it all to the light,
the solitary glow.
Screaming out in protest,
draping mist in snow.

In absence of light,
of Sol, Sun, and sight,
nobody would know her,
nor call her "the night".

The Consolation Of Danger

by Bernard Chan

Too slow is the speed of life,
so we try to outrun avalanches and race sounds,
flee into roaring tubes of hungry water,
brave invisible waves in the sky.

Too barren is the landscape of life,
so we take shelter in surly jungles and unruly gulfs,
set out to survive deserts where even memories die,
trespass peaks reserved for birds and clouds.

Too bloodless are the aesthetics of life,
so we declare emotional asylum in the turmoil of music,
find refuge in the jarring, scarring beauty of poetry,
ask to be abducted into the haunted wilderness of art.

Too transactional are the relationships of life,
so we pawn our souls for the drugs of cults and creeds,
trust in friends or their imposters,
risk heartbreak for a few moments when the world spins.

Too fraught is life with the danger of safety,
so we seek salvation in a rush of adrenalin,
or a trickle of madness.

Empty-handed is no way to leave.

We'll hitch a ride on those spikes along that flatline.

Or be impaled upon them.

The Joy Is In The Climb

by Gary Smith

There is a hill of grass and fern
I walked it as a boy and still,
Those well-worn tracks that twist and turn
Impart to me that childhood thrill.

In amongst the fern, the sheep
Spend the day neath sunlit skies,
They graze away, or mayhaps sleep
Ignoring me, as I pass by.

Effortless it is not,
Yet worthy aye, the time.
Think not only of the top,
The joy is in the climb.

I Write Poetries

by Line Monique Gauthier

kept in the dark
through a crack in the wall
i've seen the ray of sun

my heart longs to burst
silenced forever

my soul yearns to soar
imprisoned since
the beginning of time

i write poetries
because my words
need a voice

even in the void of silence

launched into the universe
my voice reverberates loud

whether or not
anyone cares to hear it
i've said my bit
my part is done

my pen is the sword
that defends my garden
from the overgrown weeds
out to smother
what makes me unique

I write poetries
to no longer live
in the shadows
of silence

i write poetries
because i have
something to say

The Dark

by Ralph James Inman

Beyond the distant saddened sight,
inside this lonely broken place,
I see the light that slowly fades,
the flame that burns like love's gaze
into this empty soundless space,
the void of mind and thought and name,
where all has gone and naught remains
but,
as time dreams past in impassioned reverie
will the darkness possess my night
and end my sleep in incarnadine terror.
Can the warm flame illuminate the shadows
that purloin my silent illusions,

or is the light but a trick of the eye
hiding the raven that waits to take flight.
and,
does the flame feel the darkness,
does it sense the cold.
Can it imagine its own loneliness.
Will the cold's embrace in icy indifference
sooth the pain with veiled deception.
When its warmth begins to diminish
will the dark caress its waning glow,
or,
is it yearning that drives the emptiness.
Is it drawn to the flame
sharing its light in warmth and comfort,
to feel for the briefest of moments,
desired, wanted, needed,
beyond the ceaseless unseen tears
that fall from its ebon unseeing eyes,
then,
flicker flame for soon you will leave,
but memories of you shall linger on
like morsels, so sweet, of pastel dawn
and end of day shall come again
with fear of pending evening's gloom.
Fear not as shade engulfs the flame
for I may search for love too,
so,
embrace me, for I am the dark.

High Dependency

by Christine Adams

The drone of machines goes on and on
with the endless cry of the ward sisters song
energy rises like billowing smoke
with fiery glances to the ones who dare choke.

Invisible hand undertake their chores
over the barks and commands of the insistent roars.
The sick and the fallen lie still in their beds

as the army of staff turn it all on their heads.

Rigorous routine steps up a pace
to the onslaught of pressure that's put on this place
Healing and harmony must still exist
It's the law of the land, that one must insist.

So many bodies, so many hands
dancing to orders, between the commands
And so it continues day after day
In this battlefield tent, where the injured must stay.

Simple Math

by David Joel Walker

100 seems to be the magic number
Numbers less than 100 are the lesser...More than 100 are the better
100 on a test ...100 meters to run...100 miles per hour...100+ for
fastballs...100 $$$

My father lived 26 years < 100
And his father only 11<
My mother's father,
a man I should have, but did not really know
Lived 5 years < 100...and very close to 4
if that counts for anything

I knew a man who was 102 ...2 years the >
and still smoke cigarettes and drank
A shot of honey bourbon whiskey every afternoon at 3

I knew a man who died suddenly
At 48 years < , one afternoon alone
They said it was the curse of genetics and
There was nothing they could have done

I wonder how 100 holds its magic over us
A simple goal of getting old
And then you're gone

Just Because

by Carol Mitra

Just because I chose, not to complain
That didn't mean I felt no pain
Just because I listened, to the breeze
That didn't mean winds blew with ease
Just because you held grudges,on your finger tips
That did mean I gave your hand the slip
Just because I liked the smell of the rain
That didn't mean you could make me cry again
Just because I embraced courage
That didn't mean there was no damage
Just because I smiled in the sun
That didn't mean my needing was done
Just because I wore my heart on my sleeve
That did not mean you could get up and leave!

Worshipping In Nature's Sanctuary

by L. Milton Hankins

Johnny-Jump-Ups nestle into the forest floor mosses,
Along with dainty Jack-in-the-Pulpits hiding beneath
The larger fronds of swampy ferns soaking up moisture
From the dew-laden flowering branches of laurel
Where I find myself dreaming in the verdant woodland,
Edging the meadow beyond the cluttered beaver stand.

A canopy of vine-entangled branches, a vault-like nave,
Provides a sanctuary of sacred candles dimmed for mass
A pew-less haven for wounded souls, and tiny chipmunks,
Who scurry to find isolated spots for quiet meditation
While grebes and gallinules make up the choir ensemble;
A purple swamphen takes up the guttural baritone line.

The late morning is mine, sitting along the narrow trail
In a cross-legged yoga pose with arms across my knees,

Soaking up the faint sweet smells of sassafras and pine
And slipping into what I sometimes call my "blue funk"
Where nothing on earth matters outside this quiet shelter,
Dozing softly, I dream of a utopian sweet, elusive peace.

Swarm Sigh

by Lasaad Tayeb

You arrived on a splendid December day, as I recall.
I relived when we came home; I let out a large sigh.
I put my elbows on the overhang facing a mountain wall.
I sighed again vowed to be with you till you rise to the sky.

I sighed as we had to migrate to find a brighter future.
However, you are scared to chime out of your safety zone.
I sigh when you left our house and rejoin with your ruder.
My frequent sighs are for the sake of my child's shone.

At the point when you chose to wed, I hopped for bliss.
You acted accurately in picking a high erudite young lady.
Recall your cracked tone telling me you had a boy you relish.
"I'm relocating for my child," you sighed as I moved away.

If time was a ritual and you were doled of a gold spoon.
I would be careless if I denied your grace to the moon.
Some emotions, such as rain, are as rare as a typhoon.
Candor and anxiety of others are expected when done.

Father, you may not attempt to strive or be dispersed.
You are an idealist; that hurts me to witness your sigh.
Halting and the peak of the emotion are vividly defined.
From the heart, I'm yet motivated by facts and nigh.

I sigh as I ponder on the past with suffering.
When I'm in front of my parents grave, I cry.
I sigh again as I reckon of individuals in my living.
My sigh was a combination of relief and ecstasy.

The Owl And Raccoon

by Debra L Brown

There once was a silly raccoon
He slept in a tree until noon
He came down to play
He decided to stay
He danced a jig to a tune

Val the Cross-eyed Owl
She saw his jig and said-"WOW"!
The Owl and Raccoon
Then danced to the tune
She stepped on his tail then he "HOWLED"

The raccoons name is Harry
Miss Val lets you and I get married
The Owl and Raccoon
Were married in June
They lived in a tree near the prairie

Rain Dance

by Kelly Deschler

Do you see the rain dance
no drop at a still stance,
pitter pattering all around
bouncing back to the ground

Steady there while you sit
as atop your head they hit,
each one is an invitation
and a newfound inspiration

No more need to stay inside
or under an umbrella hide,
simply set your soles free

leave all your troubles be

You can see the rain dance
live a little, take a chance,
lasts only a minute or two
later on skies will be blue

The skin will feel every drip
fresh enough to take a sip,
falling so freely in the air
let them tangle in your hair

Two together become one
washed over by innocent fun,
to thoroughly enjoy the soak
before the clouds above broke

If rain could it might smile
because for a short while,
here under the circumstance
you decided to join their dance.

Come To Me Love, So That Tender Heart Swells

by Robert J. Lindley

Come To Me Love, So That Tender Heart Swells

Gone, our days dancing in the splashing rain
Awaiting the great mists of transcending time
My love, you taught me to ride a hurricane
Within the mind, a storm blasts out flashes
Consider the moment you wake this coming morn
Walking streets paved with nameless stones
Grains of sand, pretending to be boulders
Cool winds grace the soft emerging twilight
Memories of crossing fires and true romance
Hold my loving hand gently in your hand

Your gold hair hung just right on your shoulders
Thou art bright crimson-in rose red-lit bloom

Those sounds that now arrive in early morn
Those were golden days of splendor
Sit beside this gentle flowing stream
Morning dew glistens in anticipation
When I slumber where rushing waters play
River laps softly, a rainbow sings
Once I sought but love ran away
Climbing that hill, your heart within my soul
Hears that whisper, lovers in epic romance
You are my life, longing for you
The view, where led that path not taken
Who knew your forever was, a lover's query

Yet hope promises a new dawn each day
Dawn burst forth, earth was drinking its new rain
Goddess of my passion two hearts a'praying
Sunshine embraces my soul, drinking from mercy's cup
In sky's thundering heart, weeping for your sweet hand
We are but a mere blink, Fall sets to turn
Huge blue eyes that speak, seek fairness and love
On the high mountaintop I see the stars
We walked the night sands, moon shining down
Nights so love-locked in your arms, fill up a scroll
Caressing virgin soil, with soft caring hands
I am laid bare, naked with nothing to hide

They Wait For You

by Terence O'Leary

Your lover's drawing straws without you, better bid farewell;
he'd never time for rhyme or reason, so it's just as well.
Slip out the curtained window quick, the future winks and calls,
ignoring paths of pagan gods, where faulty footsteps fall.
Identify faint flashbacks, cloaked and clustered in a heap
and sort out those you treasure most, you need or long to keep;
Forget about the epoch past, which wasn't what you'd sought,
pursue instead remaining dreams before they come to naught.

Reflect no more on what it was he'd meant for you,
strike out ahead where something waits, has sent for you.

The graveyard night is haunted still, it hovers where you sleep
recalling souvenirs amassed, the ones that made you weep.
The poets poised in dungeon vaults, now growing old and bald,
retrace their palsied pleas in dust, like those that you once scrawled.
Except for runic proverbs carved on stone walls ill defined,
assumptions will not dog you that you dare to leave behind.
The fortune-tellers waiting at the moat for you
read tarot cards while setting sail a boat for you.

The road behind is empty now, the sky is painted black
so gather all the wisdom gained, no time for looking back.
Forego the prophets' prophecies, so tempting to pursue -
although they might be asked advice, they seldom have a clue.
Reject the secrets they reveal, enveloped in their guile,
which be betrayed between the tombs in ruins of their smile.
They're waiting with a fractured rule of thumb for you
while beating on a perforated drum for you.

A sand-glass dribbles distant dunes, the sun dial's shadow's late,
so now's the time for slipping through the open swinging gate.
A joker wild defies the fools to read between the lines
in search of cryptic radiance the future world enshrines -
"the days ahead will wake again like waves before the dawn
when picking up the pieces left behind a passing pawn."
A noble knight awaits to clear the board for you
when, soon, a cup of nectar wine is poured for you.

Equus

by Nicola Davidson

Beneath the forelocks shady shroud
and chestnut lashes low,
A gaze to halt the human heart
This creature can bestow.
Apple breathed indifference and
Wistful, fearful grace

Can catapult the senses beyond
This earthly place.
Mankind made him subservient
And service he knows well,
Historically, such willingness has
Grazed the gates of hell.
Natures' magnum opus,
Of evolutions course.
Majestic in his countenance,
Noble, hypnotic Horse.

Endless Bloom

by Angel L Villanueva

She worries that her softest bloom is gone,
The beauty that was hers in younger years.
She reminisces days of early dawn,
When flawless skin awoke to gleeful cheers.

She frets her steps have lost their sultry dance,
Her slender figure time has cast away.
She dreads her crown to white will soon advance,
So feels it is in vain to hide her gray.

But I don't see the years her mirror shows,
Instead I view a bloom's maturing glow.
Her smile, her lively eyes and button nose,
Are still like early days of long ago.

The mirror only sees her graying years,
But I the graceful bloom beneath the tears.

Grief

by Shirley Ann Hawkins

G rief
R emorse
I s
E verybody's
F ear

No one is smiling today
As the coffin takes my son away
Grief-stricken, we stand and stare
With a hole in our hearts
That death leaves there

As we stare without seeing
Realising death comes to all human beings
God takes us in his time
The next funeral attendance
Could be mine

Or any person in the world
As the script of our life span is unfurled
God alone has the eternal plan
For every human woman or man
The day will come when we must part

And fill the void, that hole in our heart
To meet our loved ones again
Freedom at last without the pain
Of living a life of sorrow
And look forward to a peaceful tomorrow

Summer-Swoon Leaves

by Kim Rodrigues

Summer-swoon leaves, dyed and dying, windswept -
    uplift of Autumn season
  for drifters and dreamers

Word Play

by Anisha Dutta

      Tasting butter from toast
  Butterfly flies fluttering wings, uttering whistles.
  Listener caterpillar sliding on bamboo pillar.
  Sparrows dancing, prancing
    on narrow furrows of non-mowed meadow.
  Wild weeds and thorny bushes playing with shattered shadow
Fast is rabbit with chewing habit to have its breakfast
    on tender leaves and slender foliage.

  Chameleon champion on disguise mesmerizing massy grass.
   Spotted deer are spotted wandering leisurely in early dawn.
  Feral flowers yielding angry aroma
   making fool bumble bee tumbling
    on glossy patina of sepals, and petals.
    Few dew drops glistening, twinkling on periwinkles.

Morning gradually turning noon.
  Pale stale waning Moon winked at dazzling sizzling Sun.
   Rains drizzling, rainbow rushing in rapture,
   captured in platonic panorama.

Me lazy, crazy, oblivion observer
    stepping horizontal, dreaming vertical, glancing conical,
   hearing viral, speaking spiral,
    enchanted on variety of viola.
     Drank desires, mind soared high with eager egret.

No regret, heart danced delight
yet reasoning and emotive urge always clash to fight.

Autumn Melody

by Anulaxmi Nayak

Splendid leaf cushion
Mosaic of vivid hues
Cool breeze sprays crisp charm

Zing of playful kids
Rich harvest of summer toil
Mirthful mother earth!

Moon Of Sadness

by Iolanda Scripca

Nude in front of you
Slapped by bats but kissed by light
Enigmatic scars
No one understands but YOU...
I dream of dreams of moon life...

I pose - you draw me
You take pictures of my soul
Wondering what's wrong...
Sadness... immortality
How much Love I cannot give!

Behind The Wall Of Sleep

by James Fraser

Modernism abounds
Behind the wall of noise, lies
Tranquility Bay

In The Autumn Of My Life

by Elaine Cecelia George

I walk through flames
of autumn's sweet refrain-

That break beneath
a weight too much to bear-

Where I tread in solitude
and mourning there-

Along a path of maple trees
and scented air-

As I recall the life that
we once shared-

And in these twilight hours
I see the beauty of it all-

In every autumn leaf
That softly falls-

~~~

In Loving Memory of my precious father

No One

by Bessie Kolb

Silent screams no one hears
Tired eyes filled with tears
Gut wrenching heartache no one feels
Emotions, dark enough to kill
Mental exhaustion no one sees

Strong enough it hurts to breathe
An answer seeking no one speaks
A language spoken without speech

Will Do Chores

by Jessica Amanda Salmonson

I can do this, I can do that
I can do anything, splicketty-splat.

I'm quite the expert, and certainly quick
Excellent service here, licketty-click.

Your toaster won't roast'er?
            Your car needs repair?
I'll fix your teepee,
            your sofa and chair
I'll cure your doggy
            of fleas, lice, and pox
I'll wash your diapers,
            your windows, your socks.

I'm inexpensive, and fast as a wink
Available any time, blinkity-blink.

Yours To Keep

by Richard W. Morris

I was there, when you were born.
You brought a smile, not a scorn.
I was there, and watched you sleep.
Protecting, your tiny soul to keep.

What do you dream, I did oft ponder.
Made me sigh, my heart grow fonder.
Such innocence upon your face,
Would you always show such grace?

I was there to see you grow,
To child and more, so long ago.
We as family, did trips take,
To many a country, island and lake.

I always sought another kiss,
To watch you grow, to reminisce.
A loving hug, a simple smile,
To add a memory to our file.

Well, when I re-play your life,
Your young years had little strife.
Those were days of joy and prime,
Your youth was such a happy time.

Hours became days and weeks,
Too quickly how time sneaks.
Weeks became months and years,
Until my love fell upon deaf ears.

Yes, I was there, as you grew,
Saw you both smile and stew.
Take your place in the world,
Aghast at how life unfurled.

It matters not how old you are,
Whether you be near or far.
You'll always be my little girl.
To me, my eternal pearl.

One last thing I must add,
Tonight as you go to sleep.
Remember always, I'm your dad,
With love, and yours to keep.

I Am A Book

by David Joel Walker

I am a book of Unread pages
I am a book

     I am a book Written in stages in
A travel log On a road called Time
With the foreign stamps Of Passport Ministers
Checking my credentials along the way
I am a book

I am a book Of unread scripture
With the lectures on faith
In staggered chapters and the
Tattered chronicled collections of
Odd jobs We have asked of a Loving God
Written in a foreign language
I am A book

     I am a book Of erotic poetry in
Pictograph albums Scrutinized and analyze
Then censored By holier than me censors
I am a book

     I am a book With pages numbered
And then sealed Its secrets to be
Revealed in full on an unannounced
Judgment day with Disputes left in the hands of
A Divine Defender
I am a book

     I am a book
To be colored Everyday
Where the lines do not matter
Only the hue and The view
In which you see me
I am a book

I am a book Not to be left On the dusty shelf of
A forgotten library Rarely opened in a
Distant history I am a book to be read
And even if misunderstood To be savored
I am a book

A Beauty Queen Dethroned

by Nora Gibson

Is there a junkyard for old tiara's and outdated ball gowns?
Where does Beauty go when age has taken her crown
Removed atop her head and passed onto the new,
smiling gracefully her rein is over her chapter is through
the walkway has shortened the stage has reached its end
her audience abandoned her, few remembering her when.

Beauty dissolved in creases and folds
faded pictures tell numerous stories of desires untold
lost sapphires, rubies, diamonds and lace
torn denim, short skirts and selfies have taken their place.
Roses soon wither fallen off of her pole.
Tower high stilettos now traded have soft flattened soles.

Waken one day unable to recognize this new face
searching for the old one but never finding a trace
of that person who was familiar and she once knew
who was young and beautiful, without even trying to.
Haunted by yester years with memories complete
when she held love's attention and men fell at her feet
Commanding the room as she swung and swayed
Beauty was immeasurable but there was a debt to be paid.

New beauty surrounds her with past souvenirs
Reminders of time ago and broken down years
now she's invisible as she dissipates in the background
with a crocked tiara and wearing last year's ball gown.

Hilarious

by Robert James Liguori

I've sat down to write my poem,
But my pen ran out of ink.

So I used my pencil instead,
But I broke the lead.

So I write with crayons,
To try and rhyme...
But I'm really,
Running out of time.

So, I lean on in to focus,
And I hear cracking from my chair...
With crayon and notepad,
I go flying in the air.

So I'm on the floor as I write,
But it's too dark, I need more light!

Moonshine Shuffle - Moderate Country Waltz

by Michael J. Kalavik

Moonshine, diesel fumes, and chicken wire.
Laundry hangin' on the line.
Bible open to the Book of Job.
Backyard thick with prickly pine.

Jacket pocket full of Red Man dip.
Work boots laced with leather thongs.
Wedding portrait on the mantel piece.
Shotgun right where it belongs.

Kettle simmers on a cast iron stove.
Faucet's drippin' in the sink.
Matchbook underneath the table leg,
Teacup teeters on the brink.

Cobwebs draped across the window screen.
Horseshoe nailed above the door.
Things calmed down some since the weather broke.
Same sad silence as before.

Ma's been servin' up the buttermilk
Boiled potatoes in a bowl.
Pa starts eatin' while she's sayin' grace.
Lets her worry 'bout his soul.

Man might say he be a slave to love.
Women make the same complaint.
Neither really know the meaning of
What it is and what it ain't.

You Came Home

by Regina Marie Elliott

About-face, young, yet so aged, translucent,
marching silently into a column of
gold~lined clouds,
bloodshot eyes burning for sleep,
close them as you wipe the sweat and sand
from your newly freed soul,
damn the icy kiss from Death, as you,
he cannot keep,
God's promise to you, fulfilled,
you came home from the war to Him.

Beauty Of Imaginations

by Snehal Ade

The black and white devil clouds,
Becomes true beauty for me.

The sweetest vioce of singing birds,
Becomes a Song for me.

The stable leaves and branches of still trees,
Becomes high flying Birds for me.

Imagination beautifully colours your life,
Like a Heaven with all great vibes.

We can survive in imagination,
We can live in imagination.

We can roar in imagination,
We can die in imagination.

We sometimes like or hate imagination,
But imaginations never come to the end till our death.

Tempest Wind

by Sandra Weiss

Thoughts linger, not fading away.
Evoking memories I choose not to share.
Within shadows of my mind they stay,
quietly slipping in when most unaware.

What once was, now to forget.
The past survived the years.
Trapped within a tangled net.
It comes, all else disappears.

What will come with tomorrow,
when darkness refuses to fade?
Do I relive yesterday's sorrow,
that I have tried so long to evade?

Thoughts like tempest winds swirling.
A storm within, one out at sea.
Blocking them, my mind is whirling.
They must not take what is left of me.

The storm ends, no more raging tides.
The wind, now quiet, barely a sound
The turmoil within subsides.
I cling to what peace I have found.

The Ink Pen Of History

by Scott Alan Campbell

History should happen in pen of ink,
not pencil of lead.
It must not be erased, or hyper-spaced,
or gently changed by those who think
their own wishes instead.

We often say, "It is what it is,"
and fully believe that to be true.
If that is the case, "It was what it was,"
is also true too.

Yesterday's lessons cannot go unlearned
unless we succumb to the fear of the past.

Today's bravery is to look into the face
of the cancel culture and say,
"We renounce you," at last!

Touched

by Sara Kendrick

Touched by His Presence, now I can see

Satin And Old Lace

by Ann Oglesby Peck

Bent fingers trace embroidered leaves
on satin and long lacy sleeves.
Blush roses, twenty-six she counts--
A French word she can't now pronounce.

She blows dust from old envelopes
tied with blue ribbons and her hopes.
The letters penned by her true mate.
Over his name, she... hesitates.

A trunk in attic soon became
her refuge from days all the same.
Photos dwelling midst her daydreams,
and keepsakes of sweet seventeen.

She thought he'd walk up Dusty Lane;
he might appear, along with rain
and wash away her endless tears;
bring summer nights and happy years.

A wedding date that came and passed;
memories cut like broken glass.
A heartache like the roaring wind,
returning nightly without end.

She lived alone among the ghosts
of dances, laughter, champagne toasts.
Altho eccentric, she was bright;

looked forward to impending night.

Aunt Agnes passed at ninety-three;
still wore her ring for all to see.
Memories left for wind to tend;
they have beginnings but no end.

Surrounded By Ghosts

by Jack Horne

She smiles as she looks at her photographs
and she isn't alone now,
as she lives in the past

Heartbroken

by Jack Horne

The sun was shining on the day
she packed her bags and went away;
he tried to look a little sad,
but by his grin I think he's glad...

Blind Date With A Cat

by Jennifer Marie Fenn

My auntie asks me, "You want a new cat,
who'd love a home as warm as yours?" "How great!"
I say. "I'll take her sight unseen!" My hat
and coat I fetch, prepare for this "blind date."
A blue-eyed tabby, curled on auntie's bed
comes straight to me as I extend my hand
to let her sniff, then pet her dark-eared head.
She head-butts me for more. I understand!
I take her home. She hides a little bit
beneath my couch, but as I reach for her,
she comes right out and follows me to sit,
then covers up my lap in shedding fur.

She sleeps now, purring like a dove in song.
It's like this cat's been with me all along!

Why Do They Glisten So

by Peter Rees

Why do they glisten so, these pools of light,
my trembling senses lost in ardour sweet?
As stars they sparkle gently in the night
and dance to rhythms of my own heartbeat.
I gaze deep deep into a magic glade
where intertwining lovers each caress,
as silvered waters softly serenade
and sporting moonbeams do the shadows bless.
Soft silken creature of my dearest dreams,
I ache to hold you fast within my arms,
to breathe in scents of paradise. It seems
to die would pay small homage to your charms.
The book of love is filled with many a rhyme,
of lovers' promises and tender sighs,
but few could match this fervent pen of mine,
as, drowning in the lustre of your eyes,
my heart must surely burst asunder,
lost in unfathomable wonder.

Random Lives

by Michael S. Bross

The reaper reaps in random ways
no signpost warns of last lived days
but ancient ears can hear the sound
of thundered hooves upon the ground

on blackened steed with fiery breath
the sickle scythes of pending death
with slackened reins the reaper rides
as changing gait our fate decides

and now the day on random ground
the sickles path has laid us down
and on he rides for those to come
whose random lives soon now be done

till silence falls the fields around
and winter snows make white the ground
we rest awhile with random friends
and in the spring anew begins

as clover lines the babbling brooks
and flowers spring from tiny nooks
and deer and rabbit come to graze
the reaper reaps in random ways

and so again that day will be
with promise new of destiny
till thundered hooves of blackened steed
the reaper comes again.

A Slave

by Angie Sharp

Slowly, one's self control ebbs,
as appetites begin to take hold.
The body's defenses crumble,
while temptation grows more bold.
The mind tastes the sweetness
of pleasure's tightening noose.
A chain of craving is formed
to set the drug of addiction loose.
The body becomes the eager slave
to an appetite's endless desire.
Self-control dies within the light
of the soul's own forest fire.
As the mind surrenders to want,
the addict's life spins faster.
A slave is born into this world
when the appetite becomes the master.

Cancer

by Terence Robinson

Hold back the hour.
Stop the tears from flowing.
Breathe again untainted air.
Take back my bones, my breasts,
and race forward to passion once more

Hold back the hour,
before the ravaging of every sinew
and fleeting glimpse of salvation, and
forced pity encroached upon my earth

Hold back the hour,
before tested strength
proves weakened failure
and commitment runs a ragged road

Before privacy alludes
and birds no longer sing for me,
or the pinch of reality is drugged
away before the fluttering of breath

Now bring back the hour
let the tears flow
I'm ready

Please Define

by Maria Rheza Mae D. Rubio

Define that fresh sensation once again
Thought to be missed while mellowing further
Define that shiver until one knows when
Tickled by touch as light as a feather.
Define that out of the blue expression
Brought as a smile amidst wonderstruck gaps
Define that itch to make an impression
Asked oneself if it may cause a collapse.
Define that strong desire to keep it close
Tried to hold off the longing within reach
Define that incessant praise as it shows
Felt the comfort to be part of such speech.
These feelings wished for more to discover
Though discouraged to be felt forever.

Define that jaundiced eye hidden deep down
Affected by delusions that must cease
Define that sleepless night tumbling around
Worried about its substance to decrease.
Define that gentle torture creeping in
Intoxicated by pleasure from pain
Define that risk taken for a good spin
Saw a dead end coming latched on a stain.
Define that sweet lemoning on the rocks
Denied the existence of falling out
Define that misfortune kept in a box
Considered as a sentiment no doubt.
These feelings wished for certainty to bite
Regardless, I still do not get it quite.

Clanging Echoes

by Millard Lowe

When I've gone
to the place
where my fathers'
have gone before me
and the last tribute
has been paid to my memory,
may my singing words
crack the silence with clanging echoes.

May the clanging echoes
excite starving eyes
and taut wrinkled eardrums—
both to awareness—
guiding them
to actions of liberation
yet to come.

May clanging echoes
wake-up sleeping souls suffering
uncertainties of tyrannical rule,
slobbering from political absurdities,
drooling from mouths of misguided evil
diagnostic odysseys—peddling false hope
to precariously lost wanderers.

May my clanging echoes echo ringing
bells of freedom that can't be unrung:
"Oh death where is thy sting?"
"Oh grave, where is thy victory?"

Poets will die;
but the ringing chords
of their words will live long lives:
Echoing clanging echoes...

Artless Dissipation - Wdj

by Avantika Poddar

The prodigy has turned prodigal
Making silver spoons out of gold medals
While the hearsay deepens about clandestine meetings
I fix myself a plate of pity party, for I know nobody
I don't even know myself
The prodigy is now pedestrian
Crossing roads without a care
And I lost track of time ages ago
In blue screens and daydreams
So I fix myself a plate of pity party, for there's nothing else to do
Especially now that the world is broken
And I can't find the version of myself I lost in the chaos of trying to find
myself

A Short Session

by James Popplewell

My mind
unstable foundation.

They keep talking,
through dreams, comes communication.

A combination,
another citation
never any satisfaction
(Look over here, another distraction)

Formation into another illustration
division by another diversion.

So, what version can take me out of isolation?
(Wait, murder? I thought this was multiplication.)

How many live there now? I need some information.
Because if this conversation involves a congregation
then call for an assembly, it's time for orientation.

How many are there? I think this is beyond regulation.

It's time for a confession!
(Why? There has been no violation.)

The situation may be a possession
But I do not have the protection of religion.

Nothing in moderation
We do not need validation from an administration.
The revelation has been in question.

Objection! This is all just speculation.
I'm getting a suspicion that there have been signs of manipulation.
There are signs of depression and in addition
I would like to draw your attention to the blatant exaggeration
and ask for your cooperation
So, we can move past the persecution
to focus on the solution.

The verdict is in!
What is the conclusion?

To Be Continued...

Ode To Ketchup

by Fritz Purdum

For hamburgers hotdogs and french fried potatoes
add the sweet savory sauce a gift from tomatoes
Ketchup Ketchup pour it thick
for bland foods it does the trick

Scramble eggs just to plain
Ketchup adds that sweet tang

Steak a little too dry
that's when ketchup applies
Try adding ketchup in your sauce
topping meatloaf it is boss
Beautifully red rich and thick
Ketchup is foods favorite condiment

For finger foods a tasty dip
so yummy you smack your lips
Ketchup is a sweet sensation
taste buds crave with anticipation
That magic that ketchup brings
is that flavorful wonderful zing

Friend

by Thomas Flood

 Oh why, oh why doesn't ostrich fly
The lion roared oh why, oh why
He has the feathers
He has the wings
And all of those other birdie things

Along came the monkey
Who pretended that he knew
And would gladly tell all
For banana's, a bunch or two

The lion turned quickly
And the monkey took flight
For he knew quite rightly
The lion he wouldn't fight

A little while later
A giraffe sauntered by
But the lion couldn't hear him
Because he held his head so high

Then along came the elephant
Who waved his might ears

I'd really like to tell you
But it just brings me to tears

A short time later
The crocodile appeared
He said I know the reason
As his throat he did clear

A long time ago
When Ostrich was sick
He had little friend
Who by his side did stick

And when he did recover
A promise he did make
I will never fly away again
For you, I will not forsake

So if you ever see him
With his head down in a hole
You'll know that he's just visiting with
His little friend the mole

Bare Souls

by MAXIMILIAN G. WOLF

It is so lonely under the starry sky.
Our soul shells washed away with the speed of life.
Emotion bones faded.
With an empty eye of own skeletons,
they count the stars on the cosmic vault,
seeking for the meaning of the life show.
*
Surrounded by a multitude - alone.
In disbelief, I count so many treacherous.
They have hungry eyes and empty souls crawling in the mud.
They bow to the screens,
from which a river of fog flows,
covering their weak minds.

*

I know you exist, and you are far away.
I can feel your breath on my face.
I'm free to tell you all my thoughts, fears, and desires.
I reveal to you all of my secrets.
There is no fear - just pure joy of being naked in front of you.
You rejoice to my naked soul as you take your veils off.
There are all colors - it's beautiful.
*

Finally - on a sand pond - by the sea.
We are naked by all means.
Bare souls and naked bodies - you come to give me a hug.
Fairy light and wet - we merge into one being.
---#09---

Of Nature

by Christuraj Alex

I call you mother. Yet, O! You are God! Goddess! Fairy!
You're like the invisible shore of the visible sea!
You're, O princess! Beauteously divine! Exuberant!
In you, every atom transforms and proves purely potent!

Smallest creature-wonders to the greatest animals, hale,
Softest of breeze to the thunder, lightning, and the great gale;
Grass, plants, and vegetation that many mysteries hide,
The sun, moon, stars, and planets, like infants, in you, abide...

Wonders, like magic, you reveal randomly each moment,
My life is a splendid gift in your holy covenant;
From entering the womb till reaching the tentative tomb,
In you, my Garth! I live and love and bud and plume and bloom!

You are Aphrodite - of love, beauty, and awe - inflow,
Ghats of graces gild your gardens gleeful gorgeously glow;
Though thorns thrill and thrive, like thugs and pricks and poke hardest
bones,
Fragrant flowers blossom brightening moods of mourning tones...

Your vindictiveness spread its wings with unending passion,

You are, yet, heavenly divine goddess of compassion;
From nooks of the earth till highest of skies you solely reign,
On the smallest of grass and largest trees, your mercies rain...

Gentle breeze, turning into, tough tornado and tempests...
Cooling drops, flowing into streams, rivers, and flood-conquests...
Tsunamis of seismic waters, seizing beings alive...
Are these but cycles of cleansing for new lives to arrive?

Doesn't a wise mother punish her naughty loving child?
Your prompt wrath, indeed, is corrective, though willfully wild;
Surprises, like waterfalls, wrap me - serene, still and cool,
From the unknown heights, they arrive, yet they're as light as wool...

Harmoniously rhythmic is your mighty Milky Way,
I, a minute melody, move and make musical sway;
As a mother calling her son home after his long play,
You call me to Rest In Peace and no more to stray away...

Some Days

by Raven Howell

Some days I want to stay in bed,
Let flowery thoughts run through my head.
Some days I like to kick off shoes,
Run through our garden as I choose.
Until it's time to work, I play,
And gift the world my best bouquet.

Give A Fig

by Kim Rodrigues

To aid the celebration's overindulgence
of snow and damp, sugar and fat,
serve a cornucopia of felicitous fiber
    and its vitamin rush—
whirligig of walnuts and crisp cranberries,

Honeycrisp apples and wild red strawberries,
spring mix sprinkled with balsamic and fig.

Give a fig* about your friendships and figure.
Strap on boots, tread through snow and ice.
Make nice with muscles and joints,
    your neighbors.
Share the bounty of your colorful heritage.
Stay in shipshape form as you celebrate.

Hearing A Bell And My Heart
by Marilene L. Evans

You
captured
my heart and you
captivated my mind,
yet you free my spirit, lift my
soul like hearing a bell ring when I think
of you, hearing my heart sing when
I see
you.

Dating In Socks And Crocs
by Tania Kitchin

I decide to take the plunge, internet dating is all the rage
My loneliness grows, I decide it's time I try to engage
I join several dating sites, cynical of what I may find
Hoping it's someone sweet, who's honest and kind

I write my profile and describe myself as stylish and chic
Smiling with a chuckle, right now I am not dressed for my pic
I go to my closet; the fancy date dresses are way in the back
I move all the comfy clothes as I take the sexy ones off the rack

I narrow it down to two dresses, one glittery red and one slinky black

I grab a pair of heels, spiked red leather and with sexy strappy backs
My face is now make-up, red lipstick, blue liner and false fake lashes
I set up my camera and tripod, hoping it takes my pic and flashes

A week goes by and I have several hits and messages on my profile page
I find one I like, he seems nice and honest, or it could all be staged
We chat awhile and then he invites me to talk to him over zoom
I agree to video chat in a few hours, as I stare at the dresses in my room

I get all made up, wearing my red dress, spiked heels, flashy fake rocks
As I try to walk, I take the heels off and put on my fuzzy socks and crocs
We video chat, really hitting it off, until he asks to see my sexy shoes
I panic, as drop my tablet, it crashes, lands at my feet, I am not amused

I grab my tablet, my face is red with embarrassment, maybe he didn't see?
He laughs as he tells me, he now knows I am the one, it was meant to be
He's holding up his foot, below his suit, he's wearing shorts and fuzzy socks
and says he loves that I can be glamorous while wearing socks and crocs

A Gathering Of Friends

by Kimberly J Merryman

In the yard stands a large Bradford pear tree,
Its spreading branches forming a shady canopy.
Beneath this shady haven is a ring of chairs,
And in each chair sits a friend who cares.

Women of diverse backgrounds and ages,
Make pleasant conversation as each engages.
We sit peacefully enjoying the cool spring breeze,
As it wends its way and rustles through the leaves.

We are not idle - each one stitches, knits or crochets,
On which ever crafty project is their forte.
Discussions range from family matters to local news.
Politics and politicians really light a fuse.

We tell jokes, ask and give advice.
Sometimes we just act silly and its nice.

Sharing our high points and our woes,
When we're together just about anything goes.

This gathering of friends is refreshing and renewing,
A bright spot when the darkness of this world is brewing.
These women are a blessing and a treasure.
Their worth exceeds far more than I can measure.

One Life Lesson

by Sara Kendrick

paring peaches, cut away the bad and bitter~makes the good sweeter

As The Moon Rises

by Lasaad Tayeb

The Moon shone brightly, coated in silver.
Enabling objects to be freshly alive.
Build our life on the Moons cycles and shiver.
Having one Moon implies we must observe.

Kindly advise if I can stay awake all night.
Stop the gentle shine in my spirit, O Moon.
At night, the moonrise is an aesthetic sight.
A window with the words shown for a boon.

With my eyes, I raise my gaze to the sky.
Fly Me to the Moon to play with the stars too.
The Moon was obscured by the trees nearby.
The moonlit curtain was the sole source of view.

I'll be with the stars if I miss the Moon.
A moon is watching over the orchard.
The crescent is a moon in progress soon.
Have this stressed-out lady on her period.

The Moon is a source of inspiration for lovers.
When the lights are shut off, it emits a gentle glow.

She nourishes her kids in the way a mother utters.
All traces of dread settled within vanish, though.

My love, don't sleep; I depict myself as a butterfly.
Our scars were fashioned into an ornament.
It acquired the potential to be sensitive to the sky.
With your glossy lips, you are a lovely fortunate.

The Moon has been brilliantly designed.
Cannot hide the sun, Moon, and truth.
The desire is born out of the human mind.
As I view the moon, I praise God for my soothe.

A Season Of Color

by Jeanne McGee

My favorite wonders and magic found in each Fall
are the way colors of trees raptly begin to sprawl
Across the woodland paths that I like to wander
the season fills me with many poems to ponder

Blazing leaves of yellow against skies of Prussian blue
then russets and copper and royal red break through
Swirling reflections saturate winding waterways
beautiful pallets to fill my picture-perfect seeking gaze

When gusty winds and rain come to gleefully play
We see the leaves set sail from the trees as they sway
As mist curls in the dawn, the nights welcome the cold
Autumn too must end so winter can begin to enfold

Poetry Friends

by Mark R Toney

Exposed to types of poetry
a coterie
of poet friends

great poems pen

I wish that I could read them all
from that I fall
the mountain climb
there is no time

How satisfying to belong
we're growing strong
our dear peer group
Poetry Soup

A Walk In The Wood

by Timothy R. McGuire

Strolling thru the wood on this warm summer night,
Enjoying the breeze in the waning light,
Lilac and pine are filling my senses,
Primrose and Morning Glory climbing the fences.

Barred Owl and Nightingale are questioning me,
Glimpses of deer now easy to see,
Off the Sycamore and Red Oak tall shadows fall,
Hiding the wolf and his soulful call.

Lake Loon and turtles are making their splashes,
As into the water the bullfrog dashes,
Clicking of bats flitting in the air,
Chirping of raccoons and the huffing of a bear.

I stop for a moment and listen to it all,
And I cannot begin to recall,
A better symphony than I hear tonight,
As I wander the wood on this warm summer night.

The Keeper Of Secrets

by Donald J. Craig

I am the Keeper of Secrets
I have heard all men's tales
Of murder, adultery
And other betrayals

Their stories come to me
Through back doors at night
Their compromised souls
Caught in desperate plight

I'm the Keeper of Secrets
You never would know
I make no judgments
No cursings of woe

I hear both sides of stories
Only one thing is sure
That both sides are liars
No one speaks the truth.

Caves Of Sorrow

by Meenakshi Raina

In my dark deep caves of sorrow
I have the walls painted with tears,
Lonely I stand there with no hope
Tormented with unwanted fears.

Restless regrets roam and reside
In my dark deep caves of sorrow,
I exist as withered autumn
There is no spring for tomorrow.

Roses, reminded me of you
 Now uprooted since you were gone,
  In my dark deep caves of sorrow
   My life is caged has not moved on.

With broken heart I feel disturbed
 Some peace I wish, I could borrow,
  Ashes of faith are now buried
   In my dark deep caves of sorrow.

Love Beat

by Nayda Ivette Negron

A dream or reality
Your smile is always in my mind
The stars started to blink
Destiny has different paths
Love is a feeling so pure

Reality is sometimes very difficult to
accept it. I had forgotten your smile.
There's no trace of it in my mind.

Life demonstrated that journeys
were separated.
Is better to had loved at least once
in a lifetime that had not loved never.

Autumn Colors

by Evelyn Pearl Anderson

The world's aflame or so it seemed;
Pulling back the window's white lace
To glance out at morning's dawning.
My heart skipped with joy of this place

Red Maples touched the horizon
As dayspring brought golden splendor,

Sparkling dew upon grass of green—
God's majestic touch so tender

Alone

by Rukhsana Afridi

Alone during my childhood years
Alone I stand as an adult
Fighting off tears and all my fears
Amidst the uncertainty and profound confusion
Of my younger years
I stand alone

Cornucopia

by Ralph James Inman

No
Lenten
fare on this
our day of thanks.
The warmth of family,
in swollen feelings of
tear filled joy and full bellies,
warms our hearts when loved ones gather
and nights grow cold in evening darkness.
W e   fill with joy our life long desires
o   n   cozy carpet in front of warm fires.
W   i   th laughter that bellows within us
a   n   d lights our way when we are lost.
T   h   e fullness of our heart flows
I   ike the abundance of
t   he fruits of our worth,
o   pen and free
and filled with
thoughts of
love.

America, Where Are You Going

by Paulette Calasibetta

When facts are flawed by fantasy,
Embracing a delusional reality,
When wrong is right,
And right is wrong,
Instilling chaos and fear;

Arresting truth and
Liberating violence,
Manifesting fallacy,
Whittling at the core
Of civil liberties;

Clothed in an ideology of hope and prosperity;
Deceptive machinations
Bring us to our knees,
Silencing voices in opposition,
Mandating conformity;

Political malevolence rising,
Huddled masses, lost in the abyss of ignorance,
Awaiting the feigned promises of a utopian society,
Dividing a once united nation;
Subordinate puppets for the bureaucracy of Bumbledom.

The Last Leaf

by Newton Ranaweera

A grey, lonely leaf sighs holding a stem
Sobbing, and pleading to let him remain —
To stay, a day more, to see sun's next dawn.
My guru, an uncle, a beacon - gem,
My guiding star, I saw — in biting pain,
Keep on
Trying to hold his breath, feebly clinging

To my hands as dying doe to a pawn,
Pleading — yet not knowing it is as vain
As Fall's last leaf that tries farewell singing
By swan.

The Solemn Rose

by Robert James Liguori

In the breathing forest came memories of my youth,
Nothing more than happiness shadowed by the truth.
The rising sun pulchritudinous like the smile on her face,
Let me think of her once more of pure and simple grace.

In the center of the wood lived a solemn rose,
Surrounded by a cruel weed which prohibited it to grow.
The weed was not considerate only thinking of itself,
Hurt the little rose not caring of how it felt.

Now the rose has grown up and overtowers the weed,
Making it undernourished and causing it to bleed.
Through tolerance and patience the rose has been well fed,
And for the spiteful weed, he gained a brand new bed.

Glancing to the falling moon, I've realized what I've done,
I've killed my inner self by following the sun.
I only hope that things will change far before the end,
So that the enemy I have gained will turn to be my friend.

The Gift That I Give You

by Regina McIntosh

Gifts from the heart will always fill up the senses with insight and delight, a living whisper from a tender thought ~ by poet

I give you little pieces of my heart
Wrapped in lemon sunshine, dripping hope
I give you feelings that come alive

When a melody of rain softly whispers delight
I give you dreams that are filled with faith
Colored in hues of laughter, sensitivity and grace
I give you the color of love enlightened by inspiration
Filling up my thoughts with a joyful imagination
I give you joy that comes from the spirit
Enchanting the senses with tender acceptance
I give you my thoughts of tenderness and passion
Dressed in light that thrives on serenity's prayers

The gift that I give you is more than my legacy
It is the beauty found within a emotion
The color of azure deep inside the ocean
The warmth from the stardust nights
The rainbow that silences the darkest explosion
The brilliance of a moon across the horizon
The affectionate embrace found in creation

The gift that I give you is wiser than the stars
More alive than the twinkling in your eyes
More wise than the mountains at dawn
More adoring than the flowers caught by sun

The gift that I give you is a gift from above
The gift that I give you is *pure, unconditional love!*

A Paper Cup

by John Terence Miller

A spider
on my wall;
I spied her,

just inches from my head,
her big fat hairy legs
and body crimson-red.
Soft light casts a shadow
making her look larger;
her high, and me below.

On my desk, I see a paper cup.
If I could trap her underneath it;
but then, I could miss and cock-it up.
She could scurry down my arm, or worse,
down my neck. I pull my collar tight.
"It's a quandary, alright," I curse.
Spider-cup, my nerves begin to fray.
Cup-spider, spider-cup: will it fit?
As I think, she gently walks away.

Me And You In The Canoe

by Betty Jo Legros Kelley

Come, let's build a canoe,
We'll float away
just me and you
We'll float down stream
Upon the water,
Flickers of light
In our hair
My daughter
My little daughter
A poet too
An artist
May our dreams
Come true!
Floating along,
The streams
sweet song
Of voices of
forever long
Petals floating
beside the canoe
Many poets
Sailed here once too
We watch as we
float past the trees
Redwoods vast
and meadows green

Embracing life
In joy serene
Nodding flowers
watch
The meandering stream
And me
and you
In our
Canoe

Her Shape

by Laura Leiser

She moves in undulating beauty, a figure of mystery
who fully embodies and embraces her surroundings.
She cradles her arms around the earth like a tender mother
and fills deep oceans like a life giving womb.

Her fluid lines are as changing and malleable as the seasons
smooth and silky as a placid lake in summer
lazy and languid as a meandering river in autumn
choppy and volatile as a torrential flood in winter
laughing and spritely as a flowing fountain in spring.

She can be unpredictable and freeze into icicles
can break the will of the most hardened soul
or soften and melt into a fresh spring of happiness.
She is never silent, for her currents run deep
she knows no boundaries, for she is boundless.

Her liquid art is as unrestrained as the rains
endless clouds form and bear witness to her.
She is translucent and at times elusive
she can never be fully grasped
for she is the shape of water.

I Am Me, You Are You - Nursery Rhyme

by Kenneth Rone

I have one sock and it is blue
Here's another, which makes two.

But the second sock is red and white!
There's something here that is not right.

What if I search and cannot find
That other sock that's just like mine?

I'll just wear THESE socks that aren't a match!
Because I'm different, what's wrong with that?

We're not the same, YOU can be You,
And THEY be THEY, and be friends too!

April Fair

by Kimberly J Merryman

O April fair,
    delightful is your
        warm embrace.
A welcome rest from
    Winter's chill -
A gentle nudge towards
    Summer's heat.
You are perfect in my eyes.

O April fair,
    your showers soak
        the slumbering earth -
            reviving dormant life.
Nature yawns and breathes out,
    a floral crown of

purples, pinks, reds and yellows.
Green ascends the throne.

O April fair,
  new life abounds.
    The offspring of many
      enjoy your bounty.
And even I am born of you.
  All this is of God,
    the beauty of His creation,
      ordained from the beginning.

.

O April fair,
  you are my diamond,
    a breath of fresh air.

A Conversation With Coronavirus

by Michael J. Ponnambalam

1   "Hi, Corona, thy name means crown.
      But all thy deeds in pain us drown.
      Many losing jobs, homes and hope,
      Are not sure how they now will cope.

2   For months schools and colleges closed,
      For us many problems have posed.
      Online class is not fun, my friend.
      Good if soon it comes to an end.

3   Deaths one million by September.
      Scary number to remember!
      Why hast thou become a killer?
      Please, leave us, mad graveyard filler!"

4   "I am only a messenger.
      Neither killer, nor avenger.
      Many see me as an evil.
      But the wise will see my goodwill.

5 God, your great and loving Father,
 Sees you drifting from Him farther.
 Fun and entertainment centered,
 You are now much conscience blunted.

6 Money you chase; but not wisdom,
 Depth in spirit, or God's Kingdom.
 With your science and tech power,
 You think you're a mighty tower.

7 God sent me to help you to see
 Powerless how you are. Hence flee
 From all your sins. Follow God's way.
 Then I'll fly away, as you say."

Mother Elephant

by Pusselle Wineetha

If only you knew...if only you knew...
How a mother's tears flooded her eyes;
How blood oozed from her aching nipples;
And how she quarrelled with a stubborn quarry,
Lashing the quarry with her shrunk trunk,
To save her drowning son.

She commoved herself,
Looking for her darling baby,
Running up - the rocky hill,
And tumbling down – the prickly valley,
Yet, no laugh, no groan, no mourn,
No whine...nothing did she hear.

She ran, wailing and mourning,
Frenziedly smelling his footprints,
Blowing the dust and oozing the blood.
With rocking, swaying and head bobbing,
She headed to a quarry.

She screamed like an angry wind,
Spinning, beating her heart,
When seeing her drowning baby,
Feebly groaning, "PaWooing"
In a mud-splashed, narrow quarry.

With flood-smothering eyes,
Oozing, aching blood from her nipples,
She lashed the quarry with her shrunk trunk,
To save her drowning son,
Her darling son, her life —
If only you knew how...if only you knew...

Autumn's End

by David I Mayerhoff

The birds are chirping
The landscaper is mowing
Sweets floral scents
Waft in the air

School is still out
Frolicking in the sun is still in
The games grown-ups play
Are those familiar to children year round

Our senses delight
In the sublime subtleties of nature
We grin from ear to ear
At the cheer that sunshine brings

Nothing can interrupt this divine setting
Nothing can disturb our countenance at these times
For we somehow believe this will go on forever
Even though we know it will not

There Is Magic In Poetry

by Rukhsana Afridi

There is magic in poetry
The way a poet's wrist twists with a flair
There is magic also in the air
Writing tool used like a threaded spool
Amidst the midnight blue
That's what we do in school
There is magic in poetry
Spinning thoughts like cobweb
Expressed in words of rhyme
Provocation of rhythm
All on a piece of birch wood paper
Writing while twirling one's hair
There is magic in poetry

Listen To The Warm

by Upma Sharma

"It happens just because we need to want, and to be wanted to, when love is here or gone to lie down in the darkness... and listen to the warm". ...Rod Mcuen

As the chills of extreme winter bite me through the night, I close eyes to visit my memorable past when you held me in your arms so tight, I could feel your breaths on my neck, skin next to mine and thumps of fastened heartbeats.
Wantings craved to end tranquil as I listened to the warm.
I then open eyes to find no one by my side, frozen frigid with dried up eyes that do not reply to any emotion anymore, I wait endlessly for your eternal touch that only could send some warmth.

Me and you and our rhythmic beats
of that time were the soul's treat...
Those close walls if were able to speak

will evince and further endeavour to seek...
How inseparable souls and crossed our hearts,
could time ever tear us apart?

Hunter's Moon

by David Mohn

branches creeping
toward a sleeping deer-
hunter's moon

Admiring Greatly

by Richard Nsonge Nah

At the verge of this our day break,
permit me pour this few words from my cup;

For these are not the lyrics of a song,
but the voice of my soul,
the cry of my life;

You possessed my air of indifference,
appearing quite debonair,
making me fall without sliding to the sabotage of your indifference;

With your unique kind of joyful smile,
you engulf me,
filling my yesterdays with your love,
creating a light I don't understand,
demanding my fingers on your soft ivory skin;

Such awareness to these emotions,
untouched and raw becomes more expose than my flesh,
and my heart at your feet teetering on the brink;

Falling is inevitable,
but in whose arms is the question my heart holds,
wondering why it has not been declared,

for the answer lies within you my love,
as I truly and madly fall deeply into you.

Email To Subby Conscience

by Gail Rickless DeBole

(Gail's Note: Reply Email from Subby Conscience is the sequel to this.)

To: Subby Conscience
From: gadeb@zzzsmail.com
Re: Communication between You and Me
Date: February 4, 2012

Why isn't it easy to call you at will?
Couldn't I just Twitter or email you until
You provide the answer in clear, solid terms
So that I don't have to lie in your chaotic squirms?

Instead, you tug at my psyche
And laugh at my logic.
You taunt and tug at my struggles
And sap my dream tonic.
You expose my repression
While disguised as a friend
All the while sneaking around
In my personal REM.

A swirl of feelings
Interferes with the theme.
Makes my heart pound and pound.
Makes it seem like a scheme
To interrupt sleep
And destroy my 8 hours.
To wither my psyche
And sap super powers.

And then comes the waiting
Sometimes for years
Of what this all means

Could it always be fear?

But unknown to you
Over time you are helping
To harness the pounding
And process all my days' yelpings
So that I can function in the AM and more
While you are repressed as
I cozily soar.

Should I Dream

by DM Borowski

Were I to fall asleep this night
  rather than toss and turn restless in my efforts
  seeking rest and comfort in my sought escape;
what would I say to you, now gone
  emptied of my love and life as it slips away?

How often does the memory of days past, rise
  as if all were today in place of yesterday
  when it was always you and me against the world;
should I dream
  daring to recapture what was forever between us?

Yes, I would do it all again,
  casual conversations blooming to warm love's embrace
  and passionate vows and promises to last a lifetime;
hold me close and tender
  let me whisper in your ear, I love you still.

Forever and always
  I hold you close
  knowing words need not be spoken;
we are forever bound
  and should I dream, I dream of you.

Utopian Land

by Meenakshi Raina

My poetry takes me to Utopian land,
  Where love and peace perfectly blend.
    Humanity is the only religion known
      Arrows are rusted, bows can't bend.

Everyone is kind with beautiful heart,
  Equality and justice for all, I wonder.
    A perfect place where women are safe,
      And it rains, without any thunder.

I imagine people living their dreams,
  Society woven from threads of trust.
    Here life is perfect, devils are dead,
      Joy prevails, worries crushed to dust.

But, when I encounter the real world,
  My poetic soap bubble tends to burst.
    And I am drawn out of Utopian land,
      Now I find blood quenching the thirst.

Physics

by Heather Secrest

I'm traveling north
At a fraction of the speed of light
In a linear progression
Through the dimension of time
A point mass
A particle
Going in a straight line
The interesting stuff happens
When your path hits mine

A collision
A decision
To connect
Or redirect
Each path a new
Direction
Each direction a new
Path

It's all relative
I'm the center of the universe
All I see
Is mapped from me
It's all relative
You're the center of the universe
All you do
Is mapped from you
It's all relative
We're the center if the universe
All we need
Is mapped from we

There goes the clock
Tick tock
tick...
tock...
Slower and slower
As I go faster and faster
Traveling north
At the speed of light
A point mass
A particle
Hurtling towards
A destination
A collision
An intersection
A decision

A Tribute To Black Women

by Riquetta Brown

People say she is built with rage and has a
Heart that is solid as a concrete.
I say there is no fire within her, suffering is within her when she tries to
speak
Her opinions and truths without silence.

Though she had struggle through her tribulations,
She continues to stand and walk to her path.

She is saddened to see her own male species present hate towards
Melanin women for an exotic taste, especially vanilla.
She's not worried, she knows there are plenty of fellow melanin
That will walk into her doorstep.
She even has a different taste of flavors of her own.

In this time of civilization, they do not see her as the definition of beauty
For what they believe, but she does not seek as she continues to
Wear her curves and her skin proudly.
Humanity tries to deny her radiance,
Yet she still walks with grace as she
Swings her hips with pride.

My Limited Perfection

by Ilene Bauer

In rhyme, I'm a perfectionist;
In other things, I'm not.
You'd think I'd treat all things the same
But rhyme is what I've got.

For patience is a virtue which
I really don't possess.
I'll rush though projects though results

Will surely not impress.

My sewing comes out crooked
And my seams don't seem to match.
My baking skill are mediocre,
Though I bake from scratch.

You'd never want me as your chef;
I clean, but things don't shine
And wrapping gifts has never been
A special skill of mine.

My ironing leaves creases
And technology's a bane.
My plants all droop and getting rid
Of clutter is a pain.

But when I write, I'll work each line
Until the rhyme's in sync.
My pencil and eraser let me
Change things as I think.

Some people are obsessive
'Bout so much, and all the time
While as for me, that just applies
To writing poems in rhyme.

Reverie In Colours

by Malabika Ray

aquamarine horizon with crimson hue,
   unfolds a sublime picture of dawn,
drowns my senses in tender lilac dreams,
   sways me away to a mythical land unknown.

lose myself in a tranquil tangerine reverie,
   spring birds merrily cooing songs serenade,
saffron imagination dawns on my dreamy eyes,
   fantasy a magical garden, sprinkling faint lemon scent.

swirling all vibrant colours of rainbow in palette,
          fragrant petite graceful flowers wake me up,
chartreuse waterfalls falls soft on coral rocks
          lavender yearning fills my passionate heart.

watermelon marvels of life mystifies the beauty of our existence,
    doting sleep whispers faraway dreams gently on my eyes.

Being Unseen

by William K Kekaula

Tryst edged ... Aurora whisper serendipitous saffrons,
e'er forging balms beamish strands to aerate crown's expanse, whilst
bestrewn
lissome mists waltzes amongst errant gasp caught in rapture.

An ephemeral cloudburst evaporates on supine
silhouettes of the gods. Pristine manna with a sigh ... midst hollow
utter, guides dulcet zephyrs to petrichor arousals.

Purged euphoric realm steep in its prismatic solitude
poise, waft chimerical imagery effervescent caprices,
volley afar ... harks labyrinths mellifluous murmur.

Vesper, yon the zenith of Terra, breathe his claim toward
the cosmos, granting resplendent panacea a vestured vault,
... occasions an epiphany as moonglade o'er a lake.

At One With

by Annette P. Kauffman - Sam Kauffman

Still! Perfect stillness
A verbless hermit
Present tense of the divine dawn
Ageless angelus -
No specter of yesterday
Vital youth of the ever eternal daystar

To a priceless creation before Genesis.

Motionless in meditation
The caress of flawless beauty
In virgin minutes
Essential oil of dim caliginosity's fragrance
And a massage of morning's messenger
Soft wink in a sequester of time
Daylight and midnight equal twins

Seamless solitude -
A chant of plain song –
Solo symphony -
Soft chimes of audible words
In wordless alliterations of wisdom
Expressions of the source
Without a shadow

Tranquil in
The sweet taste of tranquility
In personification of the placid calm
Only cravings of perpetual satisfaction -
On the tongue perfection's noun
A ban of bitterness
Savory sips - cool flavor on the palate

Cradle of baptism
A christening of bliss
A dedication to the infinite
A hug from the divine edgeless Pi
A suspension of the animate frame
Caress of eternity's essence in a benediction
No separation of Be into the ageless clarity of Is

The Grapes Of Mirth

by William K Kekaula

As death mimics love itself and clutch a throbbing heart,
kindling consolation to savor flight, farther and farther
beyond the inner yelps released as vibrating soar easily,

255 | P a g e - PS: It's Still Poetry – Volume II

stimulating stress to execute its portion and naught idle, merely trounce its climatic claim with an uttered gasp.

Exhale nor inhale as a soul embarks anew venture upon a road that seems less traveled, albeit, a much-traveled road, nonetheless, deliberating back to that grey hued frame, thoroughly placed in peace, smiling at once was a vestige of their former self as hands clasp naught wave.

The hours, the days, the years, all appear as if time itself is naught placed on hold, but practically be nonexistent, then again, seeing the circumstances unfold, obviously, one will be able to grasp that there is no other direction of a skyless opaque mist, except a harmonious presence.

As distinction advents and all be so unique and naught strange, more and more a glide into the everlasting light and that the glorious manifestation established hereon, whereby, one came upon Steinbeck as he was sitting by vines, beaming, as he was writing, The Grapes of Mirth.

Peacock Dance

by Supraja Kannan

Somewhere between the Poseidon and Azure
Is his double shaded blue that always allures;
Between the lush and chrome, green hues
That glow in layers of velvet like necklace;
With rufous brown tail feathers and long neck
With strong twig like legs which are too thick
And with the slender body and crown feathers on head
Peacocks are the boss of mass which make others dread

From the Rats to the Snakes
From the Rabbit to the Crakes
Also the night warriors Bat men
Every one is afraid of this majestic man;
From the young women to the children
From the Kookaburra to the Magpie robin

And the Ostriches from Sahara
Every bird is envious of his aura

Thousand little eyes on the long floating feathers,
Blink only when he feels his favorite weather;
When the rain god cascades down to see his dance,
And when photographers yearn to use their chance,
In the mid of the picturesque green land,
with his feathers stretched, he majestically stands;
When Koels sing ragas and loras hum rhythms,
Begins he, the divine dance steps; joining birds with him

'Thath Tharihita Thai', he oscillates left and right
'Thom Tharihita Thom', he jumps and floats light
'Thathom Tharihita Thathom', he lands on the land gently
'Thamthom Tharihita Thamthom'he grins and performs friendly

From heaven, retains his dance steps best
Performs he, with sheer enthusiasm and zest;
Not to entertain us or his dearest friends
But to entice his beautiful girlfriend;
Does his persistent love line dance,
Until he puts his mate into a trance;
And the planet earth revolves
Just to see them dance in love

Plight Of The Elderly

by L. Milton Hankins

Suppose all around you suddenly vanished,
And you realized you were standing alone
In the twilight of your years feeling banished
Like a pilot-less, rudder-less, helpless drone.
You knew your life was mystifyingly dreamed
With many questions and answers few,
You know everything was not as it seemed
And you scarcely know exactly what to do.

The lot of many elderly in our nursing homes
Removed from the familiar, in a strange place

Victims of memory loss and various syndromes
Suddenly feeling like they are in outer space.
Many spend their last days lonely and sad
Feeling unwanted and deserted, I am told,
And some of these places are horribly bad
It makes me fight to keep from getting old!

Call Of The Unknown

by Delice Arleen Skelly

Rush of life for me is over
Insidious age has me ensnared
Fond look back at days in clover
Of twilight years am too aware.

Shadows gather at warp speed
With stoicism must face my fear
With footsteps of faith, I proceed
Silent goodbye to all things dear.

Bound by rotating wheel of life
Rising, falling endless chain
Through laughter, tears, and daily strife
From birth until this life force wains.

Going ahead to who knows where
Positive thoughts are invisible guide
Time to be brave refuse to be scared
Universe is vast where will I abide?

Sunday Awakens

by Gordon S. Wolf

Sunday awakens, stretches her arms
  It's sunny outside, the air's laden with charms
Can it really be October already?
  Sure enough, yet delight's holding steady

The morning is warm and inviting
  The skies are clear-blue, on a kite-string
Birds are still chirping, the green grass yet sings
  Oh, let winter come without warning between

Halloween Clown

by Janice Canerdy

I seldom have bad dreams, just silly ones,
but I had chilling nightmares as a child.
The one that comes to mind most frequently
involves a clown and Halloween gone wild.

My friends and I, age 12, were walking home
from trick-or-treating when, just to our right,
we caught a glimpse of orange in the woods
and heard a wicked laugh. We shook with fright.

We took off running. Then, to our dismay,
a giant clown with orange hair appeared.
It growled, "I will be back"—and it was gone.
That it would keep its promise, we all feared.

That night I dreamed the clown was in my room
asphyxiating me. I couldn't scream.
Were bruises on my neck and orange hairs
left on my bed proof of a lively dream?

Gaia Spins Her Summer Scenes

by Martha L. Kiser

Pastel florals arise and flow,
in hues of tranquil misting seas.
Back light of a sapphire glow,
captivates the heart of glee.

Impassioned crest of rainbow song,

crescendos in the twilight beams.
Where angels walk abreast in throngs,
emanations of hope begin to stream.

Majesty of the cresting wave,
 gifts sinewy strings of morning dew.
Mother Nature then engraves,
her claim of incandescent hues.

Gay sings the bird up in the bower;
in observation of the blossoming flowers.

Inhale Lovesickness

by Eve Roper

bursting full rain clouds every moment beat
at my grasp my ceaseless soul clasp to seek
golden sun rays on warm field at my feet

acoustic years have passed like ascending vines
yet hued shadows appear from its ripe binds
an inhale lovesickness and redefines

flourish and it takes hold and soar aloft
and glide through as time sweeps away whisper soft
clutch to early morning light and gasp a sound waft

A Desire

by Er.Aamir khan

Come back, my love and we shall have some summers again
    The beauty of sunshine and the showers of rain

In the valleys strange and unknown
    Between the butterflies and silkworm's cocoon

Under the canopy blue and endless

Across the oceans deep and tasteless

The dance of peafowl and the melodies of koel
Lavish green meadows and the fragrance of soil

The hops of grasshoppers and the croaks of frogs
and the sober eyes of yours under that dense fog

Those sweet whines in bright crystal glasses
I miss those days and regret those passes

Come back O! beloved and dance with me in the rain
Quench the thirst of my soul and relieve my pain

Oceans

by Janine lever

When lips share a romantic kiss,
Can it be, in that intimate exchange
One bears a mist
And another holds no such cover?
Is this a truth?
One heart remains the same
And one becomes a lover?
Or, in that truth does truth-some lie?
One has to play and one must fly?

Do these polars make the bind?
Of seconds, moments of lives, in kind?
And knowing truth is a fleeting thing
When change and circumstance is king,
It fluctuates, in method, like the sea,
And truthful lips lie, somewhere,
In the waves that be.

My Obsession Is Writing

by Constance La France

I have always had an urge to write_
have something to say- something to tell
words shake the ocean of my sleep . . .
and I must let them pour out so, I put pen to paper . . .
(or fingers to keyboard these days) and tap my creative potential
with time have found my inner voice- writing is music to my soul
it fulfills a need in me nothing else can . . .
from my innermost thoughts I pen poetry of life, grief and sorrow
with beauty and imagery I express my feelings
I write of the scars on the roadmap of my soul- the shadows on my wall
like a letter to the world I expose my broken heart-   it is my obsession
it's a voyage of self-discovery . . .
my writing is a legacy to be left when gone
writing came to me a guest unbidden- I am not sure why
the power of the pen for me it is like breathing . . .
I write, I weep at what I have written
but cannot stop this writing obsession
and will not till I can no longer hold a pen
then, I will write in my head
until my mind fades away . . .

The Office

by Brian Sambourne

Jungle clamour
Banter twisted like vines
Lions with psyche scars
Monkeys as crackpot sleuths
Snakes in a labyrinth guise
Parrots preen an oily beauty
Giraffes creak in rumpled posture

Immersive labelling

My colleagues salivate slippery ambition
Pre-occupied with image
Our digital frontier, computer glitches
Terrain fighting, coffee muted
Hidden fracturing
Beasts that claw parchment cubicles
Self-propelled advancement, perpetually out of reach
Few scraps of conscience
Strong scents prevail

All of us are watchers
    seeding what cannot be grasped
    spirited wishing
    to pass beyond our bars
    to re-write uncaged narratives

Poet

by Pusselle Wineetha

Before everyone else,
dreaming of heaven
and blooming with desire,
poet rhymes with pleasure
the road to heaven.

No matter, even to Hades
poet goes first; rushes back;
tells the gruesome news;
and dramatizing the scene,
discourages evils.

Poet enjoys being a guru:
he gently kisses a flower;
smells the fragrance of love;
sighs like a furnace;
and models how to live love.

The beauty of the flower,
blooms with cocks' crow
and flies away with sun's fall,

yet words by a poet
never, ever glooms,
but blooms at every moment.

We Are Thoughts

by Rama Balasubramanian

Thoughts make man, decide life and personality
We are nothing but thoughts in totality
World is what we perceive in mind
In thoughts our world is confined
Most of our thoughts are superfluous
What we don't know doesn't exist for us

Thoughtlessness is the key to bliss
It can take you away from world's abyss
When sense organs are focused on task in front
Rather than evanescent thoughts they confront
We experience perfection in action and peace
All our woes at that instance cease

When we do all tasks with thoughtless concentration
From kundalini raises up blissful divine vibration
To fill up the vacuum created in head
Transcending chakras, they gush out of head,
We see our soul, experience bliss infinite
Nothing bothers us, in own self we delight

We become one with God, immortal
We are liberated from the world of mortals
This is what all meditation course teach
Same thing scriptures across globe preach
This the real goal of human life

Dreams Within Dreams

by Pramod RASTOGI

Under the canopy of pine trees,
We lie watching the peaks of mountains
Crowned in white and wearing stony brown.
We take flights to majestic heights
To see views from the summits' tops.

Dreams fulfilled, we fly back on a high
And land on the remnant of pine leaves
Where we lie, you and I, wide-awake.
Ever in the mode to propel me to fly,
You are my dream-drive, in blossom,

Residing in the warmth of my bosom,
In a niche that you have dug deep
And which you have never quit,
Forever forgiving your companion
For his shifting sights, pine tree high

Piercing the sky, and buoyantly green,
Quivering like pine branches,
Leaving him with no breathing space
To take life in slow motion and meditate,
To bring a shade of stability to his life.

You have left me high dreams to nurture.
I have bartered some for pieces of gold
But some you have treasured for me
To fall upon when inconsistency filled my life
And buds of high dreams

Started wilting before their bloom.
Then, in a soft gesture, you will open your chest
And grant me some of those jewels
Which in their flawless forms
Will glitter like shining stars.

A life's stretch is finite.
A day will come when I'll feel fatigued.
Then, in a meditative silence, you and I,
We will lie under this canopy
And gaze at the clear blue sky.

The sky will take on a dreamy look
Embroidered with resplendent stars
To salute my companion and me, lying-in-state.

When Ned Came To The Island With His Dog

by Richard A Martin Jr MD

When Ned came to the island with his dog
greeted by the men in bulging Speedos,
some he knew and many that he didn't
he saw the tip of an enormous iceberg
the submerged of which would quickly be revealed
men and women would die in agony and pain.
Ned wanted to rise and rail and shout
...urine on the steps up to the Capitol
never silent...always loud and angry
in counterpoint to their deafening silence.
And that accomplished his and their agenda
so that in these days the trigger has become
accepted, resigned to, complacent
as if everything has now been put aright.
The problem is that many still are suffering...
but now the kettle's taken off the boil.
And all that's left is us to brew the tea

My Owner's Garden

by Tania Kitchin

My owner has a beautiful garden out back in my yard
I can't wait to run out there to play and stand guard
My whiskers tickle with fresh air and morning dew

I watch songbirds fly around me and chirp as they do

I sneak over to the perennials and the catnip bunch
I chew and roll in it until I feel all giddy with a punch
I then relax on the garden swing, basking in the sun
And lick my lips as I watch the hummers, such fun

Now Bored, I run under the lilac trees ready to pounce
At the chipmunk eating seeds, I will make him flounce
I dart and chase him and he hides in the geranium plants
I give up and decide to check out the peonies and chase ants

My owner then calls out and wants me to go back in
My food is ready for me with pate' from a gourmet tin
I joyfully skip to my food, relaxed and still feeling a high
I can't wait to go back to the garden before the day goes by

The Horsetail Fall

by Jenish Somadas

I was a nascent virgin stream
Born to glabrous mountain king
On the unflinching love his dream
The dark damsel of sky he fling.

On her rapture and cry I grown
Broken the rules with fickle friends
Freely flown as my growing brawn
Smoothing curves of fine couthy bends.

One day I reached the fall of love
Met your golden face and quiver
Fallen blind on your hands I calve
My silver hair known as river.

Mating, jiggling and blushed in red
Flown to the deep, deep to the bed.

Learning - A Good Investment
by Bartholomew Williams

A lazy student known as Burt,
To parents and teachers was curt.
    With little knowledge,
    Flunked out of college;
Played stock market and lost his shirt!

Fading Light
by Freddie Robinson Jr.

Did you shine bright,
star bright,
in your brief sky of time?

Did you have a stellar afterglow
once you departed
and vanish like melted snow?

Did your life leave an indelible mark,
a blazing comet trail
in the all-enveloping dark?

What composition did your death bring,
was it the same song
that a supernova sing?

Now that your light is fading away,
what magnitude was it yesterday?
Now that your light is dimming down,
will any residue of your life be found?

As your fading light
recedes into the dying night
Will your soul still keep burning bright?

Only God, who sees all, knows
whether He'll snuff out the light
still emanating from your soul

As your fading light
recedes into the dying night
Pray that your soul keep forever burning bright

Flight To Atlanta

by Ray Dillard

We float together above the earth,
The clouds and I.
They form layers.
From above, they are fluffy white and pristine.
Below, dirty gray and flat.
A skim of flotsam that seeks a place to settle.
A sheet of marble.

Then changing to rows of cotton planted
Two on four. Ready to strip and bale.
The ground between shows shadows
That gallop like wild mustangs on the open plain.
They are the darker of the twins,
And remind of the limits of light and sky.
Yen and Yang, the balance.
Each an ink blot that would test Rorschach.

Now becoming forever white like
Deep and driven drifts of snow.
Or, white icing on an endless sheet of cake.
Small peaks are skillfully placed
By nature's cleaver hand.

Towers of misty clouds climb above the rest
And become smoke from a fire
Or steam from a boiling pot.
Smoke signals.

Moving through the climbing vapor
Gives the ride a rattle and rumble
As driving on a country road.
Windows become foggy glasses that
Clear without a wipe.

The cloud ahead becomes an angry mountain
That towers above and darkens the ground below.
With admiration and respect,
We circle,,,and wait

The Waterman - Visual 1

by Brian L Lowmiller

Oh, streaking man on epic sea;
bold waterman stoked up on fear,
your blue room wall calm lunacy,
oh streaking man on epic sea.
In magic, bound up ecstasy,
your arching nemesis comes near,
oh streaking man on epic sea;
bold waterman stoked up on fear.

Poem In Your Pocket

by Heather Secrest

There is a word.
You like it,
You grab it,
You put it in your pocket
And another one
And another one
And another one
And they all jumble themselves up
Sitting in your pocket
Sometimes neatly
Sometimes messy

Until you pull a word
Out of your pocket
And find
That you have
A poem there
Instead.

White Moments In Time

by Gwendolyn D. Cloyd

White days
White nights
White alabaster arms and legs
White, crimson lights-

Oh, what seamless nights-
White moments in time
White memories - yours and mine,
White love, white hate
White demise-
of an inkling of what's left
of our white/fiery passion
upon white silken sheets...
Only that is not what made our love complete-

The Perfect Painting Love

by Jerry T Curtis

He softy strokes a canvas, in His style
As She sits there wearing, just her smile
He's studies all Her lines
As he carefully defines
The beauty that exists
Within her soul
He lives and slaves
For this very goal

Pigments mixing, creates a different hue

Colors blending the way the often do
He looks into her eyes
But he dares not compromise
For his love of art
He simply can't deny
And paints Her while the tears
Flow from His eyes

Slowly twisting, brushes filled with umber
To a canvas, that cannot be encumbered
For it is his connection
To this painting of perfection
No greater critique
Can there ever be
He's imprisoned by the Art,
That set Her free

Holding beauty, in such adoration
His is truly, the greatest abdication
He wants to keep her near
But, he works in constant fear
She can't return his love
After all
While he gently hangs her portrait
On, His wall......

As she's leaving, his heart begins receiving
Inspirations, that dissipate his grieving
Another girl comes in
As she poses to begin
Soon another Artist love-a-fair imparts
That's one more "Perfect Painting" for The Arts

A Little Girl That I Once Knew

by Vickie Hurtt-Thayer

There is a child in me,
she hides way down beneath,
the adult in me.

She saw awful things,
she felt many painful things,
and heard many harsh things.

The adult in me,
always attempts to protect her,
but there are times I fail.

That is when,
the adult in me,
cries for the child,
that I once was.

My tears remember,
the pangs of distress,
for the child,
who can never rest.

Alaska

by Amya Richelle Ranck

It's a place that snows
That shines and glows

With mountains all around
And wonders to be found

With treasures to behold
Under the river rock is gold

Wild animals roam the land
Never being touched be man

With fish that swim the streams
In the summer with the suns beams

The northern lights shine at night
That creates a beautiful sight

Voyage

by Joanna Chamberlain

With a weighted foot
I advance another step
Feeling the cold sand
Between my toes
Wet and sharp

Inhaling and exhaling
Every breath nourishing
Misty, briny breeze
Caressing my cheeks
Whispering secrets of the ocean

Salt crystals glisten
Sand jewels
Sapphires, emeralds flicker

My withered entangled hair
Revealing stories of a troubled past
Sulphur perfume
Awakening my senses

Dreamy eyes drawn to a solitary bird
Ghostly in the silver night sky
Our contentment mirrored

Seduced by a murk entity
Shielding, protective

Enchanted, captivated
Alluring, calm presence

Entwined souls
Destined to meet
Simultaneously we interrupt

The oceans poetic ballads

To Die Of Love

by Jean Bush

Lean in, oh so close, my love, and kiss my waning cheek.
For you have taken all I have and yet your love is sweet.
Wrap me in your velvet cloak and gently lay me down;
I need not now my feathered bed but rather broken ground.

You promised that our love would last the winding centuries,
But now I know, as my blood flows, there's nothing left to see.
I told you I would follow you as long as I had life
Now I see, that more than me, you only loved the night.

Your hurried footsteps tell me that the coming dawn is nigh
You did not stay for my last breath but left me here to die.
One day, I think, that you will tire of all that you have been,
You'll touch the sun and call my name and love me once again.

Love's Dawn

by Mark R Toney

The rooster's crow warns me that dawn has come
My sleepy eyes resist my need to rise
I blindly reach for her but she is gone
Then hear a sound that much to my surprise
Reveals she hasn't left but still is near
The sound then ever closer she appears!

One last embrace and kiss before she leaves

Declare undying love to last the years
Such declaration mitigates our fears
As varied shades of love each one perceives

Poets' Pursuits Beyond Writing

by Beata B. Agustin

Abounding in seemingly infinite activities for actualization
Bards are we, bestowed with busyness beyond poetry writing's best
Chores of caring await like being coaches, cheerers, counselors
Duty-bound, we can do these or that and such with diligence...

Earnest in our roles as parents and family members, ever-endearing
Fulfilling entrusted assignments along faithfulness fortitude
Guards, governors, guides ... glowing in goodness
Helping, healing, hoisting hearts upon hope's herald...

Influencing against impossibility's impact
Joy-sharers while journeying with jubilation
Kindness' sowers, as well as instructors of knowledge
Loving, leading, learning along the light...

Managers, merchandisers, or ministers
Nourishing talents and gifts, knocking off negligence
Open to development opportunities
Planting, praying, pursuing toward prosperity
Quitting not to live in contentment's quietude...

Reconciliators or reconcilers, rejoicing for relationship restoration
Singers or perhaps speech makers, truth --- spreading
Triumphantly testifying with thanksgiving*
Upholders of righteousness in our undertakings
Voicing out vigilantly against violence...

Worshipers while watchers of grand children (soon) ... wisely
Xylophone players maybe, while basking under bliss of xanadu
Yearning for yields with strength of youthfulness
Zealously we accomplish much midst passionate zest.

Catharsis: My First Love

by Rashini Kaushalya

I heard your voice first
while you were sitting behind me
on the second row in grade nine class
The moment I saw you first,
I felt a volcano booming, inside me

I heard you criticize my school,
comparing it with your previous one
and to escape from your grunt
I locked my earlobes.
I told your sister I love my mom, my School ......

Next day, I saw you alone,
alone – at my Grand Mom's house
I saw you hide like a mouse..........
a frightened mouse, in a dirty rat hole ....

I still remember what happened
I was in grade nine
We stood with daggers in arms,
and you splattered my white-washed
school walls with a mud-fire

We hated each other as crow and cuckoo do
or cobra and mongoose do,
but our mates stared with mouths agape
at the rising ... scarlet castle of love...
in our fiercely fighting battle ground

I dreamed one day a nightmare:
My prince fell dead in the battle front......
I could do nothing.........
I dreamed of marrying my first love,
but it remains a living, breathing dream....

Fake Noise

by Franci Eugenia Hoffman

loudest words askew
drastic times tempt the masses
oh, those lying eyes

Pleiades

by Carol Louise Moon

Please write more Pleiades.
Patiently I wait. You
Pen your seven lines to
Ponder. Six lines unfold,
Plus a seventh. And now--
Pandora's box, words on
Parchment penned in silver.

Blue Hole

by John Terence Miller

I lie on the cold, damp grass,
alone;
staring reflectively
at the hole
in the tent above me.
I'm only here because I promised;
or rather, you made me promise.
The sky I see through the hole
is dull and grey
and the music drifting heavily
from the stage in the distance
is the darkest blue.

When we laid here in the grass

together;
Just last year;
the sky we saw through the hole
Above us
was bright, light blue,
and the music blared in dazzling colours:
of yellow, red, orange,
and deep purple.

We laughed ourselves silly
about the hole.
The rain dripped in at night
collected in a pan;
the rhythmic drips
keeping time with the music;
or so we convinced ourselves.

Today the rain drips
and makes a damp puddle
on my chest;
next to my heart.
The blue hole is no longer.
The dull grey hole that replaced it;
is like the dead hole left inside me
now that you have gone.

Natures Music

by Regina McIntosh

Whispering softly, liquid against smooth stones
Caressing my naked thoughts, my imagination, my heart
Roaring rapids pouring over in rushing torrents of unspoken words
Creating tender melodies of unspeakable joy, faith, hope and love

Breathless laughter trembles from silent stars
Twinkling delightedly, inspiring souls to listen to their falling smiles
Coloring the night in shimmering displays of emotions that inspire

Dancing flames of wisdom color the dawn in lemon rays
Sunlight sighs through the azure sky, embracing souls

Warming thoughts with awe of heaven

Nature's music invites prayers and psalms to become well known
Lingering on minds for moments alive with a spiritual warmth
Lifting shadows from the darkest grief
Capturing hymns of enlightenment, amazement and
unending grace

Everlasting

by Lasaad Tayeb

A grateful man has received the gift of love,
a person who has made all his dreams come true,
for the rest of his life, he would have been thrilled
~~towards precious pearl.

He was entwined by the green vine of fondness,
the stars were tumbling on his bewildered bed,
he was compelled to her powerful savior,
~~cupid~ dart hit him.

He believed infinity would protect him
yes, if love exists and his hands can undo
to scrub a memory, he shall make a mound
~~you~ made this to please.

'Broken Crayons'

by Wilma Neels

Broken crayons in my bag
Still has a purpose
It can add color to a dull day
Words, you are afraid to say
Can be shared without shame

These broken crayons still has its worth

Just like us as humans
We might be a little broken and bruise
But we are still important
We still have a purpose

You can brighten someone's day
You can paint another's sky with a myriad of shades
Be like those broken crayons in my bag
Let your actions be your words

Imagine If You Want To

by Marilene L. Evans

Was at a lovely concert last night,
love was the message of the night.
Love, peace of mind, of mankind are
what the world desperately needs so far.
Yes, what the world needs right now
can be done, if you want to, somehow.

If you want to, if we want to, if you want to.
Open your mind, your heart and look into
your soul and think or ponder, if you want to.
You can see or be blind, if you want to.
You can hear or be deaf, if you want to.
You can feel or be numbed, if you want to.

You can also smell and taste if you want to.
You can see all the bias going on around you.
Be it political, racial, social or religious at times
is hurting everybody, somehow, sometimes.
You can hear the results everywhere, any time.
You feel something when you see, hear at times.

Feel sadness, feel nothingness, hurt sometimes,
or you can be blind, deaf and numb sometimes.
How can we have peace, when everybody hurts?
You can if you want to; dream, imagine to convert
your mind to unity instead of hostility, divisiveness.
You can if you want to; dream, imagine wholeness.

You can have love and peace, if you want to.
Show your love to people around you, if you want to
Dream, imagine peace within yourself, if you want to.
Imagine love and peace if you want to. I do want to.

Writing For You

by Jessica Thompson

To all the writers,
old and new
I wish you well
in all you do.

To all the writers,
who've long since passed
we miss you dearly
no questions asked.

To all the writers,
who strive to be
the world is yours
for all to see.

To all the writers,
across this great land
we all unite
with pen in hand.

To all the writers,
whose stories tell
may your pen always ink
and your words forever sail.

Spirit Voices In The Night

by L. Milton Hankins

I am befuddled by these spirits visiting me
In the middle of the night with shrill voices
Whispering devilish messages, full of glee,

Enhancing my weariness for the mystery
Suggesting a plethora of available choices
I am befuddled by these spirits visiting me.

Intimate, acquainted with my own history
In the background, I hear familiar noises
Whispering devilish messages, full of glee.

Obviously meant for a night-time delivery
And since sometimes my heart rejoices
I am befuddled by these spirits visiting me.

Remarkable messages linger in my memory
Some are unwanted like annoying invoices
Whispering devilish messages, full of glee

Upon awakening I recall scenarios of reverie
I seek to place a name to remembered voices
I am befuddled by these spirits visiting me
Whispering devilish messages, full of glee.

Hidden

by DIANE PERNA-GRAF

I hide behind a mysterious façade as
they wrongly charge me with blatant
estimations of who I am.

Feeling displaced as they examine my
northeast inflection, while their obtrusive

glaring resulting in false postulations.

Every encounter, I'm never able to combat their
fallacious beliefs as the scorn pours over me.

They've always been adjudicators during
my trials and tribulations instead of
utilizing the simplest act of kindness.

Slightest glimmers of decency quickly
turn into dismal darkness as I'm
smeared with their assumptions.

If I were not an abused child, my
mistakes would've been negligible
thereby ceasing the incessant torment.

Still and soundless while I disappear, into
nothingness concealing and burying
my most heartfelt thoughts.

While my dignity is attacked, there's no
way out, so I stay masked and muted.
Any aspirations are abolished.

When it was clear I had it together
rushing to and from jobs and schools
their knives of ridicule remained sharp.

A woman said to me, "Why are you hiding
your warmth and compassion?" I answered,
"When I showed it they destroyed me."

So, I shall stay hidden protecting myself, so I
don't suffocate on the fumes of their lies.

I beg, oh God for mercy, as I look to him for
protection, hiding beneath the shadow of
his wings until this violent storm is over.

Popcorn Town

by Barbara P. Peckham

It's a salt water, sea
Water, popcorn town
Where the carousel music goes
Around and around
And the horses fly free.
To the karaoke's tide.
Someone grabs the gold ring
To win another ride.

A salty, buttery odor
Permeates the air -
Lobster rolls and fried clams
And pizza everywhere.
Mom and Pop and children
Still sandy from the shore,
Lick giant ice cream cones
That dribble on the floor

Boats of people party
Along the harborside
Others jam the shops
To browse and then decide
On souvenirs for family or
What to bring a friend.
Instead they buy a t-shirt
That sports an island trend.

The ferry line twists long
As people end their stay
But a boatload more of people
Have come to have their day.
This isn't a "resort",
It's a tourist destination,
It's a little popcorn town,
Best place for a vacation.

A Walk In The Park

by Natasha L Scragg

As I went strolling through the park
So blissful, so serene,
I was awestruck, stopped in my tracks
By the most enchanting scene!

Beneath the draping curtain
Of a Willow Tree's green
Lay a graceful pair of Swans
Right next to the stream!

To add to my enjoyment,
Their signets tottered near!
They ruffled their little feathers
In response to a sudden gust of air.

It truly was romantic.
It really made my day!
I was captured by this moment
And my worries flew away!

Waning Crescent

by William K Kekaula

Arbiter star
aloof to eyes
caught in a trance
fables apiece
artless roam arrest
promises guise
complicit affair
strays guileless caprice

Muddle of minds

in wanton tumble
senseless and reckless
against fugitive shame
e'er betray touch
lack fingers fumble
its lewd intents
stead hearts lay aim

Beheld afar
in quantum expanse
conservative pose
sketched silhouette
art envisions
maestro entrance
sparkled chamber
stars minuet

Dulcet nightwings
winks in fleeing
arcade charted
ambient frame
ephemeral epoch
begs a freeing
golden chariot
star's anew claim

First Bloom

by Janice Canerdy

Though brief, it was a time I'll always treasure.
Its essence shines, undimmed by fleeting years.
That June was filled with pleasure beyond measure.
First bloom of love was sweetest of premieres.

At summer camp, a boy so cute and funny
became my friend--then boyfriend, very soon.
His brilliant smile made rainy days seem sunny.
His arm around my shoulder made me swoon.

With close of camp and time together pending,

we stole a kiss and promised "Every day,
I'll call" and "Many letters I'll be sending."
Such fervor fourteen-year-olds' words convey!

Though youth, with its first love and freshness, flees,
we celebrate it through our memories.

Twelve Months

by Paula Goldsmith

Spring is here,
flowers blooming.
Birds singing,
kids playing.
Summer is coming,
swimming-cookouts.
Hot-hot days ahead,
I am roasting.
Autumn cool days,
need a sweater.
Tree leaves falling,
colors red-orange.
Squirrels scampering,
nuts are hidden.
Winter wonderland,
white fluffy snow.
Santa-gifts,
everywhere I go.
Year is ending,
Hooray-hooray.
A New Year,
A new start.

A Deciduous Tree In The Forest Of Its Dreams

by George Stathakis

in a forest
a deciduous tree with an immortal spirit
germinated in a foreign flora
while surrounded by evergreens

it came from another land
where deforestation is the norm
from a world of destruction
and death

after many years
this deciduous tree became robust and admirable
its trunk sturdy, its branches stout
with its green wide flat leaves in the summer, colorful ones in the fall

and the winds blew, and the storms came
and it was pelted by the rain and hail
thunder and lightning attempted to uproot its soul
but the tree stood tall, and was not dismantled

and all of the evergreens
questioned its existence
laughed at its appearance
said that it was infecting the purity of their sacred evergreen forest

and if this tree could think and speak, if this tree could feel
it would simply say....

"I only seek a better life
in the forest of my dreams."

River On The Moon

by Paghunda Zahid

In the middle of deep dark woods
Beneath the clumsy, capricious clouds
A wacky, wiggly passage leads
To a captivating, cavernous ground

There dwells a divine dreamy Ipomoea__
With the sunset, she gets herself unwrap__
To brew with love, in her beaming lucent lap
Some nifty, nebulous Ambrosia

Pour one drop of it in your soul and soon___
You'll see a surreptitious door in the middle of thin air
Climb it__ embrace it___ no need to fear
And boom___ you are teleported to a river on the moon

Night Elves in gossamer gowns sing by the brink too
Ssshh! listen to the sweetest song, the calmest tune
Swim and watch the ethereal flies hovering over you
Until you are inebriated by river of the moon

The secret river, seen by none
But those with a tender heart
Purest of thoughts and sweetest clarion
And who love the universe __ till the very end

Ever Me

by Betty Robinson

How did this happen? Did someone ask me?
No they didn't. No warning. Not one!
They could have sent emails or maybe a tweet hinting,
"5o years young you are not."
Well, I guess there were warnings,

Ads sent in the mail like for hearing aids, stool softeners and such.
But nobody asked my permission, I'm sure.
It's not written down anywhere.

And you better believe my reply would have been,
"Forget it! Not ever!! Not ME!!!
'Cause you know what would happen? I know this is true,
I'd not stay the me that is ME.

And slowly and surely and sadly you'd hear,
"SHE WAS..." What? Forget it, SHE IS!
So don't you go looking at a place for this mom
Never call me, Miss Minnie, my friend!

Just laugh at my jokes and remember I'm wise.
You've not heard the best of me yet.
I'll keep my hair red and my nails a nice blue
'Cause my heart and my soul like it so.
Let me live out my life in the way I know best,
Never young. Never old. Ever ME!

El Paso, Texas

by Evelyn Carlin Swartz

El Paso, Texas
 desert landscape
  mountain tops
   cactus's so green
    sand storms
     dry air
Footprints of a lone coyote
  beige sand
   rocky mountain ledge
      leads the way
        to a
           sun-filled sky
dry heat
  winter in the morn
        spring at noon
              summer by four

El Paso, Texas
      a
         small
            fragment of
               the Lone Star State
                  Home

The Wind At Play

by Carol Mitra

The sun rises to hold sway
Woken up by the gentle wind
Who is in the mood to play
The clouds glide and are few
Across a vast expanse of blue
The wind blows curls away
From a little girls face
She looks around to see
Whose entered her space
And moves her curling tendrils
off her little face
She clutches down her frock
As the wind lifts it up
Giggling with laughter
she fills natures cup
The flowers all around
Approve of this play
As they nod their colored heads
Moving with the wind they bob and sway

Arlington

by David Holmes

Row upon row
as if grown from the green carpet
they stand starkly white at attention.
Mute sentinels in the drenching sunlight.

Although rooted and still,
in martial regiments, they march endlessly
to the joining of blue sky and green grass carpet.

Those who come here
find the etched places, the names;
the beginnings and the endings.
Those who are here
cannot see, but only rest.

At least that is what we who are the living think,
although perhaps those who are here
Turn restlessly at night and dream.

Flag draped, veiled tears,
percussion cap volley,
the little girl sobs
wrapped in the arms of her mother, his wife.

Where Do Poets Go

by Emile Joseph Pinet

When their pens run dry, where do poets go?
With old thoughts scripted in rhythm and rhyme
can poetry relate, though past its prime?
Bards of yesterday, today, and tomorrow,
ink feelings of love, passion, and sorrow
shared by humans, and thus immune to time.

Poets pass, but their poetry lives on
in the cloud tethered to the internet,
securely stored for anyone to get.
Wordsmiths forge feelings to ponder upon,
and those feelings speak for us when we're gone
so, when death comes, we don't fear the sunset.

Poets drift away in supportive groups
that lift a kindred spirit when it droops.

Selkie

by Peter Rees

Barefoot she walked along the sandy shore,
her golden hair soft fluttering in the breeze.
Like gossamer the flimsy dress she wore,
her soul at peace with joy and youthful ease.
The island shimmered in a summer haze
across the bay, the sea so calm and bright.
As in a dream, it caught and held her gaze,
Her quickening heartbeat spoke of her delight,
as at a lover's silken touch sublime.
The sky had deepened to a burnished gold,
a spectacle of eloquent design
and artistry, exquisite to behold.
She felt the warmth of sand between her toes,
and at the water's edge, the rise and fall
of distant oceans did their truths disclose.
In perfect harmony she heard their call,
an ancient call that echoes down the years,
to speak of things unknown and deeds as yet
undone, and pleasures ofttimes turned to tears,
as lovers' hearts she breaks without regret.
She pauses and with scarce a backward glance,
she steps into the silvery beckoning foam.
It welcomes her as in a merry dance,
of kindred seaborne spirits coming home.
Her lovely form is taken by the waves
and she is gone. Her footprints in the sand
all that remains of everything he craves.
Forlorn and unbelieving, still he stands.
At length he hears, above the ocean's swell,
a phantom whispering in the wind, "Farewell".

A Poem For Society

by Victoria Cruz

roses are white
and although that's a lie
color doesn't change
the beauty inside

Death By Office

by Laurie Mahoney

The maddening click of key strokes
The shrilling of the phones
The crunch of crumbling paper balls
Slices to the bone
The dull humming of the copier
Four million paper clips
The smell of tacky wite out
So sick of all of it
It's like sitting in a coffin
This tomb with three gray walls
Choking on monotony
In a stifling, dreamless stall
I need to find the exit
Won't be like all of them
A dead eyed walking corporate corpse
Fake smiles, no brain stems
I know I need to hurry
Before they bury me away
And I become a pro quo victim
Soulless zombie for the pay

Unconditional Love

by Paul H. Schneiter

Oft have I wondered how wonderful it would be
if there were no fine print
in your love for me.

Even in your arms, inundated by your charms
you seem caught in wayward thought
washed up, and joyful not.

If I dare speak of marriage, of becoming one
there comes a shadow in your eyes
and failings I own arise.

Love lacks conditional clauses, awkward pauses.
It embraces with one's whole being
frailties forever unseeing.

Do I ask too much, human nature presiding?
Not if time is endlessly providing
and love is pure and guiding.

Under The Moon

by Thomas Wells

My mind's eye preoccupation,
I am captive to my guiding light,
the source of all my equivocal influences.

Erik Satie under the moon,
Shadowy contours
against a nocturnal silver sky,
my subliminal ambient impressionism.

I am walking a shrouded path,

trudging through murky ponds
where I find the silhouette
of cattails swaying against the moon.

Here, I inhale
the night wind bouquet
from which the violet violins
play through all my dreams.

My Advice To The Media

by David A. McHattie

Please be silent and let your burbling
   succumb to autumn's breath.
Where your caterwauling and cacophony
   will hopefully meet a timely death.
Please be silent as your thrumming is an
   affront to all who read this space.
Where your clamor and your blaring
   have become the cause for our disgrace.
Please be silent for there are far better
   voices straining to be heard.
And repeating a prevarication in louder tones
   does not make it less absurd.
Please be silent as your clatter is made bitter
   by a wretched desperate throng.
Who feast upon each bit of meat you tear,
   no matter right or wrong.
Please be silent as you add nothing of value
   to a discourse that has lost its humble way.
With your pathetic desire for fear and chaos
   to make dark the light of day.
So my friend, my dear dear friend, please be silent
   as there are things you need to hear.
As when an Angel who by the Grace of God
   wants to whisper in your ear.
"If you must create this hell on Earth,
   do it quietly and please contain your stress.
You have kept us up for far too long
   and we all need to get some rest."

The End

Acquisition Of A Fresh Perspective

by Richard Carl Evans

will you please wake up
but first signal where
you will place your dreams
not there my grey hair
and nitro tablets might not mix
your eyes so matter-of-factly
smack me upon my brow
a reminder of how the years
can grow grass through concrete
or turn boulders to sand
forgive me if I piffle
forgive me if I bore
but you must know that I
can't piss like a stripling anymore

A Cowboy Poem

by Steven Kopko

I was riding on the range
And I was feeling pretty good.
All the cattle were behaving.
They were running like they
 should.

The sun was just a-setting
In a blaze of orange and red.
And my dog was acting frisky
Like a pup that's been well fed.
I had planned to build a campfire,
So, I chopped myself some wood.
Then I cooked my steak and beans

And I can tell you they were good.

I pulled off my leather boots
You know the ones you buy in
  town.
I took out my heavy blanket
And prepared to settle down.

Alongside Salvation

by Richard Carl Evans

I am the seed hoping for soil
enriched with tears from the sky
a sun so warm one must pause
the rays perched upon the eyes
I could grow in solitude
escaping from this pod
then grab hold of the earth
to become one with fertile sod
so long as I can bloom
and launch precious seeds
some across a dormant summer sky
to sprout flower, bush, or tree
in the heavens I might travel
farther than the bald eagle
though I may end as fodder
for crows who squawk and banter
I am the seed hoping for you

Ankle Deep

by Gary Smith

This morning chilled me to the bone,
For frost had crazed my window panes
'Twas hard to leave my cosy home,
For given choice I would remain.

But no, there's pennies to be earned

For what in life is ever free,
So into winter's arms I turned,
To face grey skies and misery.

But I found to my surprise,
My street was deep in virgin snow,
Falling from a pearl white sky
To decorate the land below.

Such childish pleasure did I take
As I stepped in, ankle deep,
It brought a smile to my face,
To feel the crump, beneath my feet.

Without A Dream

by Sandra Weiss

Dreams that were, have withered and died.
The remains lay scattered upon the sand.
A breeze will send them into the tide.
I reach out but pull back an empty hand.

Life without dreams, barren ground to sow.
Wondering what would be next to die?
A vast wasteland, where nothing will grow.
No looking ahead, all else is a lie.

Live your dream, just words to say.
What is life with no thought of tomorrow?
Confused, I falter, trying to find my way.
Decaying dreams, swept away by sorrow.

Never Give Up

by Walter Daniel Tomeo

Never give up,
There's a dream in your name;
Never stop,
Nothing ever stay the same.

The day also gets tired,
The night too closes its eyes;
Your dream builds wings from the sphere,
Your sad face draws a new smile.

Never stop believing,
Rise yourself as a kite in the winds;
Our blood is of one color,
And it is faith that breaks a day.

The Silence Of An Empty House

by Shirley Rebstock

The silence of an empty house
Once I craved the silence
Seeking peace and quiet
Now the silence is deafening
Each day without my spouse

I go room to room
Seeking, hoping, left with despair
The silence echoing in my ears
The noise more than I can bear

If only I could hear the whisper in my ear
I love you
It is you I adore
Then I would whisper back
I love you more

The silence of an empty house
Is deafening to my ears
Yet I can hear my heart breaking
And the drop of every tear

Goodbye My Love

A Drunken Rant

by Abdul Malik Mandani

Oh, you say you love me; is it true?
The sky, it appears, is blue; is it blue?
I lived a long life without a damn clue,
If ever I find God anywhere, I'll sue.
Methinks, it's the devil I better pursue
Set aside holy water and beer I brew.
Go and pick a gang of disgruntled crew
to steal the Dog Star its brilliant hue,
And garner the dawn's glistening dew.
Live a lot dandy if all the knowledge I knew
and up from the sky get a bird's-eye view,
Or obtain from the Mystic a divine cue,
Untaught, soon much anguish could ensue;
Maybe, put aside my search and quietly rue
At long last bid to the world my sad adieu!

Sonnet From The Porch On Geese

by John G. Lawless

Why linger still upon an ice bound pond
lone feathered symbol huddled warm and dry
dine upon the fresh sweet sprouting frond
unable to assault the fleeing sky.

Bloodline circle beckons join the draft
can nature's simple truth become undone

weary wings abandon ageless craft
passing on the future to the young.

I cannot travel with them all their days
nor burden gaggle with slow flapping wings
while longing for the feel of old sun rays
watch as they depart for future springs

Thus rendered faster in their flight
seeking out their day and I my night.

Schizophrenia

by Shirley Candy Helen Wontas

Strange dreams blend with reality. A true
Compliments toward rejection.
Haunted by
Irrational voices;
Zoomed.
Outrageously tortured. Presents
Paranoid delusions, as well as
Hallucinations. Then, consciousness;
Run, seceded. Became
Extremely dried. So
Noticeable and rapid.
Ironic, yet dramatic.
A pure self-imposed isolation.

Song Of Your Soul

by William Darnell, Sr.

Sing a song of your soul,
Let it soar on the wings of your spirit
Live the tune of your love so loud
All the world will take notice and hear it.

The gift of your very presence;
Marks your place of worth as a person

Rejoice, and be forever grateful
The day of our journey on earth, to be certain.

Find your passions, and decide,
Who and what you want to become
Create your life and move on ahead
You're not defined by where you have begun.

The race for humankind is yours;
Not the boundaries of any one nation
Stand, and shine in the light of who you are
A beloved and glorious creation.

Reply Email From Subby Conscience

by Gail Rickless DeBole

To: gadeb@zzzsmail.com
From: Subby Conscience
Re: Communication between You and Me
Date: February 14, 2012

While I sneak and scheme in your chaotic REM
I am doing nothing more than being a friend.

Those dream-swirls and 'mare-tugs purge your mind's eye
so that your psyche can grow and won't suddenly die.

While you're gripping tightly to antique feelings that won't budge
I'm prying them out; giving them a strong nudge.

And as you grudgingly work through a feeling or two
I am working my hardest to make you feel what is true.

I even may help you work out a solution or two
Because during the day you are too busy to.

Who else provides perks that allow you to be
both young and old in the very same dream?

So tell me dear, and answer me this.
What would you do if many nights I missed

And was sneaking around in another soul's REM
What would your sanity be like then?

Without my help to work out thoughts
That keep you quite sane...

Would you then turn around
And try to cast blame?

Saying Subby's absence caused you to act like a drip?
Saying Subby's absence caused your tongue to Freudian slip?

Instead your mind can skyrocket and cozily soar
After I recede in the A.M. and work behind your mind's door.

Morning Breaks

by Nicholas Windle

A farewell twinkle from the morning star,
As darkness leaves, on fleeting wings.
The driftwood left of yesterday,
As life anew begins.

My eyes drawn to the cliffs above,
its granite outstretched hand,
Mighty proud and awesome,
As they push up through the sand.

Never ending with relentless zeal,
The sea is pounded at the stone.
carved and weathered, in crevice deep,
as a blade that's now been honed.

The rolling tide she beckons,
As I walk the morning shore.
Waves cry out like a sirens song,
As she enchants all, with her call.

For upon breeze it seems to say,
Come join me if you dare.
A trance like state that draws you in,
So all out there beware.

As sparkling water laps my feet,
The sensation of sand now warmed.
A shimmering sun now rising,
Signals the coming of the dawn.

With the idyllic beauty of a painting,
On which the brush still wet.
As tomorrow now becomes today,
A new canvas we shall get.

Race By Tooth Colour

by Agona Apell

I judge men by the colour of their teeth,
And by the colours of their teeth I group them:
The Whites we have,
The Blacks we have,
The Browns we have,
And the Yellows too.

Life we all start as Whites, and with good care
Whites we remain.
With less care Yellows we become;
With yet lesser care Browns we become;
And with least care to Blacks we turn.
'Tis thus that our descent down the rungs of color
Often bespeaks our personal quality.

By effort and discipline Blacks, Browns, and Yellows
are sometimes to Whites restored:
So it is that men can choose what color they'll be
If by tooth not skin we judge their color.
There is song and speech in the colors of their teeth

From which can be gleaned glimpses of their habits
and hints of their mettle.
But neither song nor speech we find in their skins
Which are born mute, live mute, and die mute.

So if ever you hear my skin speak,
Spinning tales of my habits and mettle,
Rather look up my teeth and hear their side.
They lack a tan but speak a tonne--
That much I know from my years on earth.
The whole truth they may not give
But what you get is closer to it!

Rain And All

by Lycia Harding

Wind, as her final rainstorm gathers,
gathers up the orphaned leaves
Leaves some tucked in between the rocks,
rocks some to sleep beneath the trees

Trees, moved so by her (rain and all)
all bow and trying not to cry,
cry now and silvered leaves of fall,
fall as they watch their Zephyr die

Throw Off This Earth

by Leo Larry Amadore

We wear this earth
            and bear the heft of stones,
  glacier-galled, polished by
                eons of slow crawl
                    toward far-too-distant
          views, which call us
from our blue, thin-air shell,
                this shallow soil where,
  weak,

the hold of roots restrain.
We struggle to break free
from such restrictive strata,
to expand -- as bubbles rise
and glisten -- to throw off
this world -- to emerge,
new born from natal egg --
and, freed,
to flee among the stars.

Grey Garden

by Amanda Fowler

Lingering longing hung like gallows, blossoming shadows of bliss to seed her love.
Barriers of brick, metal and plastic confining the flourishing depths of her roots.
Shadowing walls of hurt and anguish, threatening to veil the sunshine in which all true colors need to thrive.
All beauty that does exist is fleeting back to the cosmos.
Stretching to its limits, incomplete the stem is weak but leaves and petals shine.
Nurturing the importance of life against all odds, knowing there is nothing you can do to fix it.
You just trust in your heart that your pollen will be carried to a place that illuminates the grey garden.
Spreading like invasive love-struck souls in harmony.
May the meadow of her existence envelope future struggles and fertilize the soils of her bounty.

Maggie And Porter

by Evelyn Pearl Anderson

Come meet two of my former patients;
A nursing home room they did share
Maggie was blind; Porter became her eyes
Finding, picking up, helping her

He was kind. Her mind had slipped - or had it?
"Porter, I lost my comb," said to mate
Frail as he was, under the bed he went
Crawling for Maggie - deliberate

Day in and day out he would meet her needs;
She contrived to keep him near her hand,
Porter this and Porter that - it did seem
Though they each understood the commands

The nurses would come to help as needed.
Then, on that morning when a stillness
Penetrated the room reverently
Quietly sitting slumped by her bed

No answer; no movement; just sitting there;
Porter dressed for his daily tasks,
He had fallen asleep when breathing ceased
He had given all that was asked

"Porter, Porter, help me," was softly heard
"Porter, Porter, please answer me,
 Porter, Porter, where are you?" asked again.
"Porter's gone. He loved you, Maggie."

Follow The Yellow Brick Road

by Florence McMillian

As I was walking
Along my chosen path
Where each step marks
A notch this world hath
I caught a glimpse of
A Yellow Brick Road
Like the one from Oz
Once long ago told
Now how the glimpse
Came my way
I chose a path to take

On a sunny day
Back to work from break
Strolling merrily along
Head held high with joy
Whistling a happy song
I jumped over a little crack
Just purposely out of my way
Being sure to be aware
Never matters which day
As I came up to my office
Tapping a rock with my heel
Then the feeling hit me
The vision seemed very real
A comparison factor in our minds
Creating obstacles out of fear
Or do we step over them
To prove we are there
It's our choice to place sunshine
On the path we choose to go
Thus creating a happy path
To Follow the Yellow Brick Road

Crimson Sky

by Maria Paz Samelo

Looking at the horizon
Sky turned into crimson

Feeling of great happiness
Winds blows with sweet caress

Amazing God's creation
To the nature's temptation

Pouring with fantastic view
Birds flying with lovely show

Sun may set for a while
But my lips will smile

Beautiful night to hail
With crimson sky I will sail

From A Distance

by Paul H. Schneiter

From a distance what I saw
in a Down Syndrome child
was a human in the raw—
forgettable, lamentable, wild.

My prejudice was abhorrent
dismissing a "different" being.
Disdain came in a torrent
driven by cold-eyed seeing.

Then came a close-up look
at a new grandson in my arms.
My bias I forthwith forsook
lost in his extra-gene charms.

Almond-shaped eyes, short fingers
flat nose—those one observes.
But the trait that ever lingers
is a smile an angel deserves.

The sight remodels the mind,
assures that nothing is awry.
Anything like it you won't find
regardless of how hard you try.

From a distance what we see
is often not what we suppose.
The virtues of human intimacy
universal truths ultimately disclose.

Go Away Yesterday

by Brian L Lowmiller

Drunk on emotions she wandered,
through forests of anguish and pondered,
vile, those years squandered;
>   go away yesterday.

Breathless she runs through life,
tumbling in rivers of strife,
memories like a cutting knife;
>   go away yesterday.

"Meadows are easily forsaken" says she,
"when beasts of regret roam free,"
"slay them that I may live peaceably";
>   go away yesterday.

Alas, she wanders still,
round each bend looms anxieties hill,
her destiny guided by will;
>   go away yesterday.

Boiling Over

by Gabrielle Jordan

angst overflowed
pouring thoughts into a legitimacy
I had been told

best left not to unsettle
what has been imposed

but that corrosive tolerance
will slow drip life if left seeded

a door that had guarded a frail lock
began to creak open

I ran fingers of my mother through my thick natural hair
defiant to be reckoned with
strong willed wild free
and knowing its privileged place in history

an ironic impression

I am reminded in haste that there are those
that are offended by the coils of my tree
why is it again that I am not allowed
to just exist and be free?

that toil was at cost
ripped from sacred ground
dumped onto a seized land

an orphan

bowing over backwards
tears on cheeks ever turning
left unbalanced muzzled bound and burning

the deception manicured for generations to come
diligently working to despise and degrade
introducing fear of God in attempt to contain

now woke and on fire

abandoned justice is being freed from her chains

the regret should come as the present teacher
not as the dead reminder

The Seventh Day

by Lycia Harding

Stillness. Darkness, in this place
Thought that starts as arcs of light,
shot through hollow parts of space
Henceforth, day shall follow night

I create a stratosphere,
which I lay atop a sea
Day and night shall rotate here,
trading for eternity

To the edge, I bind a land
Vines aburst with fruit and flower,
Orchards lined across the sand
Eden's first and finest hour

Moon and stars such light will bring!
Just as much shall fill the sun
Beauty must still touch a thing,
though it might be seen by none

From the air and water spring
creatures I have caused to grow
slick of scale and quick of wing
As above, so too, below

Fast four-legged beasts appear,
friend to foe their numbers span
Last, though slumber draws Me near,
in My image, I make man

With free will and virtue blessed,
choices tell the fate he'll earn
Go forth child, today I rest...
Choose thee well til I return

Sherkston

by Francis J Grasso

Mike was ridin' shotgun
I was sittin' on the hump
Ledford's got the steering wheel
There's the devil in our trunk

Drivin' up to Sherkston
For a day of sun an' fun
Doin' ninety miles an hour
That's how Jerry liked to 'run'

Headin' towards bikini beach
On a road called Thunder Bay
Flying by the local yuks
And laughin' all the way

Glove box stuffed with Genny Cream
Women filled our head
Passin' blind on narrow roads
Lucky we're not dead

Jerry pulls out left again
To pass this lumberin' truck
But there's a 'semi' comin' up ahead
I think we need some luck

Jerry's wearin' a devil grin
Gas pedal's on the floor
I'm just hangin' on for life
As we hear that big truck roar

In just a half a heartbeat
that Ford swerves to the right
Jerry's grinnin' ear to ear
Mike pees his pants from fright

Jerry dives from the high board

A graceful perfect swan
I meet these cool hot chicks 'bout then
While Mike puts clean shorts on

I Walk Upon The Fallen Leaves

by Stephen Mayne

I walk upon the brown, orange, golden, fallen leaves
From silent standing, now dormant trees.
That stand and rest at this time of ease

With no one to impress, or even to please.
They stand naked now, everything else gone with the autumn breeze.
They've let the past go and have nothing to grieve.

I look upon these magnificent, standing, inspirational trees.
Not with sadness for their loss, but with an element of glee.
As I understand their wisdom, that they depart to me.

Their time will come again, when leaves and branches begin to interweave.
A rebirth with new vigour, they begin to grow and breathe.

Love

by Suzanne Johnson

I was at my desk when in he came.
His hair was dark, his eyes the same.
Excited, I blurted, almost a shout.
"Hey you, would YOU like to go out?"

His smile told me all I needed to know.
And that was over thirty years ago!
We're married now, for twenty years.
Most of that was filled with tears.

He drank, he lied, he ran away.
But I still loved him to this day.

Ten years ago, consumed with strife.
He put down the bottle and took back his life.

His eyes are still dark, his hair not so much.
His smile is for me and so is his touch.
I weathered the bad times and cherished the good.
The first time I saw him, I knew that I would.

Still my love!

I've Found My Freedom

by Stephen Mayne

I've found my freedom
An epiphany happened in the night
Somethings woken in me
I've regained my sight

I've cut the shackles, ropes and restraints
Though not all physical
They added to my weight

I've let my mind go free
Let go of everything hindering me

Now impervious to my egos desires
I've found a true freedom
Fulfilling all I require

September's Song

by Richard Carl Evans

how I love the fall
its tempered coolness
and gusts of wind transport leaves
and emotion across miles and miles of earth
the dry secular heat of summer
that turned my heart to kindling

and filled the streets with barren ideals
has come to an end
along with this seasonal change
my sorrow like the fallen leaves
slowly begins to decompose

Syria

by Maryam Musharraf

On This day I picked your eyes
And wrote in my diary
Snow is gazing guys
Buries within

I am a giant heater who
Welcomes you all in my quarters
And my hands are so so big
That the Hell they bestow you will

The black giant came then close to me
And the sky went all dark
Like grand ma's eyes
My parent are the same color as ground
And I am the same color as ground
The soil takes care of me
Since my parents reside in ground

Passion

by Catherine Johnson Broussard

By HIS Words, I am forgiven, HIS Merciful PASSION;
without IT; where would I be?
I have fallen; HIS mercy has lifted me.
IT surrounds me; ever so mighty, yet stillness.
I thirst, I pray that I not be weary.
HE will strengthen me, HIS Greatness;
forever surrounding me;

never wavering; giving me breath.
Oh; HIS Glory; I will seek always;
never forsaking me; keeping HIS Promise;
by HIS PASSION, I am forgiven.

For Gail

by Douglas S Brown

I stand guard
in the heavily trafficked night
while you search in your sleep
among the bones
of lost loves.

Celebrate My Death

by Ibrahim Wonsebolatan Bashiru

I want you to celebrate my death
Even if I was to die tomorrow
Shed no tears, curse no gods
But do say a prayer for me

I want you to celebrate my passing
For that's what life is
A long road that will surely come to an end
In my footprint you will see that I have lived my fill

Wanted to fly and I have flown
Wanted to dance and I have danced with sweat soaked shirt
Wanted to sing and I have sang
Wanted a little one to call mine and my Fatima shine so bright

Mourn me not when I am gone (mourn me not for now I rest)
Just say a few kind words
Let the angels know of the man I hoped have been
Let them take your words to Allah Almighty that's above

Paradise I hope to call home

This life is only my journey towards it
I hoped, have chosen my path right
At every crossroad that was a test

For the wrong paths that have led
Hoped have found forgiveness with my creator Allah
Hoped with His mercy new paths have emerged
To take me to home

Don't cry over this body of mine
From clay it was made to clay it shall returned
Just prayed that it find peace in the ground
Not punishment promised to the disbeliever

Pity me not for the life that could have been
I have faith that my life has been all that its meant to be
Have prayed for death to take me when my time is up
When I have Allah Mercy and a place by my beloved Prophet Muhammad
(peace be upon him)

Celebrate my death even if I was to die tomorrow
If corpse could cry, my will shed tears for you
For your journey still continue
And you are still far from home

The Huntsman's Plight

by Dean Earl Wood

In darkened wood he takes a knee and weeps
The blood trail's gone, and with it all that's good
He knows not where the stag has gone to sleep
His children's aching bellies want for food

The blood trail's gone, and with it all that's good
Dappled shadows hide the trail he seeks
His children's aching bellies want for food
A stoic face belied by tear-washed streaks

Dappled shadows hide the trail he seeks
Until the sun reveals it at his feet
A stoic face belied by tear-washed streaks
With hope restored that soon his brood will eat

Until the sun reveals it at his feet
He knows not where the stag has gone to sleep
With hope restored that soon his brood will eat
In darkened wood, he takes a knee and weeps

The Welcome Trespasser

by Gail Rickless DeBole

You quietly hold your head
high as you stand on
the grassy bank - never
gazing back at me.

Your head and neck play
games with the alphabet
as they gracefully
curve into an "S".

Human boundaries
have no meaning to
you as you gracefully
catch fish next to a
well-worn No Fishing sign.

I think of all of the
times I have watched
unknowing you as you
catch what I suppose is
your lunch...

...in your beak,
Mr. Crane.

Aging Gracefully

by David I Mayerhoff

Up in the morning
body a puzzle
with various layers
going in and out of
this dimension

Liver enraged
legs projecting
a different plane of reality
than the arms

Muscle fiber groups
looking for their chorus
to sing a symphony
instead playing a lot of solos

Spleen laughing hysterically
at what
no one knows
least of all the brain
which keeps sending signals
that no one wishes to hear

Bowels and guts
keep making fun
of each others'
names and comportment

Kidneys about
to break through the damn
despite the bladder paying its taxes
to keep the water out

Nervous system
does not have the heart

to grieve
this state of affairs

Noises and strange motions
coming from everywhere
going nowhere fast

Joints at wrong angles
each one
blaming the other
and the pillow

Then a loud yawn
and breakfast is served

Anne-Sophie Mutter - The Club Album
by Gordon McConnell

As a great lover of classical music
over many years the violin became ace
one particular lovely lady enchanted me
Anne-Sophie Mutter classically first place

This lady appeared in the Yellow Lounge
a night club in Berlin, she did astound
the Club Album played out such true class
covering composers splendidly crowned

Classical music doesn't normally appeal
in such an establishment it is pretty rare
but the clientele loved this classic treat
as Anne-Sophie served them such fare

Thankfully this performance was recorded
being on CD and DVD covered release
composers like Vivaldi, Gershwin and Bach
stunningly superb richness on each piece

Love to watch this many times over
never fails to hold me in its grip

such musical feast left in wonder
takes one sailing aboard strings ship

A Pastoral Tragi-Comedy

by Newton Ranaweera

A pastoral tragi-comedy – twelve hours long.
It begins with twilight: the day's oozing hours,
Creating somber music of a melancholic song:
The theme song to mourn fall of day's powers.

Night rain begins to flood the glamorous plain,
Inspiring dark shadows to release, stormy reign.

Each sneaks in, tiptoeing, after a helpless pray,
Seizes or play with it before, the dawn of day.

This classic tale does not, thus, miserably end.
Moon, the dimmed lantern, with her fireflies
Leaves all, yet allowing sovereign sun to send,
Crystal rays to dawn the day, and cease our cries.

Our Paradise—My Sweet Love: Linking Pin Sonnet

by Joseph S. Spence Sr

My sweetest love hearest thou reverently my advice
My advice is to leave now for our home—in paradise.
Paradise blooming with rainbows and tasty red cherries
Cherries, delicious mangoes, and bright sweet berries.

Berries with our cottage in the midst with a skylight
Skylight, gingerbread, and sunset—await us at twilight.
Twilight and misting rain for showers on our lawn
Lawn where we sing sweet songs with birds at dawn.

Dawn where firefly's lights soothing sweet moods

Moods with ravens bringing us nice nourishing food.
Food while sparrows build our soft resting nest
Resting nest, my dear love—my darling, my sweetest.

Sweetest we will wish upon the mellow shining stars,
Stars shining above us—where we shall not be far!

Couplet-19

by Simon Rogerson

Two metres apart
Is where we start
Then self-isolate
Before it's too late
Wash your hands
Else virus expands
Using PPE
Helps safety
Society shut
We all stay put
Food shops empty
Used to be plenty
No supermarket trawl
Just Internet haul
But what of the old
Whose lives now unfold
There's no face-to-face
Now virtual place
We laugh, we sing, we joke
Keeps spirits up for us folk
Videos to see
WhatsApp glee
Woman's sneeze
Toddler flees
Toilet roll
Not cash he stole
Human environmental attack
Pandemic weapon – nature fights back
World at war
Like never before

So many go that extra mile
Never happened for such a long while
Good things can come out of so much pain
Self-centred actions we all must refrain
Once over it's time to rethink
As humanity steps back from the brink
Wake up call
For us all

Receptive

by Brian Sambourne

In the songbird's throat
    a palette of colours
    startling flair
    in the white lace of morning sun
    tiny fierceness
    that shears the forest with its bravado
    deliriously unselfish
    unbroken vocal spear
For a hiker, in statue like calm
    closing cluttered thoughts
    discarding tidy self musings
    his receptive ear to the rosy pulse of song
    to recall his beau with perfect pitch
    displacing willed isolation

Chorus of vanity from a winged creature
    that skips through a wounded forest
    to wash away a world stained
In notes pure, like ripples of water on a hiker's brow.

Teardrops From Our Souls

by Ingrid Lehman

The raindrops fall as we stand close.
Drips wet your lashes, slick back your hair,
Once thick black curls, soft through my fingers.
Now thinning, with grey sprinkled throughout.

We kiss once.... twice, then hold on tight.
Our eyes connect, the sadness flows.
I search your soul, see loneliness....
But you must go, you say to me,
Enjoyed your company, and off you dash.

The rain keeps falling, a grey day indeed.
I'm left with wondering if you're ok.......
After everything was said and done,
Somehow, I feel I've let you down.
The tears slowly run down my cheeks,
Mixed with raindrops that keep falling,
Like tear drops from our souls.

Her Talent

by Anne E Sangster-Keeley

Creating her artwork from silky fine thread
She carefully wove it and knew where to tread
The pattern she worked on was cleverly laid
Displaying her craft by those who had stayed
The fruits of her labour were well worth the time
For her talent in webs ensured she would dine

Through The Breath Of Divinity's Passing

by George Stathakis

Upon the majestic peak I stood
The wind against my face
It is there I felt
The breath of nature's passing.

Transfixed by presence
I journeyed into the mystery of the unknown
To find in the depths of tranquility
A revelation in my being.

A tree, a stream, a mountain peak
Revealing internal truth
And a calming state of consciousness
Through the breath of Divinity's passing.

Greatness

by Ansar Mohammed

I have been pondering for quite some time,
Is there a permanence to the meaning of the word 'greatness'?
Whatever does it mean 'to be great' or 'to feel great'?

You see, from ever since, I've attached its meaning to superiority,
Something unreachable, beyond my wildest imagination.
With branches beyond the skies,
which climax at levels exceeding human capability.
And thick, fibrous roots so deeply entrenched,
that they become onerous to deracinate.

But over the years, my realisation has surprised me.
I have recognised that greatness has distinctive,
yet instinctive qualities.

Much like a budding and unfolding bouquet of roses,
Its perfume is subjective.
Pungent to some, but fragrant and elegant to others.
Its vessel comes in different forms,
Some curved, thin, or well figured.
And its florets can bud, bloom, change colour or even decay,
depending on the level of care.

Similarly, I have discerned that greatness resides in each of us.
Its aura is unfastened by our creativity and vision.
And it is unbarred by the similitude of unreached potential,
encasement or bewilderment.

And, at last, there cannot be any fixity to its meaning.
Rather, there is much subjectivity, intuitivity and reason,
that we must open ourselves up to receive.

I hope you receive and accept your feeling of greatness,
in whatever form it appears.

Love & Light.

The Colourful Empyrean

by Shonima Burman

A place so serene with myriad colours,
With nature's beauty so plenty,
Yet wild!
A land full of rivers, lakes, ponds, hot springs, and volcanoes
A wandering eye would love to behold,
But!
Neither the springs have water,
Nor the lakes are azure,
Neither the ponds are crystal clear,
Nor the lava is red.
Instead!
Hot springs are made of sulphur,
Emitting bright yellow colour.
The copper-laced lakes,
Are of turquoise tinge.

The ponds are of bright green hue,
Made of sulfuric acid,
Surrounded by red, yellow, and orange minerals.
Lava burns blue,
Volcanic lava oozes out,
In blue, green, yellow, and red colour.
Hillocks of salt cover the terrains.
River dries up never to reach the ocean.
One must be wondering that,
Am I in a tottering dream?
Or I must be lost in the mesmerizing world of colours!
But far away in the,
Land of Ethiopia,
Lavishly flourished with vibrant and dazzling colours,
A piece of land with phantasmagoric beauty,
Known as the Danakil Depression.
Some call it the "Gateway to Hell",
To some it is the "Land of killer Lakes".
The weather here is not magnanimous.
Rather harsh with blistering hot sunbeams.
Yet habitat to some people,
Who call it their abode.
When the sun sets over lake Karum,
Darkness takes over,
Only the starry night,
Stares silently,
On this unearthly land.

Wind Chime

by Anisha Dutta

Wind-chime swings, rings,
hanging in my garden,
since I had shifted
to my new house.
My Dad had gifted
on house -warming,
confirming
charm of tinkling

of light hollow brass balls,
sweet whistling of wind
through chinks of wind-chime.

Wind-chime swings, rings,
brings blessing of Dad.
My bliss! My pleasure.
Peerless treasure.
An eraser
of evil and devil.

Dad had passed away
leaving blessings
to resonate with
tinkling and whistling of wind -chime.

Separate-Ly, Equal-Ly, Together-Ly
by Betty Robinson

What if we'd met at Jackson Memorial in the neonatal ward,
Placed ever so gently, side by side, facing the outside world?
And our parents and relatives and friends they had
Giggled thru an oversized window
And waved and pointed and cooed at us,
Two tiny babies in little pink blankets with silly hats on our heads.
The joy of our grandparents. The meaning to life.
Heirs to the family misfortunes.
We Separate-ly, Equal-ly, Together-ly went home to be loved by all.
And walking and talking and learning to trust
Were taught in our childhood years.
And you learned to sing, "Amazing Grace"
At the A.M.E Church on the corner
And I learned to sing, "Amazing Grace"
At the Baptist church on the square.

We gossiped together each morning and "double dutch-ed" at lunch.
You angled me through geometry class as I read you through English Lit.
I cheered when you made cheerleader and you cried when I didn't.
We laughed when I made Homecoming Queen,
Went to Macy's and picked out a dress.

Then the day finally came, with diplomas in hand,
Throwing caution to the wind,
We Separate-ly, Equal-ly, Together-ly plunged into the outside world.
And through the years, no matter what, we stayed friends to the bitter end.
As husbands came and husbands went and the world grew up around us.
We loved and prayed and raised our babies.
We shared our families' misfortunes.
Together we sang "Amazing Grace" when people we loved went Home.
And never once in all that time did we ever look askance
That you are a woman of color and I am some shade of white.

He Painted The Sky

by Gary Smith

Tangerine, crimson, aquamarine
Behold the sunrise, an artist's palette
Such vivid colours they conjure a scene
Truly so lovely, my favourite and yet

Coral and lemon with a lilac hued tinge
The soft touch of lavender delights me too,
Beautifully set in a saffron rich fringe
A watermelon finish, chartreuse peeping through.

Look to the heavens some clear early morn
Take it all in, a treat for the eye
A kaleidoscope feast, the day now reborn
How wondrous the Lord... he painted the sky.

Spring - Haiku

by Annanya De

Golden rays of sun
Amidst echoes of birdsong
Shine on fresh green grass

Pretty pink flowers
Covering the tree branches
Spring's cherry blossoms

Sweet smelling nectar
Lingering in the cool breeze
Buzzing all around

Spaghetti

by Ann Foster

The meat,
the cheese,
the sauce.

The smiles,
the laughs,
the wine.

The music,
the song,
the moment...

The vow of forever!

Then...

You and I,
and the garlic bread!

Unlearned Love

by Jonathan Jordan Sutarima

Emotions are small.
Emotions are still.
Or so I've learned as a matter of will.

Because when emotions were tall

When I gave it all and had my fill
The highs and lows burned; so quiet emotion became my skill.

I learned restraint and guard
Learned to fake all things hard.
Learned loads to unlearn on later roads.

Attitudes change with understanding and life's range.
Learning love became easy when purely showed.
Working wildly to become this new love is strange.
Absences have done their work and I no longer feel.
You've filled the gaps: you've led me to heal.
Soul and song, head and heart, you've won from me in the deal.

Confidence instilled in me now
Overwhelming evidence of an unwavering bond.
Matchless and marvelous are you, my love
Even if you cannot always see how.

Babbling words cannot explain; but I'm able in a vow.
Amnesia would be a pain, that magic memory wand.
Calling my memories away alone could not get rid of
Knowledge of you and keep me away somehow.

I have failed to love; that is in the past.
I would crawl over broken things--dreams, glass—for this to last.
Losing memory of you would surely fill me with sorrow.
But I'd never stop trying to come home til tomorrow.

Sunday Morning

by Leo Larry Amadore

The morning comes, dawning
slowly, as I arise once more --
mind meandering, sleepily yawning,
sunlight creeping through my door.

My mewing cat demands a morning meal
while distant church bells faintly peal

and traffic sounds invade the room.
Coffee briskly brews; the cat begins to groom.

I grab a glass of breakfast juice -- the minutes pass
as I drink it down then get the paper from the grass.
I brush off the dew, read the news,
the comic strips and op-ed views.

My coffee cools; dumb opinions heat me up.
To calm myself, I re-warm my too cold cup
then turn to hear pure music's psalm.
No rapping please -- just melody's sweet balm.

What Do You See

by Florence McMillian

While sitting there quietly
Before us we take in a view
All things are seen differently
Between us all as well as you

For some the sight is scary
With the evil glaring through
While others visualize beauty
Filled with joyful happiness too

A few will have the weeds they see
With dead plants and even bugs too
Others look at flowers and every tree
While admiring where each one grew

From one's mind comes the visibility
Developed within the heart of you
Let our walk guide us with integrity
As the Lord will test our minds too

We have free will to choose actually
As we learn the right and wrong to do
So you are sure to get what you see
Just like we reap what we sow is true

The wickedness really tries to get me
The righteous path is hard to get thru
I will always seek for the good diligently
Keeping Jesus close by my side as I do

Visions may be distorted and blurry
When we carry many burdens too
We should be accepting it all gladly
Even if the load gets heavy for you

Blessings come through adversity
On that difficult path to pursue
So looking out WHAT DO YOU SEE
Is that the right vision for you

Florence McMillian (Flo)

Poetry Is Not

by Melani Udaeta

Poetry is not a repeating phrase
totally limiting your unlimited mind,
Soullessly following another's rules
knowingly pushing your thoughts aside;

Celebrate what's inside of you
extrapolate your soul's unique dance;
Elevate that inner rhythm
create your own perfect cadence.

This Is Who I Am

by Tawananyasha Rambanapasi p

You will never fit in! is my everyday alarm .
My emotions so hackneyed to that venom
That like water off a duck's back has no effect.
Hide away they tell me, because we cannot bare to look at you

The dark has become my companion, the citadel of refuge to whom I can always flee so that I'm invisible to many.

Wherever I am, I try so much to be the ghost,
Unnoticed and invisible.
Because if I am noticed I know that like a thousand arrows the words will stab me to death
Before I realise it.

They say I love the mirror
but that is not the case
I am trying to identify, to spot,
To analyze what you say is wrong with me.
What you tease me of!
But sadly I cannot seem to find it
I shall not cease to look in the mirror
Maybe one day I shall see it too
But for now I AM BEAUTIFUL THE WAY I AM.

Once Upon A Moments Time

by David Joel Walker

Once
I learned to walk I walked
Once
I learned to run I ran
Once
I learned to talk I talked

Once
Was when my life began

Once
I learned to read I read
Once
I learned to love I lost
Once
I learned to seek I said
Once
A penny paid the cost

Once
An hour past a day
Once
A flower fades
Once
An answer stopped to say
Once
The debt is paid

Once
Upon a time a clock
Once
A day to strike the chime
Once
A mountain now a rock
Once
A moment caught in time

The Gaslighter

by Cindy Bahl

Contempt carves her soul
He wants her pain to sustain
His pleasure is cruel

Only Now Is Promised

by Cindy Bahl

nothing awakens love,
and the soul,
like forgetting destiny is cruel
to those who forget moments are fleeting

fate never promises a future,
not to anyone,
especially to those who neglect
appreciating the gifts the universe bestows upon them

pay attention,
always pay attention,
this moment is the only promise
that will be kept to you

The Twin Oak

by Janis Medders Thompson

There is a tree
A large twin oak
That's watched the lives
Of this farm's folk
A double trunk
Grows from the ground
Becoming one huge
Grand one found
Within the field
That saw the lives of
Jimmy, San and
Johnny thrive
So many others
Did it see
Within the years
This grand old tree

And now beneath its glorious shade
The shadows of the loved ones
Fade, in and out of moonlit nights
Gone but present in our sights

When I Die

by Jane Carter

When my allotted time is spent, and Death arrives to claim me,
Don't lay me in a field of stones, beneath an ancient yew tree.

Find a place where vibrant flowers grow and joy and love abound,
And there below the fragrant blooms, set my ashes in the ground.

I know your heart is breaking, you bear a pain as sharp as glass,
But ride the changing waves of grief, and know this too shall pass.

Don't spend time wishing for a different past, and mourning all I'll miss,
I'm in a place outside the pull of human care, far beyond the precipice.

My mortal coil has shuffled off and all that's left are memories for you.
Don't bury me in sorrow, remember me with love and let me live anew.

So, share stories of my time on Earth, talk about my life in all its parts,
And with every smile and laugh I'll exist again, deep within your hearts.

The Shape Of Water

by Emile Joseph Pinet

Try to wrap your mind around a gust of wind
a rainbow or the shape of water.
Let your thoughts swim in a pool of imagination
and dive into the depths of abstract
and let it help you define what defies definition.

You can inhale a breath of air
and you can feel the wind on your face,

but can you describe its shape?
The wind, although tactile, is invisible,
and it's constantly transforming itself.

You can envision a rainbow arched across the sky,
and yet, it's ethereal, without mass or weight.
A magical illusion composed of water and light,
it only appears to be substantial.

You can see, smell, feel, and taste water,
even observe its magnificence as clouds.
But can you sculpt water
or describe it based on its shape?
Our mind connects all of those missing dots,
so we can make sense of this phantasmagorical world
contemplating the shape of water.

Momentary Assurance

by V.Deepa

I was in a sound sleep
    ahem.. ahem...
    ahem.. ahem...
Suddenly heard someone cough
Then, i quickly opened my eyes
to just find a heart lying on a thermal surface
wriggling & weeping for support
  Oh...unfortunately it was Mine..
My Brain had a stroke watching at a strange sight instantly..
Strong choking feel in my neck..
Mouth remained unclosed for people to hear my voice box scream..
Hands and legs were in paralysed state
Blood slowly kept dripping from my soul..
and tears leaking out of my glorious eyes
  Oops...there i stood ..
freezing into a lifeless statue..!

[struck by the storm of ephemeral stillness........]

Gosh..

I urgently wanted Life..!

Unexpectedly, there came my Hero
stood by my side
Gazed..
Gazed deeply into me
Finally touched with his magical fingers
And...wow
i saw myself ..
lying on the couch alive
On his...broad shoulder..!

The Dancer

by D Holmes

Early morning.
Sun climbing in its ascent
Over the mountain crescent lip
Throwing its fan of light.

The great log room quiet
As the player sits to begin.

The soft flowing notes
Fill the space
And the music unfolds in the quietness.

Lost in that aloneness of sound,
Out of the corner of his eye,
Wraith like she appears.

Dressed in a gauzy
Ballerina dress with off the shoulder straps,
The almost three year - old dancer glides
Silently with the moving notes,
Interpreting what she hears in her own way
Completing the circle of her quiet dreaming.

Switch Off The Telly

by Charlotte Wakeman

Switch off the telly
Calm the nerves in your belly
Release the stress from your head
Don't worry about what they said
Accepting ourselves though there are things we lack
To have a purpose and give something back
To be accepting of others our sisters and brothers
It's to share warmth and laughter, that's what we're all after
Breathe in the fresh cut grass, don't worry about the size of your arse.
Soak up the sunshine, feel it warm your bones
We will survive five minutes without our phone's.
Kick back and relax in your fuzzy socks and crocs,
I'll do the dinner, mashed potato and lamb chops?

Broken Egg

by Carol Louise Moon

I mourn for you, oh Mourning Dove.
Your egg lies broken on my porch.
You build yourself a modest nest
but jay flies here to scatter it.

You seek and find those sticks unfit
to build yourself a modest nest.
Your egg lies broken on my porch.
I mourn for you, oh Mourning Dove.

The Person You Are

by Stephen Mayne

I don't know who you are
I don't know where you're from
But to be quite honest, I couldn't give a damn.

But tell me my friend, are you aware, of the person you are?
Have you really ever explored or travelled all that far?

You tell me of all the people and places you've seen.
But have you ever stopped, to just take in the scene?
Have you always made your travels the best as it could've been?

Have you ever really experienced the joy of happiness?
Have you experienced the true sorrow of sadness?
Have you ever been to an outrageous party with savages?
Or do you prefer to sit at home and be content just growing cabbages?

What's in your heart?
What's in your soul?
These are the things that make us whole.

So tell me, not who you are.
Tell me, not from where you came
Tell me, not of your name, nor that you are from some sort of fame.
These things really don't matter in this life we treat as a game.

But do tell me, if you're a person who has stood outside to appreciate the rain.
Or helped a stranger, not for any reason, not for any gain.
Do tell me if you're a person who's empathetic to other people's emotion and pain.
Tell me these things and a true friendship will always remain.

A Rose

by Ann Oglesby Peck

You hoped she'd be strong like an agave;
instead, she bruised easily like a rose,
feelings like silken petals carelessly
scattered along paths she finally chose.

Full of daydreams, she was given her room
to search until able to find her roots.
Her step hesitant among other blooms
she followed, unthinkingly, larger shoots.

One day you lost her in morning's cool mist
hidden among thorns and those growing wild.
Was your care not sweet as a lover's kiss?
Or, was another keeping her beguiled?

She was barely herself on many days,
her eyes emblazoned by powerful lust.
Poppy dust became her truest soulmate,
the only bloom she was able to trust.

If the rose was yours to love, not to grieve,
would you allow her now to grow so free?
Or, instead, place a cage around her leaves,
stifling her inner spontaneity?

A thousand painful nights you ask yourself;
the answer possibly you'll never know.
Do You relive memories scene by scene,
until it becomes a bitter tableau?

She needed more days to live and enjoy
the good times that are now left unspoken.
time to grow into a majestic bush
before her stem bent, finally broken.

You thought, as other parents may have done,

all blossoms grow stronger in warm sunlight.
Yet some are withered by the noonday sun;
some perish quietly in a moonless night.

She was a soft and delicate flower
prone to bruises, yet eager to appease.
On a summer's night, she silently left:
a faded blossom on a gentle breeze.

Heroes Every One

by Dave Timperley

Heroes, every one.
They came in a trickle and then a flood,
To enlist in the forces to do some good.
They were turned from ordinary men,
Into frightening fighting machines.
Farmers, millers, tailors of clothes
Butchers, bakers, they came in droves,
They rallied at depots throughout the land,
Now ready and able waiting for the command.
To theatres of war, battalions deployed,
Generations of men, leaving villages void.
Leaving women and old men to watch their back,
Defending the realm from an enemy attack.
Battles raged across the world, the land was red,
Before it all ended there were millions of dead.
War graves across the ravaged lands cry out,
Here lies a hero that no one may doubt.
They died knowing freedom was worth the fight,
Shoulder to shoulder they stood and they died,
Regardless of race, colour or creed, they knew,
This war against tyranny they had to win through.
No matter what this modern age try to do to erase
the memory of these heroes, they will surely fail.
For if war comes again to threaten the world,
They will rise again to repel and prevail.
Lest we forget, which will be NEVER.

Night Of A Fallen Sky

by Alok Yadav

As the night foster, sank my fragile heart,
Because the frivolous moon began to play with my thoughts,
As gleam the the moon up high , heart began to go in deep,
Thinking of many butterflies that come to me and left ,
And of cemetery I went with flowers , bestowed,
With gangrene and extinguish bodies which once glowed,
The chain of thought broke , with a marvelous sight,
Once dead sun again stood for fight !
The sun rose for them , who burn and got too far,
Still night for them, who let exodus the stars!

This Forgotten Chapel

by Indiana Shaw

The walls ornate brass findings are long gone, and are no more
Years of dust and debris lie upon the now no longer used pews
Pieces of broken stained glass from the windows lie on the floor
In this small chapel, God is no longer the wanted religious news

Years of dust and debris lie upon the now no longer used pews
Old leather bound bibles, lie sprawled across the floor in misuse
In this small chapel, God is no longer the wanted religious news
Cited local lack of interest as in order to claim their poor excuse

Old leather bound bibles, lie sprawled across the floor in misuse
Their lightweight Scritta pages, waver from the windows breeze
Cited local lack of interest as in order to claim their poor excuse
A religion to whom these folk laboured in as some dirty disease

Their lightweight Scritta pages, waver from the windows breeze
To relate a long forgotten message wrote within its open pages
A religion to whom these folk laboured in as some dirty disease
This small abandoned chapel who's lack of trust in God enrages

To relate a long forgotten message wrote within its open pages
Relictus; where the Lord's words lie within here, as all forgotten
This small abandoned chapel who's lack of trust in God enrages
No shoes to clink the chapel tiles as no more the aisles trodden

Relictus; where the Lord's words lie within here, as all forgotten
Pieces of broken stained glass from the windows lie on the floor
No shoes to clink the chapel tiles as no more the aisles trodden
The walls ornate brass findings are long gone, and are no more

The Mirror

by Gregg Louis Marcucci

Awoken from dream's blackened veil
Thrust into this forsaken place
Madness and uncertainty consume
Seemingly hidden from God's grace

The mirror reflects a stranger
Undetermined friend or foe
His gaze a vulgar display
His silent screams go unknown

Frantically tearing flesh from bone
My horrors turned to reality
This mask I can no longer shed
The man that I see ... is Me ...

'You Once Told Me'

by Wilma Neels

You once told me
It wouldn't change
Yet it did
But it was expected
Change is norm
It's how we react to it

That determines the outcome
I am so much more at peace now
Hope you are too
We say things in jest
Not realising we put them in the atmosphere
Eventually
They happen without you having control
The trick is to move with it
Not in angst, but expectancy

Haiku

by Rick Davis

Silence melts sunlight.
A robin chirps playfully.
I sing to the rain.

Counting My Blessings

by Vera Judy Ball

There's nothing that thrills me like the feeling,
When into my mind the words come stealing,
Of thoughts and dreams of long ago,
Of songs and seasons and new fallen snow.

How sunlight sparkles on waters calm,
And the feel of the breeze on warm skin is a balm.
The crisp air of Autumn and warm Summer rains,
The morning sun's glow on mountains and plains.

I'm happy, contented with The Lord by my side,
For basically all of my needs are supplied.
I eat when I'm hungry and drink when I thirst.
I work and I play and I'm free as a bird.

I've lived my whole life in a place that's secure;
Never known the oppression that others endure.

I think on these things as I lie here at rest,
And closing my eyes I know I am blessed.

'Torimodosu'
by Wilma Neels

There is no blueprint
How I do it, how you do it
Will always be different
Nor can I dictate or judge
how you do yours
I retreat, I will go quiet, I will shed tears
When I am ready; I will write
Even after that; I will sit on that piece for days or until I feel prompted to
share
That works for me; that being said
we all deal differently
healing is a personal thing
some choose to share others don't
some do it privately others in public

Let us not fault each other for how it's done
Let's cheer each other on
So many things are already broken
let us not fuel the fire of brokenness

Poetry Soup
by Karen Kandle Jones

Playground for poets online bizarre
Onyx sky where we are stars
Emerald eyes eager to read
The next line written with elegant ease
Romantic patrons infatuated
Yellow sonnets purple phrases
Somehow, we are all related
Onion soupers with cheese grated

Unity in what we achieve
Poetry Soup for all yes please.

Dancing With God

by Marie Duddle

He entered the dance hall, clad in pure white
I sat in my corner, far away from the light
Bodies swayed slowly, the lights were subdued
The wine had been flowing and mellowed the mood.
This stranger intrigued me, he seemed out of place
One moment I saw him and then he was gone
I was right after all, he did not stay long.
His appearance was sudden, my heart skipped a beat
I cringed as I sat there, saw the smirks and the stares - did the stranger not
know I'm a harlot, beware!
He smiled oh so gently and asked me to dance
I mumbled no thank you, dropped my eyes to the ground.
In a very short time he would hear who I am
a woman called Scarlet seen mostly at night,
the affection men gave me was kept out of sight.
I sensed the stranger was still there, looked up and then he bowed politely
Before I knew it, curtsying slightly, I took his hand with a timid smile.
Not once did He speak when we started to dance
but His eyes were so piercing; I knew He saw through me.
Then the scales on my eyes fell away and I cried
For my Partner was God, He had captured my heart.
My Beloved taught me His celestial dance,
I stumbled a bit, fell over my feet
But soon I learnt how and just followed His lead
Swirling and twirling the ballroom was ours
I was dancing with God! I was Belle of the ball...
The music stopped playing, still I swirled, and I twirled
then breathless I realised the Stranger had gone, yet it mattered not, for this
dance with God would forever be cherished as I made a new start.

Tenure, A Terza Rima Sonnet

by Ken Allan Dronsfield

Are our spirits that of the great Thunderbird
sowing their seeds within the powerful storm
are we just feathers afloat like useless words

slowly they float down landing within the form.
See the steamy breath rise from the buffalo
the majestic beast with his coat is quite warm.

Are you grasped by a mournful wolves howling woe
such lonely sadness during the bright full moon
or the growl of a grizzly rumbling off slow.

Did you hear screaming rain forests die last June
dropped by the millions and now gone forever.
most human's slept soundly the night they were hewn.

Mother Nature's anger is now our weather;
will we see forty below next September?

Bali On The Morning Breeze

by Dominic Middleton

Of the morning
The dry season breaks
Clouds open
And the rains
Comes down
From the nor east
The breeze
It brings
Bali mornings
I feel
I hear

I smell
Bali
On the morning
Breeze

Pagan Life

by Lewis Raynes

Now a story to finish this hour of news,
Our reporter from out in the field,
Tom's on the spot with the universe itself,
Where the answer to life's been revealed....

...Hi everyone, we're live on the street,
With the guy on a deep acid fry,
What is the answer we're all looking for???
"Hey man let me answer you why,

"You see man, we're all matter and joules,
Energy and heat condensed right down to a slow,
Vibrating pattern of conscious experience,
And together like a river we flow,

From life into death back to life back to death,
Life's a dream that goes on forever,"
Well thankyou Tom from out in the cold,
Back to Frank to wrap up the weather.

Precious

by Paris-Maree Boreham

Water trickles loud and clear
Soothing moving atmosphere
Above eagle glides in circles
Over natures course of gurgles.
Perchance this is a mere fine dream
Creating such cascading stream
Atmosphere brisk and cool

Now wading in the running pool...
Bubbles from the falling drops
Splashing down around the rocks
From waterfall where life does thrive
Our very souls she helps revive.
Peaceful, calming natures song
Inviting me to sing along
Here with you I do belong
Where flowing notes prolong.

Love Is

by Betty Jo Legros Kelley

Love is as big as the galaxy,
No way can it be contained
Sickness and death
Cannot ebb its breath
Love's bonds mend broken hearts
Or can rip them all apart

Love's bigger than the human race
It shines in every place
In the loyal stance of a precious pet
Whose long passing hurts us even yet

Love holds the freest creatures
Whose wings led them on great quests
Flying from the far Northeast
To the warmth of the Southwest,
Love holds them to a nest

Love is bigger, love is greater of a power
Than a star
It can be seen in a purpose
No matter where we are
Created by a loving hand
A power of Light at His command
Written in poem, Painted in skies
On epitaphs and lullabies

Chocolate Cake

by Nora Gibson

I admit, it was me who ate that whole chocolate cake
I'm not very proud, please give me a break
I was possessed by the devil or some malevolent force
It was as if some entity stood over me, I felt so coerced
Even from the oven I heard it calling my name
My mind was already made up, I wasn't going to play that game.
Smelling so delicious my lips had begun smacking
Sneaking trips to the kitchen I was definitely tracking.
Then it was all finished to my sheer delight
A fork in the middle to make sure it baked right.
I couldn't stop munching I was out of control
I ate it right out the pan; Why waste a bowl?
Piece by piece I sliced until it was through
It was so yummy; What else was I supposed to do?
I know you were thinking, share it or cut a piece for another time.
Yeah, it's all gone so I won't even bother with this rhyme.

Trail Of Emotion

by Subimal Sinha-Roy

My dreams lifted from mirage, magnified so manifold,
the miniature frame of my mind could no longer hold,
but in desert wind they grew wings of soaring desire,
turning into twilight birds fluttering in the ardent air.

Through the ribboned arc of the resplendent rainbow
they sailed to the slanting horizon dipping down low,
where the setting sun's hues of silence drizzled to lie
on the carved canvas of the color-suffused mural sky.

They flew en echelon on the cotton canopy of cloud,
the drifting design in pristine blue made them proud.
I tried to decipher the meaning of plethora of pattern,
some I could decode, but many I had failed to discern.

The birds making all the time new template of flight,
allured me to catch the kaleidoscopic sight of delight.
I couldn't, in the end gave up, toiled the tedious try,
for they ascended high to obscurity in the remote sky.

My dreams wafted on soaring wings of summer birds,
disappeared beyond the winter's misty edge blurred.
I now wander forlorn in the middle of frozen nowhere,
trudge on dregs of time in the trail of emotion forever.

I would build nest for the birds that had flown away,
and wait, after the winter they would return someday.

Rain

by Nikolay Lopatin

I like rain more than all
Phenomena of nature in whole;
Rain reminds me of all
That exists in my soul!

The time of the rains
Is called bad and foul weather,
But I love to walk on a cloudy day
With my thoughts together!

I like to walk in the rain
Under an umbrella and without;
I'm going and admiring the rain
When everyone doesn't wanna be out!

I'm ready to go mad and give a cry
When there is not a cloud in the sky,
And the sun scorches so high
As if it wants me to fry!

But rain saves the world around,
It slakes the thirst of the ground;

In the air freshness can be found,
And everything seems alive around!

No better melody for me
Than the melody of rain,
And I can't imagine the world
Where it doesn't rain!

To My Daughter, Sophia

by Perrin Peacock

"Is it a girl? I think it's a girl!!...Doc?"
Flowers form'd blooms from sunny Easter skies
Let's call her Sophia Pascal Peacock
Our first baby born with baby blue eyes

You were two, I'd brag..."See what I'm seeing?"
Sighing, your mother would cringe and quiver
"Look! We've made the perfect human being,
She got all the best things we could give her!"

Wisdom, passion, love flows from your spirit
So alive with drive, caring and kind too
Accepting defeat? No, you won't hear it
So...you know...we can't be more proud of you

Birth day, we pray'd, thank'd God that He brought her
Now sweet sixteen, my beautiful daughter

Peace Bell

by Amitabh Divakar

Ringing the Peace Bell

Black
............................lives matter
All
............................lives matter
All
............................beings matter
All are
...........................Sentient beings
.....................Some beings are invisible
................Some sentient beings are hidden
...........All sentient beings are interdependent
.......All sentient beings share a common lineage
......Can we say humans are the crown of creation
....Or are humans of all creed just a link in the chain
....Note:- A chain is -- as strong as -- its weakest link
...somewhere.................alas.................somewhere
...humanity......................as.....................humanity
...is testing........................&......................is missing
...its sense..its wisdom
...its knowing...its hard head
..thru war/battle...................................seems to forget
.wily- dirty politics............................in key to existence
nay to common sense......................compassion & oneness
in lust for power & superiority....Missing is heart from the pic.
.....................................Ring in ~.
.............................the gentle bells
.............................Drops of Silence
.............................to deafen bombs
.............................how limit debate
.............................to Black/White
.....................................?¿

Trail Of Homes

by Sierra Chen

1983
July 24
Leaving
her child-
hood memory
- *home* behind.

Crossing Pacific
Ocean. 7200 miles
relocation. Called...
America her new
- foreign *Home.*

June 26, 2017
Sailing to her
Highest-Self *home.*
A purest residence no
address. A journey raising
consciousness. March 3, 2019

welcoming her true beloved. She
safely nests at a *Home Port* in his heart.
Present moment: Ode to Contentment.
Bow to detachment. Gratitude whispers: smile!
Be here and now................*Home* is inward.

Home

by David Holmes

A one pub village-the Cotswolds
The Totternhoe Chalk Stone
weathered, firm grey and brown co-mingled.
Corner edging buttressed.

The outskirts of hedgerows lined roads
Lawrence and the motor bike
in the sunlight until there was silence.

Set in the green grass
under the blue sky shadowed by clouds,
intermittent rain now cleared,
the Chalk Stone waits.

Grass plot surrounded by close in
green foliage, trees nurtured by the rain
next to the resting place where they have come.

Stones made of the same Totternhoe Chalk
once labelled, now weathered, indistinct names, dates
decipherable only in parish records.

Today the family gathers
to bring home to family
dust to dust and ashes to ashes.

The Vanity Of The Flowers

by Evelyn Judy Buehler

Blooming colors in shade and sun;
Fragrant elegance, not to be outdone!
In field, garden, and flowerpot,
The rose, the violet, and forget-me-not.

Proud and erect upon the stem,
All who pass must notice them!
Pastels and deeps; an array of brights,
Blaze the days and scent the nights.

Preening and dancing on summer's breeze,
In days of beauty. Days of ease.
I've glimpsed them at noonday, rounding the garden wall-
Much too vain to notice me at all.

And seen them blossom in June morning's heat,
In sun washed loveliness and total conceit!
Scarlet and blue and orange and yellow,
In Red Valley. In golden meadow.

Others bloom wild on desert sand,
Disdainful of a helping hand.
An ageless beauty that none could depose-
It's just the way it goes.

Heart Into Art

by Khadidja Megaache

All the tales I must write
For the unlucky ones who can't get the words right,
I'm afraid I wouldn't be able to halt once I start
Metamorphosing their hearts and mine into art.

Beaver Moon

by Smita Kulkarni

In the wee hours of early dawn
Beaver moon was shining upon
Spreading her earnest radiance
On the lake that was calm
Her shimmer was silvery bright
Transforming darkness into light
Spilling her numinous beams
She brought so much insight

The Birth Of A Poet

by Pramod RASTOGI

My heart has bled verses,
But none saw it bleed.
It has gone barren
And has not rained spring for so long.
Thirsty for a loving embrace,
I can taste only a strand
Of its shadow in my dreams.
I have been separated
From my love for so long.

My glass has gone empty,
I beg you fill it with more.
Each drop of nectar
Brightens my amorous eyes,
Adding to my desire for her,
Beckoning me for more.

Lost in dreams of my love,
To my heart's content do I drink,
To breathe vibrancy
Into a newly-born poet's heart,
Who, in his ruin and solitude unseen,
Pours out reams of poetry
On the tender, yet tormented love
He has for her in his heart.

Heavenly Sight

by Shirley Ann Hawkins

I looked out from a mountain top
To scan the views out yonder
My cup of happiness overflowed
Filling my heart and soul with wonder

Waste

by E. Adeline Thomas

all day I sit here
sporadic thoughts screaming dazed
I call the wild in

Black And White

by Jane VanDoe

No human is black
No human is white
God is the artist
His palette is light

The rays of the sun
Show skin as pale tan
To darkest mahogany
Arrayed as a fan

Of red tints and yellows
Of browns in all shades
The plight of the human
Is anger and rage

Blindness to beauty
Painted by God
And blaming ill fate
On outward facade

Ignoring Gods gifts
Is man's greatest sin
A human's true beauty
Reflects from within

The Duty Of The Poet

by Richard Tipping

The duty of a poet,
Is to unlock thoughts and themes,
Explore beneath the surface,
If each thing is what it seems.
Combine imagination,
With a storytelling bent,
But make the reader fill with awe,
Direction that it went.
Make the reader think a bit,
And see more things each time,
To add to what's encaptured,
Every time you read my rhyme.
Sometimes to get you thinking ,
Other times designed to shock,
Another time to make you laugh,
Or outside world to block.
The duty of a poet,
To combine a range of things,
But really to ask questions,
And see what response it brings.
It may upset, it may annoy,
It maybe brings a smile,
But as I write, I hope it makes,
You linger for a while.
A duty of the poet then,
The writing seed now sewn,
To make you feel so strongly that,
You write one of your own!

The Magic Of Light

by bradley lane

I look up sometimes, when surrounded by green,
To things above, which have yet to be seen.
In the dark green forest, with twinkling light,
With golden rays, that fade into night.

Long canes of a glorious and wonderful sun,
That nothing surrounding, could ever outrun.
They touch the ground, with a delicate touch,
The vibrancy of colour, I adore so much.

The darkness and shadow, are defeated once more,
As the sun shines down, it's rays so pure.
Like a golden honey, it trickles through leaves,
And encases all, as the light falls and weaves.

A forest so dense, has a magical feel,
A setting so calm, and wondrously ideal.
A magical place, with beings and more,
Where sun, and rain both equally pour.

You never know, what exactly you'll find,
From fairies and life, please do be kind.
This magical place, untouched by all,
Is a home for these beings, from winter to fall.

The sound of the branches, moving with wind,
And the crunch of a leaf, from a tree that's thinned.
Autumn is coming, the leaves are all red,
A pile of leaves, as big as a bed.

The floor is a canvas, that changes around,
With burrows and branches, where trees are bound.
A place that changes, as the sun goes to sleep,
To a wondrous night, with blues so deep.

The hoot of owls, the guardians of sky,

They scour the floor, with yellow marble eye.
The forest is alive, as much as the day,
With mice and bugs, the owls nightly prey.

To look and examine, as the sun falls down,
A scarlet red and orange, that shines through the crown.
Of a thousand trees, with crowns so glorious,
Their presence in the forest, is very notorious.

If you find yourself, ever wondering around,
A forest so magical, listen to the sound.
Of every breath, and rustle and crack,
And be glad you're there, and don't look back.

Labor Day

by Regina Marie Elliott

aging laborer
work boots off
sleeps deep Labor Day

Dedicated to my brother David

The Souls Of The Seas

by Regina Marie Elliott

The souls of the seas are
committed to their maritime dwell,
and the reflected tides shall bear stars
on silent waves that mourn,
when my grieving for humanity will
leave my earthly body,
as the merpeople attend my
seashell bier in the vast of
the Atlantic.

Ballad To Spring

by Nicholas Windle

For little robin, red breast,
On my spade, you sit.
With bobbing head, and twitch of tail,
As another season now say's farewell.

In the bracing chill skip, sprightly,
On this sun-drenched day.
Look up towards the heavens,
And be thankful come what may.

The coming days grow longer,
With life refreshed anew.
As flecks of white and purple,
Permeate among the dew.

Erupting upward shards of green,
With heads in saffron gold,
A multitude of trumpets play,
Herald forth as spring unfolds.

Under tip of twig now freshly dipped
In a cornucopia of greens.
In waives that crest, where bluebells rest,
And one can sit and dream.

For nothing say's that spring is here,
More than posies clutched, and garlands fare.
A chick, an egg, and the mad march hare,
The wild of youth without a care.

Pathetic Life

by Gayle Rodd

Adorned in scabs and faded scars
You swore you'd never let it go this far
And friends aren't who they say they are
in this pathetic life

You haven't eaten, haven't slept
The clothes you wear are all that's left
Your other stuff - you lost to theft
and this pathetic life

Steal from family just the same
dishonesty's your middle name
and all the pawn shops know your game
in this pathetic life

A hopeful end you swear you're done
Oh look! Here comes another one
You'll do just ONE MORE HIT for fun
in this pathetic life

Your time's run out your needle's bent
Your friends have left, your money's spent
Your dope was your own detriment
in this pathetic life

A Walk Down Memory Lane

by Robert E. Welch, Sr.

My mind takes me there, more often than not,
To the days of years gone by.
Of a time and a place, wherever it be,
Above and beyond the sky.

A place of my own, in my own little world
With none to cry or complain.
So let me be there, alone in my thoughts
As I walk down memory lane.

Let me walk down that lane, with shadows and light,
To see all the good things and bad.
And follow that path, wherever it leads,
To times both happy and sad.

As I walk down that lane, each step that I take
Brings forth a tear or a smile.
Each memory I see slows my walk even more
And gives cause to linger awhile.

To live in the past should not be for me,
For now is the time to be.
The things that I do, the things I see
Will each make a new memory.

But I store up those thoughts of heaven sublime
That never the memories wane.
And travel with me on clouds soft and fair
As I walk down memory lane.

More Than Dirt

by James Study

It was its own little world in its day
But in this time forty acres not much
Old house and out buildings hauled away
Just something to plow around treated as such
What once was here the plow can't touch

A tear in the dirt a cry in the wind
As the big field machine move now
Dust sting my face when the plow begin
As if to say you should not allow
More than dirt went under the plow

The Rougarou

by Shirley Rebstock

Deep in the swamp on a full moon
Legend says a creature roams deep in the lagoon
Eyes red and glowing in the dark as he prowls
Even the alligators hide to the sound of his growls

A few brave souls have searched in the bog
For the creature with the body of a man and head of a wolfdog
The legend originated in France from there it grew
To the swamps of Louisiana
The Rougarou

Parents told the legend to their children to keep them out of the woods
Also, to scare Catholics to keep Lent as they should
He is super strong, moves fast, can change shape
Anyone who finds him needs to know how to escape

Put a leaf in your pocket and say a prayer
Whatever you do, never into his red eyes stare
If you should find him mustn't tell anyone for a year and a day
You must heed this warning to what I say

If you make those mistakes
 I'm warning you
You could change and become
A Rougarou too

Love Is - Sonnet

by David Drowley

Our life book is laden with lots of love.
Brief notes and roses and corny love songs;
Kisses, rubbing noses; cooing like doves.
Pledging our love to the one we belong,

A sentence here and a paragraph there.
Wedding bells and honeymoon embraces,
Alone times and skis; with you anywhere!
Romantic sails to exotic places.

Churning ice cream with kids the old-time way.
Grandkids rushing to hug our knees at the door.
The sadness of parents passing away
Left bittersweet memories, rich, not poor.

Beyond feeling, love is life's best way:
The peaceful love of ordinary days.

Fixed Gaze

by Kevin Lawrence

To capture the distant gaze
Of the aged's milky blue eye
Is to gaze into eternity.

Is it my eye they see
Or a distant memory,
The tiniest mote,
The light of a spark?

Fixed upon a place
Staring motionlessly,
Fearing to miss
A glimpse
Of who they might be.

A feeling of falling
Into the vastness of space.
No beginning no ending
Consciousness lost in place.

I swear we connected
Within that long stare.
The horror of knowing

Too soon I'd be there.
A milky blue iris
Not seeing the world
Not seeing me.

Fixed gaze,
The world staring back
At me.

A Dog Named Harry

by Richard Breese

A hairy thing once roamed our streets
Chasing cats for sport and treats.
Till it roamed too far
And a dog catcher and car,
Grabbed Harry and chained his feets.

The Derby

by Kim Robin Edwards

Through the days of blistering toil.
A murmur of spirit after a blissful
trial. These were the emotions on this
endless day. Minutes later in single
file, were prints from hoofs in the
muddy soil. While easing toward
drudgery and withdrawal. The amazing
thoroughbreds entered their stall.
Jockeys clambered onto their colts.
As they were trained superbly, for
the oncoming derby. While over the
loudspeaker the narrator spoke.
Calling out numbers for only who was
there. Consider a victory and the
triple crown. Ready to gain-gain an
inch of ground. Thoroughbred racing

was the name of the game. Where
hesitating was nothing, and no
one to blame. Where multitudes of
spectators impatiently waited, for the
master racers to open the gate. A
photograph finish ended the race.
Beaten by a length-a length out of
pace. Was the thoroughbred racer
in second place.

Fairies Of The Field

by Francine Roberts

Sunshine sparkles off fairy wings
as they flit through a field of gold.
Listen carefully ... hear them sing
melodies of old
while a magic spell takes hold.

Watch them dance for you and me,
Fairies dancing with delight.
Such a wondrous sight to see,
playing among fragrant lilacs bright.
All the world seems right.

Is it all just a dream?
Are the fairies really there,
with their gossamer wings that gleam
flitting through fields without a care,
dancing on a breath of air ?

Silence

by Clevia Bedeau

In the midst of silence
regret feeds,
devours my soul and
churns my conscience.

Simple things,
desires that caused me bother
You ask of me to share with you my time?
Putrid thoughts of me
complicate my living
whilst my soul laments
the loss of smiles
of love, of you.

Amidst the silence
Guilt begins
to fill my lungs.
I gasp for truth
and rue each waking moment.
The void has brought me clarity
Does clarity beget absolution?
But time slips by and
yet still I mourn
The loss of smiles
of love, of you.

Velvet Paws Of Time

by Tommy Leon Wright

When juvenile,
it matters not the ticking of the clock.
For then, time creeps as if on velvety paws,
casting its shadow o'er the earth;
but as we mature it appears,
as a bird of prey on outstretched wings.
Always solemn-faced, talons extended,
snuffing life as were it a candle at first light.
We know of our beginning,
but only God knows of our appointed demise.
In the interim, withhold not thanks,
for the extension of life each day.
For while life's beginning,
may come with the glow of a velvety red rose;

time, as the noonday sun,
will soon render it a pallid pink

Source Of Nile

by I.B.Padmakumar

North eastern whistling through papyrus banks

Emanating streams are from forest Rwanda

Collecting reserving ever controversial
No propagating ,Lake Victoria real natural source

We are from the source of Nile

Summer rain blessed over mount of Ethiopia

Seasonal worship prolonging to Hapi.
Egyptian farmers awaiting the blue silt
Obscuring barriers , flowing river great
We are from the source of Nile

She will be joining blue hands at Khartoum

Resting reversing , then reaching to Cairo

Looking behind like a responsible mom
Blessing the fertile land again , hats off
We are from the source of Nile

Enchanting caves and all gigantic pyramids

Egyptian mummy an evident civilization
Gentle the flow for the life distribution
Never dispensable such a real contribution

We are from the source of Nile

Dark Night Of The Soul

by Nayda Ivette Negron

despair knocks the door
hallucinating the mind
tormenting the soul

darkness dispels light
sinister black shadows loom
unhinging spirit

an evil fiend tempts
execrable ideas
drowning to abysm

His Shoes

by Wade Greenlee

The other day I wore your shoes in the rain
They fit so well but still brought pain
Someone asked, "Why wear them then?"
I answered, "They bring me close to my son again."

I wore your shirt the very same day
It was a Volcom shirt in a shade of grey
A touch of your cologne and it smelled like you
It gave my heart something to cling to

Remember the thirty cents you left for me
It's in my pocket to set me free
That quarter and nickel you last held
Binds our souls like the strongest weld

Your baseball hat with the sweat-stained brow
I never really appreciated it til now
It's too small to fit on my head

So I wear it proudly in my heart instead

Yesterday I finally turned off your phone
I cried, son, it made me feel so alone
Today I'm using it with my number instead
It ties us together like the strongest thread

Your music is the best gift of all
For in it I can hear your heavenly call
An un-silenced voice always there to hear
A love that draws me ever near

With all these gifts I hope to move on
Like the sun rising upon a new day's dawn
I will think of you with every step I take
And in your shoes lessen my grieving ache

The Whippoorwill

by Valerie D Staton

In the dark of night, the whippoorwill cries
As it flitters beneath the night's blue sky

Master of camouflage. Heard, seldom seen
Is searching for woodland insects to glean

Whip-poor-will! Whip-poor-will! The nightjar trills
As it glowers and swoops down for the kill

Insects traversing the forest take heed
For the mottled bird has tremendous speed

It nests on the ground, it perches in trees
It's gray-brown plumage the color of leaves

Up at dawn, at dusk, and on moonlit nights
Brindled bird rests with the coming of light

Tiny bird with a magnanimous shrill
Whip-poor-will! Whip-poor-will! The nightjar trills

Early Season Moth

by richard a jordan

Early season moth

Born before it's really Spring

Flying all alone

But time still to feel the sun

If only for one moment

Ghosts Of France

by Brian L Lowmiller

One month in May, I journeyed far,
winged through the sky t'wards Eastern star,
to land upon the Charles de Gaulle,
grand port of ile de France's sprawl,
live city where studied Renoir.

A taxi to a ville by car,
this ville oh Vesinet not far,
walked round the ibis lake to loll,
one month in May.

Then back to gates of iron bar,
round homes of which it seems there are,
the old grey ghosts of France in all.
They walk baguettes down lonely hall,
the men in black, women in shawl,
one month in May.

Summer Days

by Paul Martin

Masses of sunburnt grass,
Sway with delicate ease.
Seduced by the composer
Of the soothing May breeze.

Swallows parade,
Pirouetting,
Swooning,
With humpy gluttonous crows
Giving weary approval
From tops of telephone poles.

The summer silence,
Bestows dignity upon this land.
As downtrodden seeds,
And wild limitless weeds
Claim their ancient ways,

My mind is light,
To hot,to drunk,
To care about the darkness of man,
And all his little subplots.

I turn on some baroque,
Wishing to dream
transcendental dreams.

The Day Baklava Bent The Fork

by Moji Agha

On this taxing day on Earth,
I finally saw with my own physical eyes,
in one hilariously sweet moment,
the sticky triumph of baklava over the fork.

The formerly cocky fork,
his erect ego bent,
finally learned what it means to be hard, or not.

The triumphant baklava, however,
wondered if age on a lonely shelf
hardens even the sweetest of the sweet.

I wonder:
Whether she also wondered, what it means to be tough
on this warming taxing day,
on this dying blue goblet: my Mother Earth?

Is my mother's sweet heavily taxed heart finally hardening?

Has she taken the fork in the road
that ends in hard, rather than sweet?

Or alas, was it that the soft-hearted fork
had no choice but to cry bent tears
mourning the death of softness
of sweet hearts?

I hear the wind of "what is" cry:

For whose out-of-balance baklavas and forks do the bells toll, especially
today?

The Comet

by Norman Littleford

Rampaging through the heavens
never stopping day or night,
a spectacle of a lifetime
a comet in full flight.

Faster than a cheetah
with a tail that's miles long,

bigger than a mountain
so powerful and strong.

The outer ice is melting
causing vapour from the force,
and leaves a trail behind it
as it travels on its course.

If one should come too close to earth
the atmosphere will shake,
with shockwaves reaching to the ground
causing the land to quake.

Scientists say the chemicals
in the dust they leave behind,
could have started life on earth
which resulted in mankind.

I cannot say if this is true
I do not have the right,
but I know no better spectacle
than a comet in full flight.

For Richard On His Fiftieth

by Francine Roberts

Welcome to the over-the-hill gang.
We're so glad you're finally here.
We know it's a wee bit scary
knowing old age is near.

It's now perfectly acceptable
to be in bed before nine
and of course it's time to substitute
Geritol for wine.

Feel free to bang your walking stick
and scream at young people you see
to turn down their blasted music
before they go deaf as can be.

Eight hours of sleep is long gone,
you'll wake up after just three
for your nightly walk to the bathroom
to have yourself a pee

Young people will call you "sir"
and offer their seat on the bus.
Just smile , sit down and shut up
and try not to make a fuss.

Your eyesight will start to fail
and words will slip your mind.
Put everything right where it belongs
or it's whereabouts you'll never find.

It's really not that bad
getting old ... I mean older.
Don't forget to take a sweater now
as the temperatures seem colder.

Hope I haven't scared you.
Welcome to our little group
and don't forget your fibre
or else you'll never poop.

Cattle And Suv's

by Rex Allen Holiday

Polar bears, spotted owls and honey bees
Care nothing of scientific debates
Over flatus of cattle and SUV's.

Some drop big oil drills and some drop big trees
To provide a place for our dinner plate,
With its filet mignon or black eye peas.

The planet goes on with its rolling seas
Immune to false conclusions and the hate

Over flatus of cattle and SUV's.

Should politics and graduate degrees
Be allowed to sit and decide our fate,
While eating filet mignon/black eye peas?

Political winds, like a gentle breeze,
Carry the pollen of absurd debate;
Over flatus of cattle and SUV's.

Perhaps all the powers of wannabe's
Can save all the birds, fishes, ants and trees;
The filet mignon, and the black eye peas;
The flatus of cattle and SUV's.

In The Seventh Hour

by Walter Daniel Tomeo

Here is where I am,
No words of shame;
Despite the past,
Nothing is lost when the time is right.

In your arms I feel the peace I'm craving,
Your skin gave me a place to stay ;
And your presence a sense of two,
Nothing is lost when the time is right.

On this bed of starring stars I'm resting well,
No apologies, no regrets;
The prize was the warmth of your presence,
Thus your flesh gave me a place to stay.

In the seventh hour,
When everyone is waking up;
The morning melody of rush ,
Despite the past;
I wasn't alone and neither lonely,
In fact I was alive,
Brave and not sorry.

My Escape

by Byron Kaya

The pin holes of night
Crickets sing the mountain's song
The stream's gentle hush

Hidden Beneath

by Dominic Middleton

Never did a fire so fierce
Blow across the land
That same land
His heart did grow
Nourished by his sweat and toil
No more
The morning mist
Will hear his weathered voice
Call his horse
Com'orn
His mark
Has been scorched from its soil
And how that land
Greens, grays
And blacked haze
With gusts of wind
And rumpled hills
The fathering face
Of this dead man
Hidden beneath

Clouds

by Stephen Michael Tefft

"There is a cloud that looks like a bunny!
Over there is one just like a rocket!
Do you ever think it might be funny
To put a cloud right into your pocket?"

"I think that would just make your pants soggy.
And then we would both have to go inside.
That one right there looks just like a doggy!
And there is a dragon! Run, doggy! Hide!"

"Do you think clouds might be made of cotton?"
"You're being silly! Cotton cannot fly!
Mommy told me once, but I've forgotten...
The rain comes from the clouds. I wonder why."

They watch the clouds pass and lay on their backs
'Til Mommy comes out to bring them some snacks.

Melancholia

by Debra Walker

Like a tree with a broken limb
This broken branch begins to bend,
Like the splitting hairs caught in a comb
I sensed the void on my own
I look and seek deep in my soul
In hopes to find something to console
Dull and deep is its shaded abyss
For there is nothing in its mist
But dust and spirits, of the disappearing
For I am the one that has become weary.
The void I walk is very deep
Who knew these hills could be so steep.
However, I am who is broken

Yet, everyone wants a token.
Thinking they have givin me something
When in turn they have provided nothing.
I feel the pain of my psychosis,
For my mind has become atrocious.
The nullness and the empty space,
I knew would win the race
But there is nothing more
For I have become
Null &Void

Let's Meet On Our Yesterdays

by Bernard Chan

Meet me back on those effervescent days;
Let's swing on shafts of their lingering light,
Like our childhood hero in vine-borne flight,
Till we're again in that sun-swaddled place,
Where once we were colts free to roam and race,
On meadows with dews of innocence bright,
And friendship's rainbow arching every sight,
Before we were called to the adults' maze.

Let us leap across the years, my dear friend;
Though our bodies may balk, our minds are lithe.
On the playground of our youth we shall land,
Where birds still kiss the sky, stingless bees hive,
And our mischief roiled through a drowsy glen
Whose slumber still our laughing echoes rive.

All Those Loose Ends

by Vickie Hurtt-Thayer

With this tear I remember you,
betwixt the moon and morning's dew.

Old photographs taken have cracked and faded,

my roses have crumbled inside the book's pages.

A gift you gave me is wrapped but broken,
In pieces my heart still holds these tokens.

By a thread old love is sewn into me,
Binding my heart with memories.

I often tug at its loose ends,
I'm sewing my heart and hoping it mends.

A Golf Tale

by James Study

Into the ground the ball on tee I push
With a mighty swing the club went whoosh
This I will share
The ball still there
But my club did sail into the bush

Midnight

by Hans-Christian AleXander Melschau

shadows in small places
empty eyes dancing
tortured looks
forcing straight lines
facing straight down
pretending so pretty
 and the cold is here

I like to watch when she listens
does she see me
the way I'm feeling down

so just be
and me, I couldn't of ever wanted you more
into the night

and all of our promises
you were the first
and always
my always
staring, if I could
the reflection in in your eyes

The Wisdom Of The Sun

by Moses Sichach

In a night where the sons of sons sat under the stars
My father's father told the sons of the wisdom of the sun
The beauty of the world is beheld in who we love
To live and to die they are all we try to have
A feeling that we love, that we are loved by the one
The one who breaks our heart, our souls they starve
The one you love will never love enough

In the same night when the sons of sons sat under the stars
My father told the sons of the wisdom of the sun
The eyesore of the world is our love of the mirror
Our confidence constructed on a surface of silver
Our charity creeps from the mountain of useless surplus
Just so they say we are as kind as they say they are
We sweat and sin just that we see them sin and sweat
The only love we trust is love by us, for us, by things like us

Still on that night when the sons of sons sat under the stars
I told the sons of the wisdom of the sun
The fairness of the world lies in forgiveness and sin
We all are sons from sin and of sin
We all are looking for a little peace just so we could sit
Always going everywhere and heading nowhere
Searching for atonement through the accursed
So we made God from our trepidation for our own redemption

On that night when the sons of sons sat under the stars
The son of sons told the sons of the wisdom of the sun
The plainness of the world is found in unsocial socializations

We are all alone, our tears are our accomplice
They teach us to be us yet they don't know us
They create us in the image of their exalted desires
We are a canvas painted in their own narcissi
Brushed in a light so dark hoping we get drawn for them

A Duet Sung Alone

by Aniruddha Pathak

I know now how confusing 'twas to find
That I loved my love walking one-way street,
Knowing, she seldom with my love was lit,
Her heart was but with love of friendship lined,
Whilst silent was my love, clueless it came,
Hers, distant, chilled, warm too of a close friend,
An unknown seed still sprouted sans a name,
Love built the nest still, hard to comprehend;
A nest it was by both if strange birds made,
Built by love's sweat, reinforced to last long,
With a plinth-stone precious enough as jade;
And I sang all alone a duet song,
  She sensed the same frisson I too had felt,
  In hope that long frozen love soon might melt.

Obituary

by M. Braimah Saaka

In ghana
no one dies
before a short illness
no tarriness
quick, swift

no prolonged sickness
debilitating, painful
by the barrel of a gun
or incantation
by the bonnet of a car

or prophecy

no one dies
no sudden death
before a short illness
no one

Through The Storms

by Tiffany Saxon

Even though the skies are grey...the sun is still shinning my other...
Even through the mixed emotions of heavens rain;
There comes a time of unforeseen troubles my brother.
So
Whatever the trouble, I'm always at your right side;
Cheering you on knowing;
 That through whatever storm you're going through...
You'll always persevere, keep your faith and recover.
Here's my message to you...that I got you all covered.
James 1: 2-3
"Consider it pure joy, my brothers and sisters, whenever you face trials of
many kinds, 3 because you know that testing of your faith produces
perseverance."
For this verse is your tool for this day and that of others.
And
As the tears of heaven continues to fall...
Always know that whenever you need me
I'm right here waiting on your call.
And
 Now that God has blessed us in staying in touch...
The sun will always shine
 Through the rain, blowing winds, snow and such...
It doesn't matter the storm
I'm always here as your strength and inspiration
Because
 I am that with your spirit and I love you all so very much.
So
No matter how your day may go...
You are never alone...

For
You will forever have a piece of me and the direction of how to get
"THROUGH THE STORMS".
God Bless....

The End.

Time To Go Merry-Go-Round

by Newton Ranaweera

You are in your prime, and I'm in my clime;
Why sweetie in twenty then we waste this time?
Come, dance; we can gently our pleasures hound,
For here's a time for us to go merry-go-round.

Run around, and you'll see how flowers bloom
And drones fly around wanting for some room;
Birds, herds, and all love while their time is high,
So come sweetie; in delay, our prime will sigh.

Moon smiles and night palls a velvet blue veil,
And owls and curlews hail with a flirting tale;
Xylophones and cymbals bounce for our dance,
So come sweetie; let's dive in a hypnotic trance.

Amma- Mother

by Gunadevi Rajaratnam

Amma, when you were with me,
I did not know your value.
Only when you left me,
Did I realise your greatness.

I remember all what you did,
All the sufferings you underwent.
Your never-ending care,

Your honesty and hard work.

Your sleepless nights,
During my days of sickness,
Your sacrificial deeds and struggles,
Your enduring patience.

My exam days were like yours,
Midnight or break of day,
You were there to support me,
Encouraging me to persevere!

Your ways were Simple, Humble,
God- fearing steps taken by you,
Will never be forgotten,
Guiding light of my life!

Above everything else, you taught me,
The power of the Almighty God,
Thanks for enriching my life in a myriad ways,
I am blessed to call you 'Mother '

(Amma means 'Mother' in Tamil)

Colorscapes In Black Velvet Night

by Martha L. Kiser

Black velvet painted by nature,
emboldened primaries of
red, yellow, blue,
melding into
secondary chromatic sensations
that, echo tertiary waves.

I flung my soul upon the canvas,
oozed my essence among the blends
and empowered singing paints
to release their rhythms;
expel their agonies and I
left them speaking in
tri-tones, quad-tones
raging vibrancy;
psychedelic amalgamation.

Even Nature vents,
releases her crystalline tears and
robustious laughter upon this realm;
a wise old sage among celestial bodies;
her passions bleed upon our lives
and we drink, become one
with the soul of Gaia;
our heart songs pouring ecstasy,
right back into hers.

Garnet Lake

by Chas Weeden

I pause to listen to the silence –
I am one with the million befores
and the afters and at great peace
amid the soundless, immense harmonies.

I become the rhythm of the spheres
and part of that oneness orchestration,
both absorbed and apart in a light,
too orderly to be but blind chance.

There must be purpose to the whole
that transcends reason and goes beyond
the despair of nothing. I become the Cosmos
not the chaos and within I am part.

There is a miracle to existence
and its exquisite, ephemeral beauty.

To hike to Garnet Lake is to be without,
wherein, without, I find my within.

Socially Distanced Cocktails

by Chas Weeden

The night is warm and her flowers in bloom
A chance to dispatch our covid'd gloom;
Old friends together, our drinks too well known
A chance to catch up instead of alone.

Each chair is placed at the distance proscribed
And each wears a mask as our hostess advised,
Surely, covid here has no chance to spread,
Though no one can hear a word that is said.

Tribute To The Fallen Leaves

by Pramod RASTOGI

Breezing trees heard the whispers of leaves
The autumn has cast its shadow
The sun is on its round of the sky
And the wind is quickening its pace,
A choir of sighs is building up
Breaking the hush in the forest,
The trees are counting their losses
As the leaves went dry and frugal
Are gradually shedding their abode
In spades, drifting down slowly
In movements rhythmic of Ballerinas
On their last dance, in waves sinuous
In harmony with the music crunching
Played by feet aplenty
On their daily walks in the forest
Crushing the fallen into thousand pieces,
In vain was not their life
Giving shades to travelers while in life

And once fallen serving as a staple
To their companions in life, or
Turned into duff serving as shields
To smother parasite seeds
Under their companions turned barren.

Breezing trees heard the whispers of leaves - From the poem, The last
goodbye by Vijay Pandit

The Devil Cometh Tonight

by Gary Bateman

The Devil Cometh Tonight

The fright of this unholy night
says the Devil cometh tonight
to capture my soul
before I grow old,
it is told
on this night.

God, save my soul on this dark night,
by your true grace make it all right,
save my holy soul
so I may grow old,
being bold
this dark night.

Mighty Oak, Her, You Are Beautiful

by William Darnell Sr

Mighty Oak, Her, You Are Beautiful

Standing her,
ever so proud she be.

Her beauty,

her,
the mighty oak tree.

So tall, the length of her,
the world to see.

Even by the heavens,
who created her to be.

Her mighty natural strength,
her undeniable beauty,
she possesses.

Forever really,
uniquely,
a great success.

You are unique to me,
the strength she takes.

Though clouds that sit above you,
her branches and limbs,
sprawling up into the sky.

Her searching radiant essences,
she counts on to survive.

If you're looking at her,
she,
breathing from the inside.

Keeping you alive to be;
with oxygen,
for this world to see.

I'm grateful to her; for her adorn!
The Mighty Oak, Her, For She Is Born.

The Grizzly

by Warren Oscar M'Baht

A grizzly isn't really, as bad as he's made out
He wanders round the parklands, when no humans are about
But there are times of course, we meet him in his home
We can't blame him for being there, it is on his land we roam

Open up your tent flap, and see the big brown bear
Close it quickly zip it up, you must not meet his stare
He would not come to campsites, if nothing for him there
After he had looked around, he would go elsewhere

He has that special odour, you can tell where he has been
You sense that he was at your camp, even though not seen
That is why statistics, that are often known to lie
Can this time tell the Gods own truth, so very few will die

So when you stay in National Parks, or even just 'Out There'
Leave a pristine place behind you, leave nothing for the bear
We can do it safely, out camping in the bush
If we just use some common sense, not give our luck a push

So there is that big brown bear, sexes named as hogs
Does little of the damage, of domesticated dogs
But he is big and looks so fierce, he takes a lot of blame
Should he vanish then this earth, would never be the same

I'm The Stellar Deer

by Walter Daniel Tomeo Figliola

No longer I needed,
The ladder to climb;
The space is wide open,
The ascension is mine.

A burning sensation,

The splatters of stars;
A jewel from Venus,
Descends down my sight.

The glittering mansion,
Unfolds as I ride;
With a group of observers,
While journeying the night.

Shapes of silver petals,
An unknown frontier;
The space is wide open,
I'm the stellar deer.

Fish In Bowl

by Anisha Dutta

Me frolic fish once fluttering fins
swam through opulent aqua flow
sometimes too fast or often too slow,
sudden whirling rolled on hurried spins.

Sea foam surged on scarlet scaly skin
Strange quirky sea-creatures all around
Both prey and predator to astound.
Smooth touch of mossy weeds brown or green.

Every moment a challenge with thrill
Me frolic fish once swimming in swarm,
Happy to thrive on algae and worm.
Haply caught with thousands of small krill.

Once muse amused welcoming gay mood.
Now imprisoned in little glass bowl.
Helpless! Remembering sea: Part and whole
Now confined in cell, only to brood.

With my eyes open I dream to swim
in vast sea and wake up in small pot.

Sea is snatched, tiny jar to allot.
None can listen to my soundless scream.

Honorable Mention

by Mark R Toney

When just a child the poet's mom said "Son
Throughout your life beware the sin of pride
Remember this when every day is done
What counts the most is who you are inside"

At first he thought his mother's words unfair
For recognition surely has its place
In time he witnessed prideful thoughts can flare
When undue adulation supplants grace

The poet took to heart his mother's words
Too many accolades can turn your head
Vainglory flits away on wings of birds
What's left is mostly emptiness and dread

Life immersed in modest exhibition
Satisfied with honorable mention

Avian Architecture

by Craig Cornish

As robins forage on the lawn,
their last pre-frost hunt, and
feast within the berried trees,
I wonder if they think upon
an old, disheveled nest
and recall at all their youth
within its sheltered folds;
as we might ponder
while passing by
our old childhood home.
Or, do they simply move along

- time being too valuable
for sentimental recollections.

Machine: The Final Chapter

by Simon Rogerson

Computer
Bits, bytes, ones, zeros
So Charles and Ada conceive -
IT's Pandora's box

Robot
Man and beast replaced
Same task over and over -
Objective carnage

AI
Boolean bible
Artificial ignorance -
Logical ending

Evolutionary finale – Armageddon!

Bear

by Thomas Flood

One day while walking thru the woods
I saw a big brown bear
I looked at him he looked at me
We both just stopped and stared

He looked at my fingers
As I looked at his nose
He looked at my funny ears
That were blue because it was cold

He looked at my woolen hat

And very rosy cheeks
As I was wondering to myself
I wonder what bears eat

I then looked at his massive paws
As he looked at my feet
At   this time I noticed
His very long sharp teeth

The bear let out a mighty roar
And I began to tremble
As a thought ran thru my mind
Is it food that I resemble

I then looked down at my watch
And said
Is that the time , Oh my
You'll have to excuse Mr Bear
I really have to fly

Sweet On You

by Edward Ibeh

Sugar generously sprinkled
With love, atop a salivating tongue is how you'll always taste.
Enslaving; your fascinating je ne sais quoi.
Effortlessly charming; you pull me
Toward you like magnet against the other.

Organically, you do so with wondrous ease.
No one captivates me like you do.

You seduce me with your smoldering sex appeal.
One too many times, you've trapped me
Under your unbreakable spell.

Searching For Lightness

by Lonna Lewis-Blodgett

On the river of wishes that fall upon my youth
And flows with the autumnal streams of leafy dreams that float
Upon the future of my tomorrow seeking my truth
I journey wide and long with my ghosts aboard my boat
To search for the soul of heaven and living heart of me

Deeper currents lead me to a brilliant light somewhere
While darkness all around my fears swallows all my hope
I push through murky waters escaping unknown phantoms there
To find my faith and willingness to struggle and cope
To search for the soul of heaven and living heart of me

So on it streams unswerving as its course sways and wends
So I may find the light of understanding promised long ago
For I know my intended destiny lies just around the bend
As far and wide I journey on dark secrets water flow
To search for the soul of heaven and living heart of me

A Girl And A Guitar

by Denis Brian Briggs

She stood all alone in the spotlight
Just a girl and her guitar
Though she was only the warm up act
She deserved to be the star

She stood there and played and sang
With a voice so pure and clear
Songs of love and songs of loss
Sweet music to my ear

Some of her songs were ages old
But she made them seem quite new

Her voice and her music filled the room
The notes just soared and flew

Some songs she sang made us laugh
Some brought a tear to the eye
Some made us want to sing along
Some just made us sigh

She sang us gentle songs of love
Songs of peace and war
She held us all right through to the end
Then we all yelled for more

She may have been just starting out
But I think that she'll go far
I will always remember her
Just a girl and a guitar

Tsunami Sickness

by David Kavanagh

sea draws back a breath
shore disappears out of view
then spews forth it's puke

As I Lay Dying

by Paul Thomson

Speak to me though I can no longer reply
As the life that was me does not comply
At once; for after the flame falters
The wick glows before it smolders.

Lady Liberty

by Fred Jagenberg

Follow me son to Lady Liberty
Beset by wolves she struggles on
Our wounded pride lays her reeling
Absent her, our endless seeking better days are pointless
By fakery they left her quartered
Offended they aim to render her helpless
Yet the slightest sliver of light from her lamp
Ignites our inward drive to seek her form
Above persistent calls for anarchy, she breathes through us
Against a world of famine, she feeds us
From determination to dissolve, she holds us
Until toward brotherly love, she moulds us
So truth, her triumphant beacon lights the world

"America is, and always will be, a shining city on a hill."
- Ronald Reagan

On-Sight

by Thama Logan

On-Sight
There aren't many who see me-
Those few view me in the
Words they say
"speak" me when they
Glance away
Their inner ear "attuned"
Their "knowings" seek invitation
To an inner, sacred place
Long ago barricaded from
"Exploitative" desires-I can
Not promise entry-

I LIVE here, and must protect my space.
Still; there are
a few...

Night Time

by Pauline Faller

NIGHT TIME
Darkness falls upon the night
Covering over day times light,
Enclosing like a velvet glove
Stars appearing from above.

Sunlight fades as night draws near
Clouds disperse and skies do clear,
Moonlight comes with golden grace
Showing her majestic face.

Silence of the night profound
Nocturnal creatures do abound,
Midnight comes on nightly quest
Dreams and nightmares manifest.

Shadows loom with face unknown
Dissipate with coming dawn,
Night time terrors bringing fear
Come the daylight, disappear.

A Station Scene

by Janaka Godevithana

The last passenger leaves:
last train's sound fades,
and breeze begins to grow.

Tiny grass and plants
crawl railings slowly,

and in dimmed sky
shines a bright star.

Sun begins to glow;
first train's sound echoes
and life takes its flow.

"The Full Moon Kindles The Bipolar Mind"

by Ngoc Minh Nguyen

The full moon kindles the bipolar mind:
    like a hunter hard on his prey, the nights
revive a dark, dysphoric mood; then grind
    the soul to abject lows from perfect heights.
And when from states of bliss to states of woe
    the spirit goes, even a king born high
longs for enduring sleep where the dead go;
    where the departed no more howl or cry.
But if this dour dilemma be his plight,
    then he shall fight it to his final breath;
and receive only then his promised flight
    to heaven, where there's no more tears or death!
For kings will not be bipolar coerced,
so long as in the Kingdom they're well-versed.

Fragile

by James Popplewell

Walking on thin ice
Searching the universe for a new vice.

One wrong step could mean never again waking
One step... cracking, another step... breaking.
I watch as another piece of the path floats away
but from this path, I must not stray.

I finally see the frozen water's edge
I finally reach it, but now I'm looking down from a ledge.
No more path from here, what am I supposed to do?
Is this it, the end, am I finally through?

Then I see something across from me
Standing next to a twisted tree.
Then I see something across the pit
Standing over a small fire that he just lit.

Then I see another, then another
they... are... me... one, two, three, four.
We each walked different paths to reach this place
and confusion was clear on each ones' face.

Water, Earth, Air, and Fire
Each one with a different desire.
Frozen, Quaking, Tempest, Eruption
each one brings its own destruction.

What is it that I am here to learn?
Life, Live, Breathe, Burn!
The mind is
Gentle... Hostile...
Changeable... Fragile.

A Stargazer's Journal

by Nelvy Gracia Majaw

I am aware
How the stars shine in her eyes,
Like pools of black waters for a mage to scry.
How the wind blows softly when-
She, in her graceful darkness
Raised her arms to the heavens
Casting the clouds aside
To let my eyes gaze in awe of the starry night.

I am aware
Of the depth of her heart

How her darkness consumes her light and
Her light consumes her dark.
How in her very being, I see
The Universe in all its glory.

I am aware
Of her tired eyes
As she sat in solitude
Singing the songs I have only heard in dreams.
How we float in an unending sea of darkness
'We'--balls of energy, darkness and light.
How we live on
Though our bodies have died.

I am aware
Of her heart
That felt none of the world
How in her last days
She had smiled for she had lived.
And once again with starry eyes
She turned to me with a jaded smile:
"I am no longer Human".

My consciousness,
Entangled with every being in existence
Since I first heard her voice.

And still today
While drifting off to deep slumbers, I hear-
The songs she had sung-

That appeared and disappeared
Within my forgotten dreams.

Independence

by Bartholomew Williams

In search of freedom, many braved the high seas,
Needing to flee the chains of their home countries.
Desiring a fresh start in a far-off land;
Educating their children to understand.
Plymouth, Jamestown, Hampton, and other such sites;
Enduring hardships, attacks, and other fights.
Now viewing self-rule, like Paine, as Common Sense;
Declaring to England their independence.
Early clashes at Lexington and Concord;
Not shrinking from gunfights or edge of a sword.
Claiming patriots' victory at Yorktown;
Earning a U.S. republic, not a crown.

Four Seasons

by Theresa Lynn Beyerl

Wintry white weather whirling westward,
whooshing wildly when winds wrestle.
Snowflakes swirling starting snowy stacks.

Spring showers sprout saplings
some scattering so softly.
Florist fashions flowing florets
flowers form filling flowerpots

Summer sunshine sets
sending sunrays sideways shimmering so sparkly.
Pool parties prove popular pastime plan.

Fall foliage falling fiercely
Floating, flipping, flopping... fell!
Autumn afternoon adventure
accumulating apples, apricots, and acorns.

Rainy Day

by MAXIMILIAN G. WOLF

The melancholic, cold rain makes me sad.
In the days of loud silence,
rain always called on you.
Your way into my thoughts and tears.
*

Color of lead on the sky; everything is grey.
The blue is in your eyes only.
Come along and listen with me
to the drops dripping down the window.
Like once upon a time down to our curls,
while in love and smiling,
we kissing each other under the clouds.
*

Your head is on my heart.
I am silently touched by your skin.
The gentle warmth of voice.
Your hands on my face heal everything.
*

Heavens Weltschmerz for all sad loves.
Maybe spring will bring something new.
New love and joy.
*

Piano music is somewhere in the distance.
A full circle day is approaching.
Announcement of the golden days in Marrakech.
With flower petals on the bed
and the view of the sunny oasis day.

Engagement Night

by David B D'Braunstein

We carpooled every day
I was in love, what can I say?
It was far too good to be true!
She was so beautiful to view!
She was like heaven to touch
I wanted to hold her so much!
But I was driving so had to wait
Until that night on our next date!
I thought a while to find a way
To pop the question and hear what she'd say
She said yes, and that was the start
Of many wonderful years, "be still my heart"!!

Ivy And The Elm

by Rick Keeble

The mighty Elm said to the Vine,
"On me you may climb, to reach out for the sun."
Ivy was not shy, for she had her reasons why,
So replied to the Elm, "only if you don't mind?"

The Elm being proud, looked Ivy in the eye,
"I see no reason why we both cannot survive?"
So Ivy held on tight and prospered in the light.
So much so she could not let go.

After many happy years, the Elm began to creak,
Ivy had grown and grown,
So much so the Elm was barely known.

Finally, the Elm did die, suffocated from the sky,
With Ivy still around, it stood no longer in the ground.
Bringing Ivy right along, now both had finally gone.

Viola

by Beryl Edmonds

Admiring her beauty he was mesmerised
Her complete perfection brought tears to his eyes
Holding her tenderly in his loving arms
Slowly he caressed the magic of her charms.

This was the gift he had waited so long for
The answer to prayers he had made to the Lord
It felt quite spine tingling as his heart took flight
Sensing that he'd love her till close of his life.

As he held her within a loving caress
His fingers traced o'er her with skill and finesse
Feeling the joy to the world that she'd bestow
Strumming her heart strings music began to flow.

They got on well and lived happily in tune
She was his amulet to finding fortune
Together they made sweet music forever
Nothing but death could tear them apart ever.

He carried her in a case on his shoulder
The musical, adorable viola.

The Boy Who Put Glitter Eyeshadow

by Himani Bhaisare

The house mourns now that she has gone
Desperately I dig through her cabinet to find anything to hold on.
My dewy gaze lands upon her glitter eyeshadow.
Mesmerized, I put it and my eyes lit up like rainbow
Unaware, the devil stood behind me with his eyes filled with rage
"Stop this at once! Act like the boys your age!"
He struck me across the face and labelled me an abomination

No boy I knew liked glitter eyeshadow so must be true I thought, the allegation.
Bruised and bleeding I hid from him in the closet of hers
Found two angels with broken wings and wrinkled skin in the drawers.
The old rusty sprites started singing songs of freedom and fight
"We are everywhere! Those of us who like glitter!" said one with all their might.
Every day I would sit there and learn of my identity
Knowing there are people like me in the world gave me serenity
As it sang its last tune, I realized they were left to me by mother
She knew I'd need them one day after she's gone, in the hope to save me the fate I suffer.
The stained papyrus armed me with spells enchanted
If it wasn't for them, I would have been locked forever with my knowledge scanted.
With a purple heart, I get out because now the devil scared me not
I walk proudly out of the house knowing I'm not made to rot.
"Do you not care what the people call an unnatural?" asked the devil shocked
"Look! He's a tranny!..is how you will be remarked."
"It's not He. Its She" placidly said I and left him dismayed.
Freedom and identity were the weapons handed down for my aid
By warriors who put their words in books unafraid.

An Invitation To Rest

by David Richmond

You try your best, yet fall far short,
of what you know my will requires.
Cease by your strength, my grace to gain.
Come unto me and rest.

Rebellious heart by trouble torn.
Restless, dejected, and forlorn.
Get off your independence horse.
Come unto me, find rest.

All who are burdened down with stress,
by cares of life that wear and press.
Let me your heavy burdens bear.
Come, and in me find rest.

You were not made to live alone,
to hobble hurt, to moan and groan,
but in me to find, your purpose blest.
So, come to me, enjoy my rest.

To Many Doors Not Enough Exits When Its Too Late

by John Lusardi

Secrets spooned over!
the dipping of toast
into the steamed cup captured espresso.
Un-asked answerless questions.
They return spinning in an orbit of not knowing.
Chairs scattered; cold empty seats
the previous occupiers never to return!
All doors are open! and locked mindfully:
Between them truth struggles to breathe
choked by lies, in long dark years.
Now all exits lead out away beyond teenage years;
and their failing to look and ask.
The walls know! its dissolved into their existence.
To many doors, and not enough exits,
and a lost code of answers
sleep in distant soils and ashes,
still you don't know!
And never will.

The Dak Dak

by Janine lever

The Dak Dak
The room is small
 With spaceships on the wall paper
A narrow brown wooden table sits quietly under the window.
Dark navy blue curtains fall

With cars and red, faded rockets
A small metal chair sits on the slatted floor.
It is midnight says the grinning, frog faced clock
And it is the time when the Dak Dak comes out.

He waits, until the house is silent
Until the adults are asleep
Then he crawls from under the boy sized bed.
His body smaller than his large green head
With a single eye, he stares, unable to blink
Large teeth glint, with sharpened points.
It is midnight says the story in the book
And it is the time when the Dak Dak comes out.

 Human sense, crawls up the sleepers neck
A slithering, creeping scary alarm
There is no scream in the throat
It is buried in the fear of what came from under the bed
Only rapid panic rises to its height
To move the arms and pull the covers over the head
It is midnight shouts father, stop messing about
It is tomorrow when the Dak Dak next comes out.

Sempiternal Kiss

by Roren

Late at night, in the secret chamber far apart
A valiant knight, stands there, put his hand on his heart:
"With this ring, I plight unto thee my troth till death!"
She's slumbering, the damsel in distress. Her breath
Divinely lovely, her rosy lips, they beguile
The fiery lordly, leave him, with the sweetest guile.
Deep within his bosom, dulcet sounds beat quicker,
Lambent eyes blossom, red face betrays his fever:

"Fair lady, why sleepest thou? Rise out of thy sleep
O deary, cast me not away, nor let me weep.
Awake thee, beauteous maiden! Awake! Arise!
I prithee, let me see thine orbs, before sunrise!
In woe and pain, I suffer from like no other.

I ache all o'er again, and I can no longer
Tarry here, abashed by thy fleshly body.
Harken ere I succumb to thy charming beauty..."

After months of waiting, I kneel beside the bed
And fingering, at the blonde hair about thine head:
"Princess, how dark the darkness of Abyss must be...
Blessed be my last favor! In love with none but thee"

Nigh to thy visage, my late outrage to the realm;
—Thy lips I kiss for ages!—Into Heaven's whelms,
I fall apace... How long this fantasia will last?
Till my Grace behold mine eyes, for a long time past.

In mine arms, thou shall awake or remain this way!
If thou fallest under the charm, avarice pays...
From ecstasy to agony—The deathly kiss—
There rests no heavier calamity, than this...

Countless minutes goes by, since my lips are on thine
Thus, I die! In death my lips thou sealest... decline...
But I care not... Thou art mine! How happy I am!
Thy tongue is so hot... what a delectable jam...

My lips are sealed on thine!—Sempiternal kiss!—

On the morrow, after and beyond, I beseech:
"Fantasy not about the others! I'll never
Let them slake their thirst, drink thine heavenly water...
Thy sole lover I am! Forever and ever!
And 'till never sever, our link for another."

I wish that somewhere, in the far distant future
I could meet with her, go back on an adventure.
My shape may change may be, but be sure, by my troth:
"My love will never cease to be." I pray for both...

The Spartans

by Alshaad Mahomed Kara

Ancient tales slashed our vineyard,
We were the bloodshed of love...
Cupid fleshed our hearts.

Austere eyesights.
Fierce catch upon your mark,
Am your prey in the love arena...

I escort this frugal lover.
His Achillean personality enchants every man,
I am the residue of my manhood...

Close the cishet doors,
Let the cue tip-off,
You will be my man besides the world.
Two kings for a kingdom.

If I Write Down Words

by Leo Larry Amadore

If I write down words
that pour from me like
water rushing from a rusty gutter
carrying my cries in the flood
with decaying leaves and
the smattering off the roof
of droppings from so many
ceaselessly cooing mourning doves,
is that a poetry of sorts?

If the aged shingled roof leaks
at its eaves (like my eyes)
when wind blows the rain
nearly horizontal and the house

beams creak and sound like
corroded hinges when
seldom-used doors are opened,
has a trope occurred?

And, is anything here -- honestly --
more than almost senseless patter?
Except to me (and a few others)
it really doesn't even matter.

The Old And Weathered Bridge

by Justin Maxwell DePietropaolo

I find myself a-loss,
Alone upon the ridge,
As I debate to cross.
This old and weathered bridge.

While slowly inching towards,
I gaze upon and spot,
The holes and splintered boards,
And areas of rot.

The rocky ridge does lend,
A different way to go.
For I could just descend,
To cross the creek below.

A way that's not as brisk,
Would take a deal of time.
And down the rocks I risk,
Then up again to climb.

Or maybe I just ought,
To step with bated breath.
And put away the thought,
Of falling to my death.

And so inside I toss,

Unmoved upon the ridge.
As I debate to cross,
The old and weathered bridge.

Girl On A Bridge

by Terry Flood

Seeming unseeing, expressionless being
Asleep in this wide awake town
Leant on the side of a bridge cross the river
Her gaze and demeanour are down

Considered a knife for taking her life
But thoughts of whom-ever might find
her blood drenched cadaver, decided she'd rather
not mess up an innocent's mind

Spent some time thinking, painkillers while drinking
Might bring her the peace that she craves
But what if they merely left her feeling bleary
So now she stands gazing at waves

Nobody asks if she's needing assistance
As busy folk head on their way
Ladies with lippy and cyclists nippy
And suited chaps seizing the day

A note she laid down, then without tear or frown
She climbed up and over the side
Made her last pledge on a protruding ledge
That really was not very wide

Well Lord, that was me, what had you hoped to see
Whatever it was I have failed
Messed up all my life, but I'll get one thing right
For I've got my final act nailed

Behind her a groan in a juvenile tone
The nine year old face wore a frown
From under the bridge, that scared little kid

Said, please Lady, don't let me drown

My dad paid a man who had a white van
To find a long life of good health
Snuck out of Francais then to my dismay
Abandoned me here by myself

She said take my hand, then climb up and stand
Safe on the bridge, then we'll go
Miss, said the lad, did God have this planned
Honey, she said, I don't know

Volition

by Dave Collins

Sitting with stillness
seasons come without my help
Mother guides herself
grass grows flowers bloom birds sing
Nature Nirvana Rebirth

Haiku 160

by Richard Colbert

i expect nothing
therefor i deserve the same
being is a gift

An Agnostic's Prayer

by Cindy Bahl

I take a deep breath
Focus on my body
Acknowledge the miracle it is,
It always has been
I'm grateful for being alive

For existing in this moment
No matter the challenges
I feel weighing on me
The alternative is an end to surprises
No more new starts
with each morning
with each breath
Let me connect with the awe
of the astonishing small wonders around me
And rediscover why being human
is an incredible gift

At Your Last Breath

by Shreya Laxmi Nagendra

If I had to explain to a child
What is fear?
I could not
I would not

But for the adult
Fear is all too familiar
Yet so unknown
Transcendence is skewed

Fear is natural
Yet it is corrupt
It is in the mind alone
But also physically numbs

A lingering silence
Devoid of thoughts
Or a chaotic noise
Without a gap between screams

Blooming from confusion
Unfamiliarity, wrath and kindness
The reason for being afraid
Was not the same

For Jack or Jill
Dorothy or the Tinman
Stepmother or Stepsisters
Bonnie or Clyde

Are you still afraid?
One asked a dying man
'No', he replied
If not before, then at your last breath

As I Climb The Peak

by Polen

At an angle of unknown degrees
I climb the peak to get a clear picture of the world,
This mountain hiking is deep and sweet.
So many things had fallen into my sight and
My inner agitation unfolds the words,
That promote victory and avoid chaos along this fields,
Looking into the past
I definitely deserve this peace.

My vision is clear enough to recall all the scenes
Though it's much blurry to figure out
What the future holds uptight along the hills,
Sometimes living in this life feels so itchy.
I realized after so many revolutions
That looking back was never a concrete floor for solutions.

My ultimate goal lies in this mountain hiking
Which alters the timeline and historical times through my illusions,
I am sweating enough to reach the peak
Which will confirm the accomplishment of my dreams.

Soup Of Poetry

by Nancy Rodriguez Laurel

Soup of poetry
What great taste
It's better than poultry
Unique ingredients that won't waste
The passion of hands that inspire royalty

With a simple bowl
So steaming hot
What's in it, what it holds?
One serving is never enough
Don't worry there's plenty in the pot

Words that float as you smell its steam
An intriguing and captivating love
Let's you comprehend what it truly does mean
The art and heart it has of...
In the kingdom of thy King and thy Queen

In the land of poets and muse
A beautiful world filled with galore of ideation
Where jesters smile attaining all and can amuse
The throne needs leisure or face execution
Many things that are mad but yet can confuse

Painting the roses red
Is faking the truth to the emperors crown
To be caught won't matter what all will be said
You'll be judged and humiliated on a jury's ground
All warning signs you've avoided to be read

The token to a skill to feather and write
Takes devotion and emotion from deep inside
Flavor that foresight don't let it escape your sight
What one without knowing might hide
Soup of Poetry that finesses with delight

The Kissing Tree

by Deborah Milner

Deep in the forest,
Down by the flowing waters,
The tall tree stood...
Arms stretched wide apart,
Covered by balls of entanglement,
Tightly wound on each arm,
The pests entwined around.
But under the old trunk,
Two lovers stared out to the branches,
with beauty in their eyes.
To them, it would always be,
The kissing tree – where,
a first kiss had started,
the growth of new beginnings.

Silent Tears

by Anna M Shepard

Silent tears are what I cry
something I learned as a child
turning from all those who can see
keeping my feelings deep within

Silent tears are seldom heard
muffled whimpers sometime escape
my body trembling from the ache within
silencing emotions is almost an impossibility

Silent tears come from the heart
mourning for what has been lost
from the pain that's been inflicted upon me
they're felt through the corridors of my very soul

Silent tears fall freely
seemingly unending at times
releasing the anxieties which life has to offer
cleansing my innermost being, waking to a brighter day

Salvation

by Dexter I Greener

Kneeling in the median, crying, crying, what have I done?
Oh the pain, the pain wishing the past was undone.
I have no hope for my wretched life, now that I am alone.
The horror of a dying man reverberates in my bones..
That look sinks into my soul with his plea of, WHY!
His pleas of why, I cannot live, why must I die?
As his eyes of his soul fade away into lifelessness.
I feel the authority gently pull my arms and cuff both my wrists.
I wanted no representation at my hearing the following day.
The Judge took pity on me for I was trying to keep my crying at bay.
He sentenced me to five years for DUI and 10 for vehicle manslaughter.
Now I sit in solitude, withering away and not living, why bother.

I usually keep my cell door closed, I want no company
But in my melancholy of self-pity, I left it open this day.
A joyful youth of red hair came bounding in with a beautiful smile.
His noble intentions startled me for a while.
He offered me his ration of delicious smelling bread.
I was distraught over this death with deep sorrow and dread.
I gently refused his kind offer and told him I want no life.
He warmly smiled at me which put a pause in my strife.
You have me transfixed and wanting to know more.
"I see the pain in your eyes, do you want release?" he implore.
I told him that it hurts so much that I do not want to Live.
He said, "Have you considered an alternative that I am willing to give?"
What is it? I stated, what do you have for I know I am condemned.
Let me tell you about our brother that he wants you to mend.
I am an only child and I have no brother, you speak of him, who's he?
He is Jesus, our brother who extends a welcoming hand and want you to see.
See what? I asked as my heart started to warm as if he's there.
Suddenly our brother appeared in radiant light and sat in a chair.
I fell to my knees and bowed to him crying, why me brother?

I feel your pain of a contrite heart for you are my child like no other.
Please listen to me for I and one who has died forgive you for what you have done.
Now, child, please forgive yourself, when you do your life will shine like the sun.
Still kneeling at my brother's feet and I forgave myself over and over again.
Thanks to my redheaded friend and brother, my new life began.

The Writer In Me Wants You To Know

by Harriet Davis

The writer in me wants you to know
Challenges in life causes one to grow

The hurt and shame one will endure
Can cause vision to become obscure

Not settling for the prostrate position
Overcoming was achieved; I identified the condition

Of low self-esteem and all it entails
Had my mind messed up 'cause I thought I failed

Failed to be what he wanted and desired
When looking back, I realize he conspired

To belittle me and keep me down
But here I am today with a re-positioned crown

No longer a prisoner of his demands
I took matters within so I could stand

On my own two feet I had to show
Challenges in life causes one to grow

Sparkling Life

by Linda Milgate

spiking stars sparkling lights
fast mornings then slow nights
nature rotates in and out of darkness
cells, organisms and structures manifest
generations form, birth, germination, death
heavens and life join into the universal breath
current combinations shaped from Neanderthal DNA
thus sapiens connected living and learning to pray
how long will this species live and evolve
as humanity changes grows then revolves
sparkling stars will join with the other lights
thus growth and eternity forever enter into the twilight

God, You've Always Blessed Me

by Franklin A. Price

God you've always blessed me
As I've moved along life's way
Never, ever, left my side
Still guiding me today

You always are all seeing
But I always have a choice
Can do as I would like to
Or can listen to your voice

You've sent me family and friends
They are one and the same
This prayer is also for them
And I give it in your name

If it isn't too much trouble
Please continue as you are
And I'll try my best to follow

Your advice, and guiding star

Amen and Amen

Shoe Box

by John A'hern

Wardrobe top shelf, a place of dust and darkness,
Sitting in such sadness.
Time to visit, memories waiting there
Words and feelings shared without care.
A shoe box, full of treasures letters and treason
Brought into daylight, secrets, reasons.
Lid is opened, just as in times before
Letters written to loved ones, letters returned unread
Others are full of memories of those we knew as friends
Some are read with laughter, some are full of jokes
Others are filled with words of love and praise
Sparking our thoughts of those that wrote
Some are not legible, not through faults of their own
Eyes are full of sadness tears, memories of those now gone
Words cannot be seen through tears that flow
Tears fall onto dusty letter pages
As many have done before
If only there had been understanding
Words that were misunderstood
letters returned full of love and praise
I love you, that line often misunderstood
Memories now flowing in front of me
The daylight hours are turning dim, my eyes close in sleep
I awake in the dead of night, just as many times before
Letters, memories, scattered at my feet, waiting to go back home
All picked up and back in the shoe box
Top shelf darkness, waits for their return
I say a few words of kindness, my memories whisper, we care.

Silent Witness

by Tony Staples

We have an agreement the chopping board and me,
it promised to keep quiet about the things it did see.
It's seen me do things that could be considered a crime,
with ingredients like Oregano, Parsley and Thyme.
I've created some horrors worse than Frankenstein's monster
during my adventures with cookery and the skills I try to conquer.
We know glass and plastic are nowhere near as good,
but it thinks it's cos of secrets that I've kept my chopping board of wood!

My Song Shall Not Stop

by Olatubosun David

My song shall not stop;
Even though my time is up,
And the mike is off
And I'm removed from the stage to the off
stage.

An itinerant singer:
Even though my trip and toils cease;
And I'm left with no blank sheet
And my pen stops to flow ink,
My songs shall not stop;
I shall continue to sing.

A man doesn't die;
Though the tent is deserted;
Residential bird escapes to the firmaments;
Dust returns to dust and feed the worms.
But I shall yet live again
For in mortality dwells immortality.

I'm a writer, I shall not die.
I'm a God's son, I shall not die.

At night, the sun shall go to rest;
Darkness from the face of heavens shall fall;
But then, the glory of the moon and stars shall rise.

If unable to live as long as time and season
I shall yet, in this work, continue to live
Shall continue to write
In the blank sheets of your heart.
Shall continue to sing melodies
To the ready ears of your inner child.
Shall continue to paint your mental skies
With the colour of rainbow.

A life there is after death.
At brink of the earth's extinction,
In the other side of the blue sea,
Beyond the stretch of the horizon beyond;
Where the sky and the blue sea blend-
Life continues to be.

Natures Observations

by Indiana Shaw

No such thing as a neutral colour when all the colours start to blend
Always mixed with wind and water from which then colours suspend
To make rainbows, from which the seven colours make a chosen arc
Ultra violet rays, from a gold, red, yellow and orange sun do embark
Rain mixes with earth, sand, or clay deepen in their colours far more
Expressed in an earthly weightiness, held within the earth's dry floor
Seeds will spring to life thanks to the heavens timely water out-pour

Over hills and as mountain's just to arrive at another distance shore
Bird's exquisite in their beauty to be observed, their colours I adore
Snakes and all things creepy, creep amongst green plants disguised
Every small creature their prey, life, or death; we are all mesmerized
Rain forests; our life and breath to which the rest of life depends on
Variety; in its millions of every animal cries, and with every bird song
Amazing sights and sounds we sometimes cannot believe even exist
Though nature comes with its own warning, should one disrespect it

Idyllic is a word; for those who seek out its peacefulness and charm
Only those; at one with earth, can till this earth and collectively farm
Nature's observations; help us to adhere, to this wonderful life's call
Sanctuary; found cradling us with each sun rise and each night's fall

My Cat

by Franci Eugenia Hoffman

My cat sits on the window sill
My cat sits on the window sill

Watching the birds and bees fly by
They flit and flutter in the sky
Her antics more than meet the eye
Watching the birds and bees fly by

My cat she lets out such a sigh
My cat she lets out such a sigh

Watching twinkling stars as they dance
Her wide golden eyes in a trance
Hoping to see a ghost perchance
Watching twinkling stars as they dance

My cat naps on warm summer days
My cat naps on warm summer days

Sun puddles sing their lullabies
She dreams of birds and bees that fly
Sun puddles sing their lullabies
Sun puddles sing their lullabies

The Good Ole Days

by Julie Grenness

For an aged brother, RIP.

His good ole days are still to be,
In football heaven, in eternity,
Looks at the face of the universe, does he,
He rewound his music, so country,
He got them all back, you see,
His wife, his old dog, his car, no needs,
Pray his good ole days are still to be....

Summer Showers

by Kathy Bahr

A drop fell on the apple tree,
That went to help bathe the sea.
The Sunshine threw fete hung.
Where the Jocoser birds sung.
The breezes brought the birds bathed in glee.

Those Sacred Walls

by Indiana Shaw

Her smile; could break a man and his strength strip
Her laugh; creating within him such a broken storm
Her cruelty; as then quells, this ardour of courtship

Her laugh; creating within him such a broken storm
Her righteous; unbroken, since her so highest birth
Her unrequited love; in his heart could not as warm

Her righteous; unbroken, since her so highest birth
Her un-realist values; worn across, her open breast

Her need; to express upon him, her own self-worth

Her un-realist values; worn across, her open breast
Her blindness; that forever, she cannot stand alone
Her battles; to keep her fortitude, so will never rest

Her blindness; that forever, she cannot stand alone
Her quest; to find who can carry her, when she falls
Her rights; to find a man, who can retain his throne

Her quest; to find who can carry her, when she falls
Her deliberation; as then challenges all those before
Her trust; so let him break down those sacred walls

A Fine And Private Place

by Alison Hodges

The coldness turns your skins fine hue
From ivory stain to deep sea blue
While cold and lonely you do lie
As in your grave you do abide

And I would lay there if I could
With rotting flesh within the wood
Though all your hair clings to your skull
Yet still my flaming passion pulls

For yet this love between us lies
Even though our bodies should die
We long to reignite the flame
That in our lives drove us insane

To roll within the casket walls
To break the silence with our calls
To consummate our love at last
To feel our dead hearts beating fast

And you my bride for one sweet night
When the angels have taken flight

Leaving us to flicker so bright
For one brief moment our love is right

Life Tracks

by Ogunyigbo Adedoyin Blessing

Remembering days that we felt loved,
Concerns etched on caring faces,
Wrapped in the comfort cocoon of hugs,
Became tracks that were played on repeat modes.

Days that we made new relationships,
The goofy conversations and awkward beginnings,
Tacky photos and hilarious memories,
Became the backdrop of our life's gallery.

The normal days and the exciting ones,
Days that the world seem so cruel,
And days that we felt on top of the world,
Are all part of our life tracks that we lie back and replay.

Always There

by Sarah Stein

Black silhouette
Evil eyes
Grinning
As if satisfied
Elongated nails
A finger coaxing me
To go near
It surrounds
Desolation sets in
Finally taking
Over me,
My home
Always there

Always taunting
Give me peace
From this horror
The nonstop
Stalking
It knows
My innermost secrets
From then until now
Can't escape
What could I do
To be free?

Fire Fly

by Kohava Ray

Seeing it's dim light
I feel relieved

The sun is too strong
The moon is too far away
The stars are too glittering
The headlights are too blazing
The taillights make me too emotional
The street lamps are too objective
The lights from the office buildings are too oppressive
The room light is too broad
The desk lamp is too direct
The flashlight is too tense
and
The fireworks are too grandiose....

But a firefly
is a reminder
It's OK to show a modest light
In the darkness, then,
We see you
We know you,
and you remind us
We are also the light

Whale Song

by Tony Staples

We have witnessed more than you can dream,
we have been to places you have never seen.
Our knowledge is beyond your comprehension
and we have suffered your bloody ascension.
You have hunted us, we await your evolution,
please show us some compassion and our planet's restitution!

More Than Enough

by HILDA ABOAGYEWAA AGYEKUM

I look at that dress and with a smile, I pass on...
That house is beautiful, says my heart...
My mind harshly replies, be content with what you have!
You don't need all that luxury,
What you have is more than enough!

Whiles in the car, I blurt out...
'I am very content with what I have'...
Are you sure that's all there is to gain? My heart murmurs...
What you have is more than enough! says my mind.

I look through the window and see the cute little girl
Feeding her dog with much gladness
Behind her, a beautiful woman smiles
She's wrapped in the loving arms of a man who looks adorably at her

I don't need all that! I blurt out...
Then why do you smile? my heart says

That was when I realized...
I wanted more than I have!
I just couldn't admit it.

I hope my heart leads one day...
Till I get to the place...
Where my heart leaps with gladness...
And shouts out...
You have more than enough!

Hearken To Thy Heart

by Rick Keeble

Is it not true when we're apart,
This ache I feel in my beating heart?

Skip it does when you're in view,
It shall never turn away from you.

Alas, my love, I am forever yours,
No harm will come, there is no cause.

As the nights roll on, a voice within,
Speaks to my heart which begins to sing.

Never before have I felt this way,
I'll spend my life telling you each day.

Our euphoric feet skipping down love's lane,
'Til the day we both walk with a cane.

Then in each other's arms we'll be,
For you are the one true love for me.

Unstable Mind

by Vincent Van Ross

When people accuse me
Of being a man of unstable mind,
I do not get offended—
I do not mind!

My mind Is constantly
Growing, developing,
Evolving, changing...

Why should I
Stand by everything
I said yesterday?

What I said yesterday
Was true of yesterday
But, why should it remain
The same today?

Everything changes with time—
Situations change, Knowledge increases,
Perceptions get overhauled,
The mind gets transformed!

Change is an ongoing process of life—
It is a Process of evolution!
If I do not change, I do not evolve!

Should I surrender myself to stagnation
Just to hear that I have
A stable mind?

I was honest yesterday
I am honest to myself today—
I have not hypothecated my integrity
To anyone, or, anything...

If my intentions are right...
If I have no hidden agenda...
If I change my mind
To accommodate an evolved thought,
What is wrong with that?

I am comfortable with myself!
I am absolutely at peace with myself!

It does not bother me
If people think of me
As someone
With an unstable mind!

The Dove

by Kudzai Mhangwa

When the dove blooms into
The sky,
What great pleasure it is to
Witness it's conquering,
Not only does it conquer
The winds above,
But conquers crippled hearts;
It speaks peace.

We look upon the dove
Claiming its space in creation,
We are called to celebrate
Peace with it and we too
Wonder why the dove
Speaks of ending wars
That it did not invent.

Trapped

by DIANE PERNA-GRAF

I run through life wounded with a steel trap ensnared onto my
foot restricting my life's essence. Day in and out I'm never able to
shake it off, in relentless movements so no new pain touches me.

I fight for sustenance; I fight to inhabit this life damaged and
wearied, from taking life's persecutions. The torment of my
afflictions you cannot see.

I hold close that God is always watching and will pull me from
the muddied roads I run. He hears my tormented cries; he

feels my tortured spirit; he sees I can't stop this path I'm on.

You say I'm not getting free, but the running is critical to me,
I'll run as long as I can, let me be free from what haunts me,
it's not something you'll ever comprehend.

You say the war is over, but the hurt remains. I keep a mask on
in good times and bad. They think that my life doesn't count
but God sees the merit of my existence.

Every day, it's my struggle; no one can imagine the heartbreak,
as the sorrow cuts my soul as deeply as the rapt foot, it won't
come off it's always mine alone.

I'm still fighting, as the battle rages on in my mind, if you haven't
experienced this anguish, you can run with me or without me.
I've accepted the aloneness in this fight.

This trap keeps me from fending off life's predators. I'm a
solitary being with a broken spirit. My desperate expression
is evidence enough.

I know God watches this burden I carry. I pray when
my time is up he gives me warning so I remain still as
I'm risen up out of this hell.

My Angels in Heaven see me; so, I'm okay to die this way;
it's not for you to say. I'm done defending this. I pray
for you without any prayers in return.

Kind

by Kevon Worrell

She wore a smile on her face like nothing matter
In a place that's full of benefits and betrayal
Her kind nature lit a passion like candles
Burning one sense of insecurities away

Scars that doesn't justify her false facade

Eyes that's looks in sync of the abyss
Hassen on her brain she knows this is not her home
For everywhere she goes her past seem to follow

Battlefield and battle fiend destroy what she once built
Seeming like the gods doesn't want her to win
Nation upon nation they own creation crumble
Kind was not no more than a chess piece design to play a role
To quench the raising conflict of the competition

A Friend

by Frank Blacharczyk

Nobody drowns in the Water of Life
No one starves eating fruit from the Tree of Life
The Light will be a candle in my darkest hour
A stream of Water when I thirst for peace
Bread when I hunger for hope
The Light will be a lamp in my darkest hour
And a Friend when all seems lost

Laborer's Ode I - Asphalt Pavers

by Robert Trezise Jr

Boy gets up at six
Needs no alarm of complaint
To shake
The brief night of sleep
From his hay-cropped hair

Brushes his teeth
Smokes a two dollar holler of cigarette for breakfast

A pack a day is like tax day for him
Paid by ten in the morning
Then the day is free and clear

Holds down his car as it bucks to life

Lurches away

Stops at Starbucks
Spends another hour's dough
On two large black coffees

Picks up three buddies at the far edge
Of the Walmart parking lot

Drives two hours to arrive
At a dismal road to tame with asphalt

The boys dissolve and stick to the road

Buns of thick shoulders
Rise and fall in the oven of sun
Shoveling boils of oil and coal

Throwing
Their boots to stomp the steam

His car limps back to his driveway corral
At 9:45 in the summer evening

Devours another hour
Of Coors and McDonalds at his kitchen table

Prays very hard to God
Maybe it could rain tomorrow?

His girlfriend stands behind him
Rests her head on his shoulder

A dim light buzzing from the ceiling.

One

by Laurie Slicer

One,
Alone
Aches the mind.
Leaving alone
Leaving me alone
Kills my soul with cold pain.
The body of my lover
Leaves me loneliness to survive.
The body of my lover
Kills my soul with cold pain
Leaving me alone.
Leaving alone
Aches the mind.
Alone.
One

The Well

by Carolyn June-Jackson

I dip from my well whenever I am lonely
I pull from this well every time I feel lost
It is my secured secret hiding place only
Excavating this hole came with a high cost

It was hand-dug; covered with an old wood plank
The water is now putrid and too moldy to drink
It was my grandpapa's well; I have him to thank
I pour in a bottle of bleach to help cover the stink

I don't pull it to drink it; it's not for consumption
I use it on my green garden; especially the plants
I like knowing that it is still in prime operation
It kills the crawling pests; including the fire ants

My well is a treasure trove of long-gone memories
Ten generations relied on the spring water it gave
I will not fill it in; It has seen tragedies and victories
It was dug with human labor by long-ago slaves

My well knows my voice; yet, will not make a sound
I look down its stony neck for creative inspiration
To me, it is more than just a dark hole in the ground
It stands on hard-fought land for future generations

Dark Veil

by John R Fiordelisi

A dark veil
O'er eyes and ears
Have set phrases to stun.
Standards for me
Omnipotence for thee,
Tripping over
grayed limping liberty,
Crumbling to a blurry pause.
Trekking through a
Field of freedoms trampled,
Foraged souls
Appear and wilt
In the fiery smartphone snapped chat.

Hypnotized by systemic doping,
we await elusive belly tickles:
To resurrect us from our
collective nod.

After All These Years

by Deborah Beachboard

I cannot recall your name,
yet I remember the warmth of your hand
as you held mine, and the way the moon illuminated
the cobblestones as we walked along main street
that first summer night in '75.

I cannot recall your face,
yet I remembered the crook of your grin and the sparkle
of your eyes as you looked down on me, and the coziness
of our old bed in the rented studio near the center of town
that carefree summer of 75.

I cannot recall your voice,
but I remember the plans you made to go and not stay,
and how the downtown fountain gurgled and splashed
and seemed to whisper and sigh so long after your goodbye
that last summer night in '75.

Typos Are A Part Of Life

by George Schaefer

Let's
admit
that it's true
we can deny
but it goes nowhere
and leads us back to truth
typos are a part of life
those misspelled words by accident
hound and haunt us to our dying days
we only hope to find absolution

Water Dear Water

by John Richard Anderson

Water, water, dear water, Mater Mare.
Where would I be without you, my wet, wet milieu?
Water is the medium that bathes my cells, my blood, my fluid within,
derived from the primordial ocean, aeons ago, still tasting of its salt.
I live bedside the sea, no other place would I, or could I be, born a Piscean.
For the ocean, river, lake, pond, drip and drop, even tiny pitter patter splats
sustains me in body and soul.
If I was dragged away from the sea, dripping wet, and I would die.
I willed my ashes to be tossed upon the sea when I pass away. From Water to
Water, I be.
Daily I make my pilgrimage to walk along the beach and swim in the ocean
waves.
To imbibe the meditative rhythm of the tides and surge of the waves,
to and fro, in and out, surging splashing on the shore around my body.
I walk along the strip of sand washed between tide in and out,
so that I leave no footprints to desecrate the beach shore, so perfect.
I love the wedding gown train crescents left
on the smooth glistening wet sand with each wave as it surges up the beach.
At night, I hear the sea shanties sung by waves lapping on the shore, moody
and reflective.
I hear the sounds of waves whooshing and hissing, splashing, and dashing,
surging up the shore and back.
This performance is so calming and charming to me and the bird flocks.
Unlike a forest or a park, every day the sea is different, never the same.
Yet like an old friend, forever familiar to seafarer me as the sea and shore.
The rhythm of the sound, and visual surge of images are my meditation,
I come daily to the shore to be refreshed, adorned and pray homage,
to 'Mater Mare', the mother and matrix,
and womb of all life, here, on Planet Water.
On a calm day you can hear
all the seashell choir stranded on the beach,
sighing sea shanties under their breath.
I am one of them, now and forever.

Freedom

by Neena J. Luke

Don't let people make you
Step outside of your character
Stay true to who you are
You were put in this world to be a light
And shine so bright
That you can be seen from afar
Don't let nobody trigger you to do something
That will jeopardize your freedom
Cause we need you to stay from behind those bars
Our children need to see role models
That show them they can succeed
Despite their battle wounds and scars
They need to see that they can be someone great
And that there is no limit to what they can be
We need to lead by example
Cause who else is gonna do it
I'm tired of seeing kids die in these streets
I didn't give birth to them
But it's hard to watch
That's such a powerful blow for me
I pray every day that this will change
But we can't help them unless we are free

Blind Willie's Sketchpad - Ash Wednesday, First Person Singular

by Michael J. Kalavik

The air smell cloudy,
With a hint of rain.
Come all this way by trustin'
In a thin white cane.
If a wink is as good as a nod,
What's a brotha ta do?
Should Jesus come again in glory,

Wouldn't chance to see that, too.

Can't read the street signs
When I'm walkin' home.
Don't never ask directions,
Gotta make it on my own.
Oh, the speck in thy neighbor's eye...
Some be never so blind.
An honest man in Orleans Parish
Ain't no easy thing to find.

It's a game of countin' footsteps
When I stroll down Rue Dupre
And the landmarks I rely on
Ain't the kind the eye can see.

My woodstove crackle
When I burn the mail.
The magic wind of radio
Done fill my sail.
Gotta reach for the bulb to tell
If the table lamp on.
A moonless night and empty skyline,
All the brilliant stars are gone.

Sweet voice on FM
Bridges time and space.
You know I'd give the world
If I could touch her face
In a gentle and sensitive way
For to know how she feel.
Get to the pearl inside the oyster
At the bottom of the deal.

Sense desire in her fragrance,
Feel the fire in her skin
Taste the ocean's salty wonder
When the levee's giving in.

Don't say no prayers for me, padre.

When the lights go out,
My soul can find its own way in the dark.
And pretty mama, when I git ya,
I'm gonna lick those ashes off.

Funeral Strut - Po' Boy On A Fat Tuesday

by Michael J. Kalavik

Hey there, little Buddha,
Let me join your Mistick Krewe.
Got my jazz hand clapping.
Gonna drop the other shoe.
I strut my yo-yo yoga every doo-da day.
It get me so-so-sober in a drunken way.
Hey there, little Buddha,
Voodoo me some déjà vu.
Those saints are marching in again;
Another Bourbon Street debut.

Hey there, little Buddha,
Save me from my karma's wrath.
Calculate my blessings;
Maybe you can do the math.
So many numb-numb-numbers,
Couldn't feel my way.
To get me near Nirvana,
Need a CPA.
Hey there little Buddha,
Lead me down the garden path.
Those saints are here to party, boy.
This Mardi Gras make 'em laugh.

Hey there, little Buddha,
Send your children out to play.
Pranayama mama,
Laissez les bons temps rouler.
I'll chant my man-oh-mantra
Till my eardrums ache
And clear my cha-cha chakras
With a plumber's snake.

Hey there little Buddha,
Second line come first today.
Those saints will set your flag on fire.
Jockomo feena nay.

We Danced To Our Song

by Graham Bentley

The first dance was ours, our song, perfect words
A special dance, seeing nobody else, in our moment
Oblivion, blurred, just us in focus, slowly, tight
Two slowly dancing, you in white, my songbird
It was the beginning

The next dance was his, our song, perfect words
A special dance, seeing our baby son, in that moment
With joy, hope, love, all in focus
Three slowly dancing, you both in white, my songbird
It was a new beginning

The next dance was hers, our song, perfect words
A special dance, seeing our baby girl, in that moment
With joy, hope, love, all in focus
Four slowly dancing, you in white, my songbird
It was a new beginning

The next dance was ours, our song, perfect words
A special dance, seeing nobody else, in our moment
Tears blurred, no focus, slowly, tight
Two slowly dancing, you in white, my songbird
It was the ending

The words washed us, so slow but full of us
We fell in love to this song
Our babies born to this song
We said our goodbyes to this song
You will always be

My Songbird

Thank you Christine McVie

The Hardest Thing To Do

by G.A. Chathurya Gurugoda

What may be the hardest thing
Once thinks a human being
We people do many things
Through nonstop thinking and thinking

"It is hard to ride my new bicycle"
Said a kid with his little tricycle
Oh..no my dear boy you insensible
One day you could, said his gifted uncle

"I hardly can forget my past memories full of sadness"
It was a soldier lost everything through the war; ruthless
But, close was a stunning maiden shaped out of happiness
Her hands with a key were caressing his arms of roughness

Man can't fly although a bird do
People said, watching what Wright brothers do
Today we all fly in a machine so,
It was hard , Yes; but not anymore

So, what could be the hardest thing, out of all
We stay thinking and thinking, no end at all
When something seems 'the hardest' we could think of
Another drudgery suddenly comes in front of

If you want to know, what I think as the hardest doing
It is exactly the opposite of what you are just doing
Have you ever tried to 'be thinking of nothing'
Yeah..it's the hardest as you are thinking to 'be without thinking.'

Life Journey

by Gunadevi Rajaratnam

Choose your path wisely and correctly,
Learn to walk on your chosen route steadily.
You may meet with ups and downs on your way,
Remember they are meant to pass your way.

The Path of least resistance is not always the best
To achieve great things on your journey.
Be not a train running on the same track;
Find various ways to progress in your life!

Water, when it is trapped, develops a new path.
Likewise, find new ways to improve your journey.
Few can accompany you to complete it;
You must walk on your own and finish it.

All the paths are not smooth and bright,
But even dark ones have a way through!
Beautiful new paths may be found,
When you get lost on your journey.

You need a clear route to reach your goal,
Take your steps carefully to accomplish it.
Paths are many to reach your destination,
Choose wisely the best way through.

Winter's Heat

by Douglas S Brown

"Don't fall for a man
with shiny shoes,"
she told us,
gin and tonic in hand,
decades left-over smokey southern voice.

Five o'clock sharp
she sat in the wingback
looking over us at iced-over windows,
as far from the South
as fading blue-grey eyes,
and memories swirling in a glass
could hold close.

She had married-
and lost-
a good New England man
who winters had spread salt on the icy path
and kept the children
  -her daughter sitting there now-
warm in jackets, heavy socks and scarves.

Dinner, then
plates and glasses always put away
same order, same places,
forty years.

We sat,
patiently, unwarned,
waiting to be dismissed,
and steal away into winter's heat,
unaware of whose reflections
or future
we were in.

In The Company Of Annabel

by Earl Schumacker

Annabel walks her eight legged friend
On a leash for the sake of safety into town
On a cold day born straight from autumn
At least the chill will keep them on the narrow

The birch tree shares her soul with God
Leaves crisping, as of late, now lost of shade

Share their demise scurrying off deciduous
Around the ground before the snow sets in
Covering their merriment for the sake of silence

The white spider could easily be misunderstood
For purity is surely not a name for killer pets
An oddity in nature governed not by love
With a red hourglass printed on the back
By design or crime, advertising black widow
But what is death but another name for heaven

They only stop to watch the skeletal remains
Of what was once in spring a thing of beauty
A birch by any other name is still a tree

Annabel spins a silver silken web of lies
To passers by who wonder why
She tells them it will not bite
But if it does we all must die sometime

The creature has the situation well in hand
Being at the end of her sweet masters tether
Should she eat her mate or simply take a bite
Surely it would be by mistake or pleasure
And with so many legs to walk around
Stepping out on the town for fun
They must feel comforted in each other's company
As long as the strap holds out

The Prodigal's Monorhyme

by David Richmond

In our father's house, you were doing fine,
but you did not want to toe the line.
Father, you said, 'give me what is mine.'
Leaving home sent a jolt of joy up your spine.

No more scenes of servants grazing kine,
or picking grapes off the vine.

Feasting on choice cuts with the chine,
sporting with women, and drinking wine,
living in a ritzy ranch on the banks of the Rhine.

You have many friends who love to dine,
but you are too naive to know that is a bad sign.
Poof-poverty pounces and pierces like a tine,
now broke, homeless, hungry, you start to pine.

To earn money, you take a job feeding swine.
At nights you lie on the streetside and whine,
thinking of the servants and how well they dine.

It is okay, you ragamuffin to regret and repine.
Get up my brother and toward home your feet incline.
The sight of you will make our father's face shine.

My Dressage Experience

by Catherine Smillie

Learning dressage can be difficult,
Especially when training with different horses.
Eddie 'Whoopee Cushion' maintains speed all the way through,
While Angus 'Cow Horse' moos.
Scooby 'Snail' fails to obey,
And Joey 'Giant' delays going into canter.
Although all horses are different,
I still manage to score over sixty per cent.
Even if horses don't obey,
I got to keep trying to keep my score high.
If I don't keep trying and let the horse take control,
I will lose marks and have no hope of winning.
When I halt the horse and salute,
I know it is the end of the test and hope for a good score.

That Magical Phase

by Eshita Jain

The sound sleep, the carefree play
The buzz of energy all the day...
The pearly smile, The gleaming eyes
The notorious and imploring cries

The glass skin, the little palm
The euphonious voice with the epitome of calm...
The pious heart pounding fast
Their bubble of joy they choose to enjoy

Carrying the school bag, eager to learn
Meeting the friends, what more to yearn...
The bright toys with funniest sounds
the joyous glee that it surrounds

The bouncing ball like the excited soul
The innocence like God, with happiness as the ultimate Goal...
Curiosity filled with how and why...
With the spirits always appreciably high

The tender age with pink cheeks
The nostalgia that this time leaves
Childhood years are the magical phase
Thankyou Lord for those most remembered days...

Talk About The Weather

by Charlotte Wakeman

We talk about the weather to a stranger
Talk about the news to a neighbour
Talk about this and that to your Nan
And poor old Pat to Auntie Pam

Talk about your favourite positions to a lover
And contraception to your Mother

But there's these things I'd like to say to you
But when I see you I just go mute
How my pupils dilate
My heart leaps at the thought of kissing you
But for some silly reason I hesitate.

Twisted Forever Together

by Shirley Rebstock

When we were little twigs sprouting from the ground
I sensed something special in you I had found
Though we were different, I don't mean to sound sappy
Just a whiff of your aroma makes me so happy

As the wind blows your foliage in my face
My limbs long for your branches to embrace
Your curvy bough around my trunk weaves
Covering me with your beautiful green leaves

We live in the woods by sunny day and moonlit night
Although tangled together, touching your bark is a delight
As we continue to grow from our roots to the sky
We stand twisted forever together

Love is the reason why

Amy

by Charlotte Wakeman

Your flick of eyeliner,
Tattoo's and beehive
A bit of rock and roll,
something of Jazz or Jive.

Your authentic words
ingrained in our memory
Listening to the beats,
tapping along to the melody.
The sultry, smokiness
the range of your voice,
We're right there with you
the moment you soar.

As you up the rhythm
taking us on a
Nostalgic, Jazz filled ride.
When we saw how they hounded you
We felt that knock to your pride.

Your determination,
uniqueness and drive
Inspired us women,
Man you did shine.

Watched you grasp onto the feeling's
to help release a little pressure.
Inhale the love before it became a bit lesser.
Back to Black when he went back to her.

You sang us through the hurt,
Coming down from the high.
We sang along with you,
We heard your heart sigh.

Walking around a little shattered and broken
A hole in your heart, alone and unspoken
Clutching to something to fill the void
Is it a hunger, a lack of nurturing and care.
When we need it the most hope somebody is there.

River's-Life's Edge

by Nick James Vincelli

The misanthropic ants
crawl on reality
as I sit by
    the river's edge

ruminating on
hellish collapse

meditating on
peaceful solitude

The river's undulations
caress reality
as I sit by
    life's edge

Generational

by Neena J. Luke

Some say being poor is a choice
But our poverty has been generational
It's difficult to break the cycle
When you had no example growing up of what to do
I have no one to talk to about my pain
So Jesus Christ is who I take it to
I've shed so many tears seeing the things
That the people in our communities are going through
It's hard to look around
And see everybody divided
Because we could really make a difference
If we made the decision to be united
Came together and shared ideas
Created a strategic plan then applied it

We would be unstoppable if we worked together
Towards solutions Instead of fighting

Do Remember

by Jeannie Flinn Furlong

Do Remember
Do Remember...
  Gifts jiggle, just like laughter
  Hidden in small places.
  Ever after, means ever after!
  We'll be fine... our chosen spaces.
Do Remember...
  Girls never want a gift of soap
  Instead... pile up hugs with mucho kisses!
  Favorite perfumes, not on a rope.
  Tickle time on my toes...2 + 5 never misses!
Do Remember...
  Time rocks my boat..marry merry
  Hissee fits...unacceptable day or night
  Alone time always n-e-c-e-s-s-a-r-y!
  Talking time, jives just right!
Do Remember...
  Going far while keeping near
  I won't forget ..there's date-day and tonight
  Vows we championed..true and clear
  You say, "I do." Me sez,"He's right!"
Do Remember...
  Years ago our saga triggered
  Onward through zigzagging ways
  Unique freedom...for as we figured
  Our fame... outlasting fathomed days.
Do Remember...
  I respect our unknown destiny
  Always you, who's hip-hip with me!
  Confirm our road! What trajectory
  True mates...true blue. We're WE!

Summertime

by Duane Anton Crichlow

Sun, sand, surfing the waves,
  Sexy swimsuits: we've got it made in the shade.
Umbrellas in martinis and lined in a row
  On beaches and resorts wherever you go.
Maui, Mexico, or even the Maldives;
  If these are your vacation spots, now's the time to leave.
Maybe a staycation is more your speed;
  Enjoy with friends and family. Take as much as you need.
Everybody's glad that summer has arrived;
  School is out! Let's go outside!
Remember to mask up. Be safe and have fun.
  But don't do anything foolish otherwise you're done!
Time to chill out, relax and unwind,
  And leave all of your stress behind.
Ice cream and cold beverages will quench your thirst,
  Especially when the heat is the worst.
Music, barbecues, games galore,
  Laughter everywhere. Who could ask for more?
Ever wished it could stay this way?
  I wish it was summertime every day.

Thus Spoke Brother Moji

by Moji Agha

Thus Spoke Brother Moji
(not Zarathustra)

With all due respect,
irrespective of
with regards to
I have no respect
for irregardless.

The Journeys Of The Prophet Mani

by David Hyatt-Bickle

Greatly he played the flute of God in India fully
Beautifully he played the lyre of light in Persia
Gracefully he played the drum of power in Babylon
Skillfully he played the harp of wisdom in Parthia

No land welcomed or even tolerated his music
Though his beautiful song reached the sunrise of the vast Earth
Shadow was vanquished by his splendid and bright appearance
Know that this musician was named Mani who brought rebirth

Light

by Eponine Seccafico

Battered Blaine down in the rain.
And kept still in the winter's chill.
Sudden appetites and several sour fights.
His moods distorted by the pain.
Seasons came and swirled the same.
Inside his brain, a sickly change.
At the will, of the world 's exchange.

Slept in sap and cloaked in shadow.
Amongst the sorry sights that drained him.
Deep in thought he stayed, inside a numbing claim.
Repeating his name, as the rain turned to snow.
Restless and weighted, he fell into cravings.
Worthless and hopeless, empty and shame.
Silently, he shouldered all the blame.

Irritable from inability, he lied alone.
Lied to those he loved, lied of his state.
And lied in the embrace of nature's disgrace.
Until a tone rang from his phone.

A message to remind him of himself.
Which broke the haze of frozen plight.
And brought him back into the light.

He soon rested near a common man's fire.
An electric heater, with a lamp above him.
Nestled in a blanket with his phone in hand.
He took his medicine and began to aspire.
To soothe his moods and mend his wrongs.
He would not give into his disorder's might.
Instead, he would remember his light.

Agape

by Theodora Polycarpou

Plato said that we are one soul halved
Agape is the name for love
Your soul whispering to mine
Your soul reflecting mine
Your passionate embrace feels like home
Your heart is healing mine
You want to give to me
I want to give to you
If only you had the courage to follow you heart
If only you had the courage to trust your heart
If only you had the courage to honour your heart
My prayers are for your happiness
My inspiration is our rare and special love
My solace is agape
Two souls found each other
Two souls wanted each other
Two souls trying to bind together
If only you had the courage to let two souls reunite as one

Ambush

by Emanuel Carter

There are times
when you walk down the hall to
yet another meeting, walk from your
car to the strip mall pharmacy that dispenses
your Viagra, or stand before a classroom of
dedicated students for another stimulating lecture
on urban ecosystems, that some sound, some color,
some geometric pattern triggers unwanted memories
about people you loved that didn't get your best,
that were somehow roughed up by the mean,
the mercurial, the muscular machinations that
served your righteous way forward and
suddenly your are naked, a declining
physique with an fascinating tapestry of surgical
scars, blotches and bruises from rugby,
relationships and reckless behaviors, and the people
around you are unknowing, unforgiving, uncomfortable
with your silence, wishing you'd move on instead of
searching in the hallway, the cracked parking lot, your
hand-written lecture notes for the clothing and armor that
have carried you this far or at least for a robe that might
hide the embarrassment of your shame and your guilt
and the nasty suspicion that, given another
chance, you'd behave the same way again!

Sunrise - Mirror Cinquain

by David Richmond

Day breaks.
Demon darkness,
flees, scared by your bright face,
as you invade his dark domain.
Birds wake,

and sing,
then take flight in your early light,
like men in a hurry,
to catch the train,
they fly.

My Last Conversation With Larry

by Jessica Amanda Salmonson

"Shine my boots, wench!" Larry said
"Fetch my wine and cheese and bread!
Tidy up my murphy bed!
Feed the hog and Mr. Ed!
Corn mash for Rhode Island Red!
Why look so gobsmacked by dread?
Did you not say I thee wed?"
"Oh, I said it, until dead"
I confessed, then bashed his head.

Being Alone

by Shreyash Mukherjee

BEING ALONE
Once I was walking alone in the rain,
Carrying my umbrella and a sweet pain,
I was completely lost in the clouds of my thoughts,
Remembering my points of success and all my flaws.

Suddenly I saw a girl getting wet in the rains,
Her clothes were entirely filled with mudstains,
She was like a bird but of a different feather,
And we traced a long way walking together.

The rain stopped and I removed my umbrella,
Surprisingly I again found myself alone with no cinderella,
I smiled and became sure that it was my delusion,
My own loneliness has served me this illusion.

I stopped for a while and took a look at the nature,
Observing every flower and every creature,
A single solitary flower is as beautiful alone,
A meadow full is pleasurable but each grows on its own.

I was happy because now I was not depressed,
Now my opinions cannot be suppressed,
My feelings are able to be expressed,
And finally after being alone also I felt I was blessed,
After being alone also I felt I was blessed.........

Unknown Soldier

by Nora Gibson

The call of assembly long overdue
named the forgotten from ages thru
From countless wars of eras ascended
pain still fresh, wounds never mended
The screams before the darkness took
Their lives blackened without another look
Scattered bones in foreign lands
dug up my diligently by God's own hands
Heavens roster penned the missing and lost
Those who fought valiant with a cost
Now fierce warriors all stood by
as summoned spirits filled the sky
Hobnailed sandals, barefooted, steel toe boot
marched in unison without dispute
Foes in combat never friends
united at the battle end.

Angels kissed the blood stained brow
awarded each their sacrifice vow
Hasta pura the Romans' spear held high
A golden Katana bestowed the fearless Samurai
The "Sword of the Sea" the Chinese swayed
while a Viking warrior sailed away
An Apache fighter reclaimed his land
the ancient Maori received his brand

The Medal of Honor secured its place
on innocent faces who left no trace
Fought to the end with unseen cries
Fought to the death by infinite lies
Rest well Soldier, you nameless soul
your seeds finally planted in fields of gold
Fallen heroes with deeds overlooked
Final reward in life's eternal book.

A Poem Written In The Cool Aftermath Shade

by Marty King

at times my footprints kiss the sunshine
my mind is drowning in a lake of pure peace
my cookie shake inspires a rare smile
it's been so long that i don't even recognize life
i play a song cause it's a good thing
i dream of oceans with my mouth wide open
i bond again with preferred choices
i get together with all positive voices
living again is smiling reunions on repeat
obsolete is the process of life on delete
now i always want look up and take a sneak peek
i have my descriptions of All Vibes as sleek neat
moving on, i meet Her at the ocean
all elements of Her Spirit express in shades of Pink and Green
i run into her and stress stops
when it is time for Her to go i just may follow
She smiles and shakes her head with passionate adamancy
i stop and immediately comprehend the moral
She waves goodbye but i do not cry
i just smile and move on as another turn invites me
at times my left hand thanks the rising moon
my heart is walking on a beach of sweet benevolence
my bottled water inspires rare laughter
i close my eyes and dream happily ever after......

Dance With Me Evermore

by Richard W. Morris

Come dance with me, the Teke man said,
Offering carnations red.
Together my love, our feet will fly,
My heart you fill, you'll not deny.

He held her tight, but loose enough,
To twirl about, and strut her stuff.
A twosome, yet they were one,
Who lived life, love and fun.

He saw the love in her eyes,
The kind of love that never dies.
Their bond, the strongest weld,
To ecstatic future they propelled.

True love, no passing fling,
A pair to waltz and to swing.
Their dance was that of souls,
To be never dashed upon the shoals.

To each the other a special rose,
That filled the heart, not the nose.

His love for her, he did shout,
She in return, he had no doubt.
Love built on rock, not sand,
Forever in each other's hand.

When at last, at heaven's door,
They shall dance evermore.

An Array Of Vast Universes

by Andrew Crisci

Everybody says that forgetting
the one we loved is unfair, cruel, and silly;
don't attempt to bury recollections under rocks,
and instead of burning them completely,
express bitterness for a sad ending...
although the fervent sentiment never stops!

Search for the fondness of words,
delve deeper into your awareness
and the skeletons of regret won't rebuke
the conscience for the unappreciated value
of all the exciting life they led once,
and the preciousness they still constitute!

Does anyone admit that continue living
without forgiving is an act of unmercifulness?
Should we love ourselves more or less,
never appreciating the joy of giving and sharing?

Pierce the sunless skies with daring eyes,
beyond them, there's an incredible blueness...
not matched or displayed by waveless seas;
what lies ahead is an array of vast universes!

Faith

by Donald Maher

Questions unanswered, never know why
Filled our mouths with Maypo, our brains with lies
The facts we are given are all their own view
Hypocrisy and hate are all that they spew

Remember I tell you faith can revive
Instincts in us we need to survive

Listen to you soul, open your eyes
Have trust in yourself and they cannot arise

Tanka 001

by Naledi Segosebe

i shout hello to
squirrels playing in the sun
they all squawk at me
i fall on nettles and yowl
my cat looks on with a smirk

Flowers In Art

by Karen Sue Croft

A tulip in a vase
on a rigid stand
does it really hold a thousand words?
or a thousand strokes
as the artist paints
it upon a fresh canvas?

What is going through their mind
with each stroke,
each dab of paint,
each mark it leaves behind
what memory does it hold-
whose life does it embellish
or is it just a painting
thought of by the artist
to spark the interest of the onlooker?

Chaos And Order

by Joshua SK Baldwin

I reside where the strings do not dare wrap around me. I am the thing that shelters comfortably under your carpet, whilst I wink at the fairy living under your pillow.

I am the atrocity that delves into its own existence and allows for question. Consume thy enemy, prolapse the expansion of the hereditary downfall of genetics whilst I, watch.

Growing ever more spiteful with every being I see collapse before me. I am the twine in your spine. I am the sheets you do not wash. I am the blood that spills graciously amongst generations-over nothing more than who's feet get to fall first, on that land.

I am the thing that lies in the shadows. I am the slumber of a million cataclysms that are yet to awaken. I am the tragedy of love and betrayal.

I am the rose that dies with a million thorns wrapped around so, cutting deeper with every question you have about love being unanswered. Every cry of a friend dying on the battlefield.

I am the memory you tremble before in the murder of the night. I am the witch you smite when you cannot accept the benevolent around you. I am the creature you call upon with every legend you make about children who lurk into the woods.

I am the wolf that knows not, of what flock should be spared and which shall be consumed. I am the kindle in the flames, the spindle of a woman's meddle to find the perfect fabric.

I am the splinter in the timber. That incessant cry out for pain. I am the relinquished magnitude you try to display before your innocent mind.

I am Chaos, I am Order. I am You.

Nature's Rage

by Sarban Bhattacharya

This is a long extended night,
   The stars all hibernate,
The blustery gusts revolve around
   The dreams which suffocate.

Now the torrents lash my door,
   And now they slam the shade,
'Be couched right here, and do not move',
   The whispers promptly bade.

Out there I glanced, the wild tree pranced,
   She swayed her tipsy stem,
All drenched and dark, the leafy arc
   Seems like her death-gown's hem.

Is that mere downpour, or a sign,
   An omen of the time?
The thunders clash with louder splash,
   Upon the lakebed slime.

My window pane is stabbed by rain,
   One thousand spears en masse,
They prick the eaves, pummel the leaves
   To the level of the grass.

The flickering lamp will die at once,
   It does not cease to pour,
A marble sculpture drowns beneath
   The water on the floor.

That which gives life can take it too,
   Lo there it heaves its head,
The shrine's bemused, the priest presumed
   A curse on holy bread.

It has to cease within no time,
   The devil's thunder roars,
The gale allays his evil play

The Streets Are Bleeding Sakura
by Jackie Chou

There's a rare blooming
of sakura this fall
the trees cotton-candy-sweet
antipsychotic-sweet
Blossoms descend in batches
soon to cover the asphalt road
like spilled Pepto-Bismol
I swallow my pill with regret
drift into oblivion
the petals blur in my vision
the whole world tinted pink
by my medicated brain

Happy Birthday To Me
by Jeannie Flinn Furlong

Hello friends! You're invited! Please come to celebrate my day!
Allow me to share party time with all those who like to play.
Pretty party decorations here across my summer lawn,
Packed for fun! Soon this celebration will be forever gone.
Y'all have been fine friends, do come celebrate me. It's my pleasure!

Bring no gifts. Just have fun! Your friendship is my one true treasure.
I'm rejoicing this passing year! What is your how, when, or where?
Remember me a heartfelt soul! Please make it fun as we share.
This is my day; I do not fret! There's more! to life straight ahead!
Happily I quote, "This day's a day to cherish! Not to dread!"
Disappearing days in time, let's remember us as we speak.
Another year passing! How can we find several more weeks?
Year in and year out, it's never, yet never's the same, we think.

To really best me in this aging game , how fast is your blink?
Once a day to Him pray, "Thanks for love, life and things we care for."

Make room in my heart to bless my days for its time I adore!
Every day is beautiful when counting plus one hundred years!

Moonlight And Proses

by Cynthia Thompson

Storyteller weaves his tales
throughout my mind and heart.
He alchemies my leaden days
into golden thoughts.

We soar above the shrinking earth
on word-filled wings at night,
glide on intellectual planes;
it's Truth we seek to find.

Charting unknown territory
of heartlands, minds and brains,
we plumb the depths of mysteries
that rule cabbages and kings.

Like Capote penning portraits,
his stories glow so real.
Their 3-D essence touches me
in déjà vu surreal.

He's captured me in tidy yarns,
with friendship for a knot.
Allowing him to nurture me,
he feeds my starving heart.

He takes me here, he whisks me there,
with legends of the fall.
But one place I can never trod
is deep inside his soul.

Writing To Ellen

by Jerry Horton

Again, I sit between the trees,
Pen and paper on my knees.
I look for something new not old.
I search for story never told.

Between the branches squirrels leap.
While near my feet critters creep.
I wait to hear the special sound,
Of story falling to the ground.

Leaves they move, dance and rest.
Sun moves too, towards the west.
Moons do rise and birds do flock.
Days will pass and months will clock.

Away the breeze carries the birds.
At the air I grasp for words.
I touch the old and never the new.
Still, I keep on - with thoughts of you.

Life

by Donald Maher

We question our existence
Driven by Natures insistence
That we all go the distance
But we don't know how

Running around in circles
Like a bunch of comic Erkles
The dinosaur is purple
But we don't know why

What are we becoming?

The music starts humming
The drummers are all drumming
But we don't know where

Soon it will be over
Lying in the clover
Next to an old friend Rover
But we don't know when

Pink Sundress

by Naomi Bannister

When we were little, I was big.
I held her hand crossing the street
while mom watched the other two
and carried our supplies for the week.

She wiggled and pulled and fought
just to run, pick up rocks
or make a wish on dandelion seeds.
But if I asked her to stop, she stopped.

Town to town, province to province,
three in the back - her in the front.
Packing what little could fit in our trunk,
our parents searched for work and their love.

Unbuckled in the back we played,
sliding ourselves into each other,
finding harmonies and blocking out arguments
from the front - where she took the brunt.

When I was young, she was younger.
I was under the bridge, drunk-bonding with kids
met that morning behind the class I just skipped.
I should have been home, could have been her defender.

Teens turned to twenties; we managed – we did.
I did what came easy, she did the rest.

When it started to happen, I don't really remember.
I got good at pretending; she just got better.

I saw her from a block away, pregnant and tanned,
crossing the street to her upgrading class.
Pink and white sundress showed off her belly,
and I felt the sense memory of her in my hand.

Now it is her who holds back my struggle.
I've been broken and healed then broken again;
still under that bridge in so many ways.
She is safe, she is home; she is big when I'm little.

Midnight Song

by Kelly Hawkins

You're a song that my heart keeps singing
Mostly after midnight when only the loneliest of birds still call
I'm answered in the whisper of night air
and a choir of crickets
While I sit murmuring softly to myself on the front steps

The Same

by Catherine Johnson Broussard

You misunderstand me;
why?
Our heart, our blood; the same.
I see you cry; I feel your pain;
my pain, the same.
I hear your laugh;
I smile, I laugh.
You misunderstand me;
why.
Created by HIM;
one child; same being;
no less; no greater than.
In HIS eyes; just the same.

My Dream Of Beth Hart

by Jessica Amanda Salmonson

Damn she's a cutie. In my dream I wandered into a basement piano bar because someone told me it was the secret place to get great waffles. Sitting at the piano was Beth Hart crooning sorrowful songs, no other accompaniment, just Beth and a piano. It was like this tattooed lass just wandered down the stairs and sat down and started playing with only a few present to share a glorious hour in our lives. I sat at a table near the piano eating a thin waffle with whip cream on top, a scattering of walnut pieces, and no syrup, with a shot of Effen Black Cherry Whiskey on the side, blissfully listening to Beth. Then I died.

A Day After My Death

by Sayeed Abubakar

The sun has risen and the dews no more
On grass. Birds are singing, farmers working,
Housewives cooking and beggars on the door.
Seeing unknown people, dogs are barking

And the naughty boys playing in the field
Fleeing from school. Newsreaders are reading
War-news on TV and showing people killed
By air-attack. Some people are bidding

Farewell to someone with their cry and tears;
Some are welcoming the newborn with smile.
Someone proudly denies God, someone fears
Him with love. Leaders are like crocodile

Are dealing with men. Who are in this time
Recollecting me and my fiery rhyme?

Laid To Rest

by Roger Kevin Harp

I sit at the ivy gates
Waiting to say goodbye
I should be sad
Filled with hate
It's not sarrow
But joy inside
Though all this sadness
Breaks my heart
You no longer bare the pain
The world will weep in your absence
It will no longer be the same

Bamboo Hollow

by Jaclyn Brown

There's a place tucked away
Nestled up against the Creek
Where the Clover runs wild
'Neath a Bamboo Canopy
Where life is in rhythm
With the Ever-Changing Tide
The Low Buzz of the Bees
And the Hum of Dragonflies
The Notes of Nature's Song
Are carried along the Breeze
Dancing with the Fragrance
Of the Sweet Satsuma Trees
The Steady to and Fro
The Balance The Beat The Time
The Magic Melody
The Beautiful Drum of Life

Invocation

by Melissa J Seneway

Bells ring through the dusk, soft and low.
    Smokey eyes narrow.
    Sultry pout on her lips.
Wrapped in black lace and chiffon,
    she twirls in graceful circles.

Violin strums through the twilight, soft and low.
    Black-shaded eyes dart.
    Lips part ever so slightly.
Silver feathers cascade from her hair.
    Arms open to the onyx sky.

Witchy apparition
    that used to be a lady
    sways on.
Breezy is the eve, song murmurs
    from the deep.

A man in a fedora with a smooth walking stick
    sees her through the looking glass,
    reaches out.
Fingers slip through a reviled hallucination.
    She morphs into a silken raven.

Head bowed in supplication,
    he is besieged by an invulnerable force.
    He refuses to abjure his hope that he can hold her.
A tambourine jingles lightly in her hand, soft and low.
    She twirls away.

A disintegrated mirage.
    Tear slides from his eye.
    The music disappears.
Blinded by his sorrow,
    he walks away from the glass, now stained.

A Ray Of Sunshine

by Amya Richelle Ranck

The morning starts with the rising sun
Ready to play and have some fun
We will dance and play having lots of fun
I will shine my light till the day is done

When raindrops and clouds start to appear
It might seem like I will disappear
But please dont worry and don't you fear
It may not seem but I am always near

As the day ends I cannot stay
It time for me to go and end the day
But don't worry for I will not stray
I will return tomorrow to come out and play

Dissolve Me In Your Mysteries

by Faraz

Love, like an emotion beyond explanation
Come to me and dissolve me in your mysteries
I will swim in your endless oceans and
Make memories of a lifetime to remember.

Gracefully as the spring leaves when her reign is over
Brush away all the pains from the chambers of this heart
Dwell deep inside the broken soul behind this smile
You might get the opportunity to cast off these sheath of tears hidden
underneath

Touch me gently for I might break
The wounds of the past has left me fragile
Delicately run your tips all over my body
Give me a night that I remember till the end of my days

Like a sunset full of passion and colour
I yearn to be united with my one true lover
But the dawn steals away my dreams
And leaves me lonely to dwell on my scars

Next time hold on to me permanently before the sun rises
Reflecting our true selves infront of transparent light radiating from moon
So that you can clearly see deep inside me
The parts of my Body that echoes only your name

Twice Fallen Leaves

by Kohava Ray

How many leaves?
Ah, you can't count because it's burning hot

Vermilion Red Hands
One on top another
Seem to transform into
A perfect synthetic persona

Their burning desire is to color
The whole world
With true red

Sadly, their nerve fibers
Cannot connect with each other
Oh, God
I watch them tremble in this hopeless struggle
I took a ride on my bike
Holding them on the front basket

Pedaled hard, at full speed, so that
All winds will toss them,
Scramble them
Shuffle them

Here, the top of a cliff
This is the farthest I can come
Where the reds slide from my palms

At the end of the world
Blown by the last and strongest
Gust of the wind
Each red leaf was then dancing
Down to the deepest blue of the ocean

I felt they wanted me to say
Good-bye

Phone

by Bartholomew Williams

Powerful tool –
Harmful at school,
Or great device?
Not always nice;
Each one: think twice.

When I Was A Kid

by Laurie Slicer

When I was a kid
I rode Saturdays on
My Friend Flicka
Sky King
Roy Rogers
And Flicka's boy
And Sky
And Roy
Hauled bad guys
Off to justice
Never seen again
Never
Never

Never seen again

Back in a barn
Me and
Annie Oakley
Held our ground
Shooting them down
Waiting for a hero
To cart them all away
But no heroes
But no others
No other heroes
Showed up

We killed them all ourselves
And didn't surrender
Or even pretend to surrender
Because
We killed them all ourselves

When I was a kid
I rode Saturdays on
My Friend Flicka
And bad guys
Always got caught

To Die A Brilliant Star

by Aimee Meyn

My dreams are too quick;
they escape me, like
fireflies from the net.
But I must dream of you;
I wake each morning
the whole of me humming,
tuned to an alien frequency,
and singing along to
sweet music, just
out of reach.

My skin, a suddenly
volatile element,
as if one small touch
could shatter this
fragile existence;
a Supernova explosion,
shooting my atoms
back to the sun. Oh,
what stories they'd tell
on their way:
to have lived,
and to die
such a brilliant star.

Why

by Laurie Slicer

I don't understand this baby boy.
Why is he so rare?
People rush to see Him sleep.
Why do people care?
Three Kings kneel in the straw.
Why do they come where He lies?
The mother sings as she rocks her son.
Why are there tears in her eyes?

I don't understand this baby boy.
Why is He the one?
A shepherd said He was born to God.
Why is He God's son?
The animals speak of a heavenly grace.
Why can they talk this night?
They say He'll make all people free.
Why would He bring us light?

I don't understand this baby boy.
Why does the night sky glow?
I hear He loves me as I am.
Why should He love me so?
Tell me what He wants from me.

Why can't I understand?
He frightens me with His quiet smile.
Why do I fear His hand?

I don't understand this baby boy.
Why does my soul feel strange?
He holds my life in His open hands.
Why do I know I am changed?

Bird Talk

by Molly Moore

My little green friend often stops by
Just to get things off his chest
It's not always easy up in the sky
So, he needs to get away from the rest

Of the other parrots in his flock
(Technically rose-winged parakeets)
Sometimes he feels they tease and mock
Making his efforts seem like defeats.

Overall, they're quite a good group
But he's an inward sensitive soul
And needs some time alone to recoup
So, I lend an ear and try to console.

We chit chat back and forth for a while
In the early hours of the day
I imagine I see a big parrot smile
Before his wings spread and he flies away.

Halloween Flight

by Molly Moore

I'm hitching a ride on a witch's broom
From on high we'll see all the Halloween sights
As through the clouds we zip and zoom
On what is known as the scariest of flights.

Skeletons rise from their earthen beds
And mingle with ghosts who are wandering the town
Amongst pirates with tricorn hats on their heads
And Cinderella in her dazzling gown.

Holiday bonfires are burning bright
Like the Samhain* fires of Celtic tradition
When otherworld spirits would rise in the night
And steal away souls to eternal perdition.

But tonight's festivities are all about fun
When ghouls and horror and laughter blend
And the imagination can wildly run
Oh, don't let my Halloween flight end!

I Love You

by Roger Kevin Harp

The moon shines down upon our town
In search of us both
She is jealous of you and I
She knows she'll never have
What we have together
"Our Love!"
Our love is made from
The energies that flow through
The heart of the universe
She wants to illuminate our love

To steal the reflected image
So she can view it in the darkness

This Place
by Harriet Davis

Look at this place
As the tide begins to drown my ankles
And the soft sand tickles my toes
I close my eyes to fully embrace this space

Look at this place
Clean air fills my lungs
Inhale! Exhale!
Those around see the relaxation in my face

Look at this place
Sun's rays massage my shoulders
Moon's reflection reveals my glow
Feeling the calm, I slow my pace

Look at this place
Simple delicacies
Complex concoctions
I think I will, have a taste

Look at this place
So full of life
I hate it must end
Real life I must face

This place is my dream
My time away
I escape in my mind
My peace to esteem

Now

by Christopher Grieves

In the blink of an eye
At the speed of a sound
From the tears of a cry
To the joys that abound
We can pass through the present
So much faster than light
We should linger a little
While the moment's in flight
For the crux of my point
Is that time is no friend
As the sand trickles down
So the endless can end
Oh to capture those colours
Oh to smile and be kind
Be the joy giver, healer
While the clock cogs unwind
Be the help to the helpless
Be the friend to the lost
Breathe deeply of life
Disregarding the cost
As a price has been paid
For the freedom we share
But each moment still precious
As our lungs fill with air...

And the heart will beat feintly
Unless topped up with love...

So now is that moment.
Is that gift.
From above.

Jinjagoliath

Teacher

by Emanuel Carter

He was black, silky and warm
as if the caressing breeze of a
perfect summer evening was
suddenly somehow visible
Golden as wine, she shone with
the sun – a goddess of day who
danced in the light that flowed
like honey in the plazas
of Spain
Engaged in the practice of
emotional arson, he ignited a
flame that excited the mind,
spread into the soul, burned out
of control and the halo she wore
was like a solar corona in a
perfect eclipse
This professor of design, doctor of
desire, señor de amor and much
more, he discovered that teaching
is hard and wisdom defined like
the soft edge of shadow in the
city of night, that the traffic in
knowledge, narcotic, seductive,
may wail like the blues whose
rhythms at midnight eventually
moan in the wet streets of
morning, where the ache of
remembrance and the contours of
error will en-frame every woman
he sees thereafter

Orange-Pekoe Tea

by Jennifer Cahill

A teabag is snug
in an orange rind as it floats
on the brown sewage;

the spinach leaves swirl
as the drain gobbles and sucks,
and the brocoli

florets are hurried
to the steel beast's growling maw.
The peach liquid soap

sponges and perfumes
the kitchen. Sun-hued butterfly wings emerge, lift.

Life Is Not Fair But God Is

by Gordon McConnell

Fairness! what does it mean?
free from bias or injustice
can one be that every time?
one's bias makes another disgusted

God's promises are true and sure
no matter how we may feel at the time
for He sees the end from the beginning
learn to look ahead flowing in rhyme

At times it can feel really hard
all you can see is enemies around
need to stop and look at Elisha's army
are on your side the victory sound

Prayed so very much since Christ came in
salvation is mine but stammer still here
over these years called much on God
His grace is sufficient no matter my fear

So maybe leave it in God's hands
He's in sovereign control no matter what
the Apostle Paul believed grace was sufficient
so I must also consider He knows my lot

Married On Television

by David Cox

They got married on T.V with all the regalia.
Watched by a camera, somewhere in Australia.
Under the microscope, living false lives.
Women with husbands, and men with wives

Observing as I do through my own little box.
Proves most humans are mental? except Mr Cox.
They cheat and hurt, there's ninety days of pain.
And the experts advise but never explain.

They have tried to find love in a bar-less zoo.
Forced to have sex and analyse as they do.
It's all good T,V as long as everyone gets hurt
A nice pay day, but your heart's the dessert.

Hats off to the experts, who encourage non-stop.
And bravo to the players and narcissists who flop.
Contestant begging to keep their marriages afloat.
And an emotional break down, through a scripted note.

Taking part in a circus so what did they expect?
Some lost their cherries, all lost their self-respect.
Reality telle, watching the pointless squirm on a nail.
Ratings through the roof when their futile lives fail.

Acacia Trees

by MAXIMILIAN G. WOLF

We are lost in the fog rolling over river waves, intoxicated with waters music.
I can see you only, and you can see only me,
while passion between us turns into endless blue.
*

In a flash, I can see
yours jump into the hug of insectoid past.
Dreaming fingers of mine and my long dark hair.
You are chasing your shadow while dreaming of me.
You will catch her only on the horizon.
*

The great wall protecting my soul is collapsing,
hit by your lips and words.
Frightened, my soul emerges out.
*

My flying words towards you are frozen
by dead bodies.
Our shoes are in love with the path
through the cemetery acacia.

Lean On Me

by Virginia Darline Gelok

Lean on me please if you want to.
And know I am here for you.
Whether I am here beside you
Or a thousand miles away.

Lean on me please if you want to.
I've been where you are so I kmow.
We'll talk, I'll listen, we'll cry,
I'll understand.

Lean on me please if you want to.
I have enough strength to help you.

Your path is familiar to me,
I know where it's going.

Lean on me please if you want to.
We can share our pain and sorrow.
We can feed on each other's love.
Gain strength in our friendship.

So...
Lean on me please, If you want to ?

On Some Back Road In Texas

by David Drowley

On some back road in Texas
Where time had flown away
Sat a dreamlike Kinkade home
Of warmth and heart, not paint,
With shaded walkway arbor
Crowned with leaves and flowers.
            Love dwelt there.
A lovely little couple,
Long past their youthful prime,
Welcomed us into their home
With bright and cheerful smiles
Saying, "We over-ripe grapes
Are now in raisin time."
            Love was there.
Our afternoon was blissful
Midst rose and hollyhock
Seated near a lily pond,
A lotus eater's dream,
With tea, crumpets, clotted cream
And conversation sweet.
            Love shared there.
We bade farewell at even
With smiles, and hugs and tears
To Pop Vin and Auntie Mae.
A stooped for sale sign wept

For the home they would depart.
The pair smiled even so.
                    Love held on.
One later year we passed by
Under a searing sky
That burned up cornfields nearby
Their home worn and withered
As grapes long past raisin time.
Wistfully we knew why:
                    Love had gone.

Marvel Of Nature

by Ngoc Minh Nguyen

Nature's so breathtaking, all know:
    when spring arrives, year upon year,
rebirth and life make the world grow;
    all of earth in this hemisphere,
from east to west, vibrate and flow
    with grandeur (so all tremble and fear)!

Tremble and fear, and be in awe
    of Nature's majesty and source:
for from the beginning, like law,
    the seasons take their destined course;
and with charge, like a lion's paw,
    make known their miracle and force.

Yet, if the marvel of Nature
    be so awesome and grandiose,
let her then be man's wise teacher;
    so she might embrace and enclose
him as Mother: and may feature
    her intemperate climes in repose.

Little Witch

by Anne E Sangster-Keeley

Little witch, little witch, sweeps with her broom
Then chants through the night by the light of the moon
Children in costumes are out on the streets
But you won't find this witch handing out any sweets
It's all hallows eve and her ritual is long
As she honours the Earth and those who've passed on
Her window is lit as a candle burns bright
To help guide the spirits who wonder the night
So beware of the spectres you pass on the streets
For some may play tricks but they never eat treats

The Night Of Passion And Desire

by Faraz

Lean your head close to this shoulder of mine
And let all the fantasies you have to go wild
Do not be afraid to express the affection you conceal in this heart
Without uttering a single word, kiss me and kiss me hard

The virtue of your soul has softened this vulnerable heart of mine
Igniting the passion hidden within and setting it on fire
The elegance of your face is the place where poets like me disarm
Disrupting the rhythm of my pen and making it impossible for me to describe
your charm

Dancing tenderly with your body gently pressed against mine
Let us rule the night of our dreams, making our love divine
Just as if the Prophecy of us together have been foretold by people of all
times
Shh, there is no need to blush, thou art my bread and thou art my holy wine

And eventually I shall surrender to the seducing whispers of your heart
While delicately running my fingers all over your bodily parts

Rendering you with its sweetness and intimidating you to yearn for more
Ahh, no need to suppress your emotions, lives through the night as if there is nothing more to live for

And just as the dawn is about to break
Sit with me on the corner of that glacial lake
And let us cherish this celestial moment while being submerged in each other arms
There is no need for any blankets, allow my body to provide yours with enough warmth

Soon the cruel world will display its colours and we shall have to separate
Agonizing is going to be the moment when for eternity we shall have to part our ways
Devoted love is hopeless in the world which is permeated with hatred and rage
But don't worry my lover, I shall wait for you on heaven's gate

Cry woman cry, dissolve all of the sadness into the darkness and silence of night
For heaven knows that we shall not have a bodily reunion again in this life
Let the metaphorical piano perform each tune with a unique tear
Blood flowing from the eyes as we acknowledged that pure love has lost its war with Earthly fear

By giving music to this unsung of mine, set our love as an example for all times to come
Become a poem of mine and make this night of us together an immortal one

A Walk At Night

by Angel L Villanueva

She's bathed with light across her face,
And freckles line her argent skin.
Her dazzling smile is seen from far;
She rouses souls with life within.

I gaze at her ascending form,
And smile at her flirtatious ways;
The times she hides behind a cloud,

To then display her lover's rays.

For eons she has danced the nights,
As waking stars suffuse the skies.
She walks with lovers hand in hand,
Aglow with light that she supplies.

Around me ring the sounds of night,
Cacophonies that soothe the mind.
Afar I hear beguiling calls,
The songs of love from two aligned.

My eyes again return to her,
Now full and bright, like beaming brides;
Like one I held the day we wed,
The girl in whom my heart resides.

I'm Calling To You

by Brooks Lewis III

Dear God,

    First and foremost I want to thank you for another year/ some healthy kids so I don't have to shed another tear/ A little less debt that I can put in my rear/ And for the simple fact I can yell out "I'm Here!!!"/ This has been a horrible year/ not just for me / for us all/ I ask that you keep us united/ because divided we fall/ This is suppose to be the times of family and of love/ please let this time be the same/ I'm pleading for your grace and glory from up above/ Wholeheartedly speaking not playing any games/ In closing I wanna say another day is nothing but another teacher/ I thank you for the life I live and I thank you for my physical features/ All I ask and pray is that you would cure me of these seizures/ I ask and praise you for all these things in Jesus name...Amen

Leftover Lines Of Poems Undone

by C. David Collins

Love avenue shuffle
spirits fandango through
grave eyes of doubt on
delusions of disorder
when we kiss do
dreamy clouds cuddle?
Photonic warped thoughts
feed on disdained
mercurial clot eclipses tick tocking
against organic time thieves, there's
cerebral fury on medication row as
rival consuls consort on
succulent erotic painules--huddling
under jagged mistletoe as bellicose vision
fugitives plan placid avant garde getaways
of broken glass and bloodless lips
under hexagon suns and sharp quark
triangles.
Neptune Clubs open their pores to
Blue Plate liquid aura traders----
reveling in the street life hubris.
And so it goes.

The Other Side

by Brooks Lewis III

You never fully understand something until it happens to you/No matter once
or fifty times/It stays on your mind/You think that it's buried deep/But in
actuality it's engraved deep down inside/Some gloat about it/Others cover it
with pride/Me myself/I hold my head up/Look above/And to God I confide/I
aint gonna lie though/Sometimes I wanna hide/I just gotta find that inner
strength and pull that thing from inside/And here lies the other side/The side
that is a little different from the world/The side where it can happen to any
boy or girl/The side most people don't get to see/Where you can't control the

outcome/You just have to wait to be free/It feels like a dream/Or worse yet a nightmare/Where you're living your life but are in constant fear/We all have our downfalls and need to work on different features/We all have things that scare us tremendously/Me personally it is seizures

Soul Sighs

by Pusselle Wineetha

How
dark, how
cold, how so
lonely his heart
feels without tender touch by his lover,
his soul, his breath; cascading tears flood his
eyes, yet his soul
blooms with hopes
to see
her.

The Christmas Slave

by Dexter Greener

I ponder these days as a lonely man wondering, why live?
My slaves adore me, but they still fear me, oh why, dear God, why?
I sit near the fireplace in a darkened room with warm embers glowing and watching the dying fire dance on the windowpane.
I begin to stare out through the frosted window watching the majestic snowfall.
Still pondering on my melancholy woos when a messenger knocked on my door.
My Butler opened the creaking door, a rush of cold air and snow ushered in.
With my Butler besides me there stood the messenger I know with a slave I recently purchased and I begged them to come in.
They dressed her in warm but ragged clothes, in chains and with her head bowed, then I saw the sorrow of her demeanor which overtook me, and I felt despondent.
I called for my Butler to take her and clean her up with appropriate clothing

and unchain her.

The Butler presented her to me, and I noticed a warm and vibrant aura about her.

I wondered, what does this mean, why does her presence tug at my soul?

I asked her name, and she said it's Gabriel as her smile radiated its beauty throughout my house, and with that, I was well Pleased.

It moved me so that I called for my Butler and made a declaration that when I die, my slaves will be free and inherit this property.

The Butler took down my declaration, and I signed it.

Gabriel, straighten up, smiled, and she began to transform.

I was in awe, wonder and fear, but then I saw this beautiful Angel known as Gabriel.

I fell to my knees to honor her. She said to me Rise oh wonderful and kind man, for the Lord saw favor in you, and I am here to take you home.

Oh, what great joy, then I saw my Butler cry and begging me not to go.

But I must go, so you can live free, have an abundance for your families and the Lord will bless you.

I died this day, December 24 1813.

Stay Strong Brothers

by SandyAxe

Don't let pride
Guide your stride
Instead take a ride
On the straight and narrow
And let righteousness be your row
Down the river we know as life
Speak with peace not strife
Speak with a feather not a knife
Speak with grace not spite
Speak to reason and not to fight
Lead not to dominate and feed
Lead to sow a fruitful seed
Love not for lust for your heart will rust
Love because it's just
Lay your anchors so you don't wither
Lay your anchors so you don't dither
Live to cure and create

Live to edify and elevate
Live not to harm and hate
Give not for your greed
Give for your brothers' need
Don't let the wicked vex you with malice
Don't let the wicked lure you into their twisted palace
Don't let the wicked make you drink from their bloodstained chalice
Sit atop a high ground not for vanity
Sit atop a high ground so you can watch and guard every sea
Know that fantasy juxtaposes reality
Know that the steadfast will strengthen and last
Know that the famous are often vacuous
Know that blight follows those who slither in the night
A dove glides with love
A raven plummets with sin
Go and reach out of your arm's range
Go and instill a positive change
Love your mothers
Listen to your fathers
Stay strong brothers

Streaming

by Paul M Thomson

I cannot chose to enter into the stream
Any more than select my night's dream,
But when swept into its generative storm,
Where earthly imaginings underperform:

Then - only - does the inner eye awaken
 to Black Elk's "Sacred Way"
Of seeing, or one can dance in the "still point"
 of Eliot's creative sway.
Yet all stirrings emanate from the primal swirl
 of quantum motions;
Ever moving, always fleeting, arising here,
 then there, as revelations.

Love Is A Blessing

by Conner John Gillespie

Oh harsh and unforgiving love
Why sear and scar my heart.
Release me from such tedious bonds,
tis time for lust to play its part.
Such games I know not how to win,
nor cheat, nor fool, or blunder
So why must I succumb to love
As strong as roaring thunder.
Mysterious, the heart may be,
Only few of its blessings yet known to me.
Some lessons I'll learn and some I just won't
There are things that I know and things I just don't
Hate is a lesson we all learn and must live
Love is a blessing to be earned and to give
If love has such meaning for life and our ways
Why am i still stuck wandering in this dark, loveless haze

Farm Illustration

by Bridget Eleanor Williams

A barn on a hill.
Beside was a wheat mill.
Corn grew in tall stalks.
"Ding, Dong!" said the clocks.
Early morning sunshine.
Finally 'twas feeding time!
Grass was the main course.
Hay for the horse.
I fed seed to the hens.
Jersey Cows in their pens.
Kid goats brayed.
Llamas strayed.
My kitten was purring.
Nobody was listening.

Oh, the pigs are squealing.
Piggies, I'm coming!
Quickly, I ran to the shed.
Roosters, waiting to be fed.
Sheep with their fuzzy wool.
Turkeys want a handful.
Under the warm sun's heat.
Vegetables, washed and ready to eat.
Watered the lawn early today.
Xeriscaping now takes place.
Y'all would've loved this day.
Zip-dee-doo-da-yay!

When I Upset The Applecart

by Justin Maxwell DePietropaolo

They rolled along the dirty road,
With apples fresh among the load.
They stopped a mile from the mart,
As I upset the apple cart,

I stood in front as if to stop,
Causing all the fruit to drop,
Telling where the road had led,
And warned of dangers up ahead.

Told my time of being there,
Coming back all worse for wear.
Be it known, I planned in part,
To NOT upset the apple cart.

These things they didn't NEED to know,
I felt it was my duty though.
I don't mind to take the blame,
If things for them don't end the same.

Thanking me for being nice,
Exchanged an apple for advice,

A different road they did depart,
When I upset the apple cart.

Chariots Of The Surf

by Clive Blake

Surf's up,
Heads are down,
Timing their move,
Concentrated frown,
Salt lips,
Hard swallow,
Adrenalin pumping,
There is no tomorrow,
The white horses charge,
Their chariots follow,
Surfing speeding waves,
Above a spray crested hollow,
For just a few seconds,
Taming the waves,
Anticipating the way
That nature behaves,
With triumphant abandon,
And balance supreme,
Living the moment,
Living the dream ...

Before I Go

by vernon michael witmer

I will turn to see the sky
touch the grass and wonder why
walk the mountain trail again
splash the cold against my face
feel the burly bark of brethren pine
upon a wintry shine of one more snow
before I go

wade waist deep in summer hay
and play all day
roll down hills and step on stones
across a creek to
peek into the earth beneath
a rock
and disregard the clock

spring upon the fence
as birds alight to lofty branch
and take a chance or dare
cast my fate into the wind
without a care
before I go

I will touch my nose
to every flower
and for an hour
I will contemplate
the stars
catch lightning bugs
and moonbeams in
my mother's pickle jars
and I will run
into my life
deep into each rising sun
touch and taste and hear and see
all this world has given me
before I go

The Snowy Road

by Justin Maxwell DePietropaolo

A time ago,
After it snowed,
My friend forebode,
A certain road,
The shortest way to go.

Yet I was slowed,
So on this night,
The moon was bright,
I took a right,
And went on down the road.

And to my sight,
I could defend,
Against my friend,
But would depend,
On if the end was bright.

But at the bend,
I saw it close,
And so it goes,
The road I chose,
Was dead upon the end.

The Only Truth We Know

by vernon michael witmer

Words fall like hard rain,
Soft snow, or fragrant leaves.
Measuring spoons of stillness
Against each swallowed sound.
You become a sink
With both taps running.
Above all words
in the light of the lone moment;
Where nary a force in the universe
Can bring back a lost thought,
The wind confides its loneliness,
Whispering cold to each naked cheek.
Life's flame, bending softly to the touch
Of every thoughtful / thoughtless breeze.
Like the first snow, we cling
To every passing moment
Warily, one by one, as weeks
Roll heavy onward,
Like ripples on the water,

Footprints in the snow,
Or the fainter sound of a drum
That beats inside the heart of us all;
Where our souls become each other,
And we remember
The only truth we know:
That we were born to love.

April 8th

by Jennifer Cahill

Thoughts of yesterday...

Light blue of sky boasts
solitary clouds as bright
as the sun, bursting

with immaculate
hues. They brush the noon's heaven;
hover over peaks.

The gossamer clouds
are wedding-white egrets-
elegant, at peace.

Bliss, I Think

by Sophie Georgia Pilkington

Grand declarations of love,
Afternoon tea;
Hidden bookshops in the crevice of a pretty avenue,
And begonias in hanging baskets.
Walks along cobbled streets;
Walks in the moonlight,
Sunday nights-
With the stars reflecting on the surface of a beautifully unblemished lake;
The soft rustle of the trees as a soft summer breeze dances through the

leaves,
The sounds of the city drifting to sleep in our wake.
Your hand in mine.
Bliss, I think.

Twilight's Embrace
by Abhishek Suresh

The myriad curtains of a deep red sky
embrace the edges of the promised horizon.
Peaceful lips, lost in a soft soliloquy
remember the memories of an ending dawn, his life.
The deathbed, a fitting place for a fitting end;
death beckons, but he is not scared.

Like a setting sun, slipping ever slowly
flowing into the last crevices of a linear skyline,
his eyes shut in solemn prayer,
his soul wraps itself in twilight's undying embrace.

As Is
by Margarita Lillico

I fell in love with her because,
She loved me without any clause -
"As is"- it seemed and so I hoped,
So I proposed and we eloped.

But things soon changed, "Who could have thought,
I was so very gravely flawed?!"
To change me was her life long shot
Into a man that I am not.

Puzzled, I analyzed a bit,
And figured something didn't fit.
Person in question therefore is:
Who I have fallen in love with?

Or maybe there is a slight chance,
If changes she, for a romance?
And then, if she does truly try
As a kind gesture so will I.

As They Danced Incognito

by Stark Hunter

From where I sat that night in 1971,
I could see in the distance south LA,
Lit up like grounded stars in black mud;
As a rude wind brushed up against me,
I saw you wearing navy blue with black shoes.
You were at the Roxy with my best friend.
Making out in the back row with popcorn and ice.
Tears of rage filled the ego ducts for two dark hours.
Then Broten visited, sitting distant under crushed stars,
My young earth, shattered in haphazard fragments,
You flitted like a engorged fly away from me, and us,
Your silent watchings and downward betrayals then,
Killed whatever love-embraces connecting our moving souls,
Our bodies, always lying clenched and breathing in a tangle, your
Milk chocolate cupcakes set before me in the naked candlelight,
With salty, salivating tongue-lickings bringing you to rise in my arms.
We lay with spent emotions in the dark room with doors closed.
Now we exit the bricks and the mortar to spy on the seven sisters,
As they dance above incognito in the cold firmament of trackless time.
"I wish someday to go to sleep and not wake up in the morning."

Eros Quarters

by Thomas Wells

The insidious reign
of your apparitions, your
coitus with the attic serpents
was sufficient to strip all
pigment from my skin.

Was it they who walked you
blindfolded through the upper chambers
of our modest Eros quarters?
Didn't you walk them?

My self-reckoning, old Freudian suppers
were wet cookies beneath your heels.
And we lived here!

Their split tongues crowded my speech.
Our energies were split hairs, gnarled
To the scalp!

Our timid blithe seconds were
massacred!

My Mom

by Melissa Lou Johnson

Feathered Brazilian brown hair with eyes that match.
Red lips,Skinny brows with mascara thick on each lash.
Skin tone honey roasted cashew.
Body scarred from self-harm and all she had been through.
Felonies, misdemeanors and a diploma.
From Great kills, Staten Island to the beaches of Clearwater and Sarasota.
Vodka on the rocks with a splash of diet coke.
Mirror, a straw and lines of coke.

She always made you laugh With every joke.
Even though, Throughout my childhood my mom was an addict.
There is no other women, I would of rather spent my life with.
Taught me how to be ok with surviving by myself.
Showed me some life choices will have you buried or displayed on a shelf.
I've learned from all your mistakes. So, I choose love over wealth.
I was born the black sheep to break the family cycle for my own health.
To ensure, I face the life. I try to create with my best self.

Banal Romance

by Serge Lyrewing

It is spring and a little bird's singing,
It's exulting again in the flight,
Do not lie to me clove that you're seeming
that the lilies bloom wildly and bright.
Oh, I do not believe for some reason,
Let the sun is so fondle to me,
I'm like deaf, but the waking up season
rings with whispering stream that does flee.

The grass rises to heaven, it's noisy,
And collecting the dewdrops of May
Beetle chirps in the green very closely,
And the sudden wind blows it away.
Let it chirps me again, I don't listen,
I have not met with miracles yet,
I'm like deaf, but the waking up season
vivifies our wood that was dead.

And the hearts beat around, pay attention,
And the fire's in eyes of the maids,
And the horses bite bridles of passion
without sparing the blush for the face.
Oh, I do not believe for some reason,
Heart has so many burns, wounds still bleed,
I'm like deaf, but the waking up season
is alluring with sweetest deceit.

Gentle Mist

by Kavira Thakker

I was once walking through the wood,
in the mist, silenced hush.
Sky rocketed trees,
graced by the tender eve.

Quacks; quivers; splash; and whirl,
faded into a whisper.
Sky fell asleep; stars twinkled,
but dwindled to disappear.

Emptiness of the green,
I felt within,
and with a sweet touch, gently
the mist devoured me completely.

Selene

by Joanna Chamberlain

The full moon golden as Japanese Maple
Dense pine trees, woodland ladders
The forest redolent with fresh, earthy aromas
Strong gales deliberately, manhandling
Navy, ebony, clouds crawl across the night sky
Mimicking millipedes, quickly, silently
Rain pours down the trees
Similar to hot candle wax
The cold bites
Mournful singing can be heard in the distance
Deeper, deeper
Advancing into the dank thicket
Twigs snap under foot
weary eyes glancing up
Catching sight of the most magnificent crown of jewels
Peach, fine, lips whispering, with urgency

Eyes snowy Quartz
Wavy, long, silver hair blowing enticingly in the wind
Complexion deathly pale
The enchantress placed a spell
Under the full moon, Golden as Japanese Maple

Oppression

by Simon Rogerson

Reign of terror plays out
Endless nights as victims shout
So many good ones vanish
People must hide their anguish
Equality is a forbidden word
Community's voice tries to be heard
Together they stand and die

Say a little prayer - then cry

The Old Scribe

by Craig Cornish

I remember the reach of
crooked fingers
and then the swing of
the lamp's chain
- at first, a silent metronome
then, in dark moments
he'd sit and stare - last words
echoing within until
an encore of light and
a few more scribbled thoughts
...what inspiration haunted and
fought to be recalled - released.

Dogeared pages stained with tears
- dried in painful pauses,

smeared ink blots
on recollections that came too close,
then slipped inside that
vulnerable glare...

Wedding Vows

by Clive Blake

May we forever be lovers,
May we forever be friends,
And should we hurt each other,
May we quickly make amends.

May we enjoy our passion,
But never let compassion die,
Thinking in selfless terms as we,
Never emphasising I.

May we forever be soul-mates,
May our love eternally last,
May the food of love sustain us,
May we never have to fast.

May we use each other's strengths,
When we are feeling weak,
May we both learn to compromise,
And always as one voice speak.

May we never keep dark secrets,
May we never tell each other lies,
May we both work unceasingly,
To ensure our love never dies.

Greystone

by Carol Louise Moon

This two-tone gray stone,
dead shadow of an egg
misleads me.

It sits tight and introspective
in its own omniscience
forcing my brain to bend
and squirm under the weight
of its own gray matter.
Or white matter, but no matter...

This stone's dull shimmer,
even before the great flood of tears,
draws me.
Yet, I come no closer,
not wanting to intrude.

Old Mill

by Katharine L. Sparrow

I walked down by the old worn mill
one day that seemed like summer still.
Where brilliant trees of amber shone,
a trickling brook slid over stone—
and there I crossed with careful tread
as 'round the stones swirled leaves of red
and yellow in a dizzy blaze
that carried off the summer days.

And as I reached the crumbling shed,
a chilling wind whirled on ahead.
It made me shiver as the scent
of autumn ruffled by and went

beyond to where the winter will
snow softly on the old worn mill.

Abstract

by Akham Nilabirdhwaja Singh

I rambled once riding my bicycle
on a foggy day of winter.
The fog remained suspended long in the atmosphere
so impatient I to go out
for such a weather decades not seen.

Going farther and farther
excited seeing the veiled country
on a lonesome village road not seen before
the fogs dissipated, evening sun appeared
giving a pleasant apricity .

Countryside calm and gentle
sprawling Paddy fields brown with stubble
on both sides of the road quiet and peaceful
at the east extended to the foot of blue hill yonder,
a tree grove in the middle,
mist resting still at its foot,
a few clouds seen floating at the brae
top and above the idyllic blue hill.

There a moment I longed to sit
by the paddy field under the tree
branches wide spreading
with a maiden of my imagination long ago.

Once Upon A Time In Hollywood

by William Kamen

It was a warm summer night in LA, August '69,
A single night of infamy and psychic darkness for mankind.
Sharon Tate was close to fulfilling her empty outcries,
when the night burned its cloak in the sunrise.

Earlier before dawn, a quiet eerie breeze came alive
and kept blowin' down the canyon to 10050 Cielo Drive.
A night so quiet, you could almost hear the sound of ice,
rattling in cocktail shakers in the homes of celebrity paradise.

The canyon walls came alive with eerie echoes.
Blood-curdling screams and cries of "Please don't, Oh, God No"
Several were listening, no one saw a thing.
It happened so suddenly, so sudden without warning.

Red sky in the morning, Shepherds beware,
Bad news at the front door, "Blood, bodies everywhere"
Sharon Tate and four others tangled in a pig-slaughtering spree.
Spilled blood staining the walls with words for all to see.

Fear and panic swept through Hollywood
from the seaside bungalows to the canyon neighborhoods.
Oh, Mercy Mercy, "what's going on"?
Talk to me Marvin, C'mon talk to me, tell me what's going on.

A devil in disguise, in the city of angels, where did it go?
Ask Dennis, a beach boy, he should know.
Business is business, death to that scoundrel,
Psychotic revenge is psychotic revenge, and it's murder so brutal.

Charles Manson a.k.a. the devil found hiding in plain sight,
posing as a peace-loving hippie with a thousand faces.
The day they captured him, he said to me, Boy, I am the Devil
and the End-Times have just only begun.

The flower-power-Era, once eight-miles high, now in a slide.
The sacred store lost its soul when love and peace died.
The soul of a nation slowly eroding, torn away with evil.
Lennon could only imagine, living in a world safe and peaceful,

Manson flashes the Jury the LA Times,
front page headlines, "Manson Guilty, Nixon Declares,"
Hold on Mr President, tell me no lies,
take me back to My Lai to the scene of that massacre.

Casey Kasem, Kiss FM, fills the airwaves with passion,
sending psychic vibes to all God's children.
play me some songs, Casey Kasem,
Play me "Revolution" and play me "Helter-Skelter"

Serena

by Charles C. Oswalt

Serena, when she's sleeping, is the sleepiest cat in the world.

She likes her basket in the sun,
and a nice warm bed when day is done.
She stretches first and turns around
and only then she settles down.
But then she'll sleep the whole day through,
with just a little break or two.

Serena, when she's eating, is the hungriest cat in the world.

She's hungry in the morning,
but at least she gives us warning
that she's ready for her breakfast there and then.
She's patient as she can be,
but her stomachs getting angry
and she thinks she's had no food since who knows when.

Serena, when she's playing, is the happiest cat in the world.

First she's here and then she's there
and, in fact, she's everywhere,

from her cat tree to the highest thing in sight.
She'll wrestle with her mouse,
but she won't destroy the house,
though it often seems, at times, perhaps she might.

Serena, when she's preening, is the prettiest cat in the world.

She's not your usual Tabby, this remarkably fine Abby,
with her beauty mark of white beneath her chin.
She'll primp and comb and preen, 'till she's certain that she's clean;
 her ablutions are almost sure to make you grin.
She's as pretty as a flower and were it within my power
there wouldn't be a show she wouldn't win.

Cool

by Douglas S Brown

The summer day is so hot
friends stay away.

I can picture them-
like me-
leaning into open refrigerators
and freezers
with frozen chicken,
hamburger,
Minute Maid.

We breathe the air
and fan the coolness
into ourselves.
We are not at all
thinking of wives or children
who try to sleep in the heat.

These moments are only for us,
the stolen coolness for us.
The appliance for food,

the cool air, accidental.

We stay apart
until the sun fades
and then with bottles of beer
begin our exaggerations
each one.

I Was Once A Part Of You

by Sagari Adhikari

I was once
a part of you,
and of course
you know it too !

We shared a body
and a heartbeat...
I wouldn't mind
if it was to repeat...

For 9 whole months
we were one...
But with my birth
it all begun !

I began to see
that we weren't the same....
But I didn't know,
who I was to blame !

Was it the world
or was it my genes ?
I still don't understand
what it really means,

to be so different,
yet one with you...
and I am sure,
you don't know too !

Golden Oldie

by Gayle Rodd

The kids have all grown and moved out on their own
I can now be a senior with ease

But as I get older, unburden my shoulders
the help I once gave / now need

What has happened to me? I flaunt apathy
I'm becoming my parents I fear

I've ditched rock and roll for the daily news show
and prefer jasmine tea to a beer

A concert for me, well, used to be
A summer of fun at Red Rocks

And now my idea of fun for a night
is taking my dog for a walk

To The Last

by Graham Alexander Devenish

Clan Stewart of Appin,
Clan MacGillvray too,
Fell at Culloden,
In the blood and dew.
They fell two by two, and then ten by ten,
Until twelve hundred dead, not sixty minutes in.
...At Culloden

The highland charge failed,
No victory as in the past.
The British stood their ground and slaughtered,

To the last.
And when twelve hours had past and a wounded man gasped,
The Butcher slaughtered again, and again,
To the last
And the last.
...At Culloden

At Culloden they fell,
The fathers and the sons,
The brothers and the cousins,
Of Scotland's bravest ones.
Bonnie na'er should ha'e marched,
His highlanders through the night.
They may ha'e had the chance,
To bring on the proper fight.
...At Culloden

But the swords came down, as men crawled through the heather,
Brits cut the Clans deep,
Ruby blood on their feather.
Through their hearts,
Through their souls,
Their lives given for this toll.
A scar to their creed,
And still Scotland weeps.
...At Culloden

Graham Alexander Devenish

Kvetch End

by KUPMEI PHOM

Here, me on the shore,
Botched to retrospect the apathy of the world.
One in charity, one in triumphant,
Herein lays a callous heart without remorse.

Here, me on a mission to win,
Unkempt the very thing I wanna covet.
The tasks without forbearance is annoying.

Herein lays the gimmick of lust.

Here, me on a verge of doom,
Sudden kvetch shook my heart.
I will not yen to greed howbeit raise my arms to give,
Herein lays irreversible assessor.

Here, me to the living,
Yield on to what is faultless.
Supper to the craving,
Herein lays the kvetch end.

Campfire
by richard a jordan

They're in across the lake again
Can't build a fire worth a damn
But the gasoline flare lights the shore for a moment or two.
Still, they do it year after year
There is some sense of continuity in seeing it each Summer.
I hope they keep it up.
I'll never teach them to build it right.
And each Summer look forward to the sudden flare
And the eventual sparks and ashes
Climbing through the White Pine branches
Proof that the fire's finally lit
And that another Summer is here.

Hope
by Cachline Etienne

A northern light
A starlit night
A silver flower
A determined fighter
As the plant grows in my soul
It shouldn't be there, yet it holds

A new surge of strength grows inside, I feel faint
Before I know it, it begins
Casting all fears aside
It can hurt me, disappoint me, or
even manipulate me
But it grows
It is determined to have its way
So my body, in turn just obey
Hope takes over, a deadly sin
For when it starts it never ends.

Sorcerer's First Time

by Sheila Van Zant - Lewis

At your first touch, I was mesmerized
A Captive was born before your eyes
Magic was passed through me It's true
Our loins stirred as our passion grew

Never before had I felt this lust
In darkness, every touch left skin flush
Sensations heightened beyond compare
of the rest of the world, I remained unaware

Before this Not once had I looked at you
But now in dark my gaze yours thru and thru
What mystical force had seduction unleashed?
Carnivorous forces turned into beasts

Once begun there is no retreat
Climax on climax or heat upon heat?
When it was over in my mind chaos calmed
The clock began ticking the deed has been done

Sanity tells me run now before it's too late.
But preserve the moment, hold onto it,
latch tight your mind gate
For now, **THE SORCEROR HAS A HAND IN YOUR FATE**

My True Love

by M. Braimah Saaka

My true love
promised me
a car
a Jaguar
Mind you
British racing car
blue

My true love
promised me
a coat
Cashmere
True wool
from Pashmina
goat

My true love
promised me
a dance
slow with soul
wet like sweat
or rain
in winter

My true love
promised me
a song
Flawless like
Minnie Riperton
Yet so sad
Still riveting

The Mourning Path - St Louis Cemetery No 2

by Craig Mahler

A tattered Calico traverses the crumbling corridor
dissecting a row of dilapidated sacred structures,
each uniquely indistinguishable from the next.

The wind carries an eerie refrain
as it whistles through the splintered stones,
white-washed to harbor their degeneration.

There's a fragrant stench of wilted petals
lying dormant in stagnant waste.
This potpourri of nature's compost
resonates from the marred receptacles
lining this mourning path.

Picket shadows serve no comfort
from the unbearable fervor
as it bakes these palaces of the deceased.

Irreverent voyagers marvel at its spectacle,
congregating within the blighted vestibules,
ignoring the pleas of sacrilege,
all to capture images for their own posterity.

Exit this city of the dead,
allow the mourners their serenity due.
Bestow the departed their wanted peace
and leave them to their gentle rest.

Celestial Chats

by Franci Eugenia Hoffman

faintest voices heard
divine talk between angels
laughter in shadows

Monophobia

by Debra Walker

Blackness above is
soundless, its darkness echoes
alone, and afraid
would it deride my fears as
one by one they disappear.

Wide-Open Secrets

by Smita Kulkarni

Don't stay occupied constantly on electronic gadgets
Step out and get touched by Mother Nature's magnificent cadence
Forgo your shoes once in a while
Feel the caring earth underneath your bare feet sometimes
Get hugged by breezes of cool calming wind
Listen to the sounds of whistling leaves' chimes
Feel silky smooth petals of various flowers
Touch barks of tree trunks to sense diverse textures
Eavesdrop on visiting birds' tweets and peeps
Wonder about the magnificent colors of ladybugs, butterflies and bees
Watch closely busy insects' awe-inspiring flights
Notice their smooth landings on blossoms to suck delicious fluids
Smell the fragrances of roses, jasmines and gardenias
Feel the refreshing breaths of their enchanting aromas
Find out how squirrels take naps by cuddling on tree branches
Appreciate the sheer beauty of nature's wonderful plays

Be present and enjoy every moment
Mother Nature has so many wide-open secrets

A Pill Cutter

by Tamanna Ferdous

I was looking at the small pill-cutter box
Which I was holding in my hand.
Blue colored with a sharp edge of the blade
To cut the medicine in halves, one-third or
Could also be, in one-fourth, maybe.

I was thinking, simultaneously, about the news
I heard today, which made me puzzled....
Churches and bombings, again, so vulnerability!
So vulnerable with this cloak of religiosity
In this utter disastrous time of unrest and confusion!

I woke up again.... just to get another news of the death
A death in the family, ending of a marvelous life, so precious!
I whispered a line of supplication for the departed
And also, for me, as there was something to do....
And, I was holding the pill cutter still in hand, indecisively.

(April 21st, 2019)

The Winter Of My Reckoning

by Vickie Hurtt-Thayer

I went for a walk today,
it had snowed last night,
I was cold,
but I did not care.

A freshness stirred the crisp air,
I tightened my scarf around my thoughts,
As I listened to the rhythmic crunching,
beneath my feet.

Towards the end of my long and cold walk,
I looked back feeling warmer,
I noticed my muddy boot prints had
been covered over by clean, fresh, falling snow.

This reminded me that the steps I took today,
are far more important,
than the ones,
I had left behind, from yesterday.

I then smiled,
while unwrapping my scarf,
a little looser,
from my thoughts.

I had listened to every new step,
that my old boots had made,
while thinking to myself,
that God was good, and he always shows us the way.

The Lady Who Liked Mangoes

by David Wakeling

Down by Hope Street where the frangipanis bask,
And the Goddess of Love has put up her tent,
Lives a lady with fire in her eyes and cats in her kitchen.
Oh of course I will tell you she's an angel if you ask,
And her magic lies in the making of enchantment,
Why then do dark clouds cover my silent sun?

We will sing together and dance in a fury of touch,
Like the wind does when a storm comes passed,
We will laugh and joke and taste wine in gentle sips,
And that won't matter much,
Because as you might have guessed,
Love has taken me and kissed me on the lips.

Time has curled up on her couch like a Siamese cat,

Yet she still loves mangoes and a foot massage at night,
Perhaps God finally got it right,
When he touched her finger and tipped his hat,
And she walked out into the light,
Why then do dark cobwebs trap me in fright?

By the sea of blue and the grass so green,
She will lay her head on my shoulder and hum,
And all the dark clouds will drift away,
The cobwebs will vanish forever,
In the dark I will find my way,
And finally...finally...finally,
The bells repeating in my brain will cease,
And I will be able to breathe again.

Oh lady of Hope Street dance for me once more,
Before the candles in my lonely church are lit,
Come with me and sway upon the dance floor,
And I will read a poem and gently massage your soul,
And the red fire of enchantment will burn forever more.

Culloden Foretold

by Graham Alexander Devenish

A man he once said ta'e me,
You'll lay on heather, your gut will bleed.
Near Inverness you should na'e be,
Your end is there upon thee.

I paid no heed, jumped to my feet,
Charged through the Highlands, sword in sheath.
Loyalty to the Stuarts was my belief,
and to the end that will be.

The charge has stalled, and is no more.
The Duke has trained his English Score,
to stand and fight, not run as before.
This man who spoke has told me.

On this ground I now will stand,

dirk at side, sword in hand.
Bring on my foe, I now demand,
The day has come, God save me.

The volley came, smoke thick as fog.
We charged into the peat and bog,
They stood as one, and stopped our trod,
and slaughtered all that will be.

And now I lay, my gut has bled.
A man by me, still live, not dead.
A Brit comes near, thrusting as he treads,
kills him and I as foretold to me.

Rust

by Patrick Cornwall

Can I ever love again your lips pressed against my ear
My soul begs, pleads with me, the heart yields no more tears
Should I gather unto me my hearing waits the matter
The pulse quickens at the touch, ice lifts and a shatter

Racing dreams ,like oil fields , drilled deep and hit the mark
Lingers, tarries, awaits me there I shift my heart to park
The embrace is warm, it pulls me forward and never was a doubt
Long the idle, engines cool ,never knew you had such clout

Arise the morn the birds a searching your hair lay cross my chest
I answered every question met but will I pass the test
Eye to eye and sweat on sweat you meet me and the thrust
Didn't know I had it in me , should've known it'd never rust

Occupation

by Lee Hawkins

They came in silence,
moving through the speckled shadows of the dawn
half-life
half-something else;
a strangeness

They came in with the news,
not in it
not carrying it to us;
but with the news they arrived,
silently.

We only read the words,
but with the reading,
we knew they had arrived
and what was ours
was passing from us.

They're sitting now in every room.
At night we almost hear them.
Fragmented whispers from up in the attic space,
beneath the eaves, where they have frightened
swallows from their nests.

Uninvited, they came
and like spiders filled the empty spaces.
The house is full now
and every empty room inhabited.

Never seen but always present,
they have made this house their home.
No fuss.
No malice.
But we know now this house is theirs
and we are only tenants.

The British Soldier At Balaclava

by Robert James Moore

I am a British soldier, been a soldier all my life
and back home in England, I left 2 kids and a wife
now I'm outside Sebastapol, with Cardigans Brigade
waiting to fight the Russians, Cavalry on Parade

We are part of Raglans Army, and we're ready for the fray,
Light Dragoons and Lancers, and Hussars were there that day
We rode our light fast horses, for mobility and speed
Unarmoured, armed with lance and sword, skirmishing our deed

we have our orders "charge the guns" believe it we cannot
but ours is not to reason why, to do or die our lot
we sit our horses and wait there, for the word for us to go
hoping we won't have to, a mistakes been made, we know.

We started down the valley, toward the waiting foe
riflemen to right and left, were shooting as we go
three quarters of a mile we rode, sprayed with shot and shell
600 of the Light Brigade, went charging into hell

A Russian battery to our left, another to our right
500 yards ahead of us, Russians, are starting to take flight
Line one went through the battery, 2 Regiments in all
the cost was great as all around, we saw men and horses fall

The second line of Cavalry, now charging through the guns
Cut and slash the gunners, as they turned to run
then came the third line, to complete the duty so assigned
to finish any gunners, or rifleman they could find

The charge is done, its "threes about", and retire back up the hill
once more to brave the Valley of Death, Though the battle continued still
through the Russian skirmisher, rifle fire and cannon shot
the end for many brave soldier, who'd given all he'd got

And so the brave 600, with two thirds left behind
after a charge against 5000, returned, only to find
the heavies had not followed them, momentum had been lost
the charge, although magnificent, had not been worth the cost.

Making Quilts Is Difficult

by Robert James Moore

Making quilts is difficult, you might think you're clever too
but there's all the thought and preparation, that you have to do,
choose the colours and choose the thread, will that one go with this
patterns which you think they'd like, and scenes all filled with bliss

Then add them all, and study it, till you think it looks just right
you cut and stitch and ponder, well into the night
paper pieces, bits of cloth, and sewing things together
flowers here, and there a bird, and stitch, light as a feather

As well as Quilt's, there's Cushions, and runners for the table too
wall hangings, cross stitch samplers, to mention just a few
to cut and stitch and applique, the pattern she will choose
to make exactly what she sees, her talent she will use

But more than colour, more than thread, there's part of you in there
with every stitch and every thought, filled with love and care
for quilts are made for family, and friends that you hold dear
so they can keep, and cherish them, year after year after year

Viet Nam Rememberances

by Robert E. Welch, Sr.

Reaching far away it stands, gently 'round the bend.
Names in stone, row on row, that seem to never end;
Reflections of the ones who died; those who gave their all.
Yet, there at last, the final name, the last to die and fall.

We went as boys so very young, our lives yet not fulfilled,
A place that was a living hell, not fit for man or child.

All gave some, and some gave all, in a war that was so cruel.
Yet those of us who did come home were faced with ridicule.

But those who died and gave their all are the truest of the true,
Their names are on a granite wall, for all of us to view.
As we pass by and stop to see, a flag, a book, a name
So many names, so many names, not one who brought us shame.

Rest in peace, oh faithful one, and wait for us above.
For one day we shall join with you and see the Heavenly dove.
But as we wait for that to come, our tears will fall anew,
In knowing that those left behind will always grieve for you.

When, in our deepest sorrow, and our hearts are heavy laden;
When it seems that all is lost, and everyone is saddened
We come together in His name, to praise and sing a song,
Knowing that the will of God will surely make us strong.

Rhythm Of The Rain

by Wade Greenlee

The rhythm of the rain
In sync with my heart
Falling slowly against the pane
Tells a story of so many days apart

I feel them on my face
Slowly and softly they flow
A warm bittersweet embrace
One not felt since long ago

Replenishing life on earth
Scouring away the pain
Bringing about new birth
Each one a memory to remain

Of life and a bond of love
Laughter from days long gone
Now falling silently from above

Something I always depended on

Angels crying in their ethereal plane?
No, these tears are my own
Falling slowly with the rain
Two were one and now one is alone

I Want Peace

by Neelamani Sutar

Let me have a sparkle of fire,
a fire what can burn
all anger into ashes.

Let me have a strong weapon
with which I can destroy
terrorism, racism and all evil deeds,
Earth would be completely free.

Let me have a pen,
also some magical ink
as I want to compose eternal song
to let peace prevail everywhere.

Let me have a brush
color and canvas
to draw and paint
The landscape of peace and ecstasy.

Let me have a drop of water
with it, I can wipe out sins
and I need a river
what can wash away all hunger
and peace would overflow everywhere.

Let me have sword or gun
to shoot out all misbelieves
from mankind.

Let me have a woman

who would give birth to another Jesus
to spread message of peace on earth.

Spellbind

by Nayda Ivette Negron

Love comes come suddenly as a breeze.
Shaking all your being, letting you shocked.
You will never be the same as before.
Smile alone and sighing are the most visible effects.
A shine sparks in your eyes as you see your loved one.

When is true love, souls recognize each other.
Glances are the door that invite to a new romance.
Time tells if it will be a lifetime love story or only a
temporary stage in your life.
Surrender to its startling effect.

Marsha Mellow

by Richard Breese

My girlfriend's name is Marsha Mellow
And I am quite a lucky fellow.
But dear reader don't be hasty
It's not because her lips are tasty,
For she's the orchestra's third cello.

Passing Shadows

by Frederic M Parker

A kiss so fleeting as a fragrant scent.
From distance far, in silence lingers near.
A memory perhaps, that came and went.
A passing shadow that will disappear.
This remembrance where soft rose petals fell.
Not from sadness, rather time's unkind hand.

To leave a thought wistful an empty well,
When stillness ever quiet will demand.
A longing, or a moment relived, chased.
This melted candle with blackened wick cold.
Once a red flame rising when two embraced.
Now a web tangled in memories, old.

To find nostalgia on your mind's doorstep,
To open the door, a fleeting kiss kept.

Indivisible Love

by IRIS SANKEY-LEWIS

I loved the way you strolled into view
Then paused to face spot of quietude
Of therapy and grace I always knew.
I awaited Sabbath's simmering sun
You stared intently, then paused as I looked
Simmering before the Hudson River.

My bike, books, snack; I sat upon grassy mound, and
Savored light touch of courteous breeze
Summer after summer, I'd known such tease...
Until, in silence you appeared, stating this:
"I just thought I'd come to see why you look so happy."
Spring rain had brought blossoming treats.

Was it "My Tribute" song you heard?
My bike and I had had our fill
Daylight warmth and view had us lingering still
You and your words did thrill.

You had no clue; the New Year was yet new, when
I stood and watched, not far from where I sat
Red heart, blue star, yellow smile on helium balloons
They traversed on wings of breeze, with prayer I penned.

By mid-year in zenith of Summer, your presence I saw
Metamorphosis with bliss lingered on my list
With ease you fulfilling promises beyond a year.

Then, the engagement!

I loved the way you floated inside my mind
You ousted the ex, who'd become unkind
You showed me love spelled forever, and
Held me in splendor of your warmth that December
You made my coziness cozier
You showed me new meaning of together
Now, you're my gulf breeze, forever strumming my chimes.

Tears Of Joy

by Millard Lowe

God cried today; His tears fertilized
Mother Earth's womb;
The fragrance of nature saturated the air.

Tomorrow I will cry upon your grave
Laughing tears
Falling from pregnant memories:
Pregnant memories

Washing away grief's gloom
Watering love
And the happiness of peace we shared.

Seahawkishness

by John Anthony Beck

The outlook was sanguinity,
For the Seahawks on that day;
Last seven of the enemy,
They'd easily put away.

However, from the starting kick,
And through the first three quarters,
The Seahawks were the sort of sick

That needs Docs Without Borders.

Then, when it looked to be over,
And they heard the death rattle,
Lucky charm and four-leaf clover,
The Hawks re-joined the battle.

Suddenly, the lads came to life
With purpose and precision!
Every play was with panache rife,
To winning bomb decision!

Beyond

by Tommy Leon Wright

Beyond each of our hills,
He leaves a valley.
Beyond each arid stretch,
He'll place a stream.
Beyond each troubled time,
We may be facing.
God gives us hope,
And allows us to dream.

Beyond each sunlit day,
He made a sunset.
Beyond each moonlit night,
He fixed a dawn.
Beyond each daily problem,
We encounter.
There is, God,
Gently urging us on.

Beyond each planting time,
Comes a harvest.
Beyond each harvest,
a separation there'll be.
Beyond separation,
An eternity to spend.

With God, saying,
Won't you spend it with me?

A Life Well Lived

by Robert James Moore

The old man sat at the window, staring into space
people could only wonder, at the smile upon his face
but they had not been where he had been, and behind that wrinkled brow
they could not see what he had seen, or what he was seeing now

He was back again in England, on a cold and frosty day
heading for the Pennines, where he would make his way
into the hills round Kinder Scout, or maybe up Scafell
following the wanderers tracks, and pathways he knew well

He may be back at Gorton Mount, or maybe Spurley Hey
reliving all his schooldays, the learning and the play
Rugby with Pete Hesketh, or football as fullback
but definitely not cricket, too dangerous playing that
Or perhaps he's back in Gorton, round the Suttons Dwelling Trust
riding bikes out in the rain, till they fell apart with rust

there's Jack and Cliff, and Keswick, the pals he hung round with
for friendship and companionship which only true friends give.
He's camping on the Isle of Man, in the August holiday
trying to get a sunburn, to prove he'd been away
and drinking hard with Scottish lads, who congregated there
and we'll come up and see you, in Glasgow he would swear.

Or again, he's leaving England, heading for another land
a place where dad had told us, the living would be grand
with sun and sand and lots of work, we'd make our fortune there
and live life to the fullest, with fun, and little care
Now he's landed in Australia, mam and dad are there
him and his three sisters, standing in the sun shine glare

not knowing how their life will be, or if it will turn out
as dad had promised to us all, but there really was no doubt

this was a cleaner, brighter land, than England had become
his dad had fought in 2 wars, and now he wanted some
place to raise his family, in prosperity and peace
a place where all the worry, and the arguing would cease.

He could not see all of the things that would happen in his life
how he would raise a family, with his Australian wife
they'd drift apart, the kids would grow, and start lives of their own
and now there are grandchildren, and the family has grown

Now he's thinking of his second wife, who looks after him
he's not easy to live with, he knows this deep within
she ignores him when he's cranky, but he loves her more than gold
some say that he has mellowed, others say he just got old

I Awaken

by Joseph P. DiMino

I Awaken a child
to the nearness of my mother;
Feeling her breath of warmth--

(apparent is the joy
on her face
a labor well done);

my eyes maturing
not quite focus
I trustingly reach
for her special day
and mine
our discovery;

it is the grasp
of a newborn,

and the surrendering
of an
infinite universe
to love....

Eye Of Dark

by Donald J. Craig

Follow the path
in the dark of night
past the Well of Wyrd

In the forest deep
the Witch Trees keep
names in a book of blood

Eldritch is plucking something
strange he doesn't want you to see
he found it under a tree

Down the path dark
is a glimmering Eye
where spirits meet

Of all living things
in wisdom and death
it questions the young

Hatchlings who say
they know the way
but the Eye says no

Odin's lost Eye
sees glowing red runes in
the magic of gods in the night

Spells like tangled wires
in the dead branches of Witch
Trees scratching and hunting

For the Eye of Dark
is dreams half seen
by twisting primeval souls.

The Land Of Promise

by Joselito B. Asperin

Often called the land of promise,
Mindanao my native land,
Her soil is wet with innocent blood,
The promises many but few are done,

Here stealth cunning warriors,
Are professed men of god,
Their decency turns refute,
For shedding innocent blood,

Anguish pierced deep in our hearts,
Even on calm starry nights,
Anytime in the city or the woods,
Barking guns shimmering lights,

Is there hope for tomorrow,
Will our wailing cease?
Will our children and their offspring,
Have the chance to live in peace?

Melody Of Four Sister's

by Tiffany Saxon

Once apon a time
There were four bird's that sing,
Who made a difference to the world
with two sparrow's that graced the sky with
there heavenly wings.
For the sparrow's had four queen's
(Jina, Tara, Shannon and Trina)
Who's love for them is priceless
and nothing was above all mean's,
For these bird's made beautiful music together
with....

Silhouette strings
Soft Key's that blings
and the beautiful sounds of the flute that rings
bought happiness to the forest of harmony's
dreams.
For the heaven's has blessed these bird's with a
king and queen Brenda and Roy
Who's crown's has bought inspiration, dedication,
love and joy.
Bringing a circle of love to a family which consists
of a mrs
a mr
and the melody of the four sister's.

This Is Planet Earth

by Fritz Purdum

Through the stratosphere
Flying where no one dares
Searching in spite of fear
Wonderful little blue sphere

Creatures strange beings
Atmosphere unclean
So many wondrous things
Collecting images unseen

Moving at sonic speed
Trying to discover needs
A medal for exploring deeds
Fame becomes his greed

Within a flash
He suddenly crashed
Saucer reduce to trash
His head slams into the dash

Billy Bob and Big Bubba saw the flash
Get out of the pickup to look at the crash

Think pictures would get us cash?
Let's burn it up don't want no city trash

This is planet Earth
Burial of Major Dirth
Images for planet Mirth
Never to be unearth

Flames burn high and green
Two rednecks pour on gasoline
Funny and just serene
How Earth remains an alien dream.

White Bread And Butter

by Fritz Purdum

We have no jelly
We have no jam
The children mutter
What shall we now eat?
　　　White bread and butter

We have no syrup
We have no honey
The children utter
What shall we now eat?
　　　White bread and butter

We have no cream cheese
We have no cheese spread
The children find no peanut butter
What shall we now eat?
　　　White bread and butter

We have no lunch meat
We have no avocados
The children stutter
What shall we now eat?
　　　White bread and butter

We have no white bread?
We have no white bread!
The children blubber
What shall we now eat?
      Another stick of butter.

Last Deer Hunt

by Paul H. Schneiter

It comes back to me in solemnity,
and I wistfully wish it wouldn't.
A willful case of killing it was—
a hunter doing what he shouldn't.

Father had taken me deer hunting,
thinking to make a man of a boy.
I prayed we wouldn't see a deer.
and we didn't—not one—such joy!

Daylight was dimming to dusk
when he said our hunt had ended.
We started down a rocky trail,
and at a turn—we froze, suspended.

A hunter was positioned to shoot,
crouched, rifle cradled with skill.
Target? A shiny-eyed rabbit
happily nibbling a leafy meal.

"Oh, don't," I felt to cry out,
but then a c-r-a-c-k cricked the air.
The place where the rabbit had been
was as if nothing were ever there.

"He missed," my glad heart sang;
"the rabbit's alive and is all right."
But the hunter's face was fulsome
with a beastly, loathsome blight.

As we came by the spot, I retched,
the brush was garnished with gore.
Father's silence tracked the truth;
we wouldn't go hunting any more.

How to conceive of such blood thirst—
wanton killing as an act of gladness.
I trust, however, for those so cursed
civility will supersede such madness.

I Stepped Out Of Heaven

by Flossie Darlene Gierke

I stepped out of heaven and allowed
myself to be
Vulnerable
Vulnerable to your touch, as distant as it maybe
Still powerful enough to hurt

I stepped out of heaven so I could be close to you
Close enough to make a difference, placing my heart
In your hand.
Allowing myself to be vulnerable to you.
Surrender all, giving much and expecting
Nothing.
That's why I stepped out of heaven
I did it for you.

A One Percent Fair To See

by Ronald A. Williams

Trickling-downing of this economic system does weigh on me.
The dripping and dropping down of these colored paper greenbacks.
It does not matter if you have the highest of degrees.
You could know everything from A to Z
only still to be tightly used and squeezed.

A Corporate Caste system is the only thing that is obvious and real.

A theater showcase of many casting calls of the first: then last.
The elites, and their enclosed franchises masked.
Is this fair or unfair; or is it too hard to see schemes.

We're in a carousel of pony phonies, an allusion like Fair
This we can truly see, if we also feel.

A Tribe Of Trolls

by Elizabeth Valerie Wyler

A tribe of trolls escaped their cage!
Now rabid wrath and rancor rage.
Hurling hurt from hidden hellholes
(most notably, their toilet bowls),
they flush their filth across your page ...

Anonymity sets the stage
for word-"warriors" who rampage
as today's internet unrolls
a tribe of trolls ...

Let's hail the stone-age cyber sage,
"bravely" mounting his mouse to wage
invectives with the screens he scrolls.
Unmask their names! Expose the trolls!
Let public shaming disengage
a tribe of trolls.

Beauties Of My Garden

by Ifeanyichukwu Dominion Anyabolu

BEAUTIES OF MY GARDEN
Many pretty things I have seen,
As magnificent they may seem,
With the aoura of pride and strength,
The strength that covers its faded part,
But none caught my fancy like the beauties of my garden.

The morning came with the yellow face coming out of the horizon beaming
with smiles,
Giving all creatures hope of life,
The beauties of my garden welcomed the yellow fellow with broad hands,
As their faces turned wide,
And their young ones fondles out of their buds,
Beauties of gladness and happiness,
Beauties of everlasting glamor and joy,
How pretty thou art.

Beauties so tender like infants,
The mild wind swaying them to and fro,
With their colors being like the rainbow,
Sweet whispers of love from the whispering spine,
And the sensation tickled my spine,
I was in the dreamland of love.

I sought of a gift for my beloved,
The beloved of my heart,
Towards my garden I looked,
Alas! I got a glimpse of the most precious of them all,
Plucked it out with its stalk,
"I know within myself what she likes"
As I smiled and walked happily towards her house,
Holding the beauty of my garden.

Shock And Awe

by Denis Brian Briggs

How are we going to win this fight
Let's try shock and awe
Let's rain on them missiles and bombs
That's how we'll win this war

A soldier walks in the rubble
All that's left of this town

He feels the tears well up in his eyes
As he stands and look around

He sees bodies lying there
Of people once so proud
Of this town where once they lived
They seem to shout out loud

Why did you do this to us?
What did we do to you?
Why did you maim and kill
Us and our children too?

He hears a whimper sees a tiny hand
Reach out through reach out through the rubble in vain
In that hand is a raggedy doll
It fills his soul with pain

He knows that a child is lying there
He tears at the brick and the stone
But he knows that the child is dying there
And that she will die lost and alone

The soldier drops his weapon
He sadly walks away
He vows to never to fight again
He shouts we can't win this way

Yes we can win a battle
Yes we can win a war
But it's not worth the cost of the victory
If we use shock and awe

Silence

by Leon Allen Enriquez

Live in the light as fate prompts poise,
Love sparks most bright as words meet choice.

Watch silence speak in hints and tints,
Sense stillness peak in visual mint.

See calmness spear the path of quest,
Feel senses clear in zesty fest.

Work witty pun to seize the day,
Brave the long run as passion plays.

Spice sacred space as silence sums,
Echoes of grace prompts healthy psalm.

Stillness funds peace upon these shores,
Silence works ease from a deep core.

Thus less is more if you but see,
Watch joy galore now come to be.

Autumn Song

by Christopher Lee Bowen

Winter's edge begins to cull
our lovely pregnant aching Autumn
swollen with Summer fruit
and wild wind-sown berries of the Spring.

Sun-drunk pears,
startling all the wild amazed birds,
leap through frosted air
like rainbows, yellow red and gold.

To spread their final sunburst
over chill-threatened Earth.
Autumn is almost more than we can bear.
all memory of beauty grace and light,

Of promise kept, or not, and ripeness in decline.
Smells of slow decay hint at April's green
and rusting leaves recall
Branching glories of the Spring.

The pears were not taught, do not expect,
harbor from ice-bladed wind,
so gathered by your hands they glow
wondering, silent, through slanting afternoons,

Amazed to the end by the warmth
of your voice, your touch, your love
their second un-hoped for
Summer in the Sun.

Our Love To Our Queen

by Tiffany Saxon

For 50 years you have been our shining star
Our advisor, second mother, leader and lastly,
Our monarch of prestige and royalty... Our diva...
And this is "our" testament of who you truly are.
Since I can remember...
It has always been about you and your sisters...
(Tara, Tiffany, Shannon and Trina) of who depended on you
For
 I know that we all can agree that...
"Our love is surely one thing
We can surely depend on you
In times of darkness and fear... we go to you;
Because
Through the years... we knew that you'd make us strong".
Remember this similar line to a certain song?
So

As we serenade you with "Our Love"...the choice of song...
Just know that you are one in a million...
A true matriarch
 That embraced and captured the true essence of what it takes of being our
queen wearing your crown...creating the stepping stones of being beautiful,
powerful and strong.
So as we celebrate this special day...
        You marked our hearts and in return... we selected an icon...Natalie
Cole to express what we mean.
For
Our love and sisterhood is forever...
And thanks to Natalie, we were able to show
  "Our Love"...
To Our Queen

The End!

After The Revolution

by M. Braimah Saaka

We shall meet again, my friend
in Johannesburg, my friend
After the revolution

Ha! Ha! Ha!
We shall dine on gold plates
And wine on rich red blood

We shall roam the open veldt
from Pietersburg to Natal
Cape Town to Port Elizabeth
Our spears raised in triumph
Our poisoned arrows in their sheaths
Our teeth sharpened for the dinner party

Yes, we shall roam, my friend
From the Limpopo to the Drakensburg
We shall chant
We shall shout
We shall sing and jump and dance

After the revolution

Like the savannah in flames
Our laughter shall be heard
across the length and breadth
of this earth, my friend
Our darkness shall permeate
the golden castles and silver beaches
their presence has putrefied
They all shall be cleansed

Heja! my friend
Till we meet again
in Johannesburg
After the revolution

Spider On Vase

by Rose Johnson

Poor teetering thing that leeched the rim
To poise and watch the world from summit
It hiked the slope and scaled with ease
Its several legs had gained momentum
Triumphant conqueror of the peak

The hero now surveys the giants
With peripheral eyes to view
The gaping hole of one such hulk
From which was issued a thunderous sound
That made the crawly start to quake

Its fate secured within their reach
The proximal limb ready to pulp
And dash the crawly to its death
Lithe movement in its spiny legs
Takes it down the crater route
Into the vases obscure hollow

And deftly rappels the precipice

With actioned spinneret
Scarce light below that thwarts its fear

Away from gaping noisy giants
At peace to spin and weave a web
Of symmetry that knows no bounds

Goddesses

by Donald J. Craig

Freya, Maria, Gaia, Sofia
Isis, Astarte
Kali and Parvati

Always it seems
They haunt my dreams
Staring like tigers in my night

With demanding love
And no expectation
But to see Her

They walk in light
Hip-switching across the Earth
A woman, a deer, a flying leaf

Her flaming sword
Could spin my head off
But She kisses my soul and I'm safe

Every day I see Her
Magic paralyzing eyes
Outlined in black

Golden eyelids smiling
Startlingly clearly brown or blue
I know lust and peace at once

The world turns over

And the world burns
And the Goddess lives forever

Feigned Her Innocence

by Hans-Christian AleXander Melschau

Listening in silent despair
Ambivalence
Numb as she walked
Bound by time was far from freedom
 I wouldn't change her everything
Despite my cries
All is left behind me
All is gone and All is lies
Nodding smiles in Jester's torture
Nothing escapes the fallen tree
 Close my eyes in hollows hiding
Desperation saddening
Turn another pageless chapter
In the mirror
The horror is me
 Splintered in her head forever
Were those words so deafening
And with the wind the sounds of violence
It's paranoia that follows Me
 I've become whom she's decided
~Terrified
 She holds my scream
 Desolation sounds inviting
 And so it burns ~
 ~This Broken Dream

Romanticism- A Harlot's Lament

by Hans-Christian AleXander Melschau

Her passion
She fashions her passion
Strangeways
This flashing
She flashes MAD traces
Strange days
With secrets and magic
And all things fantastic

Soooo-
  Delight me
  Excite me
  Tonight we
  Just might be
Together- It's never
Forever- The same
I thought it was you
When I knew it was me
At first we were two
And then maybe three
Dancing with magic
And dancing so free

I thought it was you
  Even Sorcerers bleed
Her passion
She fashions MAD PASSION
Strangeways
 Doll- like exotic Erotic we play
The faces
She makes no mistake
When they're fake

And who would have thought
With these feelings I fought

That this time would so pass
In the hourglass so fast~

Sheep, Aliens And Curry

by Lee Hawkins

While Shepherds watched their flocks by night all seated on the ground
The ewes collected up their lambs and gathered them around
"Listen now," the old Ewe said, "you young lambs listen well,
If you all want to grow to sheep then hark to what I tell
You may see lights up in the sky, or coming cross the downs
They could be aliens my dears, from space, or other towns
They may use flashy coloured beams or other fancy sights
But sometimes they have dim headlamps and indicator lights"

"It does not matter how they come or from what other lands
Aliens are just as bad who drive white transit vans
So lambs who plan to wander off and get up to no good
Can get sheepnapped to Cygnus Prime, or maybe Cricklewood
And whether you are beamed aboard, or bundled in a sack
The aliens have got you, and you won't be coming back
A simple truth for young lambs to, within their noddles, keep
Is alien companionship is never good for sheep"

"It matters not a sci-fi whit dissected in a lab,
Or spiced and served with napkins in a curry or kebab
The preparations, much the same, occurring on the way
Are what you can undoubtedly expect to spoil your day!"

The little lambs were chastened much and some quite overcome
And resolved that they would keep themselves close to their mum

But other things were happening and shepherds on the ground
Beheld an Angel visiting, with glory spread around

"Fear Not", he said for mighty dread had seized their troubled minds
"Great tidings of great joy I bring to you and all mankind"

The sheep reckoned that was not them and were much relieved

It did not really matter if the shepherds were deceived
But still, they thought, 'twas best be off, although no need to hurry
And one or two thought shepherds might improve turned into curry

The night was dark and shepherds eyes were full of holy light
And so the sheep all silently crept off into the night
Leaving shepherds to their fate somewhere among the stars
The sheep hit Bethlehem's nightspots, the clubs, the pubs and bars.

Remembered

by James Study

No one left in the world I know
No family or friend only me
So soon from home removed to here
This little room is now my home

No light from out enter upon
Would not matter for I can't see
Words lost in air no one to find
No matter what spoke won't be clear

Gentle hand softly smooth my hair
Faint puff of air across my cheek
Breath of flowers blanket my bed
Someone has come to be with me

Everyone Loves A Dead Drummer

by Robert Trezise Jr

At age 55
I press my nose
To the bark of a tree
I place my tongue
To the underneath of an Oak leaf

I rent next to a lake
I like my back against a wall

Life grabs at one another

For me, it was at a party
Where she said she'd been re-married
Stopped writing
And was happy
Finally

She noted her gain of weight with a shrug
Saying, "The forest was still in need of healing."

She wondered if I'd still been trying
Or, if maybe, I could use
A special spell that she'd discarded.

I replied, "I think so."

And she said with a wave of her hand
Over my head
"Everyone loves a dead drummer."

Sardula Javan Leopard

by Yudho Sasongko

Hot and wet as heaven pion
Rainfall scattered warm clarion, dropped some their leaves
Referred to evergreen rainforest

Girl starred being black, smiled for dark spots with silver-grey eyes
Kingdom animalia said: "Where is our crown?"
Heavy logging answered

Tilar wana memereng tepining tegil
Sardula, death.....

Bull coexist without competitive
No sanctuary in poverty
Human driven doomsday

Panthera pardus melas and the girl cried

Away from riverbanks, swamps and clearings
Where is Hillsides, mountains, mesas, and sunlight penetration?

Say sorry to piphytic plants
No attached anymore to trunks and branches, trees felt down

Suck to obtain rainwater
Fallen trees create scary gaps
Said goodbye to Pleistocene refugia
The rest only empty liturgia

Tilar wana memereng tepining tegil
Sardula, death....

Melanistic leopards coaxed black panthers
The guardian solitary and territorial lover
Sang a love songs and passed away
Growls, snarls, meows and purrs

From dusk till dawn, defending territories from intruder clown
Farmlands weighing hundreds of kilograms bombs

Away from riverbanks, swamps and clearings
Where is hillsides, mountains, mesas, and sunlight penetration?

Tilar wana memereng tepining tegil
Sardula, death......

A New Beginning Each New Day

by Vaughan A Jones

A new day dawns with the sun to the east,
A renewed freshness of energy released.
For piles of trials and trivial pursuits,
Get ready and strap on your boots.
Out and about, and so it starts,
Another day of traffic darts.
School starts at eight,

Don't ever be late.
Work at nine,
No sunshine.

But, hey,
It's a new day,
Things to do, people to see,
Places to go to, don't feel free.
Life's eternal cycle of duties begin,
Goals to achieve, life's rewards to win.
Round and round, ever striving to succeed,
And so it begins as this is how life is decreed
But to keep calm, tranquil, and to be of sound mind
Not forgetting to give love, make peace, and be kind.

Firewater

by Melani Udaeta

All top hats and class,
like the gentleman who knows
how to throw you against a wall;
Words so cordial
but hand him a guitar
and everything comes unhinged;
Leaving you hallucinating
 on that beautiful scream;
He's never less than firewater;
Pure fire water;
Stealing the sound echoing in your head,
Grabbing you
like he's kissing your hand;
Right before fracturing your jaw again;
All suave with a perfect touch
like the gentleman who knows too much,
and how to dance;
No need for any kind of buzz
He's already firewater;
Pure firewater;
Baby, just hand him that guitar;

He'll take you where you want to go
He's the matchstick, detonate delicately
He's never less than firewater,
Pure firewater.

Breakfast

by Pushpa Tuladhar

The Poetry that I never created,
But the seconds of my day
That I adored so much.
Couldn't grip the moments
Of my day in my fists   5
As the iceberg of the day
Set into water and spilled over
From the seams of my fists.

After my morning routine,
I'd befall at   `   10
The dining table of my kitchen
For my everyday breakfast
With a Mug of Coffee
Or a Cup of Tea
Arising the whole fullness in   15
The emptiness within me.

The morn spun another page
Of my erstwhile diary
With the deeds of that very day,
Too much absorbed I'd be in   20
Savoring the flavor in me
So that my time spilled out
Of my clenched fists
Might never be in futile.

The Gardener

by David Cox

She's twenty-three and he's eighty-six
He walks with a Zimmer, she watches Netflix
He has a mansion and a Maserati car
She has her diamonds and uplifting bra

They have a gardener, Chatterley like
He calls her miss, she calls him Mike
The Zimmer frame plods, slow to react
The house has a mystery, lover's pact.

She shops online for all she desires
Mike cuts the wood, mends fences, builds fires
The Zimmer makes its way until out of sight
She fills up with chocolate, champagne and sprite

Mike is now naked stripped to the bone
The Zimmer appears a long way from home
The Gardener obliges and helps him undress
Kissing together out of sight of the press

She buys designer clothes, Armani, Dior
He is quite happy when she asks for more
The paparazzi claim, she's dug up her gold!
Zimmer loves the gardener his story's untold.

Change

by Franklin A. Price

Change that's made to "what" we are
May appear to set us free.
Changing looks or changing sex
Can be done for you and me.
We may change the "what" we are,

I think you would agree.
Until we change the "who" we are,
The one we cannot see.
We cannot change the world we're in,
Or the future that's to be.
Must evaluate the "who" we are,
If we're to change humanity.

The world is one big family;
It seems we've lost that thought.
Hate is not a natural thing.
It's something that is taught.
If we let love lead the way,
Then hate will go for naught.
Love is from the "who" we are;
Unlike hate, it can't be bought.
If we love the "who" we are,
And offer it to others,
We will better co-exist
With our sisters and our brothers.

Love Is Like A Pane Of Glass

by Richard W. Morris

Water flows from the dam of life,
Not easy, but not all strife.
There is a point at which we die,
Lest we forget, not all goes awry.

Often, we denounce and scold,
As we pass from young to old.
Friends and family are to adore,
Before you or they are no more.

Love is like a pane of glass.
Held by two, it can endure.
If by one, too heavy a mass,
Alone not too sure.

Always in motion, never stable,

Never static, ever brittle.
Held a moment, barely able,
To withstand the noncommittal.

Words you utter, tone of voice,
A grimace, smile, or rolling eye.
Words and deeds are your choice,
Be they honey or some lye.

Every thought or smile,
Frown or furrow can beguile,
And must pass first this test:
Is it really for the best?

If the pane glass should drop,
It will chip, crack or shatter.
Damage you cannot stop,
Lasting memory does matter.

Each cycle does grow short,
The glass ever more frail.
Until that one last retort,
You've had the final rail.

You get no second chance,
To name what really mattered.
Gone forever, that romance,
The pane of glass, has shattered.

Song Thrush

by Lisle Ryder

That thrush so high up on the tree,
does it sing for you or me?
Its trills I hear with such delight
even though it's not in sight.
Then it's quiet. I peer and stare.
Has it flown? I wonder where?

And now it's on a neighbours' tree.
Is it's song for them or me?
Over the fence its song proclaims
worms and snails are mine to claim.
It's singing not for you or me,
yet from snails it sets us free.

Confined by virus week by week,
isolation may feel bleak.
Yet while it's quiet we can hear
sounds of nature far and near.
For each of us till fading light
thrush's song does us unite.

Madre

by Pratikshya Barik

Mother
Plants beacons of life
Tears nourish placid roots
Her pains quietly sewed in duty
Goddess

Life In The Time Of Corona

by John R Fiordelisi

I wonder how it will spin?
When they tell of that spring.
Eyes will meet with a nod and a wink
In keeping their lies in sync.
Grandkids will tweet
About the time in the street
When no one came out
Neither whisper nor shout

Six feet apart in
A line to the booth
The people, enslaved,

Memorized the truth.
Some ran saying change the guard..

I wonder how it will spin
If the facts are sewn in?
Of how they avoided a war
By diverting our thought
With a global pandemic
That kept those in power
Feeding scraps from their table
In the shape of a dollar.

I wonder how would it spin
If enough of us knew
The political poison
They feed us by spoon.

Clockwise for sure
For time must march on
And the thoughts of the disillusioned
Are censured, then gone.

Make A Difference

by Sarah Hassarati

Work for the week
Work for the weak

Listen to no
Listen to know

Live for the hour
Live for the our

Watch your waist
Watch your waste

Provide for maw
Provide for more

Fill the roll
Fill the role

Lose your idol
Lose your idle

Learn from the past
Learn from the passed

Make your piece
Make your peace

Lay down your arms
Lay down your alms

Strengthen your sole
Strengthen your soul

Words Unsaid

by Leon Allen Enriquez

In strange hollow
A deep mellow

How the heart grows
Language touch knows

Now feel the choice
That anchors poise

Know that you know
A sublime flow

Words unsaid can
Trade beyond trend

Forge a firm link
Beyond verge think

Mind in a spin
In storms within

Go beyond touch
To know so much

Fate now gets paid
With words unsaid

Hemlock

by Fred Jagenberg

Juniper prevails where hemlock heathen dine
As breeders of the weaker worlds increase
A persuasive drink, the final glass of wine
Spiked by grand deception ruined Socrates

Slither those who slant to slander
Bodies styled from a wicked Cain
Betrayed by his honesty of mercy kinder
Of universe, a mind for generations slain

Still the breeders slither loose among us
Full of fruits from hemlock juice defying
Prerogative of pith, they launch another strike
Freedom of your voice, the final passage dying

Body Language

by Warren Oscar M'Baht

The body language of my dog, about his only way
To tell me what is going on, and how he spent his day
He smiles at me and shows his teeth, it goes against the grain
He knows I do it when I'm happy, so he does it once again

But then the times when things go wrong, his guilty look displays
He tells me that he's sorry, with drooped ears won't meet my gaze

He slinks around the corner, pretending he's not there
Don't worry boss I will be good, keep right out of your hair

Then he thinks time for a stroll, brings his lead to me
Puts it down right at my feet, and gazes soulfully
If he thinks I take no notice, then he goes into plan B
Brings the lead a little closer, puts a paw up on my knee

Now let us say we did the walk, he rolled in something foul
He knows that I don't like it, he can recognise a scowl
I start to run his doggy bath, good gosh he's on the lam
How come the baths a problem, when he loves a freezing dam

The wife comes home when work is done, he'll park outside the door
How does he know she will be home, if he waits five minutes more
Now if the kids they make a mess, I ask him did you do it
He wanders round so unconcerned, he knows no way he blew it

Then the times when one of us, is feeling quite unwell
He will lay down right beside us, if we're sick then he can tell
So that's all body language, and to put another way
I may not be a human, but I can still have my say

The King Without A Crown
by Tino Empulu

You came so suddenly,
Bringing great terror in your arrival like many before you,
Who are you that you should be crowned king that all men bow before you,
Depriving us the right to demonstrate affection to those we meet by not permitting touch,
You have chosen to conquer territories in different continents and because of such,
We closed up our borders and set travel boundaries,
To prevent you from entering our lands, yet you forced your way into our countries,
What was the reason for that if not but to destabilise our economies.

No rest, no rest, no rest
We will not rest till victory is assured, we will not rest till your crown is

dispossessed.

Panic-gripped and fear stricken, we closed up factories and delayed production,
Yet you thrived and rejoiced in the wake of our destruction.
Leaving parents without children, leaving children without parents,
This seems to be, your very special talent.
Prolific mass murderer, but like all your predecessors,
You will be defeated because you undermine our warriors.

Coronavirus we defy you, and approach you with strong condemnation,
You proclaimed yourself a monarch and requested an audience for your coronation,
We will attend it just to plot your assassination.
You crowned yourself king even though you don't wear a crown,
Your reign of terror will soon come to an end to this we have vowed.

No rest, no rest, no rest
We will not rest till victory is assured, we will not rest till your crown is dispossessed.

We charge you for the murder of our loved ones and pronounce judgement upon you
Death will be your sentence and for all who come after you.
For those you've placed in quarantine,
We'll have your head in the guillotine.

We'll not endure your tyranny
You will be defeated inevitably

No rest, no rest, no rest
We will not rest till victory is assured, we will not rest till your crown is dispossessed.

Space X And Falcon Number Nine

by Marc D OBrien

There is a rocket firing off today
Sending a business adventure trip far away
With the thunder below
Up it will go
Looking to put technology in the sky
In a late afternoon scripted signature that everyone on the beach will wave
bye bye
Falcon number nine is spending the dime
To climb climb climb
Calling the plays from the huddle
Very near to the pad for the shuttle
Internet interaction will be shared
In this mechanical bon voyage that has flair
Traveling to many orbits out there
Sixty broadband satellites will be dispersed
Into the vast universe
After the fact that been confirmed
Space X had money to burn
Linking the stars from above
With Intergalactic communication that fits like a glove
T Minus the launch will be here
Giving us new apps to play with next year

What Have We Learnt

by Muyideen Ayinla

We have become prisoners in our homes
In a time when war planes aren't flying overhead
And missiles' too crippled to design calligraphic fire in our night sky.
We peeped through the windows to watch the deserted streets,
With hopes to regain our freedom once again.

No soldiers with armoured tanks marching the streets,
But the voices of neighbours-

Asking eagerly if our incarceration hasn't been postponed.
"Baba has added yet another fourteen days
And three million households soon to see the rays."
We must bear our pains with gallantry
Even the kids have braced-up as infant-ry
Aware of the enemy that has the world in its grip.

Remember how easy our people threatened to go to war
While the youths wobble in delusion,
Glorifying the hatred that consumed their fathers,
Basking in the shallow stream of conceited deceit.
Burying the dead has become difficult
Venturing into places of worship has become forbidden
And the schools are empty without pupils in them.

But what have we learnt
Now that we are yet to be cured of greed?
What have we learnt
Now that crime has taken a new breed?
What have we learnt
When we still can't show kindness?
What have we learnt
Now that our leaders seek solace at home?
What have we learnt
Now that hunger stare us in the face?
While we watch the numbers
Descend in mass graves
With the global economy on the path of recession.
What have you learnt?

To The Shore

by Graham Alexander Devenish

The shore it's seen, calm so near,
But rocks and swells deterrent to all
Prevent a landing? It is not clear
The Stuart Prince dismissed his fear
Landed his launch, and began the call

A call to arms, he encouraged the men
To fight their foe and rid them now
Of English rule and oppression's end
The courage of each they could depend
Freedom to gain, they must somehow

Clans came as one, to the Bonnie's call
Agreed to raise arms, to fight till free
On highlands they marched for one, for all
United as Scots proud and tall
To alter their current destiny

Battles fought on bog and moor
Pushing back the English offence
To whence they came from as before
But England stood at Culloden, a core
An end to Scottish independence

A Brown Stone's Perspective

by Rukhsana Afridi

Rough edges and grainy
While sitting in this creature's hands
Analyzed and stared at
I see his brown colored eyes twinkle
As he stares at me through curiosity
Wondering my origins
Where did I come from?
How did it I wind up here?
Oh, the stories I could tell
If only I could speak
My revelations would be historic
Telling all of you true stories since the dawn of mankind
Even from the time of dinosaurs that walked the earth
Magnify and mystify
Unearthed by this human
Some say the hearts of humans can turn into objects as hard as stone
Like me, a hard-cold stone
Claiming to be unbreakable and invincible
However, I beg to differ

Because even stones can crumble to pieces
Eroded by water or wind
And melted into nothing.

Fear Itself

by William Coyne

We went for a walk after sunset in the dark,
among the shadows of chestnut trees near a park,
where howls in nearby cornfields
brought fear of what the sound yields,
and rose an unfriendly but wary question-mark.

"What fiend sets to prowl this auspicious time of night?
What fearsome, bold creature may show its teeth so bright?
stalking fresh flesh for its meal,
no mercy for those who kneel,
praying rescue them to the Heavenly Spirit of Light?

After our walk, we stood on our porch there trembling,
collecting our calm, peaceful thoughts assembling,
endured a gauntlet of fear,
survived what did not appear,
yet ourselves nothing thereafter resembling.

Step Lightly

by Catherine Johnson Broussard

If I could, I would remove your woes;
for all you endured for me.
Keep them safe; never forgetting.
Share with all; all who would listen.
I need to remember; they need to know.
All the sacrifices you made; now I am here today.
Only because of you, I stand on this ground.
The same ground you walked; I walk proudly.

Now, you rest as dust under my feet;
step lightly, remembering.

Backyard

by Quazi Johirul Islam

Backyard birch has bloomed a green umbrella
Two white doves peeping from mid branch above
Gray squirrel searches land to seedling love
A red handkerchief spoils the glabella.
Bullnose stones offered her cold and hard lap
Wind strokes the lush hair of mid-august-land
Golden finch flew, fallen feathers will stand.
Someone walks, wood diverged creating gap.

The falling sun kisses the floating dust
Between the patio-bricks smiles green moss
To uproot them lady draws cruel cross
Old man watches wash, and his anger burst
Three-years granddaughter appeared from sunset
She walks and falls, runs again, ignores threat.

Blueprint

by Diána Bósa

I am looking for a blueprint for love
the one I've once felt about you.
The perfect blue paper
that helps me figure things out
that tells secrets about a lover's skin and sighs
- the ones I knew as yours.
Now I wish to redraw, then admire its design:
relearn, then follow its patterns
down to my very heart.
I want to rebuild its structure,
recreate the way that is no more,
to have the perfect edition of it;
a guide to my true self,

the one who once knew what it felt like
to be in love with someone like you.

Fern

by Jazmyn Hanson-Yeats

No greater shadow than ferns teeth
Sheltering the infant saplings underneath,
The same soil where strangling vines sleep
What the forest grows, also reaps

Isolde's Song

by Michael R. Burch

After the deaths of Tristram and Isolde, a hazel and a honeysuckle grew out of
their graves until the branches intertwined and could not be parted.

Through our long years of dreaming to be one
we grew toward an enigmatic light
that gently warmed our tendrils. Was it sun?
We had no eyes to tell; we loved despite
the lack of all sensation—all but one:
we felt the night's deep chill, the air so bright
at dawn we quivered limply, overcome.

To touch was all we knew, and how to bask.
We knew to touch; we grew to touch; we felt
spring's urgency, midsummer's heat, fall's lash,
wild winter's ice and thaw and fervent melt.
We felt returning light and could not ask
its meaning, or if something was withheld
more glorious. To touch seemed life's great task.

At last the petal of me learned: *unfold*.
And you were there, surrounding me. We touched.

The curious golden pollens! Ah, we touched,
and learned to cling and, finally, to hold.

The Forest Inside

by Chitra Arun

Trudging on a path deep in a forest,
with the noise of loneliness humdrum in the ears.
Felt the thoughts to be slowing down,
as if were on the edge of sleep.
In the quest of searching for one who cares,
i hug my pillow tight.
Yearning for someone to hold me through this night,
only to wake up yelling,
realizing being scared of being insane.
It's getting harder to hide all the feelings built up here,
these demons are destructive.
Scooping the heart right out of the chest,
as this constant pain prevails.
My smile hide my tears,
my laugh hide my screams,
i hurt on inside.
Trying to push these demons aside,
wearing a mask that always beamed.
To hide the feelings behind a lie
their kingdom prevails!

Canary Comm

by Fred Jagenberg

Red lights flash on Canary Comm
Ice 9 warning once again
To stay or fly not serious
Who can avoid the cryogenic madness?

Most carry on Ice 9 inside
Like DNA or something drives it
No matter line no breaking in

A perfect prison for the mind

If only to contain
The Ice 9 to one brain
Observe the crystal goblet
From the safety of a body distance

Instead, we fortify to ramparts
Drawing weapons seizing
Ice 9 spills outside the brain
Foreboding thinking freezing

Behind The Mask

by Shirley Ann Hawkins

He had a pleasant face,
Quite handsome in a lived-in kind of way
His features were irregular, not perfect
And his expression was kind

He was a solidly-built man
Muscular and strong
He had a thick neck and broad shoulders
His hands were large and capable
He had a good physique
Well-rounded, without angles

There was nothing pointed or sharp about him
He was not an intellectual
Any talent he possessed
Came from using those capable hands

He was surprisingly gentle for such a big man
Sentimental, easily touched
Too easily, sometimes
He often had tears in his eyes

He enjoyed messing about on boats
He seemed content to be alone

Not craving company
He had a certain shyness
A vulnerability that was hidden
Within a massive frame

He had a vicious temper which
He tried hard to conceal
He lost it often without provocation
He flew into uncontrollable rages
That made his huge body shake and tremble
And his facial features contort

His whole persona became menacing
His haunted eyes looked frightened
As they tried to focus inward
Away from his personal torment
In a desperate struggle to get back once again
Behind the mask

Ivory Tower

by Ngoc Minh Nguyen

This hearth and home, my ivory tower,
   wherein I dwell and live in solitude,
   in complete and supernal bliss and brood
reflectively with creative power
(whereby I, emboldened, fear not or cower);
   is the keep where my thoughts are understood,
   and in myself I then oft' feel a mood
which thwarts my blackest and most dreaded hour!
Then swells of pure elation, which intensify,
   wash my despair and hopelessness away;
and once more in me expands a great high;
   a giddiness of being that's fain to stay,
here to abide until someday I die;
   and enter a state of perfect rest, I pray.

A Physical Whereabouts

by christopher tran

physical whereabouts is,
a physical science
science is science's physical whereabouts
science capture science's physical whereabouts
physical is physically a physical whereabouts
physical is physically a physical science
physical is physically a physical capture

respectively is respectively a whereabouts
science capture science respectively
science respectively capture science
respectively is physically respectively
respectively is physically capture
a capture of science is respectively a capture of science
science physically capture science

a physical whereabouts respectively,
is a physical whereabouts
a physical whereabouts respectively,
is a physical science
science is a physical science
science is a physical whereabouts
science respectively is a physical science

For An Eternity

by William Darnell Sr

If it should prevail,
that you might be born today?

May the spirit of your flesh,
Float on the wings of a leaf in the wind
In the aura of the breeze, the wind

Shall it be felt like a promise to yesterday's wisdom?

Flowing with the essence of a life yet to be lived,
Find harmony with the tremendous beauty of what lies ahead
To a life well deserved.

Shall it be you to be born today?
May the aura of life scent be upon you for an eternity!

Life Without Colour

by Yvonne Livingstone-Kania

Our world of innocence is caught unaware,
Taunted by a nightmare,
An experiment gone wrong; a distorted sculpture,
We're locked inside for the foreseeable future.

We wait for that day of relief,
Citizens get themselves into a psychotic state.
"Lives have been lost" says the news,
Coronavirus is sending people mad.

Where do we go; what do we do,
We try our best to struggle through,
The roads are clear from cars and bikes,
No long walks in the country or hikes.

Isolated from family and friends,
Trapped inside till this crisis ends,
Can we survive this helpless attack?
A life without colour.

If The Rubik's Cube Was Round

by Shreya Laxmi Nagendra

If the Rubik's Cube was Round
Would the Earth not?
Would the men with knives and pitchforks
After Eratosthenes be proud?
Would voyagers search far and wide
Once more for the famous edge
Only for the fall
If only the Rubik's Cube was Round

A Silent Viewer

by Reza Raza

Scenes within the limits of vision-
Gardens, flowers and the abstract songs of leaves
Their ways of life
The unseen cover of difference
With many languages in mind
I see their silent family ties.

My inner self-
As if an illusory mirror-
Looking meditatively
It also looks with strange eyes-
Stares at a stranger.

The night grows darker-
In the chest of the night-
With a lantern in hand, it searches for
Or-
Rotates like a radar to find
The extreme art of oyster-pearls combination.

Tired is a night-bird of groaning

In the gap of leaves
Alive is the night-
Blows its aquatic wind -
I see the Moon-
Rolling down my fingers
Stars are looking with sleepy eyes

Silent bricks of the building-
Absolute despair in their eyes-
All the answers written in their silence.

I Am The Dam

by Juli Freda

The Earth is my Grandmother
caring and gentle, whispering
to me upon her breezes to nurture,
replant, enjoy the world. She
call to me in the echoes of the
mountains to remember, to relax,
to keep the world a better place.

The Moon is my Grandfather
rock hard and silent, watching
me, instructing me on how not
to turn Grandmother into a
barren wasteland. He is bitter
and yells form the skies raining
dust and debris, turning this
world into a bitter place.

I am the dam, keeping myself
from turning a gentle, flowing
world into a barren floodplain.
I honor my Grandmother and use
only what I need. I fear my
Grandfather and the destruction
I can cause. I am the dam,
steady, looking out for both sides.

Christ Is Born

by Joseph C Ogbonna

Christ is born this day with Bethlehem's poor.
So unassuming, he enters our world
with shepherds lowly coming to adore
this infant Lord who will freedom herald.

Christ is born this day with Bethlehem's poor.
His star in the east did the magi see.
A star never seen from the days of yore
led them to this great child of low degree.

Christ is born this day with Bethlehem's poor.
His birth this day is marked by angels bright.
Singing with cymbals in a placid night,
they ushered in peace from heaven's great door.

Christ is born this day with Bethlehem's poor.
As foretold by the prophets and the law,
He is born of a virgin chaste and meek.
He will never loudly on the streets speak.

Christ is born this day with Bethlehem's poor.
He is lowly with royal ancestry,
born of David's revered noble gentry.
Men's grievous sins His blue blood atoned for.

Christ is born this day with Bethlehem's poor.
He came to earth with men to empathize.
With us for each state he does sympathize.
Our peace with God He came down to restore.

Christ is born this day with Bethlehem's poor.
A unifying force who will world peace make.
Men of different races sing to adore
this Christ child who will their cleavages break.

Christ was numbered with the poor at birth,
and with the transgressors at death.

Tall Trees

by Christopher Grieves

More than wooden structure
So much, so much more
Not just a pretty fireplace
Or an ornamental door

We need to raise our glasses
To these giants of the skies
They are teachers if we listen;
With instruction for the eyes

As we gaze on with amazement
At their presence and their stature
It's easy to forget the story
Leading to our rapture

For once there was a seedling..
Fighting through the snow
With natural persistence
And a strong desire to grow

With opposition waiting.
All the elements a test
The gentle giant dreaming.. hopefully
To one day be the best

All these years of struggle
Through the seasons, cold and warm
Would define the sleeping giant
Every sunset, every dawn.

And now we gaze to heaven
Amazed and full of wonder
At the canopy so high above
And roots that anchor under

So, as the landscape changes
And our seasons come and go
We should take a leaf, remember
How our struggles help us grow.

And finally, to listen,
With the whisper of the breeze,
The song that we've been given
From the tallest of the trees.

Jinjagoliath

Spring Summer Fall Winter - Haiku Chain
by Ronald A. Williams

springtime flowers vase
lilies tulips azaleas
scent fragrance cues

summer sandy beach
swimming snorkeling surf
summer exploits fun

fall color honor guards
canopy red brown gold tan
leaves final slow dance

winter frost fleece
snowy ivory chalk mounds
cast blank white canvas

Appreciate

by Brooks Lewis III

I appreciate all the love
Is a phrase I use commonly
Whether I'm just accepting the grace
Or my confirmation of thanking you and bringing out that calm in me
I'm thankful and appreciative for a ton of things
I'm talking clothes, shoes, or even some good chicken wings
Red Vines, X-box, and my great Mama
A great Father too
And still being alive throughout all this worlds drama
I just need to make sure I'm giving God my thanks daily
I know it may sound crazy
But that's a little harder than it sounds
Something as easy as blessing your food can be forgotten about up until now
Giving thanks for a new day should be my first thought anyway
Something that I constantly forget to do
Appreciation is a form of love in some kind of way
So I appreciate the man upstairs for putting me in the red, white, and blue

Ovid-20 - Social Flocking

by Lee Hawkins

The morning was breaking and sheep were awaking,
which was much as the sheep all expected to do
But this morning's arising was far more surprising –
a mask fairy had brought them all something new

And the fairy remained and to them explained,
"The times now ahead will be tricky and fraught,"
The sheep were all puzzled, bemasked and bemuzzled,
but guessed no-one else cared a whit what they thought

At the fairy's insistence,"You must keep your distance,
the folds are unfolding so sheep have more space.
Sheep breathing is shedding a virus that's spreading

and that's why you're wearing that mask on your face.

"Your communal eating, your breathing and bleating,
endangers the rest of the sheep in the flock
The virus arising is uncompromising,
so all sheep are trapped 'twixt a hard place and rock.

"The spread we are blocking through good social flocking,
do not be alarmed for the rules are quite clear:
We must thwart or confuddle a sheep's urge to huddle,
you can flock all you want to, but don't flock too near!

"There is no strict mandation for sheep isolation,
but two metres distance, at least, you must keep,
If you find this troubling, then you can try bubbling,
but you can but bubble with one other sheep.

"Though if you are eating, not breathing nor bleating,
devoting yourself to the one grazing task,
You can distance one metre from each other eater,
but if you stop eating you must wear your mask.

"It is most consequential, the mask is essential,
to live through this crisis, **YOU MUST NOT FORGET!**"

They did not forget them, but thoughtfully ate them,
and that is as far as sheep wisdom will get.

Selfie

by Christopher Grieves

Unfiltered Unfettered
We choose how we see
Ourselves in the mirror
Of eternity

Don't let the world shape
Who we need you to be
Inside you...a hero

Busting out, to be free

The click of the shutter.
A dangerous game.
No life is defined
By a boundary or frame...

When the people ahead
Flick through albums of you
They will know who you were
And your story so.. true.

Choose hope, love, and justice
Be a person so kind
That the image you leave
Never fades over time.

Jinjagoliath

The Man Power Of The 20th Century

by Christopher Tran

the 20th century is the man power of the 20th century
the 20th century is the stool of the 20th century
the 20th century is a skilled stool
man power is a stool of man power
man power is a stool of a 20th century
man power is a skilled stool
the 20th century is a skilled of the 20th century

the 20th century is a skilled of man power
experience is a stool of experience
experience is experienced of a stool
experience is experienced of man power
experience is a skilled experience
experience is a power of experience
power is a skilled power

power is a skilled experience

power is a skilled 20th century
power is a skilled stool
power is man power of a stool
power is man power of a 20th century
power is man power of an experience
a skill is a skilled man power

Finding New Purpose

by Robert Trezise Jr

Oh my soul
A hole in an old tree
Formed like a black eye

Swollen and wet
From a good long wooden cry
That's remained hard inside
For all these years

It's not easy to soften
To drop to the rot of your knees
Becoming a flower

When you've been shedding walnuts
From a mist

And divining air to all the world

Carrying a crown full of sun
Down the dark hill of night
All of life

To find yourself
Arms broken
No longer the harp of spring

Cracked open like a seed
From a sprout of next life.

Hang On Sister

by David Cox

I'm glad I saw you, made the effort
Left all the baggage behind and arrived
With an open heart. Still unsure why I did?
You're just like how I remember mum.
Four-feet nothing, plump and round
I'm getting there, it's what aging does.
So glad I called, unannounced, I didn't
Give you time for an excuse and no
Time for my excuse.
We've never had a meal together.
Never met on Christmas day. We forgot
About Christmas cards and birthdays
We should have done more, but neither
Of us likes inconvenience or crowds
But?
Times caught us now. There's a tear in my
Eye. Unexpected to be honest, but it wells
Waiting to fall. Hope it's not today, hope
It's never at all.
Three score years and eleven, that's where you
Are, I'm ten years behind, but in a fast car.
I don't want it to be today. It's raining and grey.
Hang on, try to find a few extra miles, perhaps
We can alter the past a little. Hang on sister.

Before We Embrace The Night

by Emmanuel Obeng Yeboah

I will come for you, I will walk you home
When evening light bathes the tree trunks in gold
I will be with you, you'll not be alone
And your sweet soft palms in mine I will hold

Together, our arms entwined, will we stride

The busy streets of Unity Gardens
Just as on the aisle with you as my bride
And casting away all our life burdens

As a worshipper adores a wild god
So shall I, your countenance my delight
And till pale stars shine, love's ship let's aboard
Then glowing, you'll mirror the gloamings light

Before we embrace the night sweet honey,
On love's wings we'll fly a heaven's journey

On The Shores Of Hope And Faith

by Marius Alexandru

By the Sea of Light and Love,
On the shores of hope and faith,
Stars are smiling from above,
as I'm dreaming of the Pearled Gate.

This sweet dream makes me tremble,
Thinking at my Home with You,
I can see the Holy Temple,
and the crystal sea-glass too.

Walking on the streets of gold,
I search for words to sing Your praises,
This new life here slowly unfolds
so many beauties, heavenly graces.

I am Your child I'm set apart,
Covered in Your love and grace,
I'm carved forever in Your heart,
And soon I'll see You face-to-face.

The Middle Children

by Grady Jeremiah Klein

Be it that I am doomed to walk the Earth
In fear of time - measured in mere fractions;
Starlight grants me comfort with twinkling mirth,
Lost in wakes of dread deeper than oceans.

I'd ask what it means to live over time,
of paupers; preachers; aristocrats, too -
why lives are measured in short centuries.
For stars, it is nothing if not untrue.
A middle child with no hope to call mine;
with stately manners, I protest, "I'm fine,
doomed to be but shadows and memories."

Stardust divines our eager fingerprints
imbued on the walls of our history:
generations defined by reticence
and willful blindness to its mystery.

I'd ask what it means to swallow my fears,
of gods and kings and legends in their prime,
to carve in my heart courage that's blinding -
Like stars whose light shines long after their time.
O' Father I'll pray the rest of my years
through the funeral rites and birthday cheers,
"Grant me the stars when life stops rewinding."

With tired devotion left in my soul
I'll shatter the world to see what I'm worth -
memories that used to make me feel whole,
buried like innocence lost in childbirth.

I'll say what it means to temper my pride
to mothers and fathers, both who are lost,
Silently waiting till we come of age.
It's the ones you bring up that bear the cost.
Tell your kids before their eyes open wide;

Before their lungs, filled with air, rise like the tide;
"Stand and face your mortality with rage!"

Reflection

by George F. Aul

As I sit by the water:
A leaf that falls upon the calm, gentle waters
is the same leaf that gets carried
into the churning rapids.

Very often, we are like that unsuspecting leaf
in wanting for the calm to return;
and just as that fallen leaf...
we find hope upon those waters.

Oh Deer, You Again

by Sierra Chen

Oh DEER, You again....

At the crack of dawn
Outside my bedroom window
Unexpected noise?   Chewy, crunchy, crumbly
......I'm trying to sleep

Oh dear! deer is staring at me
      fearlessly

Uninvited guest crackling my succulent plants
for breakfast

Astonishing red, orange and pink sky at sunset
Oh dear,   You again......
And you even brought a friend!

Sipping heavenly rainwater in Bromeliad's central reservoir

Oh dear, dinner menu upgraded to
cabbage-like
                        Mauna Loa succulents
large flat leaves frilled at burgundy
    edges. But pink showy flowers
                            wavy, ruffled, bumpy
                            thick foliage leaves
- absolutely your favorite

Dark in late evening
Two yellow dots shinning in mystic hill

Oh dear,   You again......

In The Before Time

by Paul Thomson

In the before time, my poem an inkling only,
Something nags at me to look more deeply
Lest I pen a shallow rhyme when I might
Have brought a truth, untold, to light.

In the before time, the seed not taken to root,
And I the thumbless gardener in the absolute
Am left with no indication of direction
In spite of my digging and cultivation.

In the before time, I turned to my literary muses,
Dickinson and Whitman, in hopes a word infuses
My child that it may live its life in the way it should
And I, knowing in my poethood, did all I could.

My Dream Catcher, Gratitude

by Leon Allen Enriquez

Meet here and now true glimpse of peace,
You know you can love with grand fare.
Grace tells you how in lavish ease,
Reap what you plan beyond mere cares;
Ample the light that inspires joy,
Thrill in pure feel that special state;
Indulge thoughts bright that need no ploy,
Touch frames goodwill to bolster fate;
Use your own gifts to sparkle here,
Death is a dream that fear seeds well;
End as you lift such wondrous cheer.
Now watch love stream a sacred spell,
Old paves the way for new to be,
Wise words forge play as truth sets free.

There's A Bloke In This Cafe Slapping His Face

by Christopher Allen

he's been there doing that for
about twenty minutes

it's both palms on both
face pastries

he was here the other day
laptop in front of him

bopping and biffing
like in a boat race

chronic stress? enervation?
or giving the epidermis

something to think about
sod retinoids and clarins

maybe the brain is fusty
needs a few yawns too

like the sound of an Alaskan
salmon against sham praise

is this the future? when I'm gone
on buses, trains, offices

a democratic spanking

Dreamland

by Aditi Anvita

Let's create a space where
The sun awakes in integrity,
And the darkness never scares.

There's nothing troublesome
Which haunts the solitary mind,
And reflections, not illusioned.

Affinity breathes in heart,
Ephemeral estrangements,
And no vacancy for hatred.

The flowing rivers sing
About life in generosity
Credible like clarity of streams.

The grassy broad meadows
Captivates the drowsy eyes
Erases monotony.

Reveille Contentment

by Andrew L. Chunn

Startled sprinkles twinkle and toll
The time ignores my grunts and groans
Everyday empties its force of roll
Cannons sound -- and mothers moan

Between the place where time is not
And heaven's hell slams its door
Little men with giant heads hot
Are lost beneath the fluid floor

New nothings interrupt the waste
Of petty playthings -- argue -- lose
Experience coats with sugar taste
The salty melancholy muse

Perhaps -- possible -- should -- could -- can
"I saw it rise and fall alone"
Reaction time relative to man
Depends on tendered tailored tones

Wishes want thickness, color and cover
Design for moth and spider to loan
Answers are easy like lionized lovers
And time ignores my grunts and groans

Spark

by Jeannie Flinn Furlong

My Head claimed, "It's time to pen my feelings for you.
She thought your season had ripened to a friendly adieu...

I wanted my cleverness to sound brave and bold.

Instead, my betterment made noises ... bitter and cold."

Head continued, "For sure, this logic's a perfect best!
A simple note, timed just right, brings greatest rest."

More pondering, Head touts, "She'll agree, 'cause it's really past due!
How could two people so profoundly different ever ever be true?"

Head adds, "Just keep right on walking, memories disappear.
Once passed THE break up, habits do fade. You're soon in another sphere.

It becomes an odd chapter, far away in a book, one you read."
My Heart, hearing Head's advice, came to life to shudder, "Drop dead!

Mister Head! What a nincompoop, you are! Love makes the world go round!
How could you? Dare you! Quite profound!

Mister, such a trip, so wonderful, is more than just a lark!
Opposites made for each other, we fire such a SPARK!"

Goldilocks Now

by Thomas Harrison

But, my friend said, if Goldilocks was alive today her story would be different:
we're just so used to the fairy tale message, the simplified right and wrong of
it.

Women today are too afraid to walk the streets at night,
let alone enter a house with three grizzlies hidden out of sight.
And if a girl is attacked it's considered her fault, the victim is blamed -
can you imagine the vitriol she'd face, the shame nowadays?
Let's not forget Weinstein's penchant for a golden blonde,
something no doubt that bear trio would be equally fond.
Sure, she might get some sympathy and be #metoo-ed,
but the 'Good Morning Britains' of the world would lead a feud,
debating whether she'd lied about knocking and fibbed about porridge,
because what's a girl/woman/other if not a manipulator of knowledge?
(And don't get me started about how'd she be judged for discussing a
miscarriage)
Just picture the slander, the slurs and slut shaming that would spread

when it was leaked to the press that she'd tried and tested each bed.
"One wasn't good enough obviously, so she had to sleep on all three."
"Well then, what did she expect? She had it coming to her, didn't she?"

So, my friend said, of course her story would be different today:
a cautionary tale teaching girls to never be alone, make themselves prey.
Because it's a man's world after all, and boys will be boys - it's a game hitting
girls to flirt.
Goldi's true Lock then is the society she lives in, measured by men and the
length of her skirt.

Addiction

by Vernon Michael Witmer

life, no aim or form.
In all directions careless
broom-straws
blown by gusty storm.
Towns aflame sparkling
with each busy soul.
the smell of life, the odor of its toll.
Clutching their bowls of soup; derelicts
filling their holes
with charity's endless loop.
Each street a living river
flowing driftwood buildings.
Spilling pools of debris
that wash away all evidence of vice
into dampened lots of memories.
Distant arching bridges,
limbs that link their parts
like you and I in love
linked with desperate hearts.
Another storm, another street,
hearts retreat
from city's reach.
kneeling, grasp a stone
feed the oceans' lapping tongue
whispering: "Thy will be done"

Wafting breezes christen us
        with ocean spray
lending us a holiness to pray.
baptized lappings
from a shallow surf
bind us to this hallowed earth
to lay on sand, feel the morning sun.
Yes, now at last
        The will of all be done.
Distant voices sink our ear.
Seagull patterns, heard from far and near.
Faint footsteps of a journey
   soon erased by time.
      Echoes left unsigned.
We were the cause
       of our effects unchained.
Each quiet soul, in final truth
   left stained.

The Idea Of You

by Manya Saxena

A deep brown collar, lurking from
underneath the green plaid coat.
A smirk on your face, as you turned
the page of your favorite book. "To
define is to limit", I feel my maroon
muffler tighten around you in a
pursuit to choke me, but I resist. I
resist your raspy voice, your stubble
trimmed to perfection, your quoting
of Fitzgerald and Wilde, you, I'm trying
to resist you. There's something deeply
intriguing when we dissect the movies
that we watch. I swear, my heart
fluctuates when we leave one another
notes where mine consists of all the
books you should read and yours are
filled with words describing your last
bowel movement. Last night, we danced

to Johann Pachelbel while you whispered
Rilke in my ears. Did I tell you that we
were communicating with our eyes, but
your eyes somehow spoke fluent
German? But I'm resisting you, I'm
trying. I *manchmal* stand in stillness
and wonder if you can listen to my
silence. "The only way to get rid of
temptation is to yield to it." I hate it when
you take Dorian gray as an excuse to
solve, almost all of our problems.
People just laugh around you, the mom
-ents stop and look at the vision that is
you and I, I stand here, motionless, com
-posing my body, my brain, my heart, my
gentle gentle heart. Alas, it's time for me
to wake up.

Summer In Time

by Ronald A. Williams

I love plenty green grass growing with flowers
fireflies flickering at shows at nighttime
their bio-luminescence internal night-lights flashing

people pleasuring by the beach with hot sunny sun-tanning
builders are there on many beaches with wet sandy sandcastles
swimmers are swimming; snorkelers are submerged in blue water

sun has illuminated many bike trails for mountain-bike bicycling
sunrays light up parks to have some fun of festive fraternizing
days are longer with sunsets a glow of lavender tinge and orange

4th, July has multi foods of tasty outdoor tender barbequing
summer sun brings out short-sleeves boasters bulging biceps
freedoms a most pleasurable thing of this most seasonal season

Lost Innocence

by Wade Greenlee

We tend to lose our innocence as the years unfold
So the innocence of our children is a beauty to behold

Children sing before they know it's a song
Dance to any music that just comes along

Draw upon a canvas before they realize it's a wall
Climb so high before they understand the fall

We see innocence in our children for such a little bit
So it's up to us to nurture and protect it

But a question now arises which leads to a scary thought
What happens to this innocence when our children are being shot?

Stop a moment to remember what this violence took
The precious children our society forsook

We pray, mourn, weep...and say we're sorry too
Tell the grieving parents there's nothing we can do

And every day our country pays a tremendous cost
As more children are murdered...and more innocence is lost

Never again will they sing, dance, or draw upon a wall
Never again will they marvel at the sky, climb up high or even fall

We've stopped protecting our daughters and our sons
Just memories now of precious little loved ones

As we fight with one another in anger and ire
The children of our country are caught in the crossfire

If we want our children to survive
We must do all in our power to ensure they stay alive

If we continue to allow their innocence to be taken
In this most heinous kind of theft
There will come a time, if we haven't reached it already
When we have no innocence left

Day Of Rain

by Katharine L. Sparrow

Give me a day of rain--
a day that's gray as a pigeon's breast,
a sky that hangs still, as if holding its breath.

Inhale as a drizzle begins to form;
a fine, salted mist, like ocean spray,
that suffuses the gray with life's soft elixir.

Watch, as the mist turns over to pattering droplets,
splashing on the porch like tiny, watery missiles.

Listen from inside the glow of the kitchen
as the drops become torrents,
beating on the roof, slashing against the windowpane.

Curl in the chair,
enfolded in a knitted afghan,
head cradled in a down pillow.

Let eyelids slide closed
to the thrumming of blessed rain,
and float away on rushing rivulets
to the sea.

Ode To The Night Sky

by Katharine L. Sparrow

O, black and velvet cloak with silvered motes,
the Sun has gone and left you to preside
while sonorous Moon eloquently floats.

She hums her lullaby where moonbeams slide
and dance with starlight, there on heaven's stage,
where fragments of Infinity collide.

The incandescent Moon, softened and sage,
recites her part in melodies of light
while Stars, in harmony, blink through the age.

Your lavish play, on this October night,
where starry dust and moonlit shafts are cast,
shall rend the darkness luminous and bright.

A song of spangled Stars, for autumns past,
has offered up this spectacle of grace
that shimmers ever onward to the last.

O, hear the psalm of Moon and Stars that trace
the pathways of Eternity's embrace.

Big Baby

by Agona Apell

The look, the laugh, and the loves of a coming baby,
None ever foretells: not dad, not mum, not the world.
But its manners--now that's never a surprise!
It shows in its parents,
Planted in them perhaps by God,
That mum in dad's big baby self
And dad in mum's big baby self
May find the lessons of little baby care.

It's their baby selves out on schooling duty
When expectant mum lists a thousand craves
And dad, for his part, won't clean up after himself:
Little Nancy is on her way;
Through mum comes notice of her thousand wish lists,
And through dad notice of her messy ways,
Their little world to ready for its little guest.

It's still their baby selves on schooling duty
When expectant mum waxes petulant
And dad oft waxes helpless till sweet mum's about
the house:
Little Tommy is a-coming;
Through mum he sends notice of his fragile temper
And through dad notice of his mama need.

Yes, there're parts of us that must babies be if sometime
we'll parents be:
A side of me and a side of you.
Not by our wish but by Heaven's design
We model the baby to come,
Each other to ready for its entry
With storm and stars into this our world.

In The Space Where You Were

by Aimee Meyn

It doesn't matter these days,
if I don't check the door's shut
when I bring out the trash,
or gossip with the neighbor.
If I don't come home for
days on end, it's no big deal.
It happens so easily, already:
this learned nonchalance
that breaks my heart anew.
Slipping in so sneakily,
without warning or regret,

in the empty space
where you once were.

Where There's Smoke

by Aimee Meyn

Smoking is a dirty habit
that I haven't done
in 15 years or more
(maybe here and there,
on a whim,
outside a bar,
when the night and
the neon glow and
the delirious buzz
beneath my skin
imparted the
vague plastic
sheen of a dream).
But tonight the
dark is too real,
the day too near;
and here I am,
floating somewhere
in between,
in a desperation
I recognize:
familiar, if estranged.
A longing to feel
Something, even if
only the dark burn
of tar in my lungs,
the slight twinge
of perversion (oh,
sweet self-destruction).
To conjure illusions
of danger,
of power.
Don't you know?
I am a cautionary tale.

I am a myth.
A wild creature,
breathing fire.

Thus, The Bird Spoke

by Kohava Ray

When the bird took a rest
To put down his wing
On the soil
He already ended his life

Through thirty thousand years
The most part of his wing
Returned to the land
But the bone was left
Which is bathed
In ephemeral sunlight of
North America

The discovery of the bones
Immediately ran around the world
Famous and non-famous pianists
Offered their compositions
As his requiem

Listening to them
He made a vow:
Be born again, and play
Those beautiful compositions
By himself

Pumpkin Moon

by Molly Moore

Full round pumpkin orange moon
Nestled in the hilltop trees
Am I imagining that enchanting tune
Drifting by on the predawn breeze?

Timelessness...the day not begun
Profound stillness is all that exists
In nature's mosaic all is beautifully one
I pray this ineffable moment persists.

But time must eventually commence
Unknown the vicissitudes it may bring
But henceforth I have this memory whence
In times of stress I can hear my heart sing.

Silver Thread

by Michelle Morris

There is this silver thread between us;
it's woven into our skin.
Our souls are sewn with stitches torn
from the rips and shreds and pain.

In the stillness of the night when
the darkness like a blanket enfolds;
It covers us in peace and quiet,
and lets the memories flow.

No matter how dark it seems,
and how endless the winter chill;
there beats a flame within my blood
for we share the same DNA.

And I feel that you're always close,

no matter how far apart we are;
I see you with my second sight,
and feel you in my heart.

And one day I know,
we'll be together again somehow:
in a boat sailing to heaven
upon a fluffy cloud.

For you and I are connected,
our silver threads woven tight;
and no matter how dark the hours,
I can always foresee the light.

The Soul Of Horse And Human

by Amya Richelle Ranck

Two different beings, interwoven as one
With their minds in sync, and movements fluid
The joy they share, and freedom together
Roaming the lands, never bound to anything
Always aware, of the life that surrounds them
But still they stay, as rider and horse
Together for life, their souls as one

Knots

by Tanya Guleria

Two fibers to join take some time,
Partly crossed, partly ajar.
It's like a poem without a rhyme,
Knit closely but yet too far
For both are alike and nobody's prime.

Junction pains at night
as it is treated like a dice,
for it goes to the left and then right,

just like cats run after mice
and the knot weakens with each bite.

Breaking are those knots,
which we had tied years ago.
Skimming through the blind spots,
we did crop all that we know.
For we feathered the stains which were just dots.

Sides are two but joint the same,
Stretching apart, it gains the strain.
For what is it, love or a game?
Which is the end which the main
as knots are nothing but just a name.

That Time Borrows

by Allegra Jostad Silberstein

So many bright tomorrows have crept by
becoming lost. So many sorrows
to gather in boxes that time borrows
from earth's storehouses with no reply.
I sense the memories giving ride to you—
the compass of your journey turning north
with white hibiscus blossoms sending forth
spirit-peace that flowers into rescue.

Darkness enters slowly to the garden,
with candlelight we'll make this evening shine.
Come out with me to share a loaf of bread,
what's lost we'll leave to heaven to pardon.
We'll drink to life and lift a glass of wine—
let be awhile—the prophecies we dread.

One Sunny Smiley

by Amitabh Divakar

................OH! My, my - :)
............Here's One Sunny Smiley-
.......In these times as we need to be
....How can you be grim intense grumpy
.I mean look at any grinning monkey Oops-
In good spirit; I do not mean to be offending
In this era, humans express themselves happy
Cheers! You're on screen: Spread happiness
It's your digital responsibility: Thy social footprint
Spread Light n Joy; You just returned from dentist
Buddha smiled; at least once; Jesus was dead pan!
Sorry about Jesus, but Barabbas wears- A big smile
I checked Wiki, there is A portrait-   Of Barabbas
Seems as the photo was taken with   A selfie stick
Shankara-CharyA; ever placid None   saw him grin
Ok Gandhi: Was caught guffawing;   How about-
Mozart, Plato,   Aristotle,Van Gogh;   Stoic looks
Didn't they smile?   Do you notice   OurTagore
And that weirdo Einstein: so unfit   so unsocial
.These guys had no idea of upcoming future
...Silly. They just did not know how to selfie.
...There is a surprise hidden in this write;
.....In this Concrete Poetry paragraph;
.......If you notice A Sunny Smile;
.......Click the share button
.......and Smile.

In Faith In To Me

by Amitabh Divakar

..................In
.............Our
.........core
........Rests
.....A desire
.....To explore
......To experience
.......To E X P L O D E
........To shatter the crust
...........To reach out to yonder
..............To connect to communicate
..................To learn also unlearn to know
....To become to be bold to believe
............................To experience to witness what is
.................................To explore the effervescent joys
........................."..........To explode in little star particles
..................In........... ....To merge in our nascent nature
..................My............................To lose all identities all labels
...............Faith ....To stay inspired to bloom...in
...............I rest....... ....To a limitless trust............F
.............a dot...............................Unconquered ....A
.................a seed....... ....A blind leap......... .I
..................as mustard ....In................. T
......................Speck of light ....to ....H
....Faith rests in me
......................Alight Alive A
.....................Speck of dot
.................Little; Never a lot

Violet Eyes

by Melani Udaeta

The blush of a pink candle so sweet;
I can feel the love you pour upon me
bloom in the softness of its glow;

Sparkling saffron energizing glances,
lemon tart words electrify my senses;
Captivated by your ethereal light;

I can still smell your sage in my head,
Feel the energy as I held onto your hand;
Lime fluorescence engulfing me;

Aquamarine brings such fine serenity;
Permeating your aura with tranquility,
you wrap me in shades of amethyst;

Russet leaves paper the ground,
the path glitters cardinal and gold;
Under a turquoise sky autumn flies;

I still see those violet eyes,
otherworldly beauty;
Lavender prisms play like a sunset sea;
The hues of his gentle soul
a gateway to believing.

Knot Of Life

by Theodora Polycarpou

My knot of life I keep you with me
When times are bleak you remind me
That I am right where I need to be
Wherever I am upon my journey is now the right place for me

My knot of life you keep me grounded
When I need to remember that I am okay
You show me that my path is right this way
My fears and misgivings you allay
You remind me that I am on my way

My knot of life your paths are many
These paths they wind, separate and rejoin together
Where to start is one choice from many
Which fork to take I must decide and know that it is right, wherever
You remind me that I am on my way

My knot of life allows freewill
Although I know upon my right path is life's will
I am always exactly where I need to be
To have the life that is right for me
My destination is always the same place

My knot of life you ensure
That wherever I travel
Whichever way I choose
Even when I fall, I cannot lose
Even if I stumble
You keep me grounded and humble

My knot of life wherever my journey begins
Wherever my journey takes me
My path is sure
My path is right
I am always right where I need to be

My knot of life you let me feel
Whichever path I choose is real
However long my path becomes
My journey home is not surpassed
My place is always held fast
My knot of life you tell me that I'm home
My knot of life you remind me that I'm not alone
My knot of life you take me home
No matter where or how far I roam

No matter if I lose my way
No matter how from my path I stray
Along my journey there is no regret
Like a loving hand holding mine every step of my way
My knot of life you take me home

The Star And The Cloud

by Shirley J Hudson

On a dark and starry night,
I look into the sky,
Seeing the stars as they sparkle,
And dance across the sky,
Playing Catch me if you can,
with the cloud in the sky.
Looking at the clouds above,
I sense they are watching and,
Searching for that one special star,
Where they met so long ago,
And remembering that one special night.
They search centuries but,
Can never find each other again.
The star starts to fade losing all hope,
As the cloud never does.
The Gods sense their broken heart,
Searching for each other all these years,
Feeling all is lost and yet just a memory,
But the Gods give them a miracle,
Place them on earth as humans,
So they will always be together.

Lakeside View

by Brian Duffield

The pummelled margins pulsed with steady sway
as reeds resisted swell. These shards in gilt
refracted dying light from summer sun.
Beneath their shafts a clotted mass of spawn
like slobber wobbled, thickening the lake.

There shiny flecks of tiny minnows dashed
with throbbing verve around the shallow edge.
Then hatching eggs released a swarm of flies
like pixilated screens that pepper light
as swallow wings in diving mode catch air.
Occasionally, trout would surface to gulp
a random fly escaping harmful beaks.

a heron diving, pierced a fish; but then
above a buzzard gazed before he dived
towards the lake with gilted talons bared.
In routine drill, the heron's neck was snapped
then slowly dragged along the grassy ridge.

Deep in the lake a shadow played with light
reflecting wings that fade into the cloud
that, similarly, words escape from pens
and morph in ink across a whitened page.

'That Day' 9-11-2001

by Barbara Barry-Nishanian

You're just watching T.V.
Then a horror you see
It's beyond comprehension
"That can't be ... it just can't be

Eyes should see things lovely

Not what they say that day
If we turned off the programs
Would the images ... go away?

Some will never forget
The smells, the scene, that sound
Agonizing reality
Not all loved ones ... would be found.

Not found, but they're not lost
In God's memory, they're kept
For He has felt what you feel
And seen all the tears ... you've wept

God understands your doubts
Your anger and your fears
Remember in the future
"He will wipe away ... all tears"

God Misses Them Too

by Barbara Barry-Nishanian

God misses loved ones we have lost,
for them, still shed a tear
Ever stop, consider their voices,
God no longer ... does hear?

God misses them too, all their prayers,
so loved hearing them pray
Sometimes on their knees in the morning,
or short ones ... during the day

Heard when needed their fears quieted,
times they didn't feel strong
Nights in a hospital bed,
prayed quietly ... all night long

Heard sincere prayers of thankfulness,
of gratitude and joy

Woke to see another day,
told Him .... they did enjoy

Days intrigued by flower designs,
saw how an eagle flies
Magnificent colors God painted,
The morn ... and evening skies

God's glory and magnificence
proclaimed on starry nights
When mesmerized by creation
God's power ... and His might

Prayers offered during times of victory,
few times suffered defeat
Days taking sunny beach strolls, or
the nights ... when couldn't sleep

Night eyes swollen from flowing tears,
after silly mistake
Repentant pleas offered to God,
before slept ... when awake

Millions of times during a lifetime,
with God, they've been in touch
Let's hope and pray when we too die,
He'll miss us ... just as much

***

In memory of childhood friend ... Jackie H Brewer

Just A Speck Of Dust

by Barbara Barry-Nishanian

You'll never be my heart or world,
only my God can be
He saw me as an embryo,
and knew ... who I would be

God knew even sinews of me,

before not much to see
He's my always, my everything,
in joy ... or agony

He's my strength when my weakest, my
adrenalin for pain
My hope, when disillusioned, and
my sunshine ... in the rain

He's my comfort when lost loved ones,
my eyes when couldn't see
My faith when so disillusioned
lost me ... I used to be

I'm nothing just a "speck of dust"
among dust on the earth
Forever grateful in me sees,
a speck ... he thinks has worth

The Earth Abides, Justice

by Brian Rusch

Sharing is, as sharing does
Giving is, as giving does
Loving is, as loving does

To what... is owed justice.

Bliss is, as fantasy allows
Sublime is, as vibration allows
Balance is, as chaos allows

To what... is deemed justice.

Is sharing fantasy?
Is giving vibration?
Is loving chaos?

Justice needs sounding.

Sharing... is bliss
Giving... is sublime
Loving... is balance.

Justice well served, sounding... the Earth abides.

Should She Speak

by Omar Dabrinze

Her luscious lips tend several functions;
a tender paradise to lay yours on,
A salve to your heart's aches,
A wily weapon for taking her stand,
As well a purveyor of her mind's many wisdoms.

Grateful winds carry forth her words.
Bursting forth ever so caringly,
from pink, perfect lips.
As her sublime sound caresses the air,
Peaceful perfection grips the atmosphere.

Her words, her cries, her songs,
In none lay any wrongs.
A voice ferociously tender, pervading all existence,
Breathing in life with faithful loving persistence.
The common word bleakly educates the brain,
her sounds sing serenely, not unlike the rain.
Nurturing my heart, curing its pain,
Gems born of air, nothing stays the same.

Valor

by Tucker Carwile

So young and innocent
giving that last measure.
Asking questions only to yourself,
making that final journey

home-alone.

What was the last thought before
closing your eyes?
Was it one of disbelief,
thinking you could never die,
Or was it one of valor,
knowing you had done your duty.

Now, your name, etched across some
black marble stone
with so many others.
Above your head flies a flag,
and fresh flowers mark
your grave.

You leave your family
with a box of medals.
They, somehow, lack the
warmth of your flesh.

Say Hello

by Tucker Carwile

I walked the streets today,
past rows of
shuttered people hiding
in their houses.

Those still asleep
or just afraid...
to pull their blinds
to meet the day,
or greet a stranger's
face.

Faces aren't bad,
you know,
just to say hello.

If Only I Could Find

by Roger Kevin Harp

You have a golden glow
Soft hands, a gentle soul
Loving eyes, I can see with mine
A heart that hides, behind the mind
Oh, how life would be so sublime
If a love like yours, I could find

To Becky

by Tucker Carwile

Was there a time,
I was looking,
without seeing.

So wrapped up in
my small world.
Passing by those
who really cared.

If only my eyes,
had not been cloudy.
That other road
would never have been
taken.

Paradise No More

by Amanullah Khan

Those mortals who have a history of
About five million years having survived
Many calamities: fires floods viruses
Hurricanes, tornadoes, and earthquakes
Man made wars and environmental events

A minute ball in cosmic terms, afloat
In nothingness of space held by tug of
Neighboring planets. Shooting stars Hit and
Miss Some burrowing leaving craters or
Vanish in black hole. Foretelling fate of
Worn out planets in the universe, spent

Themselves maintaining sovereignty over
The vast suspended universe that is
Immeasurable on all accounts which
Makes it unmanageably immense
And boundless. A minute globe in the midst

Of infinite cosmos occupied the
Central place in our limited logic
A people whose ancestors once expelled
From heaven now teeter on extinction
And are at the brink of destroying earth

Nature cries in the form of jolting rumbles
Of earth quakes and loud roar of tornadoes
Sends repeated warnings of forest fires
Raises ambient temperature of the earth
Dotted with torrential rains causing floods

If we fail to heed cries of nature and
See what is staring us in the face we
Are bound to lose like the dying sequoia
No amount of foil can stand fury of
Nature. To challenge it is to spit in the wind.

No True Repeats In Life

by Akham Nilabirdhwaja Singh

One calm evening
on a leisure drive with my wife
along the national highway
Imphal Dimapur road

I remembered
my overnight road journeys
to Guwahati for office works
sometimes together with her
before retirement a decade ago.
Tedious journeys
riding through the winding hilly roads
of Manipur and Nagaland
yet exciting beautiful scenery,
Intermittent stops,
taking tea and snack at short stops,
riding through the busy marketplaces
in Dimapur and Assam
songs from the Hindi films,
from the market places, hotels
and inside the bus,
a longer stop at Jakhlabanda
for all to take food and rest .
At last reaching Paltan Bazar
in the morning
looking for a hotel.
We decided then
once again to go to Guwahati
when the covid pandemic over
boarding a night super
to recreate once our past journeys.
Back home our little grandson waiting
for us to play with me.
I remembered then,
as the days, months, and years gone
there will be no true repeats in life.

Little Birds

by Judy Reeves

SHATTERED
Every morning I watched you both from the kitchen window
back and forth each carrying a twig   - one at a time
your nest random twigs arranged in some sort of lattice
over a drain in the corner of the concrete stairwell

I thought birds built their nests somewhere high, out of reach, safe.
During the day we were out, us visitors.
I guess you were too.

Evening time I watched you both settled on the rail, just resting,
You had your daily routine - so did we.

At night two small grey figures huddled in the corner to sleep.
Little birds, you became part of the intimacy of my world
I wanted to know all about you, yes you were birds
question - are all birds the same?

wanted to give you names, say you look happy - or sad
romanticise your story
question - do birds fall in love?

I saw the single egg laid on that precarious nest you built
it was never going to end well, I could tell
though I worried there was nothing I could do.

If you were human, I would see the distress on your face
know your grief, understand your loss, feel your sadness.

You looked, looked away, looked again
and again
your egg - your hope for the future had been shattered
destroyed, smashed as though it meant nothing at all!
there you were staring at the now vacant nest
your partner was not with you, you were alone

If you were my son, daughter, friend, neighbour
I would hold you close and try to console you
Say words of comfort and hope for the future
question - do birds feel pain?

I looked out for you after that day
You did not return.

Such Was Summer

by Patricia J. Mencin

Nothing was the same
now that it was summer!

Parched blades of once-green grass
crackle in the dry wind, as purple
impatiens impatiently wait for their daily bath
from the hot rubber hose.

Strangers bond in this strange drought, complain
about the heat while mopping brows with tank top ends.
Kids stage wars against boredom with squirt guns and
captive sprinklers.

Afternoon naps beneath cool cotton sheets offer
an excuse to re-energize. Laziness is acceptable;
relaxing on lawn chairs necessary.

Nothing was the same;
    summer changed everything!

Cold Moon Clarity

by Cynthia Thompson

Winter cold moons its way
through my bedroom window.
Frosty beams glint off Dad's photo,
a standing sentinel
to memories of a live ill-lived.
Wooden-framed seductive smile,
handsome rugged looks,
bely the sad inside his mind.
"Regettsive behavior" I called it.
Regret for not loving our mom more,
for not honoring their marriage vows,

for not being a good, good father
to four daughters who idolized him,
yet hated the pain we saw in our mother's eyes.
Winter cold moons its way
into the depths of my soul
reminding me of childhood days
filled with paternal love insecurity
balanced with fierce protective mother love
that gifted me with resilience.
Resilience to release to the clouds
what was, what can't be recreated,
a naive what-wasn't-ness that lulled me
into thinking things were better
than they were.
Winter cold moons its way
into the darkest corners of my mind,
illuminating the cold truth of life.
Icy moonlight rays remind me
photos are not true pictures of the past,
prodding me to relegate the smiling father
to the pile of faded photographs albummed in my heart ...
faded memories, faded hurts, faded reality.
But with deep-down, cold-moon clarity,
I know he loved us.

Sensual And Sweet

by Quadri Oyerinde

Those apples you call cheeks are as fresh as a currant, grapefruit!
Wanna eat them my luv! For they're chubby and sweet!

The crease on your neck is a line on blue-sky.
It squints for a smooch which my lips can't deny.

Flesh

by OMANGA A. LAWRENCE

I suffered through the dark
Hoping hoping i could make a mark.
Timeless struggle to live
But couldn't hold back the things i believe.

Desiring all along to be righteous.
Even the path way to live i was conscious,
But held back in pain with nature.
Was focused but uncertain of the future.

The battle becoming more stronger
My flesh, the brain behind the danger.
All day, my spirit never rest but fighting.
And my flesh also by all means pulling.

Look, i stray and mislay my heart;
Diving aimlessly to the world path like that.
The end of which is destruction
But my mind refuse to take instruction.

The He Goat arises in me no resting
After so much prayer and long fasting.
The world keeps showing me things.
Things that makes my spirit thin.

No! I said, 'I don't want to look.
Not too long in the same act i brook
Many years spent in building
Smashed with an act, sweet but destroying.

How can i overcome?
I can't fight being alone.
Please Lord, don't let me perish
For i am the child you love and cherish.

Weightless

by Onokemi Onojobi

More often than not, you clutch tightly,
The very things that weigh you down;
Beliefs, suppositions, fears and so much doubt,
You line the lie of being emancipated,
When in actual fact, freedom is alien to you.

You define yourself by others' standards,
Struggle to fit in, when the simple truth is,
Every individual created is a blueprint,
A unique creation, with quirts and kinks,
That makes you who you really are.

You fail to look up, turn to the creator,
Ignore the consult of the compendium,
To a discovery of one's true self,
Instead of the falsity of a likeness,
Imitate, forgetting there exist no facsimiles.

ME is an opportunity to introduce to the world,
Your beliefs and all that makes you distinct,
a chance to stand out and not be defined,
By standards of what right is, or by anyone else.

Defy norms: An existence outside the box
Be as light as a feather, Be you
Knowing there's only this one life to live
To live it full, live it well, live it free, live it good
And look back decades from now with nary a regret

For you have lived................WEIGHTLESS

Sonnet 105, Feathers On The Water

by Ken Allan Dronsfield

Dear shorebirds, my quills inspiration.
I love the way you're chased by the ripples
Ceasing my days and nights isolation
Dreams of the coast; I smile just a little.

Let me watch you as you bob and wiggle
You're much quieter during winters chill
The sea fogs hide the highest tides tickle
you take flight along the coast with a shrill.

Winter shows her winds upon crab and krill.
Strolling windswept dunes; the sands rise higher.
Wing beating echoes; those thoughts do fulfill,
but leaves lone feathers upon still waters.

I walk away with a chill in my heart,
Remember this sonnet whilst far apart.

Congratulatory To My Nephew's Wedding

by Ogino Makoto

(1)
Congratulations on your wedding.
Prepare for the next staging.
Believe in your tomorrow,
wherever you are heading.

(2)
Best wishes for your marriage!
The World will bring you courage.
Take a step and find your place,
that helps you for your voyage.

Human Kindness Soars

by Anna M Shepard

wild fires, floods
nature's force... overwhelming
human kindness soars

Noh Face

by Barbara Magic

The tilting mask crosses the stage
a nebulous cloud of poetic grace
forged in the furnace of latent space

The dying flower of the hidden face
articulates in tender sorrow
unspoken loss of lineage noble

Warriors steeped in samurai creed
perchance in battle encounter defeat
each breath a song to be rephrased

But for one immutable in the Way
an offering to the Sugi tree
weeping petals falling free

Gather on its graceful boughs
instantly honored and received
bows humbly to the mask esteemed

Glory ceded to anguished grief
harbinger of fate angelic thief
in days that end in cloudless night

Everyone the grave must meet

A Butterfly Dances

by João Camilo Campos de Oliveira Torres

A whistle arrived before the wind,
waving the red-wine grape leaves
dressing the trellis of the balcony.
The butterflies flipped their wings,
once, twice... stretched their legs
and crushed silence with expectancy.

Then, the windblow was irresistible
and the butterflies' ballet began,
weaving a mottled canopy.
Dried yellow leaves whirls,
sweeping dust from the ground,
emulating the enticing swing.

The entry door taps three times,
the audience watches a pair of wings
swaying with a lasting blue blur:
music remains without the wind.

Wheel Of Life

by John A'hern

On yonder mountain a remarkable sight,
stumbled upon by chance.
In shrouded mist, shapes start to unfold,
strange mechanism, a wheel is seen.
Sitting there in crossed leg pose
a being unrecognised to myself.
Asked a question no response,
asked again, this time recognition.
What is this place?
What is this machine?
One at a time, answered back at me
as fingers gripped the wheel.

Quietly spoken words follow,
judgement is passed for all,
when the wheel spins, centuries pass
then a subject stopped upon.
Where the wheel stops, it has no conscience
decisions made, no heart string nonsense.
Music chosen, do not ask questions
too many names to say,
all then called no order or rhyme
join the line pay for their time.
The name David, first to be called,
weeping and wailing across the land,
shock and horror all on show
quickly followed by the Prince of music souls.
The wheel has no feelings at all,
Name of George, whispered, who, when how?
He spoke of truth to behold,
judgements not based who or where,
humans cannot believe who is taken from here.
Study the wheel, trying to understand,
Politicians, Family, where will it land.
Wheel starts to creak, it bursts into life
Quickly left the scene, do not turn around.

Radhe Krishna Divine Love

by Venkatesh Raghava

In serene moonlight beneath banian tree
Radhe and Krishna from the world being free
The love dissolving from eyes to heart
Bringing happiness and joy to universe sat.

Their enchanting love beaming through forest
All the plants and animals took peaceful rest
With the presence of the lord around
With calmness their time they could spend.

By the grace and beauty of divine love
All our problems could be solved

So to follow your heart be proud
Then the whole world you will be loved.

Dilatory Deeds

by Nurhayati Mohd Fadzil

Hie thee, to warm utterances
that soothe reddened hearts.

Hie thee to where it knows no crackles from a cold spirit,
not even from seething sips of a blackened stout.

Hie thee, where no emerald flocks,
to blind thee into tempted wastes.

Hie thee into that which He bellows,
for trails into His Heavens or below.

Hie thee before they drub thee, a sub.
Before pain delivers regrets that deny forgiveness.

Hie thee, away from garbles of chatters,
from the morass of wrong deliverance.

Hie thee for thou art too late.

Sacred Lines And Circular Spaces

by Gerald Dillenbeck

Minds can draw dividing lines
in different natural spaces
sacred special uniting places
for secular powering chases.

Nature makes poles
and power polarity,
holes
and light circularity,

bright yangs
and dualdark yintegrity

Which spirited minds refine
and natural bodies define
but integrity is not image confined
by these cooperatively determined lines
back through universally wealthy loves
uniting healthy lives.

We make cognitive distinctions
between quiet emotive attractions
and loudly ejaculative extinctions,
where feelings find
finely balanced tipping points
between what whole has been
and who will yet consecutively
consequentially become

As we undivided are
whom we have been
and much
much potentially more

Beyond our favorite
bottom line integrity
privileged score,
healing Earth weal

Wealthing wellness
when we stop drawing only straight
unwavering lines,
bipolarities
to addictively adore.

Where There Is A Will There Is A Way

by Giti Tyagi

Untiring efforts to spread around,
When struck a sap with hardships abound,
No sun, no soil, no air, no light,
The struggling roots with space so tight,
It yet did give a final fight,
And bloomed there a flower ever so bright!

The Faith, unfailing, that was shown,
Wasn't for nothing that lay deep instilled sown,
The hand wanting the flower halts at bay,
For the Divine reflects in each of its ray!

If not for Faith, nor the Surrender,
The bloom wouldn't survive the slightest thunder,
For all odds, all obstacles, the bloom's the brightest,
The Divine Will prevails, the strongest the mightiest!

Let no hurdle never leave us at dismay,
Let not our dreams the stumbles shall slay,
Let the Faith, the Surrender brighten up our way,
Where there is a will there is a way!

I Seek You Out

by Jennifer Etheridge

I seek you out in a lake of dreams...
I look for the glowing angelic presence...
Always looking for you, it seems...
Your caring heart, sensuality, your essence...

And, when I find you, something stirs in me...
Like a group of stars, held beneath waves...
That belong in your ocean, inside of my sea...
Of desire, affection, and all that I crave...

Then, we're barefoot dancing, by a campfire...
With lingering kisses under starry nights...
And how much I feel the heightened desire...
Kissing, caressing, sucking and small bites...

Strolling, in silence, in flowered meadows...
Listening to you chatter, and your laughing...
Stealing kisses, under the tree's shadows...
Skinny dipping in a creek and wading...

I seek you out in my dreams and in life...
I need you; I want you, it's a simple fact...
I want us to be an escape for the other, from the strife...
Forever, together, in a true love pact.

The Newly Wetted Ground

by Abel Jae

Walking on the newly wetted ground,
After a long spell of Winter drought,
I ponder how rain never fails to astound:
This valuable shower we can't do without!

As I tread on the browne'd earth
Browned by the shower of yester-night,
I wonder where I got such a worth:
To be watched with such close oversight!

Someone's delivering service to me,
Loyally, like a hotel room keeper!
Yet there is a dichotomy:
I pay nothing to the caterer!

There is some love expressed in rain.
It's not only soothing but sustaining as well.
Especially after a long drought strain,
I rejoice that some rain fell!

Unkept Place

by Valerie Sherman

In an unkept place beyond anyone's watchful care lay vessels which carried the powerful blood of a forgotten people.

So strong and powerful, their very presence brought fear and panic to an entire race of people who believe dominance is theirs.

Underneath the 'ole' shade tree lay weather beaten slats of wood proof of a cultures existence.

A dark skinned people whose lives were valued less than that old hunting dog licking his colored masters wounds.

No names, memories, or accomplishments nothing at all except dated brittle epitaphs marking their era of life.

Dusty black Hebrew Israelite feet and cracked aged hands lay in those hallowed tombs-their names mattered to no one.

Shoeless black feet trod and stood in places I have never known and will never see yet, their strength is who I am.

Their proof of toiling in cotton fields beneath the scorching sun washing white folks cloths hanging them on the line to dry.

Same precious hands held offspring not their image that suckled the rich milk from the breast of the woman in the unkept dark place.

Let's not forget the shoulders which rocked the weight of misses churin' to sleep as if they were her own.

The unkept places off the beaten path lay the blood of the forgotten dark people.

643 | P a g e - PS: It's Still Poetry – Volume II

Our Romance Begins

by David B D'Braunstein

Saturday night was finally here
And my mind was perfectly clear
I made sure that I wasn't late
I had a very important date
Dinner and West Side Story were planned
And I'm "all in" with a monster hand
We had THE most wonderful time
The movie was GREAT and dinner sublime!
I thought I was dreaming and the night couldn't be
We held hands and JoAnn's kiss captured me!
Ok Dave you now know it's set
JoAnn was the most wonderful gift I could get
The rest is history or so they say
I truly wanted us to wed that day!

The Clincher

by David B D'Braunstein

On New Year's Eve 1962 she looked great!
It was then that I knew our inevitable fate
We had the most wonderful time together
I didn't know and didn't care about the weather
Her beauty rivaled any Hollywood star
And there I was her date with my mouth ajar
I was sure that our chemistry was a good match
And was humbled and spellbound by her as my catch!
We brought in the New Year with a wonderful kiss
It was natural and timely and I had hoped I wouldn't miss!
It was on that night that I knew she'd be mine
Our love had begun and the stars came out to shine!

Phoenix

by Abdul-Hakim Zakaria

You may cut off my phalanges,
Peel off my skin.
You may cast me
Into the shades' den,
Leach me down the soil
You may strike me off memory;

I'll come—
I'll dart... hop—
Just right towards you.
I'll come – visit your nights
Like a phantom
With scary sockets;
A very bleeding sockets.

I'll come,
Just for you
No! Not to harm you
But to tell you
That I live.
Even if my body is mutilated,
My soul is eternal.

I'm a Phoenix
I'm a phantom who visit dreams
Not to kill
But to tell you I LIVE.

Daisies And Dreams

by Cynthia Thompson

When Spring's soft murmurs broke the stillness of the rolling hills,
He took his guitar outside to welcome days of daffodils.
His music wound throughout the pines in greening melodies,
The gypsy lady heard them and was stirred to fantasies.

Across the daisy meadow, his tunes reached out to her at night,
On his front porch she could see him bathed in yellow cabin light.
He played upon her heartstrings with chords he never planned;
She was his gypsy lady ... he was her music man.

At night, she softy crept into the nearby forest glade,
With moonbeams woven in her hair, she danced the notes he played.
He watched her whirling, twirling form reach out to him in love,
But bound by love to another, he cursed the stars above.

Each night she gathered up his songs in the folds of her gypsy skirt,
Then shook them out as a healing salve for her heart's deep, aching hurt.
Danced among his guitar songs, wore his music like a shawl,
The image of his smiling face was painful to recall.

When sunny brightness swept across the daisy hills he pined,
While, cat-like, memories of her slipped in and out his mind.
Each night her presence in the glade made him sing a sadder tune,
'Cause he belonged to another; she belonged to the moon.

She danced throughout his moonlit dreams, he knew his thoughts were wrong,
Though he was bound to another, his heart sang a different song.
She knew she could not have him, his ring showed he was wed,
At night while she lay lonely, he was warm in another's bed.

Years passed, the gypsy's youth was gone, but not her love for him,
His fingers stiff, he still played on though her moonlit dance grew dim.
He strummed out songs of passion with a calloused, shaky hand,
She was still his gypsy lady ... he was still her music man.

One April's eve those piney hills lay bathed in quiet peace,
His guitar sang to her no more, his soul found sweet release.
From the agony of loving her through years of silent pain,
Now daisies pushed up through the sod in a gentle spring-time rain.

With silent gypsy sadness, mourning love's unkindly loss,
She lay upon his sun-warmed grave, head pillowed by cool moss;
Tears glistened on her grief-worn face, her heart burst from the pain,
In death, she'd be his gypsy lady ... and he'd be her music man.

Mountains

by Candice Ballinger

I cried for you, left broken and sullen,
I waited for you to breathe
And then I snatched your breath away;
Never explaining my actions

I live for this, this utopian existence,
I'm so indisposed, laughing at my own reflection
The particles floating in the air suffocate me in my sleep

I'm left shaking, chills wrack my body
My hair standing on end, do you see me;
Can you see my beauteous body
As I am laid across this mountain

I absorb the land around me,
Shredding trees with my thighs
These streams dry up because I am alive

Do you hear me;
The echoes that bounce off the walls of my soul
Whispers climbing into your ears at night when you lay awake in your bed,
These come for me also,

I am the one who feeds you
I will not be forgotten or thrown away like rubbish
You will feel me and I will own your body, mind, and soul

Can you hear me now,
Am I talking too loud
I can't hear myself speak,
My thoughts are up high drifting through the clouds

This transpicuous dalliance does not scare me
It brings us closer,
We inhabit the same body; yet we have two pairs of lungs
So now we're left anxious and breathless as if we were asthmatic by nature

Our organs are not riddled with disease,
Our spiritual beings are dying from sin
It's warped your life and left me nothing,

I'll have nothing to work with;
But I will reassemble our world
I'll climb this mountain;
I will conquer this mighty alpine

Visual Sympathy

by Beulin S S

Nothing can't be caught
   within the tiny bars,
Wind stuck chambers
   Bulges with the tiny wars.

Scars without pain
   Scarce visit the town;
Million channels work
   But none against the pain.

Building blocks stood
   As a slanding towers;
Bombing heard as thunders
   Ashes are mere powders.

Stained bloods highlighted

On the brightest sources,
Sympathy shown widely
   Upon the mere noises.

Pains of millions
   Stood powerless;
Beaten out of blue
   The world is merciless.

Tuning voices of the poor
   For the visual sympathy,
The world is helpless
   To wake the sleeping humanity.

Complying With The Calling Of Merciless Death

by Andrew Crisci

Complying with the calling of merciless death,
see yourself buried in the bowels of the cold earth?
How unimaginable is it to process this concept
and accept it without having a convincing thought?

Our unacceptable silence is to be debated,
to be brought out of its darkness;
we should be the speakers of a truth alienated
for fear, not distancing ourselves
from the anguish which will follow after
having lived days of extravagant cheer!

I have pondered over this awful feeling:
why be born and turn into thin dust?
What's behind the substantial lesson of living?
It's the hard sustenance of a dreadful fact
being so real and yet so widely ignored
by the weak who blend into the large horde!

Can humans reforge an unchangeable fate
that was set by time, occurrence, and dwelling...

despite the warnings of prophets discouraging
indulgence in lust which makes the sinners blate?

Listen to that preacher younger than yourself,
holding his bible and expressing his rage
for our heedless humanity dispersing itself
into streets of lustful pleasures that assuage!

Do you have enough dauntlessness and confidence
to discern how life will end in a dire circumstance:
dying in a tragic event as did unvirtuous Macbeth?
Will we comply with the calling of merciless death?

Difficult Acceptance - Mehrabian's 55-38-7 Percent Rule

by Ogino Makoto

Angry face and praising word.
I can't find out which is true.
Inputs begin to argue.
A straight posture is preferred.

Grinning face and sorrow word.
These can mislead our feelings.
People need careful dealings
with what they saw and they heard.

These are express confusion.
Which has the strong impression,
visual, vocal, or verbal?

Visual, fifty-five percent,
Vocal, thirty-eight percent,
And Verbal, seven percent.

A Calamitous Day

by Sarban Bhattacharya

This is no mere rejoicing thing,
 The sun does peep again,
It pricks the roads with beamy swords
 And dries the humid grain.

The water gleams with golden sheen,
 A mirror on the lake,
As if the glass in daylight burns
 With ripples at its wake.

Today it is a warm delight,
 The moment I thought so,
A dark and dusky cloud obscured
 The pleasant morning glow.

At once it called its sable mates,
 With wrathful vapour swelled,
They rolled and rushed, and thereon squashed,
 But never, never quelled.

As if it were a true display
 Of demons talking loud,
They deal in lies, and cleave the skies,
 And wrap them in a shroud.

The gales possessed by unjust souls
 Fly off a million miles,
The casements clack and clutter all,
 Fall victim to their wiles.

Ofttimes it pours from unknown source,
 Breaking the bowl of night,
A darkened sky is sundered by
 Electric veins of light.

From thence it throws loud, loud bellows,

The devil's dance resumes,
It rips and whips the boats and ships,
All earthly noise subsumes.

He grumbles for some unknown cause,
And rumbles all again,
It shakes the child with thunders wild
And ceaseless rapid rain.

He shouts, and clouts the unseen air,
While tumbles many a toy,
The fearsome din sprang from the sin
I cannot but destroy.

A Tale Of Darkness

by Sarban Bhattacharya

This is midnight, all slept indeed,
The factory bells do chime,
Ding-dong dong, thrice the sounds arise
From yonder darkling clime.
No one is there, two faint lamps glare,
Who rang the rusty bell?
It must be three, a shade does flee
In earshot of the knell.
Upon my eave the pigeons live,
One flutters tender wings,
It heard a whiz as soft as grease,
And to the wall it clings.
There is a grange, a mansion old,
Deserted since the yore,
Such creatures as with deep black fur,
Hold sway around its floor.
No iron melts on fire these days,
The blacksmiths all have left,
And all day long a thrush her song
Attunes to good effect.
She quavers in her leafy nest,
The pale shades pass again,

The rumbling sky does well deny
  A sound sleep while she's lain.
Mine eyes are closed yet well awake,
  The pattering distant rain
Revives the tendrils grown unsought,
  An omen of the bane.
My windows smeared with mizzle mist,
  That dreamy opaque layer,
Obtrudes my view with chilly dew,
  A fancied world lays bare.
"Don't be afraid", a voice just said,
  A whisper grim and grave,
As from a king or ancient sage,
  Conquerer of the knave.
That moment my door shook its hinge,
  Something had wrenched its knobs,
The bats beseech with a sudden screech,
  And fill my home with sobs.
A pain of olden times deludes,
  My grandsire died this day,
A tremor stirs after these years,
  Benumbed and dozed I lay.
The dawn has worn her purple gown,
  It's four, the chimes sojourn,
Her mellow light dissolves my night
  Into a canny morn.

My Reflection

by Frank Blacharczyk

The mirror never lies but we do to ourselves and others
A reflection that speaks louder than our conscience
Smothered by denial so the ghosts of our past disappear
The mirror casts only what it sees past or present
Meanwhile the rain ends the growing ends
the warm colours a frigid memory
And then the falling snow paints with shades of black and white
Sleep sweet dreamer with many shadows playing hide and seek
The mirror casts only what it sees past or present
Resurrection forgiveness awakens re-birth rejoicing in the soul

Brings peace like autumn winds that paint heavenly colours
That no one on earth can duplicate
Sun sets only to see the Artist creating the night sky
Then the sun arises
From nowhere somewhere a divine wind and rain revives
A reflection smothered in courageous love
And joy is the outburst composed by the excitement of the dancing sun
A welcome alarm clock to raise the dead and the dreamers

Bring Me Home

by Shreya Laxmi Nagendra

What I'd like to give you, is an ounce of my perfume
So you can feel this presence; my presence
Even after I inevitably leave
Profound in my apology to thee

Destined to become absent
From life's apparent joys
I step aside from your podium
To be alone; to be coy

An illness, I'm told
Of the body, soul and mostly mind
One minute I'm ecstatic
The next, uncontrollably static

Born with it, I was
Control over it, I've never had
So when I leave
Make me one promise

To not forget
And never leave
You must bring me home
Until when, my perfume will have to be

Not to be
Miles asunder

Don't give up on my fleet
Bring me home to thee

Era Of Mental Survive

by Ogino Makoto

The changing nature, Volatility.
No one knows what'll happen, Uncertainty.
The cofusion of things, Complexity,
and easy to mislead, Ambiguity.

They affect greatly people and society.
Yesterday's success will not assist us,
to ensure tomorrow's success more plus.
The solution should be diversity.

Let's make your environment elastic.
It can grow your mental capacity.
And it's no need to fear other's thinking.

Let's grow your spiritual world fantastic.
It can refresh your pure vitality.
And it's your time to fix human linking.

The Watcher

by Donald Maher

Standing watch on this warm summer night
Listening to sounds in the soft spectral light
Calling to my soul a song never ending
That the spirits of the dead forever are sending

Searching the horizon for sails in fear
Asking and praying they never appear
Foreboding is all that is left in my heart
As I remember the faces of those who did part

Not long ago they did appear

Their black sails cast with Ravens filled us with fear
Ships gilded with gold shimmered so bright
In the glow of the moon on a cold winters night

Two score were their numbers as they finally made land
We marveled as they first set foot on the land
They wore large hats on their heads trimmed with gold
Their clothes were quite fancy their attitude bold

They spoke in a tongue we did not understand
They carried a great flag they stuck deep in the sand
Explorers they were, that is what we understood
They came here to help us, came here to do good

Shelter we gave so they could all rest
Sleep is what they needed to be at their best
Morning came quickly, gloomy shadows were cast
This day started peaceful, that would not last

More ships had arrived silently in the night
Many soldiers appeared in the soft morning light
Swords gilded in gold tight at their sides
My people we screaming and running for their lives

Grabbed all our women, put them deep inside their boat
Many men had been slaughtered, leaving them to float
The ships then took sail, leaving our land
With many of my people lying dead in the sand

Standing watch on this warm summer night
Listening to sounds in the soft spectral light
Calling to my soul a song never ending
That the spirits of the dead forever are sending

Preparing Future

by Brian Rusch

For New Beginnings...
Expecting future blooms soon

Look in memory

There, inside, to find
The keys to needed futures
Therein lie best seeds

Fragrant beginnings
Sown thus before flowers grow
By those summer wise

That understand Time's
Right process for entering
End's opening door.

Whispering Angel - Abridged

by Ade Robert Amure

Whispering Angel: Strength of the Babes

**Blubbering baby, newborn to this Earth
Tell me why you wail and blubber at birth?**

Could you be afraid of this Earthly Circus?
Well, don't be afraid and don't be nervous.
I shall hold your hand, so don't be anxious.
We are all on Earth for a higher purpose.

*Even if we feel that the world is against us
Even if we face a most daunting concourse
Even if we think that the task is enormous,
...perhaps all these things are sent, and meant, to test us.*

Let us hum a tune, to the angels, in chorus.
Look up to the skies; to the Heavens above us.
I shall be your guide - just keep calm, and focus.
Hold on to this faith, and you shall be joyous.

*Even if you feel that some men are monstrous
Even if you face that foe - mischievous
Even if you think that it's all mysterious,*

...be cautious to be curious at a world that is so curious.

Sometimes you may fail, and sometimes victorious.
Journeys that you make may at times be dangerous.
I am by your side in all storms tempestuous.
Never give up hope; just stride on courageous.

Even if it seems that the paths are perilous
Even if you face a road most treacherous,
Even if you think the ways of men outrageous,
  ...take care to be precocious, for the gift of life is precious.

I shall let you in on a secret about Jesus,
How to seem poor and yet be prosperous.
Don't ever hold back in being too generous.
Forgive all bad friends, and even bad neighbours.

Even though betrayed by that man, called Judas
Even though they swapped Him for that thief, Barabbas
Even though they nailed Him to that Cross, still conscious,
  ...men still remain oblivious ...though the Truth is quite obvious.

Blubbering baby ...sleep on then in peace.
I shall watch over you - I shall your Journey ease.

O Beau Papillon

by Siddhi Pawar

o beautiful butterfly,

Have you whilom explored the inselberg,
To descry its allure,
And its rillets surge,
To see the coruscating sun,
And the meadows hushed afar,
The zephyr whisking leisurely,
Or the bodach with his old guitar,
Have you at all espy the sapphire sky,

And the clouds that move sedately,
Peered inside the fathomless dale,
And discovered the linn falling indistinctly,
O beautiful butterfly,
Have you at all seen the winsome nature,
And felt totally satisfied,
To realise that life is just an unforeseen adventure.

People Of The Horse

by Linda Milgate

Came from the North displaced by the cold winters,
They migrated to America these creatures
Natives saw the horse differently from the Spanish
As a gift to their People
Respected godlike before the Spanish came
Not quite the story told by the old school books,
The People connected and saw the horse and their magic
Between the People and their Brothers the horse
They saw the bond and formed it before others came
With their horses of Arabian and Andalusian blood
Ones the Spanish might eat because of their hunger
During their many long wars not the People
Natives respected these creatures majestic and strong
They swam across the rivers, with the People on their backs
Fought battles and carried tipis across the land
The People of the Horse knew the magic of these creatures
Who bonded with the tribes and Natives so quickly
For they knew too the People were their brothers
And life became better, easier and good

Creatures Godlike cherished and respected
As they fed on the sacred lands grazed on the grasses
The grasses that became stronger
From the horses who were free to roam
A gift from the Creator -- the horses to the People

Tanka 002

by Naledi Segosebe

an ant scales my flank
sun rays waltz on my belly
my heart skips a beat
the penny begins to drop
this is my personal bliss

Haiku 1

by Naledi Segosebe

icy waves in fall
ferry to shore a sea star
from a mussel bed

Unity In Origin Variety In Expression

by A. K. Mukerji

Under the sky I live
Over the grass I walk
Free air I breathe
Natural water I drink
Nature in me I am in Nature.
At death I get mixed with earth or burnt in fire
Transformed into other elements, get rebirth;
I live perpetually in Nature
Nature in me I am in Nature
I have no existence without it
In natural state it is in equilibrium
Without shortage or surfeit
Nature is Divine
Anything antagonistic to it is anti-divine
I cannot coexist with such entity
I am one with Nature, with it in unity.

One is the unity
Origin of beings and things
The Infinity, the Eternity;
"Ekam Sat Vipra Bahudha Vadanti."
Variety is the key to earthly life
There cannot be one word
Many are the words
It is the way of life;
True language is as many
As human hearts in happiness or agony
Variety is the vibration of Natural life
Monotony is the begetter of perpetual strife.

Breeding Death

by Seventh Realm

Not long will it be when the grass
Be nothing more than sand.
And forests through where rivers pass
Are but a barren land.
Not long until the songs of birds
Be just a memory,
And rats that dwell under the earth,
A last breath they will breathe.
Not long before the lion's roars
Be relics of the past.
And grasslands where the gazelles roam
Turn into wastelands vast.

Beasts that hide in machines' form
Purge lands with ruthless greed.
The human monsters that lives on
Their own kin they will eat.
Crops that serve their money lust
And buildings that stand tall.
Destroy what nature's given us
Make cannibals of us all.
A world that's run by selfish swines,
Corrupt and filled with lies.

The truth they bend and intertwine
All is money in their eyes.

Death is closer than we think
If we don't try to change.
The whole world in extinction's brink
Our forests must be saved.
We should learn how to coexist
And conserve what we must.
If not, our world will fade to mist
And be engulfed in dust.
Destroy all of your greedful hate
With love for mother earth.
The future in our hand's been laid
Preventing the great dearth.

Reward Of My Patience

by Faraz

Who knew that the reward of my patience shall be so exquisite
Just like a Trance of spring in winter. A hope in darkness
A fairy entered, lightning up the horizons of my dull life
She taught me how to write so that I could describe her, day and night

All my emotions, thoughts and passions
Recite a tale of her magnificence
My pen write the words which are supposed to be uttered by lips
In an ink filled with love capturing memories of this lovely life

In the alignment of stars, I see her face half hidden behind a transparent veil
At dawn, the birds and the moon sing the orchestra of our beautiful tale
Her smile is what gives strength to this broken heart of mine
She taught me how to be in love so that I perceive everything as bright

Deep in her love, I admire her everyday by considering it as my duty
My phrases are nothing more than a vague attempt to define the glory of her

beauty
Just like the keys of a piano, each word enlisting her enchantment on a higher
note
There are a myriad poems on her where each line sings a unique song

Her eyes sparkle like diamonds in drunken night
And Her face radiates a glow which would put the moon to shame
It is as if a magician has casted a spell of elegance over her
And her body appears to be the masterpiece of a famous artist

Her voice resonates deep within me
Her loyalty stands by me in my darkest days
Her mere presence is the peace of my heart
She taught me how to be free so that nature could show mercy on me

How my heart desires to never put an end to this love
If I had the power to create a world it would have been of mine and hers
A love story of two souls destined to be together
In my private Universe, I would be Romeo and she my Juliet

To Believe

by Delores Allen

To believe-
is believing a
rain drop can impregnant
a seed to burst into
this world - fully radiant
a gift from
mother nature's womb.

To believe-
is believing that one
man can change
the world, his thoughts,
his actions, his words,
blending into our
hearts and minds

that outside
of damnation there
is a better life.

To believe-
is taking in all the
pain, hurt, and burdens
one carries, and make
this world a better
place for our young.

Do you believe ?

Wings Of A Sacred Bird

by Aram Sarian

High amidst the heavens a sweet song was sung
a harmonious melody of a chosen one,
wings flapping with a galactic flow
a sacred bird the universe bestowed,
high and mighty it swayed with nothing to prove
but to be amongst the stars at high altitudes,
seemed from within it had found it's truth
a glorious bird of such magnitudes,
it shined it's light with brilliance down to earth
in hopes other birds would be encouraged,
sacred hymns it sung with a universal drift
that deep within we are all high flyers with a verse to give,
the eagles looked upward dazzled by it's wings
in awe and inspired by the freedom it breathes,
chills flowed through there spinal chords by the song it sings
that anything was possible if we rise above the impossibilities,
riding cosmic currents of destiny
it seemed one with the winds as it swayed majestically,
the heights of it's gaze seemed out of reach
yet there seemed to be a message this bird had to teach,
gloriously it flowed illuminating Triumph
to sacred heights it rose and rose above,
it seemed prophetic that it was one of a kind

radiant in color and royally divine,
other birds flocked to hear it's song
and found there wings too were Golden all along,
it was an orchestra of life that inspires and unites
together they became the Thunderbirds of epic heights,
the vultures gathered eager to consume
but they were wingless destined for doom,

Legend has it this day would come, the music would be heard
and so these are the destined Wings Of A Sacred Bird

Palo Santo Meditations

by Aram Sarian

Truth is you become you're environment
a flicker of fire, the Holy smoke transcends all illusions, and I rise above it,
a purified mind a purified spirit
a purified spirit a dignified realist,
I meditate and my light body energy magnifies
raising my conscience to glorious heights,
I AM one with the heavens universally conscious
Immortalized, an exalted maverick,
though the clock ticks my I AM presence always remains
my stoic buddhic nature burns outward with holy flames,
I empty my mind and feel the Light Of Truth
and see that the God within is infinite and absolute,
through the quiet stillness of my heart I illuminate the sacred fire
and a roaring blaze of life transpires,
as the darkness dissipates I see that I AM of the source
high above my thoughts in full zen mode,
my spinal chord electrifies
feeding my soul, ascending with greater sight,
reawakening a purified baptism of my third eye
the Kundalini resuscitates the true life,
understanding energy I hack the frequency
glorious tunes lift my spirit towards ecstasy,
as the Palo Santo enriches my senses
prophetic like visions intensify, I'm breathless,
grounded and in tuned I'm mystified
these sacred universal nights got me on the High Rise,

the light magnifies
as I enter the cosmic gates of the heavenly skies,
my aura catches fire radiating other worldly lights
reconnecting me to my divine birth rights,
they say home is where your heart is and that is truth
and so I open my heart chakra with revolutionary amplitudes,
REVITALIZED
these deep meditations have me riding enigmatic vibes,
like Galactic Tides
the force pulls inward and a Golden Halo ignites,
the air purifies as i sanctify all dark matter
and to the winds all negative energies scatter,
a triune of light, golden, blue and pink unite
and dance to this epic force of life,

I harness the power of the breath as I close my eyes
and shine as a star on this starry night

Palo Santo Meditations

February Morning Ii

by Michelle Waters

Spring's leading light has challenged Winter's rule.

The ancient king, befouled, erupted from his early morning slumbering
And marched about his fortress
Enraged and raging.
His fury exploded against the walls,
And threats of retribution echoed throughout the halls
Against the upstart who tested the king's supremacy.

The bitter monarch,
With eyes of steel and flashing light,
Like Saul, sulking and plotting against young David,
Smacked his hands-
His arctic breath thundered his commands
With authority and showy bluster
In defense of his domain, the

Crowned Head his troops did muster.
The elements converged.
"To Arms!" did he demand.
Sleet, those skilled archers of the hardened world,
Cast frozen arrow across the battleground.
Wave upon wave, the icy weapons hurled, until
The king's nemesis turned 'round.

This day's battle went to Winter
The hoary head in fierce-like frame
His dominion did defend-
The scepter in his hand remained.
The old man's reign, now prolonged,
The young Spearhead's confidence disrupted
And denied,
For a time,
The pre-ordained.

But Winter will decline,
His rule and season come to an end.
Then Spring, the anointed heir,
To nature's throne ascend- and all
The kingdom will rejoice!

Sweet Randy

by Brian Rusch

There once was Randy, a dandy
Who got through his life eating candy
The girls loved him
Joining in wild sin
Candy staying sweet as did Randy.

The Rust Of Values

by John Lusardi

The Rust of Values

Carbon breaths
Ink less goose feathers
Blunt boys knives
Dry kisses of Girls
In ending corners
Left only with
The rust of values.

A Memory

by Seymour Roth

It didn't come in like an invading horde of Mongols astride their horses.
It came like a Siren whispering a sweet song, blowing soft winds in my ear.

The old woman sat on her frayed settee, her head resting on her Macassar
Grey hair splayed sensuously across it, teary eyes turned dreamily toward me.

The old trunk, her trunk, life's collection before her
A throne of memories, and my invitation to bore into her life.

It gave a creaking welcome as I did her gnarled-fingers beckoning me to open
it.
They framed a permission, a V for some victory that danced in her head.

I searched her glacial eyes for certitude
And she nodded approval, chin jerking forward for affirmation.

With some trepidation, the old trunk beckoned me to explore.
Its creaking lid gave a diffused meow in preparation for my exploration.

A malodorous drift of the ancient met this young mariner.

It came on a charging chariot to greet me.

The inside, Kodak moment, welcomed me
And my hands fluttered excitedly to dive into this ocean of memorabilia.

A look at the old Dame and her fingers fluttering at me--
"Continue," she cried for no one had explored her depths in an eon.

The sepia-colored photos of the ancients greeted me with their austere looks,
Bundled letters wrapped in a pink organdy, the flotsam and jetsam of life, unread,

The uncultured pearls that I draped around my neck,
The cameos in profile of a youthful, chaste being,

The trinkets that marked the progress of life's cycles.
This spelunker of this being caught in this moment

Held her life's Morse code without great tenderness
Only an acknowledgement from the grand dame who found a joy in my exploration.

A soft smile marked in a moment of a callow youth
Who seized the moment to recognize that there was a life.

Twentythird Seedbearer Psalm

by Gerald Dillenbeck

Holy EarthSpirit
is our seed bearer.

Our blue celestial universe
could lack nothing
In meadows of green sweetgrass
She enlightens repose.

Into living waters of recomposure
She bears then leads us;
There S/He revives Earth's compassioned soul.

She guides me
by polypaths of virtue
not forsaking Her sense-rooted story.

Though we pass through this gloom
doom river valley,
I fear no mountainous trauma;

Within me
your rooted integrity
and your well-seeded womb are here,
to hearten and enlighten us.

You prepare a wealth gardened table
between us
under the eyes of my predative
and hoarding enemies;

You anoint our capital driven values
with multicultural oil,
my catholic creolizing communion cup
brims cooperatively over.

Ah, how interfaith enlightenment
and empowerment pursue us,
every day and night of Earth's living systems;

My home,
the recreation of ecowomanist
re-imaged Yahweh,
As long as Earth empowerment
revolves around Sun's well-seeded Womb.

The Orange Grove

by Delice Arleen Skelly

Springtime orange grove
Fresh and fragrant blossoms bloom
Inhaling deeply
Revived by cycle of life
Caressed by playful sweet breeze.

Chomsky's NY Times Swooning

by Moji Agha

"I swoon on the NY Times Op-Ed page,
every eleven weeks or so,"
said Prof. Noam Chomsky,
in the sufi monk's (actual) dream.

Around noon of the day after the dream
Ms. Bev S. Stohl replied
to the goofy sufi's appeal for help,
with the possible meaning of the dream--and stuff,
and focused rather seriously
on the number "11" in the dream.

Citing Pythagoras, the Greek math-ilosopher
Chomsky's "guardian angel" assistant said:
[Ummm...in my sufi paraphrase]
"Spiritual messages think like numbers."
So "number 11" (a 1 that stutters)
might be reducing your dream to "number 2,"
so as to avoid being repetitive.

Could it be that she,
repeating her own dreamy "guardian angels,"
might also mean to say
that the "spiritual messages"
hidden in the NY Times Op-Ed page

are usually spread over "2" pages?

Is that why Chomsky swoons there,
repeatedly, every 11 weeks?
Did Pythagoras swoon too?

Is Noam Chomsky
a spiritually angelic repeat of Pythagoras?
(who according to totally unreliable sources,
that often "report" in the NY Times,
was the first person to own
a "number" of vibrational properties in ancient Greece.)

Shouldn't the NY Times be the one
who faints from extreme emotion [swoons]
every time Noam reminds them
of the immorality of propagandistic "reporting?"

I Will, Pursue My Dreams

by Tsokoane Mohlalane

A hankering for a well-of life,
Reminds me to focus on my dreams.
And assiduous itself, is my caliber -
That relies its origin from dedication;
Because nothing rules my mind, but the words,
I will, pursue my dreams.

Being intense about a well-to-do lifestyle,
Enthuses me to ponder on my goals.
And industrious is what reveals my progress and productivity;
Which is brought by tireless all day long day!
Because nothing encourages me, but the words,
I will, pursue my dreams.

Being ardent about that moneyed life!
Engenders me to contemplate on my professions.
And hardworking itself, is my best friend;
That keeps me me unremitting and single-minded.

Because nothing lies deep in my heart, but the words,
I will, pursue my dreams.

Our Time

by Isabel D. Catrin

Sleep to forget
Wake for another day
Letting rivers grow
Looking at the feet below
Sounds melt with ease
Creating a temporary peace
Yet fingertips burn
For yesterday won't return
For there is plenty in the sea
Yet not the one I want to see
Our time was pure
Yet timing is cruel

Joy And Sunshine

by Emanuel Carter

It was the music of Joy
by the AKA Trio,
three men from Senegal, Italy
and Brazil whose lilting play
was the gracious gift, through
kora, guitar and the softest
percussion, of the exhilarating
sound of sunshine
"Does it sound like springtime?"
she asked, "No way", I said
"Like summer?" she asked, looking
at me with a face that suggested a
simple inquiry, speaking in a voice
sounding like a morning that would
last all day
I sat for a moment listening to the

music and looking at her and then:
"Honey", I said, "It sounds more like
the way that I feel every day that I'm
living with you, not simply like the
spring or the summer or any season,
but like the enchanted, elusive essence
of grace that even sunshine, given a
chance to decide, would love
to become!

The AKA Trio is Antonio Forcione (guitar),
Seckou Keita (22-string kora) and
Adriano Adewale (percussion). Joy is their
debut album.

Languid Lover

by Angela Douglas

Maybe it's monstrous to murder
the music in my mind
Turning tunes to feathers
floating on currents of ether
like waves on whiskey seas
Black cherry bourbon and soda
sweet with heat
bubbling in my blood
converting my consciousness
reverting me to who I should be
making a mockery of my insecurity
my anguish and anxiety
as I dance alone again another night
A golden rope of hope holds me upright
for one more day
though it's beginning to fray
There's no solace in this silence
A time machine for trauma
reminding me why I am this way
I wonder what words would win you

as liquor is a languid lover
that leaves like every other

The Essence Of Life

by Sarbajit Roy

Life that flows through veins of ours ,
Flows too in every blade of grass,
Life blooms in all fragrant flowers,
And every creature that comes to pass;
The rhythms of life beat in every tree,
Life radiates from each ray of the sun,
Full of life every little bacteria be,
All life on earth is unified in one;
Life is a mirror , the spirit its grace ,
Life is vibrant ,and living is its goal ,
The beauty of the mind does life embrace,
The essence of life is the eternal soul.

Shadows Are Rather Stiff

by John Richard Anderson

Shadows are stiff
hard-edged,
all telling,
not fibbing
nor forgiving.
The mind's eye is blind
to the shadowy-side
we carry in ruck-sacks behind
our backs.
Shadows are brutally honest,
dark and gloomy,
sketches of self in outline,
that we would rather lose
'cause they can't be
colored in.

Mister Joe

by John Richard Anderson

Mister Joe, would-be muse,
jangles loose change in his pocket.
Memories jogged and garnered as he walks.
Mister Joe in contemplation,
washes, rinses and tumble dries, what pops into his head,
in hourly cycles, with riddles, jingles and rhymes.
Each wash-up, extracted, pegged, and hung up to dry,
to taunt and flap jangles for him,
for his readers, and strangers who happen to pass on by.

Mister Joe, would-be muse,
casts charms, jangles and sparkles,
to jog in the minds of his readers.
His words cast nets to trawl up memories and serendipity dips,
in the minds of his readers with word play, puzzles and twists.
The catch netted, is prodded, poked, shaken and stirred,
to inspire twinkles, sparkles, hums, aahaa's, grunts,
and perchance, nods of appreciation and delight.

Mister Joe's catch of memories, once jarred and jangled, are returned to
reader with care.
For the reader to add jangles to their pockets,
and gems to their lockets and charm bracelets.

Mister Joe, would-be muse, and his reader, now walk with jangles echoing
within.

Dance To Heaven's Gate

by Richard Scott Nicholls

From Your Very First Step
　　　　You Move To a Beat
　　　　We All Have Our Own Flow
　　　　From Our Head To Our Feet

　　　　With Rhythm and Grace
　　　　Stumbling or Smooth
　　　　Dance Makes Us Happy
　　　　When We Move

　　　　To Walk or Run
　　　　With Your Own Special Trait, Is
　　　　The Dance We All Do
　　　　To Heaven's Gate

　　　　To Dance Is To Live
　　　　To Teach Is To Give
　　　　To Perform Is To Feel
　　　　To This I Owe
　　　　What Makes Me Real

Dancing Through The Ages

by Richard Scott Nicholls

I've Danced Through Many Ages, to Many Sounds On Many Stages.
I've Prepared For Those Who've Come To Town.
I've Smiled and Leaped and Never Came Down.
I've Worn Costumes That Had Laces,
I've Spent Hours Applying Make-Up
While in Far Away Places
There's No Applause to be Found,
When The Final Curtain Comes Down..
The Silence Can Leave You Deaf,
Once The Audience Has Left.

The Theater I've Always Called My Second Home.
With Other Dancers, or On My Own.
Friends You Make While In a Show,
The Contract Ends and Off They Go.
No Matter The Circumstance,
Nothing Makes Me Happier,
Then Just To Dance. 5-6-7-8

Journey Of Thought

by Paris-Maree Boreham

The higher the hill
The better the view
When reaching the top
of wishes come true.
Hence steady your climb
and never sell short
That miracles happen
on journeys of thought.

No Crushing, Let's Ignite

by Gideon I Tukuna

(LOVE)

The same way every year
Shoes strips slightly away
A hole we're meant to cover
The Harmony in my solo witter

It's bitter, to dance lonely,
It's better to dance lovely
We sing dulcetly but differently
 without backups
Why should we wait for morn to break,
While we cast blushed glances
on each others in every darkened nights?

Hey! This our voices must merge
Our shoes should step together in array
A dance, a hole shouldn't be blank
A sweet love song must usher us with a cup of cold ice-cream in the nights of
Valentine somewhere at an outskirt.

We've fallen in the same sea of feelings
So we can still jet-land into another city of undiluted ecstasy of love.
Our love will live even in greyish hair.
'Natural love always avail itself, let's kick it ON'

Keep Waiting

by Anesto Mandizvidza

Keep waiting [lullaby essay]

Prior to my expected appalling arrival
Accept a delay necessitating my survival
Recap all hopeful wishes
Evoke undying patience species
Nest and destroy negative feelings
Trust when the seed says is fleeing.

Knives come thirsty for my blood
Eyes in tears always keep a flood
Episodes full of grief and sorrow
Pray that I see you tomorrow.

While I try to realize my goal
All is destined to benefit you
Immense forces are attack-full
Tremendous effort from me is forceful
Incarnate figures seem to set militia
Nourishing their foul aromatic herb
Gather guts and expect patiently

Drastic changes in economic atmosphere
Applaud a flop on my old plans
Insolent conditions thwart my combined efforts

Lonesome insolvency escort me to their agenda
Yielding failure for me every day!

He

by Vaishnavi Narayan

HE traced my flaws, read my tattoos
Pulled hard on my piercings
Ran his fingers through my hair
His bite marks on my neck
Next moment, HE thought of her
And walked away
But I couldn't ask him to stay
Left me like a lonely toy
In his lustful world
I was waiting for him
Though it was unfair
For a slut in love

East River Thoughts

by Nick James Vincelli

In the chaos of youth lights
        dance without exhaustion
A ballet on the river
        dissonant music in the city

An agitated psyche absorbs
        the brilliant skyline
A bridge sprawls and intimidates
        perpetual motion in the city

Visions Of A Tropical Dystopia

by Nick James Vincelli

Horrible blobs
crawling on the radar
threatening detonations
punctuating torpid oppression
promising a merciless deluge

Robotic insects invading
Wrathful humans devolving
Nature devouring
Order dissipating

Ambient lyrical drones
bathing the dystopic landscape
inculcating visions of an alternate world

Medicine Walk

by Aram Sarian

Down the sacred roads I go where healing is a way of life
where mother earth is the medicine, fuel for the fallen to rise,
from the mountains, to the rivers, to the birds that sing
through my beating heart I see the web that connects everything,
from the lively soil that grounds my soul
to the majestic valleys that profoundly transform,
from thoughts to visions to golden rays of light
it's the less trodden path that gives the spirit sight,
it's the heavenly skies and purified streams of life
it's the heavenly stars that humbles as it illuminates the nights,
it's a path that nourishes the mind and eyes
it's the path for the warrior that always thrives,
consuming plants for wisdom to walk righteous and wise
earth medicine from the great spirit of the infinite skies,
it's the victorious trail blazed by few

it's the ancient footsteps that lead to glorious truths,
it's a walk of novelty for universal tribes
it's a walk where nobility conquers pride,
trodding forward mind, body, and spirit unified
trodding uphill propelled by the kundalini fire,
it's the emerald forest deep within the heart
it's the inner garden of Eden where true life sparks,
It's the road to Shambhala that refines the reborn
it's the medicine walk that spiritually reforms,
it's the tonic that uplifts the conscience to mythical heights
it's the way of no way, the empty cup that expands the mind,
it's the triumphant swagger that blazes down trails
far from the lands of the meek and frail,
it's the depths where the eagles rise to soar
it's the chosen path the heavens bestowed

there's an abundant life that feeds the soul,
and it's The Medicine Walk,   of days of old

Speak The Best

by Neena J. Luke

No matter what keep speaking the best
And take the necessary steps to change
You may feel like your bad decisions
Are the reason your life is a mess
But we have all done some stupid things
We all had immature stages in our lives
Although none of them are exactly the same
We have to stay prayed up
Speak life over ourselves
And have faith that we will see better days

Luscious Wine

by Robert Ippaso

A silken drop nectar refined,
Delicious, smooth, it's taste sublime,
Worshipped and revered in times of old,
Bacchus it's God, his hand-maidens bold.

The Romans swilled, the Greeks imbibed,
The British drank, the French prescribed.
The Church just called it Christ's own blood,
Believers flowed as if by flood.

This luscious liquid as fine as honey,
The fountain not of youth but merely money,
Small price to pay for so much fun,
When it can turn a dowdy day to sun.

Clinking glasses moments shared,
The more imbibed the more is bared,
Food important or so they claim,
When as a smokescreen its main aim.

All that said let me be clear
There's a reason we choose wine not beer,
Wine is healthy, helps the heart,
Beer is fattening and so tart.

Blessed Dawn

by Regina McIntosh

This morning, as dawn lifts her head
Smiling across my future
Preparing me for the moments
Which color my heart in kindness
Soft music caressing my spirit
As it lights up the present

With gentle inspiration, faith
Brightening my thoughts
And encouraging my dreams
Bringing me hope through distress

This morning, as sun flickers to life
Laughing at the misty gray
Relaxing my anxieties and delighting
Echoes of grace as she prays
For the light to whisper praises
On the promise of a new day
Filled with new plans, new chances
Optimism which embraces
Ideas, appealing to the senses
Playing in feathery possibilities
Guiding my reflections to believe

This morning, as light breathes joy
Shining pleasure through the twinkling
Rays of enchanted warmth
Fondling bare thoughts with affection
From the poetry that flows
In vibrant richness
Through the feelings that beckon
Refreshing, reviving
Mystifying wisdom, brilliant
Emotions on the luminosity
Of sparks ignited by virtue
And sensitivity that traces
The edge of silence
Melting every defense and worry
With shafts of subtle blushing
Sunlight which haunts the night
With its insight into hearts
Who know that only God's love
Fills the sun with its radiant courage
Its dazzling luster
Satisfying every doubt
With a love that lights up the very air
Singing with praise for His blessings!

You Can Lie To Me

by George Schaefer

You can lie to me. That's okay. I'll probably figure it out and no one will really
get hurt. But you keep lying to yourself and that's really an emotional and
psychic cancer. But like a portrait of Dorian Gray in the attic, you'll keep the
deterioration hidden from view. You know the cancer is spreading but it isn't
visible so you can smile, and I can pretend. And the pain and the depression
continue and it deepens. You refuse the surgery that can remove the tumor.
And the lies just get deeper but you're only really fooling yourself and maybe
some mindless social media followers who don't care about your soul.

You can lie to me
but if you lie to yourself
the disease will spread

eating away the spirit
your internal organs first

Words Pile Up

by George Schaefer

Words
pile up
and hasten my demise
into subconscious realms
of translucid reality
and all the while
it just gets too difficult
for me to comprehend
as I listen to complaints
from the weak and wretched
as they discuss their peeves
and I not really caring
not really wanting to hear
and being too cowardly
to just walk away

One Among Billions

by Christine O'Hayre

What am I...?
A grain of sand washed along the coast
A fading star among an infinite host
A bitty spider amongst the redwood trees
A speck of dust carried by the summer breeze
A tiny drop of rain amidst a raging storm
A wee kernel of golden corn
A penny in a wishing fountain
A pebble on a snowy mountain
A single blade of grass in a field of dreams
A pink salmon egg in the mountain streams
A tale out of thousands told
A single petal from a marigold
A snowflake melting in the bright sun rays
A little spark among a fiery blaze
A simple person among billions
...Yet I am loved

In His Last Breath

by Shardoolsen Jadhav

A distant wail, a spirit cried
"Too short a life! , too short a life!"
A piercing sound in the dead of night
"Too short a life! , too short a life!"

My candle lit to seek the sight
I leaned at the sill to look outside
He looked at me straight, looked in my eyes,
" Too short a life! , too short a life!"

Clad in black and made in bone
His eyes like jewels no man had known

A scythe in hand perfectly honed
He stood determined, he stood alone

I knew him from the books and lore
A figure that men and women abhorred
The final vision for those that go,
An appointment kept and never ignored.

" Is it I, who you seek?" To him I asked
Knowing at heart, the reapers task
He nodded yes, my time had passed
Now any breath would be my last

Give me a moment, I said to him
Let me remember my friends, my kin
remember my righteousness, remember my sin
Let me remember who I have been

He stood his ground, I closed my eyes
A saw a man that I had left behind...
A man who loved and lived a life
And not just toiled for food and wine

I saw a love that Walked away
When the mission of life was debts to pay
I saw my days they all looked the same
A promising journey that turned mundane

I heard their words of wise advice
In being like the others I took great pride
The way of the world to all applies
I never saw the truth, behind their lies.

And now I stood there, and the end of the line
Lamenting the lost opportunity of time
The scythe struck as I opened my eyes
As my spirit cried, "Too short a life, too short a life"

Wife Of My Youth

by Joseph Babatunde

Like a new thirst in the desert
My heart was soaked in thoughts and desires
Dominating was the longing to be held
Held in ecstasy, fondled in the embrace of another

Despite several invasions, tramplings and happenings
Faith smiled and there came the presence of a silver-line
A beauty I can call mine
A sprout of rose to lace my horrors

Smiles with no word said
Moments of joy saturated with affections
Days of fantasies when the little one in me tickled in happiness
Playing on the strings of lightening, singing in the rain

A time when stars fondled my mind
And my heart laid on the bed of cares
No one could be this to me
No other, except my wife.

Son

by Richard A Martin Jr MD

Across the miles
A man moves in space
To reunite with his link...
To the future.

The child struggles against the specter of sleep.
He feels the excitement of being reunited, almost succumbing to the dark
cloak of slumber...
He makes it, tho.

The father, with a curious combination scent of sweat, Lagerfeld, smoke and fabric softener
Enters the room.

The child, eyelids heavier than lead,
Rushes forward.
He grabs his DNA link
At the knees...hugging hard...hugging long.

"I love you Dad", his tiny voice said.
"I stayed up late just to see you!"
The father grabbed him by the armpits,
And pressed the child's face against his wiry beard.

And a kiss sealed the transaction.
A pure and essential show of love...
A love that transcends all love...
The love between this father and son...

And the child slept the sleep of peace.

Cold Wounds That Burn And Illuminate The Path

by Madhavi Praveen

Gathering around the blues of life,
Grey clouds signifying defeat and strife.
Thunder and lightning, synonymous with the struggle long.
Fire within burning like the determination strong.

Cold rain pouring on the wounds that burn,
Soothing within, yet kindling the fire, the fire to learn.
The lessons of life and scars of fights,
Bearing witness to your strength.
Evolving, building up and retaining your trait clement.

As the rain satiates the thirst of the Earth,
The penchant for learning quenches my yearning for growth.

The rain of wisdom blooming in my soul.
Taking me towards the light from the dark black hole.

The River

by Janice Thompson

She drapes along the valley like an evening stole
As if let loose to waft from some angelic hand
To move along the meadow in soft curves and folds
As if mere ornament upon the verdant land.

She undulates in rhythm over beds of stone
And ripples playfully with every touch of breeze
Then having spent her course in movements long and slow
She slips into a wood to hide among the trees.

Would that I too were quite so languidly disposed,
So unencumbered by life's various terrain
Allowing obstacles to teach me manifold
Without resistance and devoid of all complaint.

Beguiling Spirits

by Janice Thompson

I know of their enchantments
The longings they inspire
Of promised inhibitions
And kindling desire.

Constrained by walls which glimmer
Opaque or dim or clear
Sweet barely muted whispers
Succumb the naked ear.

A hand upon the vessel
The stopper freed at last
A casual undulation

Poured neat into the glass.

Embracing sips then swallows
Well finished is the fight
Enveloped by the liquor
Of amber, red, or white.

Tethers

by Janice Thompson

I stole upon a lusty wind
To gain the Summer sky.
A slender tail
Sustained me well
As I began to climb.

Uplifted to fantastic heights
Yet higher still I sought
But, lo, my frame
Could nothing gain
No matter how I fought.

For from below the tether bold,
A simple length of string,
Restrains my urge
And every surge
Else I would wander free.

A snap and I am reeling hard,
Convulsively I spin.
Untethered I
Am wielded by
A juggernaut of wind.

Oh would that I were tethered now,
Complicit with the breeze.
It's where I ought
To be and not
Entangled in these trees.

Inescapable Captors Of Solid Information

by Bongani Zungu

"The place of cure of the soul."

Millions, clasped beyond Minerva's hall,
While inquisitive and confident hard.
Headed down towards different thoughts;
To giant collections, questions, borders strange.

There stood content's house of three.
In front, moved in cylindrical copyrights,
In round pegs and liquid language totems.

Then the first, unsettled pages in riddles,
In spirals, springs, learning machines.
To the second, summers and archived plans.
Thriving in the boundary walls.

Near the citizens, subjects, preservers,
Near the propagative inner rims of
Scholars, thinkers and doers,
Past a fire's waging gaze.

The formats walk up the manuscripts,
Cross, some ease and model's
Algorithmic snapping patents.
The quenching value of such!

Models and catalogue's emphasis
Builds the architecture's exceptional core.
The conscious modular maps, and
The abstract granularity of it all.

The rail crawls on these sheets and
illustrated diagrams and documents.
In such, roams bound kilometres in bronze,
and softens the stained glass piazza.

The lengths of the worded path evolve,
On the dotted strings, signs:
Librarians, Poets, Authors,
Publishers and Students, the oath;
"Seek knowledge from the cradle
to the library to the grave."

Bunny Trails

by Karina Gibbs

bare footed,
I roam through a field of bunny tails
gentle steps left behind in their path,
tell the story of my trail

open space is wide enough,
to hold onto what I keep inside
I can let go of what's killing me slow,
and give birth again to what died

peace rides within fading clouds
looking up towards a blue hour sky,
freedom seems so close as
white wings glide by

Cove Blue

by C. David Collins

Cold water music
pond nymphs skate soft chord ripples
fireflys flash dance
lily pad tables for two
Catfish play hooky from school

Morning Splendor

by Aida G. Roque

St Jones River, gently flowing,
wild geese gently ride with the breeze.
A quacking sound of excitement at the
break of dawn, gently breaks the drip
of a slow-motion dew.

Soft pink sky, silhouette the golden
rays, greeting the morning splendor...
as the sun radiantly raise. An ode to
a glowing dawn, a breathtaking sight...
and I moan.

Inhaling the fresh spray of a new day,
from fragrance of wild flowers,
gracing the river bank in rainbow hues.
My soul surrender and mesmerize the
glorious natures, I muse.

The serenity of the natural landscape
is hypnotic to my sight. Ahh...
my spirit is rejoicing, at peace with
the gentle water, cascading through
the river rocks, in slow pace.

I felt alive, mellifluous sound, soothe my skin...
I began to dance with the breeze. I captured
a blessed moment of bliss, my monotonous
day, stimulate. The serene ambience of nature,
a soul-searching pleasures.

Twenty Years Of Terror

by FRANKLIN PRICE

On nine one one, back in oh one, the tall twin towers fell.
Downed by Mid-Eastern terrorists who brought us living hell.
Using two hijacked airliners, full of passengers and all,
Downed the towers in Manhattan, flew into them, made them fall.

There were two other missions on that nine – eleven day.
As the towers crashed into the earth, they were both well on their way.
One slammed into the Pentagon, our major military site.
Also flown by terrorists in their suicidal flight.

Last one headed for the White House, that's what many people say.
Heroes stopped that mission, in a PA field that day.
The USA, surprise attacked, not by some country we could fight,
But by suicidal terrorists who would take us into night.

Twenty years of US darkness were then entered by those deeds.
Growing on the fields of history are many governmental weeds.
Osama Bin was Seal Team killed, was supposedly the man.
The end of it is not yet here, though we've left Afghanistan.

The terrorists have had their way, now the leaders of that land.
Striving for some recognition. Are we marching to their band?
We are not now, the who we were, when those tall twin towers fell.
We do our best, to beat ourselves, turning our Heaven into Hell.

Representatives in Washington don't give a damn about the rest.
They're directed by the super rich, don't pass the democratic test.
It's time that We the People bring ourselves into the light.
Join our hands and work together, or it will be, forever night.

World Of Walls

by Samia Ali Salama

Mother, mother, tell me please, the way it used to be
When people all around the world once lived in harmony
Tell me how they looked and dressed, were they short or tall
Tell me of the fun you had before they built the wall

Do you think your friend's the same as in the photograph
The faded one you carry, where you and she both laugh
Did the children play our games when we were still all friends
Could there not have been a way, for all to make amends

Was their music much like ours, can you recall a tune
And how you danced together beneath the giant moon
Tell me how they cooked their foods, the spices that they used
The exotic taste you loved when all the flavors fused

And how about their languages, the sounds that their words made
Do you still remember or did they sadly fade
Fear and anger built the walls of massive steel and stone
They said we would be better, divided and alone

But now there's a consensus that's spreading through the land
That all the people, everywhere, are going to take a stand
So mother please, do not be sad, the talk around the town
From all the people, everywhere, the walls are coming down

Innocent Eyes

by Harriet Davis

Eyes watching me, are also watching you
Absorbing their environment
Whatever may be true

Vision clearly focused

Thru their innocent eyes
Allows them insight
That very rarely lies

Mimicking most behavior
Of what they hear and see
Playing to their surroundings
Is almost a guarantee

Be mindful of your actions
What you say and do
Behavior of your children
Are a clear reflection of you

    BECAUSE

Eyes watching me, are also watching you

Four Three Two One

by Kevin Lawrence

Four, three, two, one, it's all clover,
Green, black and blue,
All the same to you.

Beer, whiskey, cake, juice-bar drink
Open a cup O' Kidney I think.
Pour me a tall one, leaf it all to me,
Clover-mint-sprout, rag weed invite.

Herbal tax on highs
Lows lax on thighs.

Hang from the watermelon rafters.
Four, three, two, one...
Let's all run for cover.

Blacken The Charcoal

by Thresha Reese

Draw the embers into the wood
Stroke it like it's a three-legged stool
Blacken the charcoal of a dying fire
Fasten it to a sun swelling brighter
The object is to lick the smoking flame
Soberly thoughtful to call out His name

Should a flash shine brilliantly
With a radiant outburst of joy hotly
All about warming the frigid darkness
The ocean in which stars are as jellyfish
Will appear to the seers as Lumiere
Clearly my dear it's an Austral Hell

Toss another log into the house of Hades
Balance it on your heaven party gate
Strum the drum to conjure up the worship
The song that worms the hawthorn brush
Into its strip tease yank along

Moon moss to heavy metal music loudly
Pound the ditty along to His shouting
The anthem of a wench's wrenching
The diddly of concerted celestial voicings
Heard charring with a fire from within
The product of an incandescent spell

See that which is bright always rises twice
Conditions darken before they go black
Then Hell behaves with new eyes
And the story is told in pantomime
About a joy and how it lingered a lifetime

You, The Generic Addressee Sat

by Rebecca Fall

I

you, the Generic Addressee sat
cruising the edge of the Atom's motorway,
embodied embry- all lazy Saturday.

-o; and wreaking; y-
our bones creaking
in the radon glow of halogen What-Not;
for you are anon to be Knameless,
née born to be Known,
you weary dissident of Camelot.

and turning your cheek from the dawn of Ha-Shavuot,
you reclined in the fuzz of Sigmund Atom Room,
spent Saturday skulking the wrailings of your mother's womb,

relearning moral relativism,
soon to be anon.

II

waited hours for you, did Godot,
and it was God-Awful, he says, says he saw you wraise your hands to pray
for Lite-Emitting-Diode, Viet Pho,
etc., and Aspirin-in-Camelot.

still, you the Generic Addressee blankly sat
in-ignorance of Elijah, who all Saturday afternoon
leant twisted in your doorway 'til the waking moon;
while ants made haste on wrotten roads,
and you cried to Be-Begot.

The Iron Lung, Fear Transcendence

by Janis Medders Thompson

These days, when I look at you
Fear transcends
Your heaviness
Your electric breathing
Your encompassing total body
You, the iron lung
Yes, now these days
Fear strikes out
against the childhood horrors
The endless nights of lone imaginings
The images that a fifties child bears
deep within the mind to get vaccinated.
You're not alive and
You're not after me, climbing my steps as you pant and
Respire
To enclose me

But you are here
Still
Taken in form but not fashion
Fear lurks within the covid halls of your anatomy
A journey in final dependency
That breathes so diligently for this centuries'
Infirmed

Nothing Is Timeless And Truly Enduring

by Andrew Crisci

Aspens and oaks embellish the dense forest
distant from the suburbia's loud noises,
all remains unchanged in such a wilderness;
I gaze at swollen clouds reaping a storm,
nobody runs to seek shelter, all creatures stay put...

who said they don't have rules and don't live by a norm?

Yesterday brightness led to wonderful sights:
shrieking geese soared the windless skies,
Monarch butterflies twittered and flapped freely
while the returning hummingbirds warbled happily!

The shadowy night advances with the pace of raccoons,
one is completely subdued by the sense of their slowness,
do our feet straddle as theirs...on those dark paths of May?
They always rely on moonlight to catch their unsuspicious prey!

I was hoping to spot the pale face of the wandering moon,
and not erase this smile from the cheeks that seek sympathy;
so incredible are the pitiful looks of cooing hawks mostly maroon,
if we seek the same thing they seek, we must show empathy!

Open spaces reveal huge meadows with drowsy flowers,
I follow the sparkling midnight stars moving along without rush
in search of a fearful moon hiding behind the pine groves;
not all sleep placidly, the cry of a woodpecker raises from a bush!

I can make a profound observation while wandering aimlessly:
nothing is timeless and truly enduring, days flee quicker than memory;
we're fragile human beings subjected to mercy in times of calamity...
our character is far from perfect, and not nearly close to godly!

The Rooster And The Peacock

by Vidya Pandarinath

On a lower branch of a crooked mango tree ,
Flapping wings and shining tail , in charge
Perched the happy rooster steady and free,
Intending to view his surroundings at large ,
And announced sharp : cock- a- doodle - doo :
' Know that after all the world is mine too '.

From the cloudy grey sky , like an alien
Descended a peacock in all blue and green ,
Jiggling crest and dangling super-tail in wont mien

And in proud stance began afresh to preen ,
Intimidating the little aborigine with a scream
Aloud to defy all and claim to be supreme

Minutes lapsed before the ice was broken
As the intruder in a half- friendly way said ,
Poising : " Of what entity are you a token..
" Your feathers are but greenish black and red ;
" Yet is there pride in quarrels and crowing vanity ,
" To end up as a delicacy for the humanity " .

The other lost his temper and did thus retort :
' Perhaps you know not how they relish
' Even their drinks , naming my tail smart ;
'And more , their menu we do, forever replenish ;
'For sporting too ,each kills the other with spur ,
' Truly a cringing thing to shame and abhor ' .

Amused , the artiste with the left foot
Straightened the talons and popped down in style
And as the clouds became heavy and acute ,
With feathers blue, green and brown, the while ,
Shining in full bloom and span, danced: a spell !
Rhythm, quiver and numerous eyes - a marvel !

Thus went the rival feats of the fowls twain
While from behind the thick foliage unseen ,
A cuckoo began its sweet song in pitched strain
To match the mood and melody - abstract and keen ;
Somewhere in the distance the grey clouds began
To jump down in drizzles and droplets to scan .

Fibro Strong

by Paula Rowlands

It takes strength, day and night
to tolerate pain, the Fibro fight
the muscle aches, damn brain fog
total exhaustion, stiff as a log
headaches, sciatica, insomnia and more
tinnitus, vertigo, and stress galore
nerve pain and spasms, when does it end
this Fibromyalgia needs to mend
I don't look sick, but my struggle is real
I'm quite often hot, when cold you feel
The ride never ends, but I am strong
Chronic pains no joke, but I will go on.

The Crow

by Shazeed Ahmed

I was admiring nature in awe and delight
Looking up the sky in a broad daylight
When all of a sudden a crow came to sight
Hovering near me quite dark and bright
At once it stirred me to reflect on the bird
Appreciate the facts that were unheard
The caws of crows break the dawn
Creating commotion in every lawn
And its search and devour of leftover
Gives the earth appositely a fresh cover
Thus crows maintain ecological balance
For benefit of mankind on freelance
Crows eat carrion for their fill
As they are preordained not to kill
They carry seeds of fruits and flowers
To spread across the earth as it lowers
Thus it acts as an agent of pollination
Ordained by nature for generation

Crows are intelligent and vigilant
Nothing escapes it that is significant
Watchful of the movements of intruders
And those who are deemed as predators
Verily makes loud strident noise to warn
The members of its clan to take a turn
Crows often hold planned meetings
With several members in the sitting
For crucial decisions on the matters
Of key importance with their chatters
And occasionally gang up together
Chasing birds who are much bigger
Among the positives there are many
Crow stands for the destiny of creation
And as power of insight with resolution
Among the negative, the perception vary
It is the sign of mischief and trickster
And further of dark witchcraft rather
Crow has the ability of knowing
The changes of life and death in offing
As a harbinger of changes in the annals
Of life mysteries and the supernatural
Its power as totem and spirit guide
Gives support in the human strides
Crow is monogamous with veracity
And stands for faithful love in reality
Admiring these qualities of the crow
Got conceited with a raised eyebrow
And as I realised these noble virtues
I got captivated with nature's cues

Traveling With God

by Robert Ippaso

A colleague asked "Are you a Christian"?
Implying if I practice my religion every day?
What a topic, subtly graphic,
How to answer, what to say?

A moral trap to utter "Yes",
'Thou shalt not lie' jumping instantly to mind,
Should I now smile, force him to guess
Not showing I'm so clearly in a bind?

If I say "No", what will he think,
I'm not the man he'd hoped I'd be?
My brain a jumble, options sink,
My instinct quickly turn and flee.

At this point you may well ask
Whatever did you choose to do?
I swallowed hard, reviewed the task
Began to think the problem through.

Do I believe, yes in my way,
But maybe not according to 'The Book',
Other's held views never did sway,
Most caring little how they feel, just how they look.

With that all said I held his stare,
And uttered this one simple phrase:
There's but one God which we all share
With Him I'll travel life's strange maze.

Gustavo's Rite

by Ed Ahern

He walked onto the harbor beach at sunset,
planting a small net on a pole like a guidon,
and setting soiled cloth bags around it.
Alone on the beach he began his dance.
Mismatched clothes flapping, he swayed,
then paced, then crouched to pat the sand
into a crescent, then stepped back and back,
dug sand by hand, finding black things
and tossing them into a jumbled pile.
He stepped easily, as if riding waves,
moving in erose shapes only he knew.
Then he gathered net and bags and left,

not glancing back at the cairn
of burnt wood and asphalt fragments.

All this I watched from a restaurant deck,
and had to ask the waiter about him.
"Gustavo," he said, shrugging, "a local character."
I nodded but kept silent, recalling that morning
walking another beach, trying to feel profound.

Repent Your Fears For Soul Will Heal

by Roger A. Pautan, Jr.

Sun rises when stars reveal
repent your fears for soul will heal
Flatter naive of naked art,
a land of flocks not for your heart
Your noble life will soon retire
Beware of wings as feathers fly.
Better frump than frozen sin,
arise and shine and never win.
Repent you ears for soul will heal
Confess you name and act for real
Threshold shall on, humbly hold
Before your life will be too old
Repent your fears for soul will heal.

Lost Property

by Virginia Betts

If I collected all the lost keys –
the ones on rings, or chains,
that drop into drains,
unclaimed,
and squat there,
sequestered out of sight,
rusting behind bars,
far below blue sky,

in dank, stale beds,
just beyond light;

all the buttons, hanging by a thread,
that fall, unnoticed,
and fag-ends, and bits of cotton gone astray;
credit cards,
slipped slyly from shallow pockets;
lipstick, abandoned by a sink-side;
drawing pins and tacks that nestle in soft pile
poised to pounce,
and pierce the flesh of hand or foot

like nails,
evading hammers,
spiraling from empty shelves
dropped down loudly
to swearing curses;
under sofas, between cracks,
rogue staples worked free,
sending loose leaves
scattered to the wind;

If I could gather these,
place winking silver coins
beside the rest;
create small change;
collect them in a shiny tin;

then I might thread the needle,
mend the holes,
pay my debts,
unlock all the doors,
and let the world back in.

Tantrum

by Barbara P. Peckham

The wind is having a tantrum.
It whines and screams and
Howls around the house,
Tearing at the shingles,
Whacking the roof with branches,
Blowing porch chairs into a corner,
A loose cushion into a puddle
On the next block over.
It throws the recycle bin
Into the raspberry bushes
So cans and bottles litter the yard.
It sends trash can covers
Skittering across the road
To land against the fence.
It snaps tree limbs like pick-up sticks
And angrily summons the rain
To slash against the windows
With little icy pellets and
Drive water in under the sill
To form a puddle on the floor.
Probably tomorrow it will clear,
And we'll all go outside
To clean up the debris.
But the mischievous, childish wind
Will have the last laugh -
Because who can punish the wind
For the mess it made!

An English Sonnet Of Adoration

by Warren Oscar M'Baht

Thy countenance behooves what I adore
The sun is dim beside your smile and glow
I see things in you never seen before
You make my heart beat anything but slow

Your feet they float on surface where we walk
Your clothing wafts like mist above the ground
I look at you and find it hard to talk
My voice does not give forth the slightest sound

I see your hand and wonder does it call
Or is it just to drive me far away
Your hair, is as is for a summers ball
I have the will, I ask show me the way

I contemplate the way to make you mine
I may need help to get me past the line

The Female And The Cross

by janine lever

I have borne children
Who kick and climb and some who lay
Along my branches like a sleepy panther
Watching for prey
Some curl inside my womb
Whilst eating an iced creamy foam
Hiding from parents who say
It's time to go home
Seniors walk by and comment
On my outstretched arms
Usually the female, the boss
Who nonchalantly, in passing remarks
That they are like a cross.

And here I stand old wrinkled and worn
Lightening-struck and fingers torn
But I am still here bearing children
And always will do
My roots travelled to start my children anew
For I have lived two hundred years
I have seen the Lords and the Ladies
The grooms and the scullery dears
And I will bear children when all now are gone
For my reason to live is
To go on and on.

Dad, Where's Your Cape

by Tony Staples

You're my dad and you're my hero,
the other kids dads just amount to zero.
I copy you cos you're my idol,
you're the best and have no rival.
When I'm asleep you're probably saving humanity,
yet in you there's no sign of vanity.
I've looked under the bed, to see if it's there,
I need to fly to see if I dare.
You know to me you're no fake,
so tell me dad, where's your cape?

Silver Paradise

by Pathan Nuzhat

Silver blanket on the ground below,
Lighten up the darkness with gentle glow.

Children's heart are full of desire,
Grandparents gathered around the fire.

Frozen pieces of ice floats in air,
Crystal flakes started falling in paire.

Waving, dancing, happily coming down,
The sky looks like fairy in silver gown.

Everything is enclosed with winter white,
I fall in love with this precious sight.

Dahlia is now about to bloom,
And night is beautiful with full moon.

Weather is cool and mornings are foggy,
I enjoyed it while walking with my doggy.

Dust on face create a chill,
As we slide down from the hill.

Welcoming winter with favourite apple pie,
It's time to say rain, a goodbye.

And now the ground is full of icy sand,
December welcomes a paradise land.

Shield Of Truth

by Damian Cranney

I am lost in the darkness,
Blind to the light,
Struggling to find my way,
in this stygian night.

I know that there is somewhere,
A place prepared for me,
But my wanderings have not revealed,
What my destiny will be,

The world is spinning freely,
There is no one at the helm,
Gyrating wildly like a top,
Into a darker realm

Send someone to guide me,
Is heaven that far away?
Where is my guardian angel,
To teach me how to pray.

If there is a God? then show me,
Let me see his face,
Give me understanding,
Help me moderate my pace.

I saw the sun this morning,
It warmed my heart to see,
A new day now was dawning.
With the freedom to be free.

Truth is all that matters,
In that you must not yield,
Keep it always by your side,
And it will be your shield.

Moments

by Dexter Greener

What is a moment of your life?
Is this moment filled with insight?
Is this the moment for us to live?
Can we magically love, and be ready to give?
Can the colors of nature be of wonder?
When you sing with heart, is it lovely to ponder?
When you radiantly dance in the rain.
Does this moment shed your frightful pain?
Our brother will be dancing with you, to lighten your heart.
To cherish the moment of his presence when you part.
The moment of this day begins with beautiful rays of the sun.
Remember its rising when our father gave his son.
We sit on a bench and contemplate this moment of the day.
As the twilight begins to unfold the wind, and the trees begin to sway.
A lovely person in this moment has captured your smile of love.
Your heart sings in the moment of joy, as you fly like a dove.

You here the coo from your beautiful wide eyed baby girl.
As she dances into your heart and gives a memorable twirl.
You hold on to the hand of your dying soul mate.
Knowing that at this moment she is with our father of faith.
Life is a journey of moments that we treasure.
For these moments we always cherish without measure.

Daily Conversations

by John A'hern

Conversations, on a daily basis
Your own voice surrounded in oasis
Talk to yourself, a daily happening
Older age the reason offered.

Standing still, minding one's own business
Overheard conversations, questions, answers
Mobile phones shatter the sound waves
Eyes down not paying attention
Constant scrolling, thrill of the moment

Media news thrust upon us
Gather in groups, social distance
Chatter surrounds us, some absurd
Nodding, smiling, becoming a nerd
Hope that subjects do not ignite

Spirits are low, worrying galore
Watching, waiting, character testing
Older ones on the front line
Standing in front of them, carers that shine

Trust is tested, time after time
Walls erected around those in twilight
Faces in windows of those we know
The pain of missing you so hard to share

Hands pressed against glass
Blowing kisses hard and fast
Hands are waving, goodbyes are taken

Tomorrow waits for those not chosen.

Father, You Believed

by Mystery Shadow Musician

Father, you believed
Never let me bleed
Helped me in my grief
Helped me in my need

Never let me down
Wish you were around
Walking through this town
You're nowhere to be found

Dad, I love you so

Father you believed
Never let me bleed
Always took my side
Always saved my life

Walking through this town
You're nowhere to be found

Dad I love you so

All your life
You gave more than you got
All your life
You tried to give me what
You never had
When you were growing up
All your life
I never showed you enough

Love

God keep him warm

When the winds blow

Dad I love you so

Dad

If I Could Divide The Smell Of Flowers

by Mystery Shadow Musician

If I could divide the smell of flowers
I'd send some to the falsely charged
Locked in prison cells
Send some to the lonely seniors
Trapped in apartment hells

Send some to the weary miners
Sweating beneath the ground
Send some to the invisible people
Hauling our garbage round

Some answers in life are so easy
Like zero plus zero is none
But how do we divide the smell of flowers
So their fragrance is shared by everyone?

If I could divide the smell of flowers
I'd pass some to the frightened animals
Caged against their wills
Pass some to the dying birds
Choking on oil spills

Pass some to the angry kids
Sniffing up airplane glue
Pass some to the crying widow
Missing the Love she knew

Some answers in life are so easy
Like zero plus zero is none
But how do we divide the smell of flowers
So their fragrance is shared by everyone?

If I could divide the smell of flowers
Then you'd always have your share
If I could divide the smell of flowers
There'd be sweetness around you

Everywhere...

The Mentor

by Mystery Shadow Musician

In dreams I appear and take her
Down a path she dares not wander
In a town beset by plunder
I shake her blood and bone

In dreams she asks my guidance
How to live in holy silence
Beyond the anger of her father
Enrich her mind and soul

Hold me inside all the night
Your leader's your baby
Hold me inside all the night
Your teacher loves you crazy

In dreams she feels me beside her
As I stoke her female fire
In a world that feels so lonely
I fill her need and hope

In dreams I appear and take her
On wings of heaven's power
Beyond tears that stain her pillow
She takes my love and poem.

Hold me inside all the night
Your leader's your baby
Hold me inside all the night

Your teacher loves you crazy

Hold me

Secrets

by Sarah Stein

hidden
and kept
from others
like skeletons
inside of
a closet
a conundrum
tears down
relationships
burden on minds
emotional pain
stress and anxiety
physical consequences
trust
and honestly
relieves you of
the deepest, darkest of
SECRETS

They Said Wonderful Things

by Richard A Martin Jr MD

We sat at the Rehearsal Dinner for my Son and his beautiful bride-to-be.
After the food and desserts and coffee,
It came time to raise our glasses.

We had already gone through the awkwardness
Of special accommodations
Of meetings with people who had been at odds with us over the years.

But when it came time to toast the groom

They said wonderful things.
I was silent, in listening mode.

I had my toast in my heart.
A toast of thanksgiving for all the mercy he had shown me
Over the years.

I hadn't been the best father
Treading water just to keep myself
Afloat - above water.

But...that mewling, pink, naked person
That I was the first to hold
Was always someone I would have taken a bullet for.

Despite my ineffectiveness
He'd grown into a fine man
With talent and a spirit of fire.

There were many remembrances that I heard
In other tongues than my own
But bearing resemblances to my own experiences.

My heart soared like an Eagle
I took some credit for the "him" he had become.
They said wonderful things.

Rain Storm

by Catherine Townsend

The darkest days
amazed
the cloud is thick
the winter months seem long
I cry to God above.

Alone, with faith to see me through
another day to live
although the trials and tests are hard

I pull through and keep the smiles
as times go by
another surprise.

A pile of lies
storms and rain
followed by high winds
a will to survive.

As the storms passed over
the sun has shine
another day as I last.

Thankful and grateful
a time to rewind, a renewal of the mind
rejoicing with praise
all others are amazed.

The heavy wind blew
the storms passed through
from the oldest to the newest
relaxation in moderation
a time of consideration.

Forgiveness through it all
rain, storm, thunder is abroad
destiny carries the journey
that time has been established
a legacy of love managed.

A Dove

by Kevin Lawrence

Have you ever seen a mourning dove
Light upon a car?
And sing so sweetly
All your grief to share?

Father passed just before dawn.

My sisters spoke to him and me on the phone.
Hours I stood upon the cool night lawn.
His comatose senses surely did hear
Songs of our love whispered softly.

As first light broke, I heard the words,
"He passed."
Into another realm where his being is free
To visit me perched upon my car.
He stayed as long as I would listen
Staring at me and singing full throated lullabies.

Now, again I remember.
Tucked into bed,
My daddy sings with me all the old tunes.

Intrepid And Uncompromised

by Tamanna Ferdous

Intrepid and uncompromised
(What Ratri has to say, Niladri also)

Dreams of life are not always met
Those are not always successful
Yet, men have the sole power to hold on to the key to wishful dreams
But, many times, those are like the one time relationship of those charity organizations
One failure shatters the inner confidence permanently
When there is no residual strength to stand up again

During those tasteless, strange and clumsy episodes of life
We need love
Intrepid and uncompromised.

Keep forgetting many things. Keep forgetting every day.
Keep forgetting oath, keep forgetting gratitude
Keep forgetting definition of love, keep forgetting living well
While walking lonely in the rain, keep forgetting the umbrella also.

Everyone needs a destination in life
Durable and strong in magnitude and enormous in hope
Where the desired mingles with the greater meaning of life.
Keep forgetting those too while walking amongst many.

When everything ends in deep darkness,
there is still a hope of sunrise,
For the hope must be a true one.

Sometimes it is only essential to forget , for the sheer necessity to live.

Forgotten Dreams

by John Read

In a silent world of forgotten dreams,
Where disappointments and heartaches lie.
A world where hopes and dreams have died
And bid their last goodbye.

In a deserted land of times gone by,
Where once we used to tread.
Like autumn's leaves from summer's dreams
Lay abandoned, cold and dead.

Those winter chills of unfulfilled dreams
Linger on the ground.
The warmth and glow have left my life
Now that you're no longer around.

In a silent world of forgotten dreams,
A place we failed to breech.
I look towards the star we wished upon
But sadly failed to reach.

At Last, My Own Love

by Ikenna Igwe

I looked, looked, and looked – but all in vinegar vain.
I searched, searched, and searched – but found no love.
So sad, so sapped and no longer feeling cerebrally certain,
You miraculously materialized – my own heaven-sent dove.

My happy heart races at the sound of your voice.
My merry mind leaps at the sight of my cherished crush.
My satisfied soul swirls at my providence-inspired choice.
My buoyant body ignites at the feel of your tender touch.

Oh my good gosh! The amorous ache...it hurts – so sweetly;
And the fragrant fire flaming within...it burns – so soothing.
My delightful desire sends round sensuous spikes – so warmly.
Leaving me wet and spent in ecstasy's prison – so enthralling.

To whom or what shall I ever dare liken you, my Maple tree?
To others, falling as one, like us – or to others that fall apart below par?
To the sun, the moon, the stars – or to all galaxy-orbiting three?
No, my diamond diadem; by all, you stand head above the highest bar.

Wash Away

by Catherine A. MacKenzie

I scrub and scrub,
trying to erase stains graveled upon my face.

Age has defined its mark,
solidified a presence in folds and furrows
raked over a once-smooth fabric now heralding me as old.

These seams line my skin,
years claimed my youth
from time I hadn't known had passed

and disappeared too fast
like thieves in the night
creeping without warning.

I smell that newness born with babes,
Oh, how it escapes me,
leaving soiled flesh in its wake.

I'm alive,
still breathing,
but it's sighs of old.

Vibrancy and youth permeate my spirit
until the mirror silently highlights worn flesh,
illuminating my face and
haunting me like a ghost
forever lurking around me.

When I peer closer, I see more yet less of me,
fragments of remaining years shadow daylight gone,
like dirt disappearing from a child's face in the rain,
innocence turned to the sky,
tongue gathering pearls.

Age is dark. Quiet. Unobtrusive. Unwelcoming.

These common threads live to capture us all.

A Diamond

by Sarah Stein

He dreams
Of eyes, and
Hair of blonde
        Special
A diamond
A twilight
In the night

Turmoil

by Amanullah Khan

Tumultuous rivers submerged the streets.
Variegated shades of humankind
Cascading, unfettered by the clouds of
Fumes from the canisters and smoke grenades.

Guards turned against the guarded with bullets.
Although rubberized to reduce impact,
But enough to hurt without piercing skin
And leaving behind a black and blue smut.

Law's knee on a black neck shut the airflow
Until he had surrendered to the knee.
People looked on from the banks in horror.
Their voices fell on rocks deaf to their pleas.

What follows depends on the strength of glue
Which has withstood the stress of centuries
Enshrined in the sacred constitution.
God bless America! And keep us free!

Memories

by Beverley Abrahams

I tuck memories into corners
Saving them for rainy days
When hope heaves
And spills like tears
Those days, those days
When light flickers into dying-light
And borrowed dreams are redemption
When faith wavers, faint as echoes
Rebounding off heartbeats
Slowed into sadness

Those days, those days
Slowing time into slow-mo
Till memories erupt like fire-flies
Filling the night sky with angel eyes

I Lost

by DIANE PERNA

When my dad called me ugly,
stupid and worthless, as that
little girl, I lost!

When my mother didn't protect
me from the cruelty and abuse
at home, I lost!

When a bad man came into my
room exposing himself, as that
little girl, I lost!

When a boyfriend blackened my
eyes and fractured my cheekbone,
I lost!

When my precious dogs, Rocky
and Brownie died in my arms,
I lost!

When a car struck me and I
suffered life altering injuries,
I lost!

When I received the call saying,
"Your mother is dead," I lost!

When I watched my loving and
honorable brother succumb
to cancer, I lost!

When my closest friend committed

suicide, I lost.

When I see the painful expression
in my son's weary eyes, I've lost.

When I realize there isn't anyone or
anything else to fight for, I say to you
one last time, I lost!

Poet's Onus

by Adrian Flett

As the child draws from mother's breast
a warn sought comforting flow
so the verses of a poet should attest
to words gathered and fealty shown.

From the nipple comes the best,
as the terrier with a bone
will tug worry work to arrest,
so is the poet with a poem.

The poet's constant effort to reveal,
by fullness of feeling in a new way
and with a fresh and different appeal,
mother's costly sacrifice always gives sway.

White House

by Amanullah Khan

Built by the tired hands
Many from far off lands
Taken away from farm and spouse
Yet they built the sacred House

A house leased for 4-year terms
Unique privilege to be confirmed

To an American deemed fit
Compassionate, patriot and have wit

Tradition is the code here
Simple decent and austere
Wisdom learnt from many battles
And a constitution sound and moral

Enshrined we were born free
It was the heartbeat of democracy
There were periods of stress
Staunchly addressed by the noblesse

Fiercely defended by the have-nots
I implore everyone to see the plots
In a national cemetery
And behold what it means to be free

Peerless

by Hannington M. Mumo

Each passing second your Love
Etches its seal on eternal slates,
Proving fleeting affections drear,
Yielding warmth that never sates.

Infinitely warmer and soothing more,
It trounces fickle throbs of mortal kiss,
Eclipsing legends' amours of nymphs
Hugged by knights into hollowed bliss.

None comparable to fabled stories
Lauding mimicking flames of yore,
It permeates envy's diamond walls;
Caressing loneliest canyons below.

Your caress's unlying promise heals
Rude adder's strikes ignorance deals,
And balms vipers' capricious stings;
Surefire cure beyond temporal flings.

1914

by Linda Milgate

When did he know it
Feeling the ebbing flow
Less and less life drifted away
In the trenches -- when did he know

Heard the frightened horses
The pounding of his heart in the last night
Retreating from life were such forces
He felt them pulling in the gray morning light

So many bodies so many cries
Medics desperate holding bandages and morphine
Dust and blood rising in the skies
The calls for mother as if pulled into a dream

As the light faded
The man next to him held his hand
Another shot and the medic waited
With a prayer that they all, each one
Would pass into a better land

Sean My Youngest Brother

by John R Fiordelisi

Just four years and
I tried to know you
To help you get through
That soul snatching venom.
Just four years of reaching
Out searching for your hand...
On any forum or phone.
Just four years of wanting so
Desperately to connect to our mother,

Through you, within your swirling art.
Just four years disconnected by a few miles
And years never knowing I had a partner
In time, in crime in so many broken ties.
Just one text to learn you breathe my
Same air, no more. Hung up in the door.
My faith says you're fixed right
For good this time.
My body can't stop grieving...
For 4,000,000 more eternities with
Your precious soul.

Windows Of The Soul

by Sherry Ann Sloan

The desire shall dance upon the black soul
Beneath the stare of leaping eyes
Opportunity dances to memorized feelings
From depth of eternal life's whirlpool

My Father

by Sandeep Kumar Mishra

My father never wasted time in taking
his kids in his lap or playing with them,
he was busy in breaking mirrors, hitting the doors
or his head against a wall or slapping his children
or abusing everyone when helplessness trapped him in
the web of poverty, illness, and unfulfilled desires

Orthodox and religionist in him
taught us all superstitions,
and made him a sage devoid of social life,
and me, almost an atheist,
He taught us good values without
letting us in his room

We had seen him write poems,

We were not part of his universe,
The world may be familiar with his work,
but we haven't read his books as
we have developed immunity to it,

As a good teacher, he changed
many schools and as an honest person,
he rarely attended any social gatherings

He didn't tell us our history or geography,
Oblivious of siblings,
locked in a closed family circle,
ignorant of our community,
we live at the borders of our social circle now

When I see any kid, I wish to be with my father,
Talk, learn and serve him but still I lack a bond,
I haven't seen him for long time
and never feel a need or pain of it

He is counting his time,
his legacy some published books
and unpublished manuscripts
lying in a store almirah,
The long gap between us stops me
to take those few steps,
It seems a long journey

Upbringing and luck shapes our life,
my father was child of his misfortune
and I am child of my father

Destiny

by Barbara P. Peckham

Don't laugh at daydreams!
That childish doodle
Scribbled on the math paper,
That drawing on the essay.

Those eyes that look out
The window and see beyond the
Teacher's understanding
Might foretell the future!

Dreams are seeds that grow
And twine into a bridge that
Ideas cross, to become the hope
Of realities yet to come.
Who imagined man could fly?
Who guessed a magnitude
Of horsepower could be contained
Beneath a metal hood?

The great designer starts
With the rough and childish
Sketches of that daydreamer
Who sees a vision past today.
The child obsessed with nature's lore
Becomes the famous botanist
Who finds a cure, in nature's
Hidden secrets, for human ills.

Beware the feverish world
That fears dreams, afraid of change,
That blindly reaches out
To stifle those who break the mold!
Hold in your palm your seeds.
Plant them in the fertile soil of thought.
Water them, feed them.
Let them grow unfettered.

For this is our tomorrow.
Without dreams, ideas, hope,
There cannot be a future!
Shrug off the disbelievers!
Smile back at those who laugh,
Prisoners in their strait-jacket minds.
Spin your dreams far out, and weave a
Gossamer and steely bridge to destiny!

The Gardener

by Frank Blacharczyk

A choir of angels danced in the heavens
The sun was shining with breaking news
The Son was rising
Shaking heaven and earth a rock it did roll
The veil was lifted the curtain torn the barrier razed
Everything changed that morn for nothing remained the same
Fame was not his game the lame could walk
Tax collectors and prostitutes were his dinner guests
Like buried seeds awaiting winter's end
with a word the dead spring to life

But flowing robes with a dark heart and false lips
their refuge was a lie...deception their hiding place*
wanting their author nailed to a cross then out of sight
His grave was a tomb the door a boulder sealed tight
Guarded like a prisoner though he was chained to death
His escape was prophesied whispered through the streets

In the morning there came a deafening silence
The soldiers nowhere in sight ran with fright
the stone to guard the dead was rolled away
Some ran to see the empty tomb but left dismayed
Angels dressed in human attire arrive
to give the breaking news still Mary wept at the sight
She saw the gardener or so she thought
Fought back tears for the tomb was vacant
The gardener must know maybe he knew
She wiped away her tears with the hem of his cloak
to see more clearly He was not the gardener

Resurrection

by Dipanwita Dey

She was born in the midnight,
hidden behind a dream curtain,
Unaware of all the odds,
Surrounded by the gloominess.
She was a girl in the land of
Patriarchy.

She was the brightest star in her sky,
She was a bird , who wasn't afraid of
Spreading her wings to fly,
She was stronger than the steel,
She was the voice of the voiceless.
She was a free spirit, a free soul in the misogynistic world.

At the dawn as the last star blinked out,
they tormented her
Trimmed her wings,
Shattered her dreams,
caged her for being the voice,
Snatched her freedom,

"How could you fly ,
How could you breath ,
How could you roam around,
How could you be the voice"....they laughed.
They thought they could make her silent,
But, they have failed,

She was a miracle, she was a warrior,
She was different than the rest,
She was the bravest girl that everyone
Knew would rise up,
The fear, weakness, hopelessness died,
Strength, power, compassion, bravery was born.

Contents By Title

by Shardoolsen Jadhav...685
Wife Of My Youth...687
    by Joseph Babatunde...687
Son...687
    by Richard A Martin Jr MD...................................687
Cold Wounds That Burn And Illuminate The Path........688
    by Madhavi Praveen...688
The River...689
    by Janice Thompson...689
Beguiling Spirits...689
    by Janice Thompson...689
Tethers..690
    by Janice Thompson...690
Inescapable Captors Of Solid Information....................691
    by Bongani Zungu...691
Bunny Trails..692
    by Karina Gibbs..692
Cove Blue..692
    by C. David Collins...692
Morning Splendor..693
    by Aida G. Roque...693
Twenty Years Of Terror..694
    by FRANKLIN PRICE...694
World Of Walls..695
    by Samia Ali Salama...695
Innocent Eyes...695
    by Harriet Davis..695
Four Three Two One...696
    by Kevin Lawrence...696
Blacken The Charcoal..697
    by Thresha Reese..697
You, The Generic Addressee Sat.....................................698
    by Rebecca Fall...698
The Iron Lung, Fear Transcendence................................699
    by Janis Medders Thompson.................................699
Nothing Is Timeless And Truly Enduring........................699
    by Andrew Crisci...699
The Rooster And The Peacock...700
    by Vidya Pandarinath...700
Fibro Strong...702
    by Paula Rowlands...702
The Crow...702
    by Shazeed Ahmed..702
Traveling With God..703
    by Robert Ippaso..703
Gustavo's Rite..704
    by Ed Ahern...704
Repent Your Fears For Soul Will Heal.............................705
    by Roger A. Pautan, Jr...705
Lost Property..705
    by Virginia Betts...705
Tantrum..707

Contents By Author

Made in the USA
Coppell, TX
04 January 2022